ספר בינה לעתים

A Festival
OF
Torah

MOSAICA PRESS

THE GROSSMAN EDITION

ספר בינה לעתים

A Festival OF Torah

YOM TOV DELICACIES
FOR THE SOUL

RABBI BINYAMIN WURZBURGER

Mosaica Press, Inc.

© 2017 by Rabbi Binyamin Wurzburger

Designed and typeset by Brocha Mirel Strizower

ISBN-10: 1-946351-12-1

ISBN-13: 978-1-946351-12-8

Published and distributed by:

Mosaica Press, Inc.

www.mosaicapress.com

info@mosaicapress.com

THIS SEFER IS DEDICATED IN LOVING MEMORY
OF OUR DEAR FATHERS

Mr. Hugo Grossman

ר׳ חיים ב״ר אהרן הכהן ע״ה

נלב״ע י״ז תמוז תשנ״ו

Mr. Munish Barber

ר׳ מנחם מאניש ב״ר דוב בעריש ע״ה

נלב״ע ח׳ סיון תשס״ג

TWO OUTSTANDING MEN WHO SURVIVED THE HORRORS
OF THE HOLOCAUST AND CAME TO THE SHORES OF AUSTRALIA
TO REBUILD THE LOST LEGACY OF THEIR CHILDHOOD.
THEY WERE BOTH INSTRUMENTAL IN THE ESTABLISHMENT OF THEIR
RESPECTIVE SHULS IN MELBOURNE AND SYDNEY, AUSTRALIA.
HONEST, INTELLIGENT, AND HARDWORKING, RENOWNED AS BAALEI CHESED
AND BAALEI TZEDAKAH WHO WERE RESPECTED AND LOVED BY ALL.
DEVOTED TO THEIR FAMILIES AND WERE ZOCHEH
TO HAVE DOROS YESHARIM.

.ת.נ.צ.ב.ה

MAY THE PUBLICATION OF THIS SEFER BE
AN ETERNAL ZECHUS FOR THEIR NESHAMOS.

Dedicated by Aron and Mina
Grossman and family

לזכר נשמת
אבי מורי

החבר אריה
בן ר׳ בנימין זאב ע״ה

מאת אמי מורתי
מרת אסתר ווירצבורגער שתחי׳

לזכרון עולם בהיכל ה׳

למשפחת אבי ומורי

ר׳ חיים משה בן ר׳ מרדכי גרינוואלד ז״ל

נפטר ט״ז שבט תשע״ג

ואביו ר׳ מרדכי ב״ר מרדכי ז״ל

נפטר ג׳ חשון תרצ״ט

ואמו מרת הינדא בת ר׳ יאיר צבי ז״ל

ובניהם צבי הערשעל, ישראל בנימין,
ור׳ מנחם מנדל ואשתו חנה, עם ילדיהם יאיר צבי ואסתר ז״ל
ודודיו ר׳ יצחק אייזיק ב״ר מרדכי וכל משפחתם ז״ל
ור׳ משה מאיר ב״ר מרדכי ובניו חיים, ודוד, ובתו חנה וכל משפחתם
ודודתו חנה דבורה בת ר׳ מרדכי וכל משפחתה ז״ל
שנהרגו בתוך רבבות קדושי ישראל באוישוויץ, תש״ד — 1944 הי״ד

ולמשפחת אמי מורתי

מרת לאה בת ר׳ זאלקא ע״ה

נפטרה י״ח שבט תשע״ב

ואביה ר׳ זאלקא ב״ר ישראל אליעזר משפחת הירש ז״ל
ואמה פרימיט בת ר׳ אהרן הערש ז״ל

ובניהם ובנותיהם בלימא, שרה רבקה, איסור לייב, פייגע, מרים,
עללא, אסתר, נפתלי, וחיים אלעזר ז״ל

וזקנה ר׳ ישראל אליעזר ב״ר פנחס ואשתו צירל

ובנותיהם בינה, העננא, ובנם יוסף ואשתו חנה, וכל משפחתם

ואבי זקנה ר׳ אהרן הערש ב״ר יצחק ואשתו עללא
ואמה זקנתה חי׳ מינדל בת ר׳ מרדכי צבי

ובניהם בנימין, יעקב, שמואל, יצחק, מלכה, וכל משפחתם

ואבי אמה זקנתה ר׳ מרדכי צבי ואם אמה זקנתה פייגע

ובניהם חיים, יעקב, ובנותיהם אסתר, ומרים וכל משפחתם
שנהרגו בתוך רבבות קדושי ישראל באוישוויץ, תש״ד — 1944 הי״ד
ת.נ.צ.ב.ה.

IN LOVING MEMORY OF

Reb Yisroel "Izzy"
ben Reb Menachem Herzog, z"l

NIFTAR 23 TAMUZ 5770

A PARAGON OF NOBILITY, A GADOL IN CHESED,
HE DEVOTED HIS LIFE TO SUPPORTING
TORAH INSTITUTIONS AND HELPING THOSE IN NEED
WITH SENSITIVITY, COMPASSION, AND HUMILITY.

ת.נ.צ.ב.ה.

Dedicated by Family Herzog

שמואל קמנצקי
Rabbi S. Kamenetsky

2018 Upland Way
Philadelphia, PA 19131

Home: 215-473-2798
Study: 215-473-1212

March 16, 2016

קודם ג' שלי ניסן תשע"ו

I greatly enjoyed reading the beautiful manuscript of insights on the Yomin Tovim written by my dear Talmid, Rabbi Binyomin Wurzburger. Rabbi Wurzburger established the first overseas Lakewood Kollel – the world-renowned Melbourne Kollel – and has been its Rosh Kollel for over thirty-five years. A true Torah pioneer, he has helped transform the spiritual landscape of Australia to its high level of mitzvah observance and Torah scholarship which it boasts today.

In this sefer, the author presents hundreds of brilliant chiddushim, culled from the Rishonim, Acharonim, through to the Gedolim of our time. The author's great breadth and depth of Torah knowledge is evident from this collection, comprising countless obscure and relatively unknown original sources.

The author is to be commended for distilling this vast treasury of Torah thought into a concise, orderly and easy-to-read format. Torah scholars will also greatly benefit from this work, as detailed mareh mekomos are provided for those who wish to delve further into a subject and cite sources in the original.

This book is an invaluable resource for parents, teachers and anyone who wishes to discover fundamental insights on the Yomim Tovim to enjoy and share. Illuminating and uplifting, this book will instill the reader with the spirit of Yom Tov and enhance their Yom Tov experience.

S. Kamenetsky

RABBI MOSHE HEINEMANN
6109 Gist Avenue
Baltimore, MD 21215
Tel. (410) 358-9828
Fax. (410) 358-9838

משה היינעמאן
אב"ד ק"ק אגודת ישראל
באלטימאר
טל. (410) 764-7778
פקס (410) 764-8878

בס"ד

ראה ראיתי את ספרו של ידידי הרה"ג ר' בנימין וירלענבערגר שליט"א ראש כולל בעיר
מעלבארן שבמדינת אוסטרליא המכיל השקפות ומחשבות טהורות ועמוקות על מועדי
השנה, מלוקטעים מדברי חז"ל ומגדולי ישראל הראשונים והאחרונים עם הוספות מאת
הרב המחבר שליט"א בהיקף רב ובבקיאות נפלאה. וכמתו הוא לנו לפתח עינים אשר
כולו חומר כבוד. ודבריו חיים וקימים מקורדיס ומבוארדיס בבינה ובהשכל בעניני
תורתנו הקדושה, תקנת חז"ל ומנהגי ישראל בטוב טעם ודעת.

וע"ז באתי עה"ח לכבוד המחבר ולכבוד תורתו באחד בשבת לסדר כתוב זאת זכרון
בספר, שבעה ימים לחדש שבט שנת חמשת אלפים ושבע מאות ושבעים וטוב לבריאת עולם
עשה בזה"ל — ברוך ג—ב"ה בלמשפחת היינעמאן החונ"פ מתא בֿאלטימאר

RABBI ARYEH MALKIEL KOTLER

BETH MEDRASH GOVOHA

LAKEWOOD, N.J. 08701

בע"ה

ארי' מלכיאל קוטלר

בית מדרש גבוה

לייקווד, נ. דז.

אל בחורי 50 זיב בתך ד' יהופת ד... המתנגדים בכל מקום דכבוד
התורה, ודרש ונשא וכח את הסאל וזרצ.., מחיל לשמחה והלכו הכתבים הל ... וזיון ה'
סלאה היא מרויחת בלבם יס מיל שאותה ... ומ ... ה' יפת אל אהלי אותו אלאיזי
בניס של בניס אשר ה' יפתק של הקבה למאה מאה אין ... וסגיר להם בניס נחלות
אל כך אשר הקבה למאה כש שאין ... לכם בתש ... חסבר להם בניס והחא
אהל ישראל וזה גסדה הסברה בניס להגולל ... ובוכך לכת של כי באת מכבתין
ג' כאזיו ... מים חיים ... ואהבת מיס שה תפלה

עלעיין ונמ ... ... גזין ... ואל וזה אופל...
... ולה ... ... התש לא ... ... תגילא
... ... וקין אזו ... לכל הסבגוה, והשב שלילה
... כניס לאנואחי ל... בסיבומי הפלפליס בהלכה וגטאקפת, וזה ... אובים
להסגיר בניס של הקבה, אין ואאה וסגיר להם בניס בהלכה, ותגויך אווז...
ואלפת ... ... על זינ... הזאוקים אש ... גיתכים אלו בהלם
וינה שיתגללו כשיו ה' מקוה וסבר ... צ... גבויס להזיל מאה
לאלוז ... ... בחורבים החשובים שכפי ה' יאש... כ... גת
וחזוק ... כבני וכ... לכבוד ... ... אש...
הפות לכבוד התורה ... ...
כעתירת הכויס... קוטלר

Table of Contents

Acknowledgments

This book is the result of the brainchild of my dear friend and president of our Kollel, Dr. Danny Lanzer. About five years ago, he suggested that we offer our community "The Twenty-Point Breakfast Series." Before each Yom Tov, the Melbourne community is invited to the Kollel to partake in a delicious complimentary breakfast and to hear twenty concise points about the Yom Tov that they probably did not already know. To enable the attendees to easily give over the points to their friends and family at a later time, we also provide handout sheets produced by Rabbi Yisroel Greenwald. The goal of this ongoing series is to instill in the audience a greater appreciation of the coming Yom Tov, and Baruch Hashem it has found success in this regard. It is with deep gratitude to Hashem that I present this compilation, which is the sum of five years' worth of "The Twenty-Point Breakfast Series" — or one hundred points — on each of the Yomim Tovim.

This work is not my own material; rather it is culled from works spanning the early *Rishonim* up to the present-day *Acharonim*. What is unique with this compilation is that it contains a varied and eclectic selection of many fascinating but obscure and relatively unknown original sources. The book contains nearly a thousand insights, written in an extremely concise manner, which will provide readers with food for thought to develop further insights on their own. Another feature of this book is that it is extensively sourced for those who wish to further delve into the subject and look up the original sources.

I would like to make a disclaimer. I cannot take credit for discovering all the sources contained in this book. Once it became known that I was actively collecting material related to the Yomim Tovim, many sources were presented to me by Rabbanim, students, and friends. Although my personal input was minimal, I am thankful to Hashem for allowing me to be the "waiter" who is able to serve these precious Torah delicacies to the public.

A word of caution: Although there are also some *halachic* insights contained in this work, and although it was written with the intention to provide the reader with some familiarity to the subject matter, in practice one should always receive guidance from a *halachic* authority. Also, the reader should bear in mind that as this work is an anthology culled from a multitude of sources; the insights are not always thematic, but instead are representative of diverse — and sometimes even conflicting — authentic Torah approaches.

First and foremost, I want to thank the *Ribono Shel Olam* for granting me the merit and ability to bring this *sefer* to fruition. Additionally, I would like to thank my great *rebbeim*, and particularly HaRav Shneur Kotler, *zt"l*, HaRav Nosson Wachsfogel, *zt"l*, HaRav Shimon Schwab, *zt"l*, HaRav Mordechai Schwab, *zt"l*, HaRav Elya Svei, *zt"l*, and *ybl"c* HaRav Shmuel Kamenetsky and HaRav Moshe Heinemann, from whom I receive continuous support and guidance.

No words could adequately express my appreciation to my dear father and my in-laws, *a"h*, and *ybl"c* my dear mother, who is the regal matriarch of our family. May she have *arichas yamim* and see much *nachas* from all her posterity.

I would like to express my gratitude to Rabbi Yisroel Greenwald, an accomplished author and *talmid chacham* of note, for making this book possible. In addition to his literary and editing skills, he meticulously researched and developed all the sources in the book and presented them in a clear, concise, reader-friendly format. I am also indebted to Rabbi Yitzchok Lederman who masterfully edited the Twenty-Point Series handouts with skill and style.

Dr. Danny Lanzer has been a mainstay of our Kollel and we are eternally grateful for his continuous support of the Kollel and for helping to bring the light of Torah to the broader Jewish community of Melbourne. In particular, as mentioned in my opening remarks, we are grateful for his foresight in spearheading this project and making the Twenty-Point Series a reality.

Mr. Matis Gindof is an exceptionally loyal and supportive friend who brought together a dedicated team that prepared the beautiful breakfasts before each Yom Tov. Special thanks go to Mr. Yeshaya Weinstock and Yosef Chaim Landau for all their tireless work in preparing each breakfast. May Hashem bless them both in abundance in every way.

I gratefully acknowledge Mr. Aron Grossman's financial backing of this project and his ongoing dedicated commitment to the Kollel. Mr. Chaim Yehoshua Grossman has been a loyal participant in the Kollel's activities, and particularly in the Twenty-Point Series. He has also graciously given of his time and professional expertise in an exceptionally generous way from the inception of the Kollel.

A work of this nature is immensely enhanced by having its roots in an environment of Torah study. My sincere gratitude goes to all the *yungerleit* in the Kollel, whose commitment to Torah has greatly contributed in elevating the level of Torah scholarship and in igniting a passion for Torah study and mitzvah observance in our community. There is much to praise and appreciate in the supportive staff of the Kollel, each of whom selflessly contributes to the success of the Kollel. May Hashem bless each one of them with the fulfilment of all their needs.

I would also like to express my heartfelt thanks and appreciation to the publisher and all the dedicated staff at Mosaica Press. My dear friend and colleague, Rabbi Yaacov Haber, has taken a personal interest in this project from its inception and has brought this book to fruition in a most beautiful manner. Rabbi Doron Kornbluth has done a masterful job in painstakingly editing the manuscript, and his insightful comments and suggestions have immensely enhanced the quality of the finished work. Many thanks also to Rayzel Broyde, Daniella Kirsch, and Brocha Mirel Strizower for the gorgeous cover design and ingenious layout. Sherie Gross and her team of editors and proofreaders — Binyamin Lieb, Judy Mernick, and Meira Lawrence — did a magnificent job polishing the book yet further.

Finally, my unlimited appreciation goes to my *eishes chayil*, who has stood at my side and supported all that I have been able to achieve throughout our married life. May Hashem bless her with tremendous *nachas* from our children, grandchildren, and great grandchildren, *l'orech yomim tovim*.

Binyamin Wurzburger
Rosh Chodesh Iyar, 5777
Melbourne, Australia

Rosh Hashanah to Yom Kippur

Names of Elul and Tishrei

The names for each month were originally Babylonian names; the Jewish People adopted them when they returned from the exile of Bavel.[1] *Chazal* allowed the use of the Babylonian names — despite the fact that they were initially named after pagan deities — since they were able to expound the name in a manner congruent with the essence of the month from a Torah perspective.

Chazal interpret the significance of the names of the months of Elul and Tishrei as follows:

Elul — denotes elevation.[2] Elul is the most elevated month because Hashem created the world in this month. On the twenty-fifth of Elul, Hashem began the creation of the world, culminating with the creation of Adam on Rosh Hashanah.[3]

---

1   *Bereishis Rabbah* 48:9.
2   As in *Melachim I*, 6:8: ובלולים יעלו — they would ascend on spiral staircases.
3   *Midrash HaChefetz*, cited in *Torah Sheleimah*, Bo, Miluim p. 177.

According to other opinions, אלול is related to:

- כלול — encompassing
- חלול — hollow
- הילול — praise

Elul incorporates all three definitions since we blow the hollow shofar for the entire month of Elul as praise to Hashem.[4]

Tishrei (תשרי) — is an expression of untying (שרי), since on Yom Kippur the Jewish People are "released" from their sins.[5]

Alternatively, it is related to the words:

- הוכשר — prepared
- אישור — confirmation
- שירה — song

Tishrei incorporates all three definitions because during this month we prepare ourselves to merit Hashem's stamp of approval for a blessed year, which leads us to joyous song during the festival of Sukkos.[6]

ELUL

Time for Preparation

Being the sixth month in the year, Elul parallels Erev Shabbos — the sixth day of the week. Just as we prepare for Shabbos on Erev Shabbos, so does the preparation of the Yomim Noraim begin during the month of Elul. And just as the many preparations one does on Friday translate into a more enjoyable and meaningful Shabbos experience, so too do the efforts extended during Elul ensure a year of abundant goodness and blessing.[7]

---

4   *Torah Sheleimah* ibid., p. 178.
5   *Midrash HaChefetz.*
6   Vilna Gaon, *Shir HaShirim* 4:8; *Torah Sheleimah* ibid.
7   *Shem M'Shmuel, Shoftim* 5675; *Ki Savo* 5672.

We Are His, When We Are Not

"And we are His (ולו)."[8] This verse is an example where the oral pronunciation (*kri*) differs from the written spelling (*kesiv*). The word *v'lo* is pronounced with the letter *vav*, which reads "and we are His." However, the word is written with the letter *alef*, which translates as "we are not."

Why?

The Sefas Emes comments that the two disparate readings actually form one unified thought: the more we negate our personal ego, the more closely bonded we become to Hashem. When one combines the letters of the *kesiv* (לא) and the *kri* (לו), it forms the word אלול, since the internalization of this message is the essence of the month of Elul.[9]

Shofar of Elul

After the sin of the Golden Calf, Moshe ascended Mount Sinai again, this time to receive the second *luchos*. *Bnei Yisrael* sounded a shofar in the camp at this time to instill in them the fear of Hashem, so as not to err once again in idolatry.

Pirkei D'Rebbi Eliezer says that this particular shofar blowing was a fulfillment of the verse, "Hashem has ascended with the blast; Hashem, with the sound of the shofar."[10] The reason Hashem's honor was particularly elevated through this specific shofar blowing was because through it *Bnei Yisrael* demonstrated an effort to establish safeguards to prevent future sin, on their own initiative.[11] Since this event occurred on Rosh Chodesh Elul, the Sages instituted that the shofar be blown every year on that day. The custom was later extended to continue throughout the duration of the month of Elul.[12]

---

8   *Tehillim* 100:3.

9   *Ma'amarei Sefas Emes*, Yomim Noraim, p. 25.

10   *Pirkei D'Rebbi Eliezer* 46. Verse from *Tehillim* 47:6.

11   Radal, *Pirkei D'Rebbi Eliezer* ibid.

12   *Tur, Orach Chaim* 581.

SELICHOS

The Selichos Prayer

The rabbis instituted *Selichos* as an additional prayer in a manner which incorporates all the elements of the daily prayers. The opening verses of praise correspond to *Pesukei D'zimrah*, and the thirteen attributes of Divine mercy correspond to *Shemoneh Esrei*, which during the week contains thirteen blessings of supplications. Since the focus of this *tefilah* is to obtain forgiveness, the prayer is followed with a greatly expanded *Tachanun*. As *Selichos* is considered a prayer, it appropriately concludes with *Kaddish Shalem*, which includes the request for the acceptance of our prayers, generally a reference to *Shemoneh Esrei*.[13]

Thirteen Attributes of Divine Mercy

"Remember for us today the covenant of these thirteen, as You made known to the humble one [Moshe] in ancient times."[14] Why does the liturgist refer to Moshe as "the humble one" instead of mentioning him specifically by name?

Rashi explains that one of the characteristics of humility is forbearance.[15] The thirteen attributes of Divine mercy particularly demonstrate Hashem's exemplary forbearance. The prayer is conveying that the reason why Moshe was the recipient of the revelation of the Divine attributes of mercy is because he, on a much smaller human scale, shared those very same traits.

Doubly Poor

"As paupers (דלים) and as beggars (רשים) do we knock at Your doors."[16] Rabbi Aharon Kotler explains that the difference between

---

13   *Levush, Orach Chaim* 581:1.
14   *Selichos*, introduction to Thirteen Attributes of Divine Mercy.
15   Rashi, *Bamidbar* 12:3.
16   Introduction to *Selichos* prayer.

a *dal* and a *rash* is that *dal* refers to a deficiency in one's innate qualities, like a broken-spirited person. A support of this definition can be found in the story of Amnon, in which his friend asks him, "Why do you [appear] so downtrodden (דל), O son of the king?"[17]

In contrast, the definition of *rash* is poor in quantity, as in the verse, "And the poor man (ולרש) had nothing."[18] Through this expression we confess before Hashem that our good deeds are pitifully meager, in quantity as well as in quality.[19]

---

17   *Shmuel II*, 13:4.
18   Ibid. 12:3.
19   *Mishnas Rebbi Aharon, Ma'amarim*, vol. 2, p. 132.

Rosh Hashanah

MERITING A GOOD YEAR

By Utilizing These Days

The Gemara relates a story about a person who would travel for three months to learn in yeshiva for just one day. The rabbis in the academy would jokingly call him "a student of the rabbinical academy for one day." When Rabbi Yochanan became aware of this, he entered the academy and taught that anyone who studies Torah even for one day of the year is considered as if he occupied himself with Torah study the entire year.[20] We can extend this principle to the Yomim Noraim as well. A person can rectify in one day between Rosh Hashanah and Yom Kippur all his sins of the entire year. [21]

Through Communal Responsibility

> In the natural order of the world, a person who awaits a court judgment will dress in black and dress in an ung-roomed and disheveled manner, since he does not know the outcome of his judgment. But the Jewish nation is not like this; they dress in white, cut their nails and hair, and eat and drink on Rosh Hashanah. Why? Because they know that Hashem will perform a miracle for them [that they will be vindicated in judgment].[22]

---

20   *Chagigah* 5b.
21   *Tzlach, drush* 22 for the *Aseres Yemei Teshuvah.*
22   *Tur, Orach Chaim* 581.

This statement is fascinating. Generally, one may not rely on miracles, so how is it possible to rely on a miracle that Hashem will judge us favorably on Rosh Hashanah?

The Alter of Kelm presents a principle: while an individual lacks enough merit to confidently expect a miracle to occur to him, a community is different.[23] This explains why although it is improper for an individual to pray for a miracle,[24] our standardized prayers are replete with communal requests for miracles.[25] Since a community is secure in a favorable judgment, it is advisable for one to be involved in helping others so that he will not be judged as an isolated individual but rather as a member of the broader community.

Through Tzedakah

Some have the custom of reciting the verse, "And Yitzchak planted in that land, and he reaped in that year a hundredfold [as much as he sowed], as Hashem had blessed him,"[26] prior to *kiddush* on Rosh Hashanah.[27] Our Sages say that Yitzchak was blessed with an abundant harvest in merit of his giving tithes to charity. The *Rokeach* points out that the words immediately prior to "and Yitzchak planted" are "...shall surely be put to death."[28] The juxtaposition of these two verses underscores that in the merit of giving *tzedakah*, one is spared from death. This message is especially pertinent to Rosh Hashanah, for through the merit of giving *tzedakah* one is spared punishment of death and is decreed a year of blessing and prosperity in its stead.[29]

---

23   Cited in *Darkei Mussar*, p. 238.
24   *Berachos* 60a.
25   See for example Rama, *Orach Chaim* 187:4; *B'chor Shor, Shabbos* 21b.
26   *Bereishis* 26:12.
27   *Ben Ish Chai, parashas Nitzavim.*
28   *Rokeach, Bereishis* 26:11.
29   *Rokeach* ibid.

Through Charitable Vows

The Torah strongly discourages making vows, even for mitzvah purposes, such as pledging money to *tzedakah*. This is because unforeseen circumstances may arise that will prevent one from fulfilling his vow and he will thereby come to transgress the serious sin of uttering a false vow or oath.[30] Tosfos comments that this seems to contradict the numerous verses that extol making vows to motivate mitzvah compliance.

Tosfos goes on to explain that an exception is made for when a person is in a dangerous situation, such as when a person or a close family member is ill or in dire straits. Under such circumstances, it is permissible — and even praiseworthy — to vow to perform a mitzvah.[31] The Ritva says that this is the basis for the custom to make charitable pledges in shul on Rosh Hashanah and Yom Kippur. Since the books of life and death are opened on these days, it constitutes a perilous predicament that warrants even making vows to save oneself from a harsh judgment.[32]

Through Torah and Kindness

While suffering atones a person's sins, the Vilna Gaon writes that a greater and more potent method than afflictions is Torah study, in combination with acts of kindness.[33] The Gemara states: "Whoever is involved in Torah study and acts of kindness is forgiven for all his sins."[34] This teaches that even great mitzvos such as *tefillin* and *tzitzis* are unable to protect a person from suffering — only Torah and *chesed*.[35] For this reason, the Chofetz Chaim recommends that it is proper for a person to allocate half his charitable contributions to supporting Torah study and the other half for acts of kindness towards one's fellow man.[36]

---

30 *Chulin* 2a.
31 Ibid. 2b.
32 *Nedarim* 10a.
33 Vilna Gaon, *Mishlei* 16:6.
34 *Berachos* 5b.
35 Rabbi Chaim Pinchas Sheinberg, *Derech Emunah*, p. 40.
36 *Toras HaBayis*, p. 105.

INSIGHTS ON ROSH HASHANAH

Desiring Hashem as King

What is so unique about accepting Hashem as our King on Rosh Hashanah when, in fact, a Jew accepts the yoke of Hashem's kingship every day before reading the *Shema*?

Rabbi Aharon Kotler explains that throughout the year we accept Hashem as our Ruler *de jure*,[37] and thus we commit ourselves to His service. On Rosh Hashanah, we *want* Hashem as our King, like Dovid HaMelech said, "There is none upon earth that I desire besides You."[38] This means that even if Hashem were to offer to bestow His sustenance upon us through other channels or by being self-sufficient — even if this were to mean that we could have all the prosperity in the world — we would still rebuff those options, since all prosperity is meaningless without our connection to Hashem.[39]

Rabbi Shimshon Pincus would say that there are two ways to merit a good judgment on Rosh Hashanah. One way is by repenting and bettering our ways. A simpler way is by "embracing" Hashem, which can be accomplished by desiring Hashem as our King.[40] Rosh Hashanah is the time we can "embrace" Hashem and feel the love of that closeness. This loving embrace overrides the dread of the Day of Judgment and the difficulties this may entail.

Fleeing from You — to You

The Rambam describes Rosh Hashanah as a day on which we take "flight and refuge in Him."[41] A similar sentiment is expressed by the famous medieval poet, Rav Shlomo ibn Gabirol: "If you seek my sin, I will flee from You, to You, and I will hide from Your anger in Your shade."[42]

---

37 Latin for: by right, by law.
38 *Tehillim* 73:25.
39 *Mishnas Rebbi Aharon*, vol. 2, p. 192, 198.
40 Rabbi Shimshon Pincus, *Nefesh Shimshon: Yomim Noraim*, p. 12.
41 Rambam, commentary to *Mishnah, Rosh Hashanah* 32b.
42 Rabbi Shlomo ibn Gabirol, *Keser Malchus* 38.

Although these two reactions seem contradictory, the Brisker Rav compares it to a child who, at the very moment his father is spanking him, holds his father tightly and pleads for mercy. Even though the son is terrified by his father's punishment, he realizes that his father loves him and is the best source for comfort and support.

In fact, the greater the fear, the more we feel a need to turn to Him. In turn, as we see from the *pasuk* in *Tehillim*,[43] the greater our trust in Hashem's support and mercy, the greater His support and mercy will actually be.[44]

Concealed Day of Judgment

We predominately relate to Rosh Hashanah as being the *Yom HaDin* — the Day of Judgment. If so, why doesn't the Torah make any mention of this important point?

The *Kli Yakar* answers that were the Torah to write that Rosh Hashanah is the Day of Judgment, people would become complacent and defer their repentance to that day. Since Hashem wishes us to repent each and every day, the Torah therefore "conceals" this information.[45] In a similar vein, the Torah does not refer to Shavuos as the day of the giving of the Torah. This is because Hashem wishes that we view each day as if the Torah were given to us anew.

When discussing the festivals, the Torah prefaces all the Yomim Tovim with the word *yom* — day. (For example, "And on the fifteenth *day* of this month is the festival of matzos."[46]) An exception to this

---

43   יהי חסדך ה' עלינו כאשר יחלנו לך — May Your kindness, Hashem, be upon us, just as we awaited You (*Tehillim* 33:22).

44   Rabbi Asher Bergman, *A Rosh Yeshiva Remembers*, pp. 280–281.

45   *Kli Yakar*, *Vayikra* 23:16.

46   *Vayikra* 23:6.

rule is Rosh Hashanah.[47] Why does the Torah omit the word "day" in regard to Rosh Hashanah?

The *Parparous L'Chochmah* answers that when Hashem created Adam, He warned him that if he were to eat from the Tree of Knowledge, he would die on *that day*. When Adam sinned by eating from it on Rosh Hashanah, Hashem in His mercy extended his life to nearly a thousand years. In order to spare Adam the neccesity of dying on the day he partook of the forbidden fruit, Hashem refrained from calling Rosh Hashanah a "day."[48] This episode highlights the extreme lengths Hashem takes to demonstrate magnanimity towards sinners in judgment.

CUSTOMS ON ROSH HASHANAH

Simanim — Why It Isn't Divination

One is prohibited to do an action as an omen for good tidings (*nichush*), except for the signs that were instituted by the Sages, such as the *simanim* on Rosh Hashanah (when certain foods are eaten on Rosh Hashanah night as an omen for a good year).[49] Why aren't the *simanim* of Rosh Hashanah included in the general prohibition of *nichush*?

The specific foods the Sages recommend eating on Rosh Hashanah as a portent for a good year are accompanied by a prayer. This demonstrates that the food does not serve as an omen; rather it is merely a trigger to arouse one to prayer and repentance, which was the Sages' primary intention.[50]

---

47   *Rokeach*, Rosh Hashanah 200.

48   Rabbi Noach Lipshitz, *Parparous L'Chochmah*, p. 132. The Sages (see *Rokeach*, Rosh Hashanah, p. 88) expound the verse "The days were fashioned and to Him there is one," (*Tehillim* 139:16) in reference to Rosh Hashanah. The word ולו (to Him) is spelled ולא (is not). According to this interpretation, Rosh Hashanah is unique out of all the days in the year in that it is the day that is not called a "day" in order to grant clemency to Adam.

49   *Sefer Chasidim* 59.

50   Meiri, *Horayos* 12a.

Furthermore, the Ramban says that a prophet would perform a token action to bring a prophecy into reality. The Sages instituted taking the *simanim* in the same light.[51]

Ironically, while the *Sefer Chasidim* decries making *simanim* except for those mentioned by the Sages, he explicitly permits the *siman* of eating the head of a ram,[52] although this particular *siman* is not mentioned in the Talmud but only later in the *Rishonim*. Perhaps he allows the head of a ram since it is connected to the ram's horn — the shofar, which *Chazal* say recalls the merit of *Akeidas Yitzchak*.

Honey

"And on the seventh month, on the first day of the month, you shall have a holy convocation."[53] The *Sifri* says that the words *mikra kodesh* — holy convocation, specifically refer to food, drink, and fine clothes.[54] More specifically, *Tehillim* 81, which some recite on Rosh Hashanah due to its numerous references to this day, concludes, "I will feed him with the finest of the wheat and with the honey of the rock I will satisfy you." The *Rokeach* says that this hints that one should eat honey on Rosh Hashanah, as it is a sign that one be blessed with a sweet year.[55] The *Rokeach* further observes that we find in numerous places in the Torah that the concept of judgment is written immediately adjacent to the mention of "sweetness" and "honey."[56] Perhaps these references allude to the Kabbalistic concept of *hamtakas hadinim* — the "sweetening" of the attribute of strict justice.

---

51   Maharal, *Be'er HaGolah* p. 33; *Tzeidah L'Derech* 4:5, p. 113b.
52   *Sefer Chasidim* ibid.
53   *Bamidbar* 29:1.
54   *Sifri, Bamidbar* 147.
55   *Rokeach, Bamdibar* 29:1.
56   Ibid. Examples include: *Shemos* 15:25, *Nechemiah* 8:10, *Tehillim* 19:10–11.

Apples

Why do we eat apples on Rosh Hashanah? Yitzchak requested from Eisav that he prepare for him delicacies that he loved so that he would be able to give him his blessings.[57] The *Zohar* says that this event transpired on Rosh Hashanah.[58] The Vilna Gaon says that the reason why we eat apples on Rosh Hashanah is because the clothing that Yaakov wore when he came before Yitzchak to receive his blessings had the fragrance of Gan Eden. This fragrance is Kabbalistically referred to as *chakal tapuchin* — an apple orchard.[59]

The *Zohar* goes on to say that this episode is reenacted every Rosh Hashanah! Yitzchak embodies the attribute of justice and requests from Eisav, the embodiment of evil, to bring him delicacies. The "delicacies" that the angel of Eisav brings are actually the many bundles of sin that were created from the actions of man. When Eisav tells Yitzchak, "Get up father and eat from the delicacies of your son," he means to say that the putrid "food" would be an offering to Hashem. Hashem, though, has no desire to accept the putrid sins of the Jewish People, and instead accepts only their mitzvos — leaving the waste products for Eisav to consume.

Round Challahs

From Rosh Hashanah until Hoshanah Rabbah, there is a custom to use round challahs instead of the traditionally-shaped oblong ones that are used the remainder of the year. There are numerous reasons given for this custom:

- Round challahs are a good omen for a blessed year. Just as a round object has no end, the round challahs symbolize longevity and blessing without end.[60]

---

57   *Bereishis* 27:4.
58   *Zohar*, quoted in *Nefesh HaChaim* 2:7. Cf. *Radal, Pirkei D'Rebbi Eliezer* 32:35.
59   *Biur HaGra, Orach Chaim* 583:8.
60   *Chasam Sofer*, cited in *Minhag Yisrael Torah*, vol. 3, 583:1.

- Some connect the round challahs of Rosh Hashanah to the round matzos of Pesach: We eat round matzos on Pesach (as opposed to square or triangle ones) to counter the polytheistic views of the Egyptians. Just as a square has numerous corners, so did the Egyptians believe in multiple gods. By eating a round matzah, we demonstrate our belief in the one infinite G-d who has no beginning and no end. Similarly, eating round challahs during the Yomim Noraim expresses the concept of *malchius* — Hashem's Kingship over the entire world.[61]

- Round challahs look like crowns and symbolize our crowning Hashem as our King at this time.[62]

Nut-Free Time Zone

The *Rama* writes that some are careful not to eat nuts on Rosh Hashanah.[63] There are various reasons given for this custom:

- The numerical value of אגוז — nut, is חט — sin.[64] Many find this approach difficult since the numerical value of אגוז also equals טוב — good. In addition, the Hebrew word for "sin" is generally spelled with an א, in which case it does not equal the numerical value of אגוז.[65]

- Some explain the intention of the *Rama* to be that from a Kabbalistic perspective, nuts have an association with the forces of impurity, and therefore one should refrain from eating them at this time.[66]

---

61   *Ta'amei Minhagim, Likutim* 183, based on *Maharei Assad.*
62   *Zemiros Divrei Yoel* 2:408.
63   Rama, *Orach Chaim* 583:2.
64   Rama ibid.
65   18 = חטא, 17 = אגוז.
66   See *Sefer Chasidim* 1:153, and *Mekor Chesed*, ad loc., which writes that demons dwell on the branches of the אגוז tree. Although the nut also has positive connotations, as the Jewish People are compared to an אגוז (see *Pesikta Rabasi* 11), we nevertheless avoid its

- The Chasam Sofer offers a different rationale for this custom. The Midrash compares the Jewish nation to a nut. Just as a nut can be thrown into a dirty place, but the fruit stays protected in its shell, so too even when the Jewish People are flung from nation to nation in exile they still remain pure and unsullied. Since the nut recalls the sins of the Jewish People and their resultant punishment of exile, we avoid eating it on Rosh Hashanah.[67]

Gaining Charm

Some have a custom to recite the verse, "And Noach found grace in the eyes of Hashem,"[68] on Rosh Hashanah.[69] The significance of this verse may be based on the Gemara that says Noach didn't deserve to be saved from the decree of the flood and was only saved by finding favor in the eyes of Hashem.[70]

What is this elusive trait of *chein* — grace, which endears a person to Hashem and causes Him to overlook a person's shortcomings? Rabbi Moshe Feinstein explains that it refers to serving Hashem in a charming manner, namely with joy and happiness.[71] This is like the Gemara that says that the reason we blow two sets of shofar blasts on Rosh Hashanah (although only one is required) is to confuse Satan.[72] Rashi explains that when Satan sees how precious the mitzvos are to *Bnei Yisrael*, that they perform them above and beyond the letter of the law, he is left speechless and is unable to arouse accusations against us.[73]

---

consumption on Rosh Hashanah since we are particular to avoid anything that could evoke a negative connotation on this day.

67   *Chasam Sofer, Drashos*, vol. 2, p. 346.
68   *Bereishis* 6:8.
69   *Ben Ish Chai, parashas Nitzavim.*
70   *Sanhedrin* 108a.
71   Rabbi Moshe Feinstein, *Derash Moshe, Bereishis* ibid.
72   *Rosh Hashanah* 16b.
73   Rashi, *Rosh Hashanah* ibid.

Tashlich by Water

It is customary to go to a river on Rosh Hashanah and recite the verse: ותשליך במצלות ים כל חטאתם — "You will cast all their sins into the depths of the sea."[74] What is the significance of reciting *Tashlich* specifically by a body of water?

- The Midrash relates that when Avraham went to do the *Akeidah*, Satan unsuccessfully attempted to thwart him by deluging him with a torrent of water. We therefore go to a river on Rosh Hashanah to recall the merit of the *Akeidah*.[75]

- "When viewing the depths of the sea...one begins to contemplate the greatness of the Creator. Therefore, we go to a body of water on Rosh Hashanah, which is a day of judgment, so that everyone can take to heart that Hashem is the Creator and King of the universe. When a person comes to recognize the existence of Hashem and that He created the world from nothingness, he will come to regret his sins, and through this, his sins will be forgiven."[76]

- The *pasuk* says, "[The Jewish People] drew water and poured it out before Hashem,"[77] which the *Targum Yonasan* translates: "They poured their hearts in repentance, like water, before Hashem." Rashi explains that they poured the water as a sign of humility to demonstrate that they were like poured water before Hashem. The *Beis Meir* says that we go to a body of water on Rosh Hashanah to demonstrate our contrite spirit, which is likened to flowing water.[78]

- The *Radak* sees the symbolism of flowing water being that it represents *kaparas avonos* — the forgiveness of sins,[79] as the

---

74   *Shulchan Aruch, Orach Chaim* 583:2. Verse from *Michah* 7:19.
75   *Mishnah Berurah* 583:8.
76   Rama, *Toras HaOlah* 3:56.
77   *Shmuel I*, 7:6.
78   *Beis Meir, Orach Chaim* 583.
79   *Radak, Shmuel I* ibid.

verse states, "Remember the sins as waters that have passed" (which quickly dry without leaving a mark).[80]

- Rabbi Dovid Hoffman explains that the reason *Tashlich* is said by water is based on the *Mechiltah*,[81] which states that the *Shechinah* only appears to the prophets outside the Land of Israel when they are next to bodies of water,[82] since water is a place of ritual purity.[83] The *Ba'al HaTurim* writes similarly, saying that prayer is most effective when done near water.[84]

- The kings of Israel are anointed next to a spring of running water as a sign that their rule should also flow without hindrance.[85] Since on Rosh Hashanah we accept Hashem's rule anew, it is also a form of inauguration, which should be done by flowing water.[86]

PRAYERS OF ROSH HASHANAH

Rosh Hashanah and the Exodus

"You gave us...this Day of [Rosh Hashanah]...a remembrance of the exodus from Egypt."[87] It is understandable why the festivals are termed "a remembrance of the exodus," since the festivals commemorate the central events surrounding the exodus. But what is the connection between the Day of Judgment and leaving Egypt?

The Rosh teaches that it is impossible for a Jew to truly believe in the existence of God unless he also accepts the veracity of the

---

80   *Iyov* 11:16.
81   *Mechiltah, Bo,*12:1.
82   Such as in *Yechezkel* 1:1.
83   Rabbi Dovid Hoffman, *Nesiv Binah*, pp. 169–170.
84   *Bereishis* 16:7.
85   *Horayos* 12a.
86   *Otzer HaTefilos, Tashlich.*
87   *Shemoneh Esrei* for Rosh Hashanah.

exodus of Egypt. The exodus demonstrated that Hashem is not only the Creator of world, but is also intimately involved in the affairs of men, closely monitoring their every thought and action and bestowing reward and punishment for their deeds. These lessons are particularly pertinent to the day of Rosh Hashanah on which Hashem judges the affairs of mankind.[88]

Mercy of a Father upon His Children

The *Parparous L'Chochmah* writes that three major events occurred on Rosh Hashanah, which form the acronym *banim* — children:[89]

- ב — *Beis*: בטלה עבודה — The Jews in Egypt were freed from toiling for their masters.
- נ — *Nun*: נפקדה — Hashem remembered Sarah, Rachel, and Chanah and allowed them to conceive.
- ים — *Yud, Mem*: יצא מבור — Yosef was taken out of prison and became the viceroy of Egypt.

As the Sages worded the prayers to accomodate numerous nuances and levels of interpretation, the phrase *rachameinu k'racheim av al banim* — "Have mercy upon us as a father upon his children," was also inserted into the Rosh Hashanah prayers to commemorate these specific events.[90]

King of Judgment

Throughout the year, we conclude the *Amidah* blessing of *Hashivah Shofteinu* with the words: מלך אוהב צדקה ומשפט — The King Who loves righteousness and justice. The *Rabbeinu Ephraim* explains that the reason we mention that Hashem *loves* righteousness and justice is to highlight that he is unlike a ruler of flesh and blood

---

88   *Orchos Chaim L'Rosh*, first day, 26.

89   Rabbi Noach Lipshitz, *Parparous L'Chochmah*, p. 131. Rabbi Lipshitz was a contemporary and close friend of the Vilna Gaon.

90   *Parparous L'Chochmah*, ibid.

who is primarily concerned with his own power and the smooth functioning of his empire. For a ruler like that, righteousness and justice only serve as a means to achieve that end. Hashem, however, inherently loves righteousness and justice because of His love and concern for all mankind.[91]

Therefore, it is difficult to understand why we omit the words "love and righteousness" in the period between Rosh Hashanah and Yom Kippur and instead conclude the blessing with the words, "The King of judgment."

The *Taz* answers that throughout the year, Hashem's trait of *tzedakah* — righteousness with charity, is the more prominent trait with which Hashem runs the world. Therefore, the blessing mentions *tzedakah* before *mishpat*. During the ten days of repentance, however, the more prominent trait is justice, so we do not mention *tzedakah* at this time.[92]

The *Beis Yosef* answers that the object of the blessing, "The King Who loves righteousness and justice," is not referring to Hashem but to man.[93] In other words, Hashem loves *people* who practice *tzedakah* and *mishpat*. During the ten days of repentance, however, the subject of the blessing is Hashem — that He is the King of justice who sits on the throne of judgment during this time.

MUSAF

Life's a Blast

"Fortunate is the nation who knows [the message of the sound of the] *teruah* [blast]."[94] What is the message of the *teruah* blast? Rabbi Moshe Feinstein explains that a shofar can blow two totally different sounds: a long *tekiah* and a short *teruah*. The sound of the

---

91   *Rabbeinu Ephraim, Devarim* 16:18.
92   *Taz, Orach Chaim* 118:2.
93   *Beis Yosef, Orach Chaim* 582:1.
94   *Tehillim* 89:16.

uninterrupted *tekiah* symbolizes an unfettered life of continual progress, while the short *teruah* blasts represent hindrances and hardships, *chas veshalom*.[95]

Just as the various sounds of the shofar are not self-produced haphazardly but rather are the result of the will of the blower, so too one's good and bad fortunes are not the result of luck, but rather are determined by the will of Hashem. The message of the *teruah* is to become cognizant that it is Hashem who makes both the *tekiah* and *teruah* blast in accordance with one's deeds. By internalizing this message of the shofar, one will come "to walk in the light of Hashem's presence,"[96] and merit a year of success and blessing.[97]

Introduction to Musaf

It is customary for the chazzan to say parts of the introductory prayer of *Musaf*, *Hineni He'ani*, in a hushed tone. This is so that he may conceal his inadequacy while reciting the part, "Even though I am unworthy and unqualified [to represent the congregation]."

Rabbi Moshe Feinstein takes issue with those chazzanim who only begin reading loudly from "the Hashem of Avraham." This is because there are members of the congregation who are not aware that the chazzan recited a prayer prior to those words, and it gives the appearance that the name of Hashem was recited in vain, since it was not said in the context of a prayer. It is therefore recommended that the chazzan begins aloud from the words, "Therefore I plead before You," which is the beginning of the prayer.[98]

---

95   Rabbi Moshe Feinstein, *Derash Moshe*, p. 170.
96   *Tehillim* ibid.
97   *Derash Moshe* ibid.
98   Rabbi Moshe Feinstein, *Dibros Moshe, Nedarim* 11:59.

Merit of Six Tens

ועשרון אחד — "And one-tenth *ephah*..."[99] In the Torah, the word ועשרון is only spelled fully (with an extra letter *vav*, whose numerical value is six) in the section describing the *korban Musaf* of Rosh Hashanah. *Rabbeinu Ephraim* comments that this is because on Rosh Hashanah we need the merit of six tens.[100] They are:

1. the עשרת הדברות — the Ten Commandments
2. the עשרה מאמרות — the Ten Utterances with which the world was created[101]
3. the עשר ספירות — the ten *Sefiros* (emanations discussed in Kabbalistic literature)
4. עקידת יצחק — the binding of Yitzchak, which was Avraham's tenth test
5. the ten blessings that Yitzchak gave to Yaakov
6. Yaakov's pledge to tithe his earnings[102]

Bent Shofar — Bent Disposition

The Gemara says that the reason we use a bent ram's horn as the shofar on Rosh Hashanah is to symbolize that the more we "bow our mind" on this day, the better it is.[103] The *Sha'arei Teshuvah* cites a custom that the prayer *Hayom Haras Olam* should be recited with a bowed posture. He explains that since this supplication makes mention of the holy awesomeness of the day of Rosh Hashanah, it is appropriate to recite it with humility and awe. He concludes that in the merit that we adopt an attitude of submission and humility, Divine mercy will be aroused upon us to grant us a favorable judgment on this day.[104]

---

99 *Bamidbar* 29:4.
100 *Rabbeinu Ephraim, Bamidbar* 28:21.
101 *Avos* 5:1.
102 *Bereishis* 28:22.
103 *Rosh Hashanah* 26b.
104 *Sha'arei Teshuvah, Orach Chaim* 591:3.

THE TEN VERSES OF MALCHUYOS, ZICHRONOS, AND SHOFAROS

Scriptural Hints

The obligation to recite the verses of *Malchuyos* (Kingship), *Zichronos* (Remembrance), and *Shofaros* are hinted to in the *pasuk* *Bamidbar* 10:10:

ותקעתם — *"And you shall sound"* corresponds to Shofaros;

לזכרון — *"For a remembrance"* to Zichronos;

אני ה׳ אלקיכם — *"I am Hashem, your God"* to Malchuyos.

The *Sifri* asks: if the word corresponding to *Malchuyos* is mentioned at the end of the verse, why did *Chazal* institute that the verses of *Malchuyos* be recited first?

The *Sifri* answers that a person has to first accept upon himself the yoke of Heaven (*ol malchus Shamayim*) with *Malchuyos* in order to be worthy of being remembered mercifully.[105]

The question remains, though: why then did the Torah first write *Shofaros*, then *Zichronos*, and then *Malchuyos* last? We may answer that a person needs Divine mercy and assistance, which is only achieved through the shofar, in order to properly accept upon oneself *ol malchus Shamayim*.[106]

Significance of Ten

Rabbi Yaakov Kamenetsky comments that the number ten represents a unit of totality and completion, which is why a *minyan* requires a quorum of at least ten people.[107] It is therefore not surprising that the number ten frequently recurs on Rosh Hashanah. The *Rokeach* says that the ten *korbanos* brought on Rosh Hashanah

---

105   *Bamidbar* ibid., 77.
106   See *Ayeles HaShachar*, *Bamidbar* ibid.
107   Rabbi Yaakov Kamenetsky, *Emes L'Yaakov*, *Avos* 5:1.

correspond to ten merits of each of the *Avos*:[108] the ten tests of Avraham; Yitzchak, whose blessing to Yaakov contained ten blessings;[109] and Yaakov, who received ten blessings.[110]

In addition, the Gemara states that the ten verses that we recite in the *Amidah* prayer of Rosh Hashanah correspond to the ten expressions of praise found in the final chapter of *Sefer Tehillim* (Chapter 150), the Ten Commandments that were given amid the sound of the shofar, and the Ten Utterances through which Hashem created the world.[111]

How is this so?

The *Aruch HaShulchan* explains:

- The ten verses of *Malchuyos* correspond to the Ten Utterances through which Hashem created the world, since the purpose of the world is for man to accept the yoke of Hashem's sovereignty.
- *Zichronos* correspond to the *Aseres HaDibros*, for it is in the merit of the Torah that we will be recalled favorably before Hashem.
- Finally, *Shofaros* corresponds to the ten *hallel* praises found in *Tehillim* 150, among which is "Praise Him (*halleluhu*) with the blowing of the shofar."[112]

We may alternatively suggest that the *Aseres HaDibros* correspond to *Shofaros*, since they were given on Mount Sinai amid the sounds of the shofar's blast, and *Zichronos* corresponds to the ten praises cited in *Tehillim* 150.

How does *Tehillim* 150 relate to *Zichronos*?

The Gemara states that the purpose of our recitation of the verses of *Malchuyos* is to crown Hashem as our king, and our recitation of the

---

108 See *Rokeach, Bamidbar* 29:2, 5.
109 See *Rokeach, Bereishis* 27:28.
110 *Rokeach, Bamidbar* 29:2.
111 *Rosh Hashanah* 32a.
112 *Aruch HaShulchan, Orach Chaim* 591:7.

verses of *Zichronos* is to cause our remembrance to rise before Hashem for the good. The primary merit in accepting the yoke of heaven (*Malchuyos*) depends on the manner in which we do so. One can serve Hashem begrudgingly because he feels compelled to do so, but it is a much higher level to serve him by accepting His kingship willingly and with love.[113]

In the *Ma'ariv* prayer, we say, "And His kingship they accepted upon themselves willingly. Moshe and the Children of Israel raised their voices to You in song with abundant gladness — and said unanimously...'Hashem will reign for all eternity!'" It seems that the proof they accepted His kingship upon themselves willingly was because they did it through song. The *Zichronos* that are necessary to be remembered favorably before Hashem come from our joyful and loving acceptance of Hashem as our king in a mindset of song and gladness, just as the "the sweet singer of Israel" exemplified in *Tehillim* 150.

Chapter 150 is the last chapter of *Sefer Tehillim*, and is its climax as it encapsulates the theme of the entire *sefer*. The final verse, "Let all souls praise Hashem, Halleluyah," also represents the theme of Rosh Hashanah, as we say in the *Shemoneh Esrei* on Rosh Hashanah: "Let everything that has been made know that You are its Maker...and let everything with a life's breath in its nostrils proclaim: 'Hashem the G-d of Israel, is King, and His kingship rules over everything.'"

Shofar's Secret Message

The *Yalkut Shimoni* says: "When the Jewish People take the shofar [on Rosh Hashanah] and blow, Hashem arises from the throne of judgment and sits on the throne of mercy. Hashem is then filled with mercy and overturns the attribute of justice into mercy.

Said Rabbi Yeshayah: it is written, "Fortunate is the nation who understands the blast [of the shofar]."[114] Do the nations of the world not understand how to blow? They also have horns, trumpets, and

---

113 *Rosh Hashanah* 16a.
114 *Tehillim* 89:16.

shofars! Rather, "Fortunate is the nation who knows how to appease their Creator with the blast of the shofar."[115]

The Midrash is conveying that it is not merely the *sound* of the ram's horn that arouses Divine mercy. The nations of the world also possess the same horns and can produce the very same sounds, yet their blasts have no effect in the heavenly realms. The power inherent in the shofar's blast is a secret to which only the Jewish nation is privy. The message of the shofar is expressed in the verses of *Malchuyos*, *Zichronos*, and *Shofaros* that we recite on Rosh Hashanah.

Ordinarily, the mitzvah of shofar is a Torah obligation, while the recitation of the *Malchuyos*, *Zichronos*, and *Shofaros* verses is of Rabbinic origin. Interestingly, there are views that say that when we are unable to blow the shofar, such as when Rosh Hashanah falls on Shabbos, then the recital of those verses becomes a Torah obligation.[116] This can be understood in light of the Midrash cited above: On a Biblical level, when we are able to blow the shofar, we can internalize the concepts of *Malchuyos*, *Zichronos*, and *Shofaros* through thought alone. But when we are unable to blow the shofar, we are required to express those concepts verbally.

MALCHUYOS

Saving the Best for Last

The *Aruch HaShulchan* says that the Torah verses of *Malchuyos* are recited in the order in which they are written in the Torah. An exception to this rule is the final verse — the *pasuk* of *Shema Yisrael*. We may suggest that since the tenth *pasuk* is the climax of the set of *Malchuyos*, we utilize the most appropriate *pasuk* for the finale. Since the first verse of *Shema* is the foremost example of acceptance of Hashem's kingship,[117] it is recited as the final verse.[118]

---

115 *Yalkut Shimoni, Vayikra* 645.
116 *Turei Even, Rosh Hashanah* 29b.
117 *Devarim* 6:4.
118 *Aruch HaShulchan, Orach Chaim* 591:10.

Disconnected Verses of Kingship

Why does the structure of the blessing of *Malchuyos* recited in the *Shemoneh Esrei* of *Musaf* differ to the blessing of *Zichronos* and *Shofaros*? In the blessing of *Malchuyos*, the Torah verse relevant to the concept of *Malchuyos* is not cited immediately prior to the blessing. This is not the case regarding the blessing of *Zichronos* and *Shofaros*, where the Torah verse relevant to those concepts is placed directly adjacent to the concluding blessing.

The Avudraham explains that since the concluding blessings of *Zichronos* and *Shofaros* directly deal with the concepts expressed in those verses, it is fitting to recite a relevant verse immediately prior to the blessing. However, regarding *Malchuyos*, where the concluding blessing does not deal with Hashem's kingship but rather with the holiness of the day, it would not be appropriate to state a verse of *Malchuyos* next to the concluding blessing since it is not directly related to the subject matter of the blessing.[119]

ZICHRONOS

From Thought to Action

In the Torah, the word for seeing is *re'iah*. Rabbi Yeruchem Levovitz points out that whenever the Torah writes *re'iah*, it does not merely connote one who looks, but rather one whose sight grasps the whole picture, absorbs all its ramifications, and takes the necessary actions.[120] For example, the *pasuk* says that Hashem *saw* the persecution of the Jewish People in Egypt.[121] Since Hashem is constantly supervising the actions of every man, what is meant by Hashem seeing the suffering of His people? He always "sees" everything! The answer follows in the next verse, which begins the

---

119   *Avudraham*, p. 272.
120   Rabbi Yeruchum Levovitz, *Da'as Torah, Devarim*, vol. 1, pp. 226–229.
121   *Shemos* 2:25.

process of the redemption with Hashem appearing to Moshe at the burning bush.

On Rosh Hashanah, we request that Hashem remembers us favorably. Unlike a human being whose fond memories are mere thoughts, Hashem's merciful remembrance translates into concrete success and blessing for the coming New Year. The way to merit Hashem remembering us favorably is by us remembering Him. This is accomplished by reciting the verses of *Zichronos*. The reason why a bent and humble posture is such an important feature of Rosh Hashanah is because someone who is haughty forgets Hashem[122] — and remembering Him is key to the whole day.[123]

With Appointment Comes Responsibility

"For the remembrance of every creation comes before You, everyone's deed and his appointment."[124] It is understandable that a person is held accountable for his actions, but what is the significance of his "appointment"?

An enigmatic narrative in the Torah sheds light on our question. When Yaakov was nearing his death, Yosef brought his two sons to him in order that he may bless them. Yaakov blessed Yosef that his two sons, Ephraim and Menashe, each be considered as Reuven and Shimon, ranking equally among the tribes of Israel.[125] Immediately afterward, Yaakov asked Yosef, "Who are these [people who are unfit for blessing]?"[126]

Yaakov's question seems difficult to comprehend. Yaakov had been teaching Ephraim and Menashe for the previous seventeen years and found them without fault! Furthermore, just moments earlier he had felt them fitting to bestow upon them the full-fledged status as tribes of Israel. What made them suddenly become unworthy of blessing?

122   *Devarim* 8:14.
123   *Da'as Torah* ibid.
124   *Musaf* of Rosh Hashanah.
125   *Bereishis* 48:5.
126   Ibid. 48:8, based on the commentary of Rashi.

The answer is that the behavior befitting an ordinary person may be totally unbecoming to a person of more noble stature. As long as Ephraim and Menashe were considered "commoners," their behavior was acceptable. But as soon as he promoted them to the status of *Shivtei Kah* — tribes of G-d — he looked at them more critically. This is comparable to a head of state who is held accountable for even a minor infraction that would escape notice if done by a civilian. This is therefore the meaning of, "Everyone's deed and his appointment." Each person's judgment is decided not only by his action but is also equally dependent on his status and life mission.[127]

SHOFAROS

Call of Freedom

The *Rokeach* comments that like the shofar blown during *Yovel*,[128] the shofar at *Matan Torah* also declared freedom from servitude.[129] This explains why the *Aseres HaDibros* begin with the words, "I am Hashem who took you out of Egypt." In addition to external, physical freedom, the Torah grants internal freedom, as our Sages say: "there is no freer man than one who engages in the study of Torah."[130]

The shofar at *Matan Torah* also ushered in additional freedoms for the *Bnei Yisrael*, as they were then freed from servitude of the nations, as well as from the Angel of Death. The shofar that will be blown when Mashiach comes will once again herald our freedom from servitude of the nations and of death.[131] While in exile, the sound of the shofar on Rosh Hashanah elicits tears of yearning and anticipation for our future redemption, at the time of Mashiach the shofar's sounds of *teruah* will evoke tears of joy.

---

127   Rabbi Zalman Sorotzkin, *Oznayim L'Torah, Bereishis* 48:8.
128   *Vayikra* 25:9–10.
129   *Rokeach, Vayikra* ibid., v. 9.
130   *Avos* 6:2.
131   *Rokeach* ibid.

Shofar of Mashiach

The *Machzor Vitri* writes that the verses of *Shofaros* hint to three great shofar blasts that will come to pass with the arrival of Mashiach:[132]

- One will be to revive the dead.
- The second will be to gather in the exiles.
- The third great blast of the shofar will make the hair fall out of the heads of our enemies in fright, as the *pasuk* states: "And Hashem/Elokim will blow the shofar, and shall go in the storm winds (*sa'aros*) of the south."[133] The letter *samech* in the word *sa'aros* — storm winds, is interchangeable with the letter *sin*, which spells *sa'aros* — hairs. The *Rokeach* quotes a Midrash that says that this reference specifically alludes to Eisav, whom the *pasuk* describes as being hairy.[134]

Practical lessons that we may glean from this are to utilize the shofar to:

A. awaken our sleeping and deadened souls;
B. draw us close to Hashem despite how far we have strayed;
C. use the shofar to instill fear of Hashem in our hearts. In this last respect, the sound of the shofar is like the terrifying clasps of thunder, which Hashem created to straighten the crookedness of our hearts.[135]

Shofar and Divine Prophecy

The Torah was given on Mount Sinai amid thunder, lightning, dark clouds, and the powerful sound of the shofar. The Abarbanel

---

132 *Machzor Vitri* 333.
133 *Zechariah* 9:14.
134 *Siddur HaTefilah, Shofaros* 134.
135 *Berachos* 59a.

expounds that each of those elements correspond to various aspects of human understanding. The sounds of thunder represent the many — and often contradictory — voices of human reason. The momentary flashes of lightning signify that the flashes of human intelligence illuminate for only short duration, and the dark cloud illustrates how the human mind is also cloudy and dim.[136]

In contrast, the shofar represents the clear and pure Divine prophecy.[137] The word *shofar* derives from the word *shefer* — beauty,[138] as prophecy is pure and without blemish. The *pasuk* applies the word "powerful" not to the thunder and lightning but only to the shofar, for it was specifically the sound of the shofar that made the Jewish People shudder.[139] We may apply the Abarbanel's exposition to the shofar of Rosh Hashanah as well. The shofar is akin to Divine prophecy, as it represents Hashem calling to our soul and arousing it to tremble in *teshuvah*.

Hearing vs. Giving Ear

The *Shofaros* blessing concludes: שומע קול שופר ומאזין תרועה — "For You hear the sound of the shofar and You give ear to the *teruah*."

Why does it say "hear" regarding the sound of the shofar, and "give ear" regarding the sound of the *teruah*?

Rabbi Chaim Kanievsky comments that the composer of the prayer employed different expressions to convey the same idea for poetic considerations, just as the works of *Neviim* are replete with the same literary device.[140]

On a deeper level, *Chazal* say that שומע denotes listening from a distance, while מאזין implies listening at close range. The reason שומע is connected to shofar is because our acceptance of Hashem's Kingship

---

136   Abarbanel, *Shemos* 19:16.
137   Abarbanel ibid.; cf. *Yeshayah* 58:1; and *Amos* 3:6.
138   *Bereishis* 49:21.
139   *Shemos* 19:16.
140   Rabbi Chaim Kanievsky, *Derech Sichah*, p. 678.

is readily apparent and does not require Hashem's special attention. On the other hand, the *teruah* is a broken sound and symbolizes a person who calls out to Hashem with a contrite and broken spirit. Since Hashem is close to those with a broken spirit,[141] מאזין is written together with *teruah*.[142]

AVINU MALKEINU

Silencing the Accuser

In *Avinu Malkeinu,* the prayer, "Exterminate every foe and adversary from among us," is immediately followed by the petition, "Seal the mouths of our adversaries and accusers." The obvious question is: if our enemies are destroyed, how could they possibly mouth accusations against us?

The Chofetz Chaim answers that, ideally, we beseech Hashem to destroy our enemies entirely. But if we are undeserving of that, we pray to at least merit that they be unable to raise accusations against us.[143] The Chofetz Chaim explains that even if one has committed many sins, if he remains silent when disputes arise, he will merit that Hashem will also silence the lips of his accusing angels.[144]

Communal Debt

In the *Avinu Malkeinu* prayer, it states: "Our Father, our King, forgive and pardon all our iniquities." Afterwards it says, "Our Father, our King, erase through Your abundant compassion all records of our guilt." What sins does the latter prayer include that the former does not?

The Chofetz Chaim answers that the latter refers to sins we ourselves did not personally commit but did not prevent our

---

141 *Tehillim* 34:19.
142 *Derech Sichah* ibid.
143 Chofetz Chaim, *Chovos HaShemirah* 6.
144 Ibid.

fellow Jew from transgressing.[145] This encompassing obligation stems from the principle of *Kol Yisrael areivim zeh lazeh* — all Jews are guarantors for each other. This is why the *Kohen Gadol*, when offering his personal sin offering on Yom Kippur, had to confess his own sins as well of the sins of his household for whom he was responsible.[146]

Avinu Malkeinu on Shabbos

Why don't we recite *Avinu Malkeinu* when Rosh Hashanah falls out on Shabbos? We would think that this heart-rending prayer would be especially effective in ensuring that we are inscribed for a healthy and happy New Year! Rabbi Moshe Schwab answers that since Shabbos is a time for pleasure, it is unbefitting that we say during this time anything that may cause us pain and anguish. In the merit that we preserve Shabbos as a pleasure and delight, as it says, "*V'karasa l'Shabbos oneg*," this itself provides us the greatest merit on the day of judgment that we be inscribed in the Book of Life.[147]

AKEIDAS YITZCHAK

In Whose Merit?

Chazal say that Yitzchak was thirty-seven years old at the time of the *Akeidah*.[148] The Ibn Ezra disagrees, for were Yitzchak a mature adult at the time of the *Akeidah*, he should have equally been credited for the merit of the *Akeidah*! Since Yitzchak's merit is not mentioned, the Ibn Ezra believes that Yitzchak was only about thirteen years old at the time and he was bound on the altar against his will. In his view, the conclusion of the *Zichronos* blessing should read, "And You should mercifully remember *Akeidas Yitzchak* for *Yaakov's* offspring"

---

145   Letters 79, cited in *Chofetz Chaim on Agadas HaShas, Rosh Hashanah* 29b.
146   *Yomah* 35b.
147   Rabbi Moshe Schwab, *Ma'archei Lev*, vol. 1, pp. 154–155.
148   *Midrash Aggadah, Bereishis* 25:20.

(and not as in our texts, "for the sake of *his* offspring," which refers specifically to Yitzchak) since the *Akeidah* was of no special merit to Yitzchak himself.[149]

In defense of the view of *Chazal*, Rabbi Yaakov Kamenetsky explains that the reason why the *Akeidah* was primarily a test for Avraham is because it is much harder to sacrifice one's son than it is to give up one's own life. (For this reason, the Torah makes no mention of Avraham's personal *mesiras nefesh* of being cast into the furnace at Ur Kasdim.) However, *Akeidas Yitzchak* was indeed a great merit for Yitzchak as well and our text of the *Musaf* blessing therefore reads, "And you should mercifully remember *Akeidas Yitzchak* for the sake of *his* offspring."[150] The *Shulchan Aruch* also discourages the alternative text of the Ibn Ezra, as it implies giving credence to the position of the Ibn Ezra in negation to the words of *Chazal*.[151]

Horn of Maturity

Why is the merit of *Akeidas Yitzchak* remembered specifically with the ram's horn if the entire animal was slaughtered as a substitute for Yitzchak?

A ram (איל) is a mature male sheep, thirteen months and older, as opposed to a כבש, which is a young lamb. When a person is required to bring a personal sin offering, the animal he brings for a *korban* is a female, כבשה. A young female lamb represents the Jewish nation, since its sins are done unintentionally without a mature mind. A ram grows its horns after it is a year old and attains maturity. The ram's horn is therefore chosen as a symbol of Yitzchak's self-sacrifice, since he fulfilled his act of *mesiras nefesh* when he was at the peak of his maturity.

---

149   Ibn Ezra, *Bereishis* 22:4.

150   *Emes L'Yaakov*, p. 127.

151   *Shulchan Aruch, Orach Chaim* 591:7.

Mesiras Nefesh with Joy

We sometimes find people who will do difficult things for others, but they won't do so wholeheartedly. The *Orchos Tzadikim* writes that what was so special about Avraham's selfless act was that he negated the love for his son and replaced it with love for Hashem.[152] A proof that Avraham performed the *Akeidah* joyously can be derived from the fact that at that very time, he received a prophetic vision. Had he been in a state of anxiety and sadness, he would have been unable to attain a state of prophecy, since prophecy only rests upon a prophet when he is joyous.[153]

At the *Akeidah*, both Avraham and Yitzchak yearned to be close with Hashem and to be inseparably bound to Him. Thus, the merit of *Akeidas Yitzchak* removes the sins of their descendants that obstruct them from properly connecting to Hashem.

Reward for Preparation

Chazal say that the reward for mitzvos is not given in this world.[154] Why not? The Vilna Gaon explains that mitzvos are spiritual, while this world is merely physical. Something "merely" physical cannot possible be the reward for something spiritual!

If so, how could Hashem reward Avraham for *Akeidas Yitzchak* by swearing to remember the merit of the *Akeidah* for him and all his posterity? How can *Bnei Yisrael* receive reward in *this* world for the merit of *Akeidas Yitzchak*?

On the verse, "On the third day, Avraham raised his eyes," the Midrash applies the verse, "You will grant us life from the two days. The third day You will uphold us and we will live before You."[155] What does this mean?

The Vilna Gaon answers that indeed the true reward for *Akeidas Yitzchak* is completely reserved for the World to Come. In this world,

---

152   *Orchos Tzadikim*, beginning of *Sha'ar HaZerizus*.
153   *Pesachim* 117a.
154   *Kiddushin* 39b.
155   *Bereishis Rabbah* 56:1, quoting *Hoshea* 6:2.

we are only able to glean the reward for Avraham and Yitzchak's preparatory actions; the Torah enumerates how Avraham arose early with alacrity to go to the *Akeidah* and saddled his own donkey. It is for those meritorious acts that we reap the rewards in this world.

The Vilna Gaon says that this is the meaning of the Midrash, "You will grant us life from the two days." This means to say that what we benefit in our present life is the reward for what Avraham did in the first two preparatory days leading to the *Akeidah*. But regarding the third day, meaning the *Akeidah* itself, which was performed on the third day, "You will uphold us and we will live before You" — in the World to Come.[156]

The Reward for Binding

> *Why do we blow with a shofar of a ram? Says HaKadosh Baruch Hu: "Blow before Me using a shofar of a ram, so that I will remember for your sake the binding of Yitzchak, the son of Avraham, and I will consider it for you as if you had bound yourselves before me."*[157]

Why is Yitzchak's act of supreme self-sacrifice eternally known as *Akeidas Yitzchak* — the *binding* of Yitzchak? Why do we focus on the detail that Yitzchak was *bound* upon the altar and not his general willingness to ascend the altar as a sacrifice? In addition, why does the Gemara mention that Yitzchak was the son of Avraham? Isn't that point obvious?

The *Be'er Yosef* answers that Yitzchak specifically requested that his hands and legs be bound so that he would not reflexively push away his father and thereby profane the proper honor due to his father.[158] It is therefore specifically the act of binding that fully

---

156   *Kol Eliyahu, parashas Vayera* 16.
157   *Rosh Hashanah* 16a.
158   *Pirkei D'Rebbi Eliezer* 31.

demonstrates the lofty intentions of Yitzchak — by revealing the great respect Yitzchak had for his father and his single-minded focus to carry out his father's instructions to their most minute detail.[159]

Mercy Punishment

"And *Akeidas Yitzchak* should be recalled mercifully today for his descendants."[160] Why does the prayer mention that *Akeidas Yitzchak* should be recalled *in mercy*? Isn't it obvious that when Hashem recalls *Akeidas Yitzchak*, its merit will arouse Divine mercy upon his children? In addition, some authorities question the use of the vague terminology "his descendants," which may also refer to the descendants of Eisav![161]

The *Be'er Yosef* relates a principle in the name of the Vilna Gaon, saying that when a person is punished via the attribute of *din* — Divine justice — he should wait for the trait of Divine mercy to return once the punishment has run its course. However, if a person is punished via the trait of Divine mercy, the punishment is particularly severe.[162]

For example, if a person kills his brother, the father will beat his murderous son in the most violent manner out of his great love for the slain child. The motivation for the father's seemingly cruel outburst is not so much to exact punishment on the wicked child for his wickedness, but is rather the way for the father to express his grief and pain for the loss of his beloved son. Rabbi Yitzchak Blazer explains that this is what is meant that the wicked turn the trait of Divine mercy into justice, since Hashem punishes the wicked because of His mercy on the victims whom the wicked persecuted.

We therefore ask Hashem to recall the actions of *all* of Yitzchak's descendants — the children of Yaakov and Eisav as well. Throughout

---

159   Rabbi Yosef Salant, *Be'er Yosef, Bereishis,* end *parashas Vayera.*

160   *Musaf* of Rosh Hashanah.

161   See *Shulchan Aruch, Orach Chaim* 591:7.

162   *Be'er Yosef* ibid.

history, Eisav mercilessly and relentlessly persecutes the Jewish People in exile. By recalling *Akeidas Yitzchak* "with mercy," Hashem's recollection of *Akeidas Yitzchak* will arouse Divine mercy to bring redemption to the children of Israel and to wreak vengeance against Eisav.[163]

TEKIAS SHOFAR

No Talking

One may not talk during *tekias shofar* from the start of the mitzvah until after all the *tekios* have been blown.[164] Interestingly, the source of this halachah is not from the Gemara; rather, it comes from the Rif, who cites an anonymous head of the academy (*Reish Mesivta*) from the time of the Gaonim.[165]

The Ran challenges this ruling, arguing that it is no different than talking during the performance of any other mitzvah, such as while searching for *chametz* before Pesach, when talking is permissible (according to his view).[166] Although the Ran was at a loss to comprehend the *Reish Mesivta*'s view, the Ran concludes with deference: "Since the *Reish Mesivta* said that it is prohibited to talk during the *tekios*, it is fitting that one should not speak without [pressing] need."

There are several approaches given to explain the ruling of the Rif:

- According to the Rif, it would indeed be prohibited to talk during the duration of *bedikas chametz* until one completes his search for *chametz*.[167] *Tekias shofar* is therefore akin to the mitzvah of reciting *Hallel*, during which one may also not interrupt with idle talk.[168]

---

163 *Be'er Yosef* ibid.

164 *Shulchan Aruch, Orach Chaim* 592:3.

165 *Rosh Hashanah* 11a.

166 Ran, *Rosh Hashanah* ibid.

167 *Taz, Shulchan Aruch* ibid.

168 *Gra, Shulchan Aruch* ibid. The dispute between the Ran and the Rif may be dependent on whether the blessing on the mitzvah is for the completion of the mitzvah or for the

- Although it may technically be permissible to talk during *tekias shofar*, it is still not appropriate to do so, "since it is fitting to humble one's heart and arouse one's evil inclination into trembling by not distracting oneself through idle speech."[169]

No Shofar on Shabbos

When the Torah first discusses Rosh Hashanah, it refers to it as a *zichron teruah* — a *remembrance* of blowing the shofar.[170] The wording of the verse implies that the shofar is only "remembered" but is not actually blown. This verse hints to the law that when Rosh Hashanah falls out on Shabbos, one only "remembers" the shofar but does not actually blow it.[171] Later, in the book of *Bamidbar*, Rosh Hashanah is called *yom teruah* — a day of [actually] blowing [the shofar]."[172]

Why does the Torah first mention *zichron teruah* — the rememberance of blowing the shofar before discussing the obligation to actually blow it? The *Parparous L'Chochmah* answers that the reason why *zichron teruah* is mentioned first is because the first Rosh Hashanah the Jewish nation experienced after leaving Egypt transpired on Shabbos.[173]

(Since the first Rosh Hashanah in the *midbar* fell out on Shabbos, it follows that the original Yom Kippur transpired on Monday, ten days later. The *Tur* writes that the reason we say a lengthy *Tachanun* on Monday and Thursday is since Moshe went up to heaven to receive the second

---

performance of even a segment of the mitzvah. If it is for the completion, then the entire mitzvah is viewed as one single unit and one is unable to make an interruption after one recites a blessing until the object of the blessing has been fulfilled. According to this view, if one considers that the blessing for *tekias shofar* covers the entire mitzvah, he may not make an interruption until all the *tekios* have been completed.

169 Meiri, *Rosh Hashanah* 35a.
170 *Vayikra* 23:24.
171 See *Rosh Hashanah* 29b.
172 *Bamidbar* 29:1.
173 *Parparous L'Chochmah*, p. 132.

luchos on a Thursday and returned on Yom Kippur forty days later (on a Monday), these two days of the week are special *yemei ratzon* — days for obtaining Divine favor.)[174]

Standing for Shofar

The Radvaz wonders why the *ba'al tokea* — the one who sounds the shofar — has to stand while blowing the shofar.[175] The Brisker Rav explains that the shofar blowing on Rosh Hashanah is a form of prayer. He presents a support to his premise from the conclusion of the blessing: "Who listens to the sound [of the shofar] blast...with mercy." When we perform a mitzvah, there is never a need to beseech Hashem that the mitzvah be accepted with mercy. A mitzvah performed properly is, in itself, the fulfillment of Hashem's will![176]

However, since shofar is not simply a mitzvah but also a form of prayer, just as a chazzan stands during his recital of *Shemoneh Esrei*, so too must the *ba'al tokea* stand when he represents the congregation in fulfilling their obligation of the "prayer" of shofar.[177]

THE CALL OF THE SHOFAR

Cries of Joy

We are accustomed to thinking that the sounds of the shofar on Rosh Hashanah are primarily the sounds of painful cries, which are to arouse us to do *teshuvah*.

The Seforno says that our shofar blowing is primarily to demonstrate our joy in Hashem's kingship.[178] Just as it is customary to blow trumpets at the coronation of a human ruler, we also blow the shofar

---

174 *Tur, Orach Chaim* 134.
175 Radvaz 1:101.
176 Cited in *Sharei Aharon, Bamidbar* 23:21.
177 See *Sharei Aharon* ibid.
178 *Vayikra* 23:24.

on Rosh Hashanah, which marks the day Hashem created the world and commenced ruling over it.[179] The regal yet joyous trumpet blasts sounded at a coronation demonstrate the populace's love for their king and acceptance of his rule. This, in turn, arouses the king's love towards his subjects and his forgiveness of their indiscretions. As Rabbi Moshe Feinstein points out, it was customary on the day of a monarch's coronation to even pardon criminals deserving the death penalty.[180] The Vilna Gaon adds that *teruah* is the sound of joy that comes forth from a multitude.[181] The shofar's *teruah* on Rosh Hashanah therefore expresses our national joy that Hashem is our king.[182]

Sound of Friendship

Teruah also signifies love and friendship, as the *pasuk* says: ותרועת מלך בו — "And the friendship of the King is in him (the Jewish nation)."[183] *Onkelos*, however, translates this verse as follows: "And the *Shechinah* of the King abides amid them." The *Ayeles HaShachar* asks, what does the *Shechinah*'s presence have to do with love and friendship? He answers that the *Shechinah*'s presence in our midst is the greatest expression of Hashem's friendship with us.[184] The Temple was therefore referred to as the place, "bedecked with love,"[185] since it was there that the *Shechinah* dwelt amid Israel.[186] Similarly, since Hashem is close to us on Rosh Hashanah, this itself is a sign of Hashem's love and friendship towards us.

---

179   Rabbi Sa'adiah Gaon, *Taamei HaTekiyos*, first reason, cited in *Avudraham, Rosh Hashanah*.

180   *Derash Moshe*, p. 172; this can be seen in *Shmuel II* 19:23. See also Seforno, *Bamidbar* 23:21.

181   *Siddur HaGra*, p. 424.

182   See also *Siddur HaGra*, p. 409.

183   *Bamidbar* 23:21; Rashi there.

184   Rabbi Aryeh Leib Shteinman, *Ayeles HaShachar, Bamidbar* ibid.

185   *Shir HaShirim* 3:10; Rashi there.

186   Since our shuls are miniature Temples, they are also places permeated with Divine love. *Hararei Kedem*, vol. 2, 169:3.

Redemption and Enlightenment

In *Tehillim*, the psalmist juxtaposes the release of Yosef from captivity and his meteoric rise to viceroy of Egypt with the shofar blowing on Rosh Hashanah:

תקעו בחדש שופר בכסה ליום חגנו כי חק לישראל הוא משפט לאלקי יעקב.

עדות ביהוסף שמו בצאתו על ארץ מצרים, שפת לא ידעתי אשמע.

Blow the shofar at the moon's renewal, at the time appointed for our festive day, because it is a decree for Israel, a judgment [day] for the G-d of Yaakov. He appointed it as a testimony for Joseph when he went out over the land of Egypt, when I heard a language unknown to me.[187]

The verse focuses on one particular miracle that enabled Yosef to become viceroy: Under Egyptian law, in order to qualify as a ruler, one had to know to speak Egyptian, a language foreign to Yosef. Hashem sent the angel Gavriel to teach it to him.[188]

What is the connection between Rosh Hashanah and Yosef's ability to speak a foreign tongue?

Rabbi Yitzchak Hutner explains that the punishment visited upon the *Dor HaFlagah* for their rebellion against Hashem was that there was a breakdown in communication and they were unable to understand each other's language. A human being is created in the image of G-d, and the unique quality of a human is his ability of speech. When the *Dor HaFlagah* abused their G-dly potential, their faculty of speech was also diminished. In contrast, Yosef demonstrated his G-dly nature by resisting the temptations of his master's wife (which is why the psalmist added the letter *hei* to Yosef's name, which is one of the letters of the name of Hashem). Yosef's spiritual clarity to distinguish between good and evil not only earned

---

187 *Tehillim* 81:4–6.
188 *Sotah* 36b.

him his personal redemption, but also gave him the ability to master all seventy languages.[189]

The concept of shofar is not only related to redemption but also to spiritual enlightenment.[190] As the Ramchal explains, the essence of blowing the shofar on Rosh Hashanah is that it shocks a person into reality and thereby enables him to distinguish between good and evil. This awareness is a prerequisite for redemption, both on a personal and a national level.[191]

Day of the Teruah Blast

Why does the Torah refer to Rosh Hashanah specifically as "a day of [the shofar's] *teruah* [blast],"[192] with no mention of the sound of the *tekiah* blast?

It is brought in Kabbalistic sources that the *teruah* blast denotes the attribute of strict justice.[193] The short blast signifies a pulverizing force, as we find that the walls of Yericho fell when the *Kohanim* blew the *teruah*. This is also why the *teruah* was blown when going out to war.[194]

The *tekiah* sound of the shofar corresponds to the attribute of mercy, which is why the *tekiah* sound was used to call an assembly before the Mishkan in the desert, which was a convocation of brotherly peace amid the presence of Hashem.[195] Since Rosh Hashanah is primarily a day of justice, the verse explicitly mentions the *teruah* blast.

Elsewhere in the Torah, Rosh Hashanah is called *zichron teruah* — a remembrance of *teruah*.[196] In the Torah, *zichron* always denotes the attribute of Divine mercy.[197] *Zichron teruah* signifies how Hashem

189   Rabbi Yitzchak Hutner, *Pachad Yitzchak*, Rosh Hashanah, pp. 147–149.

190   Maharshah, *Rosh Hashanah* 11b; see above, "Call of Freedom."

191   See Ramchal, *Ma'amar HaChochmah: Malchuyos, Zichronos, v'Shofaros.*

192   *Bamidbar* 29:1.

193   See Ramban, *Vayikra* 23:24.

194   *Bamidbar* 10:9; *Yirmiyah* 4:19.

195   *Bamidbar* 10:3–4.

196   *Vayikra* 23:24.

197   *Mahari Ya'avitz, Tehillim* 38:1.

thinks of us mercifully on this day, such as when we blow the shofar, which activates the trait of mercy, which, in conjunction with *teshuvah*, nullifies any harsh judgments against us. Since Rosh Hashanah is a day of *din b'rachamim* — justice tempered with mercy, the trait of mercy is only alluded to by the word *zichron*.

The Journeyman's Call

A trumpet was used to signal the movements of the Jewish People during their forty-year sojourn in the wilderness. A single *tekiah* was blown to gather the people together in one place, while a *tekiah-teruah-tekiah* signalled them to disband camp and to continue their travels.[198]

The same sounds are blown with the shofar on Rosh Hashanah to parallel our spiritual journey in life. The uninterrupted sound of the *tekiah* calls one to gather his scattered thoughts and energies and to refocus them inwardly toward Hashem. The broken sound of the *teruah* shakes a person out of complacency and dislodges him from the rut of his routine. The final *tekiah* gives one the strength and courage to uplift oneself from despair and to redirect his energies onwards upon the straight uplifted path before Hashem.[199]

Mixed Messages

A curious feature of *lashon HaKodesh* is that there are a number of words that are simultaneously both homonyms and antonyms. One example is *tokeah*, which can mean "connecting,"[200] as well as "disconnecting."[201] Both aspects are applicable to the message of *tekias shofar* on Rosh Hashanah. The fearful blasts of the shofar arouse us out of our complacency to part from our sinful ways while simultaneously drawing us closer to reconnect with Hashem.

---

198 *Bamidbar* 10.
199 Rabbi Shimshon Raphael Hirsch, *Horeb* 32.
200 As in *Bereishis* 31:25: "Yaakov pitched (ויתקע) his tent on the mountain."
201 Ibid. 32:26: "Yaakov's hip-socket was dislocated (ותקע)." See Chizkuni there.

Shechinah's Pain

Rabbi Baruch Ber Lebowitz delivered the following stirring message prior to *tekias shofar* on Rosh Hashanah on the eve of World War Two:[202]

In the song of the *Levi'im* for Wednesday, it says: היחברך כסא הוות.[203] The verse is generally translated as, "Can the throne of destruction be associated with You?" Homiletically, the word היחברך derives from the word *chaburah* — to wound, כסא is a reference to the throne of Hashem, and הוות is an expression for pain. The *pasuk* can therefore be translated: "Will you not afflict yourself [out of anguish] because the glory of Hashem is in pain [in exile]?" The piercing sobs of the shofar's blast not only express our personal pain resulting from our sins, but should also express our pain that the *Shechinah* is in exile.

Cries of the Wicked

The *Shofaros* blessing concludes: "*Uma'azin teruah v'ein domeh lach* — And You give ear to the *teruah*, and none is comparable to You." In what way is Hashem incomparable in that He hears the *teruah* sound of the shofar? Human beings are also able to hear the sound of the shofar's *teruah* blast!

The word *ma'azin* means to listen in close proximity.[204] The shofar's *tekiah* sound corresponds to the wholly righteous, whose Divine service is also continuous and unbroken; the *shevarim* represents the average Jews, whose service is pronounced but intermittent; and the *teruah* refers to the wicked who only serve Hashem in short bursts dispersed among gaps of moral lapses.

Unlike a human king, who favors beautiful and complete vessels, Hashem especially seeks to utilize broken vessels.[205] So when the heart of the wicked feels contrite and broken (like the *teruah* sound) and

---

202   *Peninim M'Shulchan Gavoah, Shemos* 17:16.
203   *Tehillim* 94:20.
204   See *Sifri, Devarim* 306.
205   *Vayikra Rabbah* 7:2.

repents with full sincerity, Hashem cherishes their brokenness and draws them especially close to Him. Hashem's unique quality of mercy is that He yearns to hear the cries of the wicked even more than those of the completely righteous, as our Sages say: "In the place where the penitents stand even the wholly righteous cannot stand."[206]

The basis for the custom of blowing one hundred *tekios* on Rosh Hashanah stems from the hundred groans and whimpers the mother of Sisrah cried while awaiting her son to return from battle in his campaign against Israel. Why do we commemorate the pain of such a cruel person who comforted herself that her son was busy looting and persecuting innocent victims? Rabbi Shabsi Yudelevitz answers that if Hashem sent an angel to count the tears of even such a loathsome person, we see that every single tear from even the most wicked person has meaning to Hashem.[207]

Piercing the Temple Curtain

The shofar's sound brings the prayers of the Jewish nation into the Holy of Holies before Hashem's presence and causes Hashem to remember us in mercy.[208] This idea is hinted to in the Torah as the numerical value of *paroches* — the curtain that separated between the Holy and the Holy of Holies in the Mishkan — which is *kashrak*, the acronym for the order of shofar blasts that are blown on Rosh Hashanah (*teKiah, Shevarim, teRuah, teKiah*).[209] This symbolizes that the power of *tekias shofar* is that it breaks through the *paroches* to allow our merits to enter *lifnai v'lifnim* — the inner sanctum of Hashem's sanctuary. The *gematriah* of *kashrak* is the word *paroches* when spelled *chasser* (written without the letter *vav*). This signifies

---

206   See *Menoras HaMaor*, p. 624 (MHK ed.).

207   *Hamodia Magazine*, vol. 13 (624), p. 3.

208   Ritva, *Rosh Hashanah* 26a.

209   Although acronyms generally follow the first letter of a word, an exception is made regarding the order of the shofar blasts in which we use the second letter. This is done to differentiate beween the *tekiah* and *teruah* that both begin with the letter נ.

that the *paroches* is "incomplete" and is unable to withstand the penetration of the merit of the shofar's blast.[210]

Shofar and the Merit of Torah

The Rokeach says that the reason why we blow the shofar immediately following the Torah reading of the day is so that through the merit of Torah we will be worthy of a favorable judgment.[211] This is also the meaning of the verse recited after *tekias shofar*: "Fortunate is the people that know [the secret of the sound of the shofar's] *teruah* [blast], Hashem, they shall walk in the light of Your countenance."[212] Light is a metaphor for Torah,[213] and the day of Rosh Hashanah is also compared to light.[214] By immersing in the light of Torah, one connects to the illumination that is the essence of Rosh Hashanah.

The Forceful Blow

The literal and common translation for *tekias shofar* is "blowing the shofar." In *Bava Kama*, the Mishnah discusses a case of where a person injures his fellowman via *tokeah*.[215] Rashi explains that this refers to a person who shouts in the ear of his fellowman, which is akin to the simple meaning of *tokeah* — to create a loud noise through blowing.

Interestingly, Rashi offers another explanation, saying that *tokeah* means to strike a person with force. Based on this, it can be interpreted that our blowing the shofar on Rosh Hashanah inflicts a forceful blow against the forces of evil. This is alluded to in the verses recited prior to *tekias shofar*, the first letters of which form the acronym *Kra Satan* — tear up Satan.

---

210   *Rabbeinu Ephraim, Shemos* 26:31.
211   *Bamidbar* 29:1.
212   *Tehillim* 89:16.
213   *Mishlei* 6:23.
214   See *Midrash Tehillim* 27.
215   *Bava Kama* 90a.

Horns of Dilemma

The two horns from the ram used at *Akeidas Yitzchak* were fashioned into two shofaros. The left was used at *Matan Torah* and the right will herald the coming of Mashiach.[216] With this we can understand the Gemara that says that the reason we blow the shofar twice on Rosh Hashanah — although the first blowing suffices for the fulfilment of the mitzvah — is to confuse Satan.[217] Tosfos explains that when Satan hears the shofar blown an additional time, he is convinced that Mashiach has arrived, and in his confusion, he desists from bringing prosecution against Israel.[218]

Since the obligation of blowing the shofar on Rosh Hashanah derives from the Torah that was given through the left horn, Satan presumes that the additional blowing was from the other horn, which can mean nothing else than Mashiach's arrival.

Learning from Satan

The *Yerushalmi* says that when Satan hears *Bnei Yisrael* blowing the shofar on Rosh Hashanah, he fears that it is the sound of the shofar of Mashiach, and because of his confusion, he refrains from prosecuting the Jewish People.[219] How could Satan make such a foolish mistake? Doesn't he realize that Rosh Hashanah is the day the Jews are commanded to blow the shofar? And even if he were to be fooled one year, why should he fall prey to the same ploy year after year?

Rabbi Yechezkel Abramsky answers that Satan believes with certainty that Mashiach will eventually come. The length of the exile does not dampen his belief in Mashiach's coming; on the contrary, the more years that pass, the more imminent is Mashiach's arrival. Since Mashiach's coming is dependent on the *Bnei Yisrael* doing *teshuvah*, on Rosh Hashanah Satan becomes stricken with fear,

---

216   *Pirkei D'Rebbi Eliezer* 31.
217   *Rosh Hashanah* 16b.
218   Tosfos, *Rosh Hashanah* ibid.
219   Cited in Tosfos ibid.

for perhaps the Jews have repented sufficiently to be worthy of Mashiach.[220] This is what is meant by the verse: "From my enemies, I become wise of Your commandments."[221] We can learn from our enemy, i.e., Satan, how great is the power of our *teshuvah* and how strong our faith should be in the imminent coming of Mashiach.[222]

Silencing Satan

The Gemara says that there are two sets of blasts sounded on Rosh Hashanah in order to confuse Satan.[223] Rashi explains that when Satan hears how the Jews hold dearly to Hashem's mitzvos, i.e., by performing the mitzvah of shofar twice (above and beyond the letter of the law), he becomes confounded and is unable to prosecute them.

Rabbi Akiva Eiger asks: why should Satan fear prosecuting them just because they cherish the mitzvos? He answers that a person who repents out of love for Hashem has his rebellious sins turned into merits.[224] When Satan sees how the Jews are serving Hashem in a loving manner, he is afraid to mention their sins before Him, for every sin he will evoke against them will be turned into a merit and mitzvah! Satan sees that it is more advantageous for him to remain silent.[225]

---

220   Rabbi Yechezkel Abramsky, *Chazon Yechezkel on Tanach*, p. 326.
221   *Tehillim* 119:98.
222   *Chazon Yechezkel* ibid.
223   *Rosh Hashanah* 16b.
224   *Yomah* 86b.
225   *Chut HaMeshulash*, p. 178.

Aseres Yemei Teshuvah — The Ten Days of Repentance

The Ten Tests of Avraham Avinu

The Rokeach writes that the *Aseres Yemei Teshuvah* correspond to the ten tests with which Hashem tested Avraham Avinu.[226] What is the connection between these two ideas?

The *Mikdash Mordechai* explains that just as Avraham's tests elevated him to great spiritual levels, so do the Ten Days of Repentance have the potential to produce a similar effect upon us — if we utilize them properly.[227]

The Ten Sefiros

On a mystical level, the ten days between Rosh Hashanah and Yom Kippur correspond to the ten *sefiros*.[228] In Kabbalah, *malchus* — kingship — is the lowest and most physical of the ten *sefiros*, and it corresponds to Hashem's kingship as expressed in the physical world. This parallels the day of Rosh Hashanah when we accept Hashem's sovereignty on earth. On each progressive day of the *Aseres Yemei Teshuvah*, we continue to climb to higher spiritual realms, finally culminating with Yom Kippur. On Yom Kippur, we are in such close proximity to Hashem that we are stripped of our physicality, as is

---

226 *Avos* 5:4.
227 Rabbi Mordechai Ilan, *Mikdash Mordechai*, *Bereishis* 22:1.
228 Ramban, *Vayikra* 23:24.

indicated by the prohibition of eating, drinking, and other mundane activities. As the highest spiritual realms are associated with pure kindness, the day of Yom Kippur is primarily a day of mercy (*rachamim b'din*).

Seeking a Heavenly Sign

The Ramban explains that *Derishas Elokim* denotes a specific form of prayer in which the petitioner wishes to know whether Hashem will grant his specific request.[229] Accordingly, we can understand the verse, "*Dirshu Hashem behimatzoh* — Seek Hashem when He can be found,"[230] which *Chazal* say refers specifically to the time between Rosh Hashanah and Yom Kippur, in the following manner: During the *Aseres Yemei Teshuvah*, one may seek Hashem through prayer and repentance with the expectation that Hashem will openly reveal whether one has been granted a good year.[231]

How can this be accomplished? If one finds that one's prayers flow effortlessly from one's heart and pour fluently from one's mouth during this period, it is a Divine sign that one's prayers have been accepted.[232]

229   *Shemos* 18:15.
230   *Yeshayah* 55:6.
231   Rabbi Dovid Pardo, *Chasdei Dovid, Horayos* 2:11.
232   *Chasdei Dovid* ibid.; cf. *Berachos* 34b.

Yom Kippur

Erev Yom Kippur Feast

The Gemara teaches that whoever eats and drinks on the day prior to Yom Kippur is rewarded as if he fasted on that day in addition to fasting on Yom Kippur itself.[233] Numerous reasons are given as to why eating on Erev Yom Kippur is considered such a great mitzvah:

1. By making a feast in honor of the fast, it demonstrates one's joy and yearning for the upcoming day of Yom Kippur when one's sins will be forgiven.[234]

2. It is proper to perform mitzvos with joy, which is why we are commanded to feast on Yom Tov. Since we are commanded to fast on Yom Kippur, we celebrate the mitzvah of fasting on Yom Kippur by feasting the day prior to the fast.[235]

3. Through eating the day before Yom Kippur, one will have the strength and stamina to properly fast, pray, and repent on Yom Kippur itself.[236]

4. If one were to fast on the day before Yom Kippur it may appear that his fasting on Yom Kippur is also because of personal preference. By feasting on Erev Yom Kippur, it becomes apparent that one's fasting on Yom Kippur is solely because Hashem commands us to fast on this day.[237]

---

233 *Rosh Hashanah* 9a.
234 *Shaarei Teshuvah* 4:8.
235 Ibid. 4:9.
236 Ibid. 4:10.
237 *Perishah, Orach Chaim* 604:2.

5. The reason for fasting on Yom Kippur is to atone for the Sin of the Golden Calf, which came about through improper eating and drinking.[238] We rectify this lapse by feasting on Erev Yom Kippur with proper intentions.

Concealed Day

In *parashas Pinchas*, the Torah details the sacrifices brought on Yom Tov. There the Torah uses the word *yom* — day — for all the holidays including Rosh Hashanah. However, the term "day" is not used in relation to Yom Kippur.

Why is this so?

The Midrash explains the verse, *"Yamim yutzaru v'lo echad mahem* — He created days, but did not include one of them,"[239] as referring to the day of Yom Kippur.[240] On Yom Kippur, the Jewish People are comparable to sacrifices, since our body fat and blood is diminished through fasting and thus become nullified and otherworldly. Just as our bodies transcend the physical plane, so too the day itself is non-existent in the ordinary dimension of time.[241]

Day without Sin

The Vilna Gaon writes that the evil inclination has 365 officers in his "army," each holding special powers during one day of the 365 days of the year. Since the Torah is the antidote against the evil inclination, the Torah exhorts us with 365 negative commandments that empower us in vanquishing those negative forces. The negative commandment corresponding to the day of Yom Kippur is the prohibition of eating on Yom Kippur.

Since our Sages say Satan has no power on Yom Kippur, the negative commandment corresponding to this day was also not expressed as

---

238   See *Shemos* 24:11; Chizkuni, *Vayikra* 23:27.

239   *Tehillim* 139:16.

240   *Eliyahu Rabbah* 1.

241   Rabbi Yitzchak Zoller, *Yalkut Yitzchak*, p. 140.

forcefully as other negative commandments of the Torah. (Ordinarily, commandments are phrased as a direct command — "You shall not...", while the prohibition of eating on Yom Kippur is expressed in the passive tense — "For any soul who will not be afflicted on this very day will be cut off from its people.") Since the forces of evil are subdued on Yom Kippur, it was unnecessary for the Torah to express the prohibition in stronger terms.[242]

Rabbi Aharon Kotler comments that a solar year (the time in which the earth completes a full orbit around the sun) is actually several hours more than 365 days. Based on what was brought in the name of the Vilna Gaon above, Rabbi Kotler suggests that the Torah obligation of *Tosfos Yom HaKippurim*, to commence the Yom Kippur fast shortly before sunset, corresponds to those extra few hours in the year in which the solar year extends without a corresponding Torah prohibition.[243]

Fasting on Yom Kippur

The *Tur* writes that Hashem commanded the fast of Yom Kippur out of His love for the Jewish People so that their sins should be forgiven.[244] If so, if someone declines the benefit of the fast, it should be sufficient that his sins remain intact. Why is the punishment for eating on Yom Kippur so severe than one receives *kares* as a result?

The *D'rishah* explains that the Jewish nation is considered one entity. A person who dissociates himself from the rest of the nation that is fasting on Yom Kippur does a grievous disservice not only to himself but to the entire nation,[245] and therefore he receives the most extreme punishment.[246]

---

242 Vilna Gaon, *Aderes Eliyahu, Vayikra* 16:31.
243 *Mishnas Rebbi Aharon*, Yomim Noraim, p. 45.
244 *Tur, Orach Chaim* 604.
245 See *Akeidas Yitzchak, Nitzavim* 99.
246 Commentary to *Tur* ibid., 2.

Undeserved Grace

"Merit and fairness are before His throne, kindness and mercy are before His glory."[247]

The Vilna Gaon explains that the "throne" represents Hashem's throne of judgment, before which the Heavenly court judges a person on Rosh Hashanah.[248] On this day, a person needs "merit" (an allusion to Torah) and "fairness" (good deeds) in order to be vindicated in judgment.

On Yom Kippur, however, Hashem judges a person alone without the Heavenly tribunal. Then, "kindness and mercy are before His glory," and a person can merit undeserved favor and grace before Hashem.[249]

Repairing Sin with Torah

The Rambam rules that repentance, suffering, and even Yom Kippur are insufficient to atone for the grievous sin of *chilul Hashem*.[250] Yet Rabbeinu Yonah writes that even *chilul Hashem* can be atoned for through the merit of intense Torah study, as it is written: "Through... truth [Torah study], iniquity will be forgiven."[251]

How is this possible?

Rabbi Yitzchak Hutner explains that the severity of *chilul Hashem* is that it weakens one's awareness of his responsibility towards Hashem. This is countered via Torah study, which is a re-enactment of the giving of the Torah on Sinai, which created a covenant between us and Hashem and our obligations toward Him. Since a covenant only carries meaning if both participants of the pact possess the trait of truth, the verse specifically uses the word "truth" to describe Torah study.[252]

---

247 *Kel Adon* prayer.
248 *Genuzas HaGra*, p. 210.
249 Ibid., cf. *Berachos* 7a.
250 Rambam, *Mishnah Torah*, Teshuvah 1.
251 Rabbeinu Yonah, *Mishlei* 16:6.
252 *Pachad Yitzchak*, Rosh Hashanah, pp. 195–196.

TESHUVAH

"Our" Shabbos

The Chizkuni draws a distinction between Shabbos and Yom Kippur. Whereas Shabbos is called *Shabbos LaHashem* — a Shabbos for Hashem, Yom Kippur is called *Shabbatchem — your* Shabbos.[253] The reason for this could be that our resting on an ordinary Shabbos testifies that Hashem created the world in six days and rested on the seventh. However, our cessation from work on Yom Kippur is for the purpose of stopping our daily routine so that we may purify ourselves and thereby merit atonement for our sins.

Effects of Sin

Both the first and second sets of *luchos* were equally holy and perfect. The only difference was the manner in which they were acquired. Israel's preparation for receiving the first *luchos* was relatively easy, and upon receiving the Torah on Sinai they attained a state of perfection that enabled them to comprehend the Torah with minimal effort. After the Sin of the Golden Calf, they fell from their exalted state and required an intense period of repentance and self-improvement to be worthy of receiving the second *luchos*. In addition, Torah would henceforth require extreme strength and concentration to be comprehended.

Rabbi Aharon Kotler points out that the Torah remains pristine, but as we distance ourselves from Hashem, we require more effort to achieve the same goals.[254] Similarly, Hashem never lowers His standards for us in attaining perfection; only once we sin do we necessitate a more difficult program to reclaim the same spiritual heights.

---

253 Chizkuni, *Vayikra* 23:32.
254 *Mishnas Rebbi Aharon, Shemos* 34:28.

Greatest Heights vs. Lowest Depths

The Seforno points out that the two goat offerings on Yom Kippur are unique in that they are offered in a diametrically opposing manner.[255] The blood of one goat is brought into the Holy of Holies, while the other goat is brought to a desolate cliff inhabited by the forces of evil and impurity. What does this represent?

Rabbi Aharon Kotler notes that Yom Kippur is also a time of two opposite extremes. On the one hand, Yom Kippur is a time when Hashem tempers the trait of justice with mercy and assists us in obtaining atonement for our sins. Were it not for His great love and mercy towards us, we would be unable to survive Yom Kippur, as it is written: "For the day of Hashem (i.e., Yom Kippur) is great and very awesome; who will be able to bear it?"[256] On the other hand, if someone misuses the gift presented on this day by not applying himself in obtaining Divine mercy through prayer and *teshuvah*, his rejection of Hashem's magnanimous offer is a demonstration of tremendous disrespect.

The two goats of Yom Kippur portray how one person can utilize the day to attain the greatest spiritual heights, while it can cause another to sink into the lowest depths.[257]

The Sooner, the Better

Although all five cities in Sodom were equally wicked and deserved to be destroyed, Hashem spared the city of Tzoar because it was founded one year after the other cities and thus it had accumulated fewer sins.[258] Rabbi Yitzchak Blazer derives an important moral lesson from this story: to appreciate how even one year can make a categorical difference whether someone is considered a *tzadik* or a *rasha*. Although someone may have gone through many a Yom

---

255   *Kavanas HaTorah.*
256   *Yoel* 2:11.
257   *Mishnas Rebbi Aharon*, Yomim Noraim, p. 216.
258   See *Bereishis* 19:20; Rashi there.

Kippur unchanged, he should still be careful not to let one more year pass without proper repentance.[259]

Root of Teshuvah

There are two ways to weed one's garden: to cut the weeds as they crop up or to pull them out at their roots. While cutting the weeds gives the appearance of correcting the problem, it does not deal with the underlying cause, and it is only a matter of time until the ugly weeds resurface.

Rabbi Aharon Kotler observes that the same applies to *teshuvah*. The main aspect of a sin that requires attention is not so much the sin itself but rather the root of the sin — the underlying nature that produces the sinful action in the first place. If a person only confesses the action without addressing its source, his sin remains intact and unforgiven. The more one focuses on weeding out the negative roots of one's nature, the more elevated is his *teshuvah* and the more powerful and permanent the change.[260]

Granting Forgiveness

We all know that the *Shulchan Aruch* discusses how to deal with someone who harms another. But there is also a *Shulchan Aruch* delineating how a victim should act.

The Rosh writes, "Do not rebuff someone who seeks to excuse his behavior to you, regardless if he speaks the truth or falsehood."[261] Similarly, when a person seeks forgiveness and the victim uses the opportunity to pour out his wrath on the perpetrator, it is possible that the victim then becomes the aggressor and his misdeed may even exceed the original wrongdoing done against him.[262]

---

259 From Rabbi Isser Zalman Meltzer, as quoted in *Peninim M'Shulchan Gavoah, Bereishis* 19:20.

260 *Mishnas Rebbi Aharon, Devarim* 29:17.

261 *Orchos Chaim L'Rosh* 110.

262 Rabbi Yeruchem Levovitz, *Da'as Torah, Bereishis* 45:8.

It is also wrong for the victim to refuse to hear the aggressor's apology and just wave it off dismissively, saying "Oh, you didn't do anything wrong." Rabbi Yitzchak Blazer observes that although this approach superficially appears magnanimous, it is a ruse so that the perpetrator should remain forever indebted to the victim. The Rosh therefore advises one to avoid both extremes and to rather accept the perpetrator's apology, whether or not it is wholly sincere.[263]

---

263 *Da'as Torah* ibid.

Joy of Sukkos

The Torah makes no mention of *simchah* — joy — when discussing the festival of Pesach. Regarding the festival of Shavuos, there is only one mention of *simchah*. However, when discussing the Yom Tov of Sukkos, the Torah repeats the mitzvah of *simchah* three times. This demonstrates that the *simchah* on Sukkos is more complete than on the other festivals. There are many rationales presented for this:

1. We celebrate being forgiven for our sins of the previous year, which is the greatest cause for celebration.[1]

2. The *Rosh* and *Ba'alei Tosfos* say that this is because on Pesach the crops are unripe and unready for harvest, thus diminishing our joy. During Shavuos, which coincides with the harvest season of the grain, we are joyous for the grain harvest, and thus have one *simchah* and yet that *simchah* is incomplete since the grain is not yet brought into the granaries and the fruit harvest has not yet arrived. On Sukkos,

---

1 *Yalkut Shimoni, Emor* 654.

our joy is complete, as the full bounty of one's grain and fruit harvest is brought into one's home at this time.[2]

3. The Brisker Rav suggests that the extra *simchah* on Sukkos is because of the *Simchas Beis HaShoevah* — the joyous water libation ceremony that was performed in the Temple during Sukkos.[3] Still, Rabbi Berel Soleveitchik argues that the *Simchas Beis HaShoevah* is merely an isolated event during Sukkos; it does not directly relate to the all-encompassing *simchah* the Torah assigns to the festival itself.

4. Rabbi Berel Soleveitchik therefore offers a different explanation: on Sukkos, it says that we rejoice for seven days *before* Hashem.[4] The ability to rejoice before Hashem throughout the entire festival is unparalleled and surpasses all earthly joys. (Perhaps the ability to rejoice before Hashem's presence stems from our sins being forgiven on Yom Kippur, where the *pasuk* says we purify ourselves "*before* Hashem.")[5]

Forgiveness and Joy

Why is only the festival of Sukkos called "the time of our rejoicing," if there is an obligation to rejoice during all the other festivals as well?

Rabbi Yeruchem Levovitz comments that the greatest cause for rejoicing is when one's sins are forgiven.[6] The Mishnah relates that during the *Simchas Beis HaShoevah*, righteous men would dance and offer songs and praise to Hashem.[7] The Gemara elaborates that the focus of all their songs was an expression of happiness that their sins were forgiven.[8] Since Yom Kippur is the time when Israel's sins are forgiven, it is immediately followed by a festival period during which

---

2   *Da'as Zekeinim M'Ba'alei HaTosfos, Devarim* 16:15; *Perush HaRosh* there.
3   See *Sukkah* 51a.
4   *Vayikra* 23:40.
5   Ibid. 16:30.
6   Rabbi Yeruchem Levovitz, *Da'as Chochmah U'Mussar* 1:94.
7   *Sukkah* 51b.
8   Ibid. 53a.

we are able to experience extreme rejoicing. (In fact, Reb Yeruchem relates that in earlier times, righteous people were on such a high spiritual level that they would publicly dance on Yom Kippur itself!) The degree to which a person rectifies his sins on Yom Kippur directly impacts the joy that he can experience on Sukkos.[9]

Rabbi Yosef Ber Soleveitchik offers an additional insight about the capacity to attain true joy. He explains that the Jewish People are on a higher spiritual level during Sukkos than on the other festivals, since Sukkos occurs immediately after the day of Yom Kippur, on which Israel is purified from all its sins. Spiritual purity not only enhances a person's soul, but it also allows a person to enjoy the physical world in a more heightened manner. The Gemara relates that when people conducted themselves with purity, Hashem purified their fruit from all unpleasant flavors and aromas.[10] The joy on Sukkos is therefore greater than on the other festivals since one's higher spiritual level enables him to fully experience the pleasures of the physical world at this time.[11]

A Desirable Nation

"You have chosen us (בחרתנו) from all the peoples; You loved (אהבת) us and desired (ורצית) us."[12] *Siach Yitzchak* explains the difference between *bechirah* — choosing, *ahavah* — love, and *ritzui* — finding favor:[13]

- A person may *choose* a person even if he is not presently to his liking, since he believes in his potential.
- A person *loves* a person just as he is for the qualities he presently possesses.
- *Desire* denotes abundant love that is beyond reason (as in the expression "desire is blind"[14]).

---

9   *Da'as Chochmah U'Mussar* ibid.

10   *Sotah* 49a; Rashi, s.v. "*taharah*."

11   Rabbi Yosef Ber Soloveitchik, *Hararei Kedem*, vol. 1 (second edition), 165, 2.

12   *Musaf* prayer of Yom Tov.

13   Rabbi Yitzchak Maltzan, *Siach Yitzchak*, *Siddur HaGra*, "*Atah B'chartanu*."

14   Although the common idiom is "love is blind," from a Torah perspective it is *desire* that

These three expressions correspond to the three festivals:

- Pesach is the time when Hashem *chose* Israel as His nation, despite the spiritual flaws and deficiencies that they had at the time.
- Shavuos corresponds to *love*, since *Bnei Yisrael* became wedded to Hashem as a bride when they accepted the Torah.
- Sukkos corresponds to *desire*, since during this time Hashem expresses an even greater degree of love toward us.

Ratzon (another form of *ritzui*) implies an additional connotation as well. It is often used as an expression of closeness and reconciliation after a period of anger and separation.[15] *Ratzon* denotes an even greater degree of closeness than that which existed prior to the split. After Hashem forgives us for our sins on Yom Kippur, He expresses *ratzon* towards us on the festival of Sukkos. Therefore, specifically the festival of Sukkos is called *z'man simchasenu* — the time of our gladness.[16]

Hashem's Loving Embrace

"His [HaKadosh Baruch Hu's] left hand is under my head and with His right hand He embraces me."[17] Early commentators teach that the first part of the *pasuk* corresponds to Rosh Hashanah and Yom Kippur. These Days of Judgment, which are at the "head" and beginning of the year, correspond to the left hand, which in Kabbalah is associated with the attribute of strict justice. The second part of the verse refers to the festival of Sukkos, when Hashem lovingly embraces us with His "right hand," a metaphor for the attribute of loving kindness.

The *Zohar* says that this is alluded to in the mitzvah of *sukkah* itself. A minimum kosher *sukkah* consists of two complete walls and

---

is blind. See *Akeidas Yitzchak* 67.

15   See *Bereishis* 33:10; *Vayikra* 1:4; *Yeshayah* 40:2.

16   *Siach Yitzchak, Siddur HaGra* ibid.; also *Siach Yitzchak*, "*Ahavah Rabbah.*"

17   *Shir HaShirim* 2:6.

an additional wall of even one handbreadth. The two complete walls are like the upper and lower parts of the arm, and the handbreadth is the hand itself. The walls of the *sukkah* are thus shaped in the form of a person's embrace.[18]

SUKKOS

Attaining Peace and Unity

All the mitzvos on Sukkos lead to attaining peace and unity. The four species symbolize the unity between the varied groups of the Jewish People, and the mitzvah of *sukkah* represents the same idea. This concept is hinted to by the idiom of the Sages: "All of Israel are fit to dwell in one *sukkah*."[19] This is like when the entire Jewish nation came to Yerushalayim — the city of peace — where everyone felt comfortable despite the cramped living conditions.

We also find an association between *sukkah* and peace in the evening prayer: "And spread over us the *sukkah* of Your peace." In addition, leaving one's permanent home to live in a temporary hut achieves nullification of one's ego and detachment to the physical, which in turn engenders closeness to one's fellowman.[20]

Sukkos leads to the unity of not only the Jewish People but of all of mankind. The seventy bull-offerings brought in the Beis Hamikdash on Sukkos represent the seventy nations of the world. The diminishing number of sacrifices brought each day demonstrate that the divisiveness of the nations will become gradually diminished as they will all eventually come to recognize and serve

---

18   See Rabbi Shimshon Pincus, *Nefesh Shimshon*, Sukkos, p. 101.

19   *Sukkah* 27b.

20   Rabbi Eliyahu Dessler, *Michtav M'Eliyahu*, vol. 2, pp. 106–108; *Mikdash Mordechai*, Sukkos, "*b'sukkos teishvu*."

Hashem with the coming of Mashiach, as the *Yalkut Shimoni* states: "King Mashiach will come only to teach the nations two mitzvos — *sukkah* and *lulav*."[21] The Jewish nation will not need Mashiach to teach them Torah, since they will learn Torah directly from Hashem at that time.[22] The role of Mashiach will be to teach mankind to live in peace and unity, which is symbolized by the mitzvos of *lulav* and *sukkah*.[23]

Sustaining Body and Soul

Rabbi Shimshon Raphael Hirsch expounds the interrelationship between the festivals of the year:[24]

- Pesach commemorates the *creation* of Israel's *body*, since it is when Hashem brought them into existence as a nation.
- Shavuos corresponds to the *creation* of the *soul* of the Jewish nation, as it celebrates how Hashem connected to us through His revelation on Sinai.
- Sukkos teaches us that Hashem *sustains* the physical *body* of Israel, just as Hashem miraculously sustained the Israelites existence throughout their forty-year sojourn in the wilderness.
- As Shavuos corresponds to Pesach, so does Shemini Atzeres correspond to Sukkos. Shemini Atzeres represents how Hashem continues to *sustain* the spiritual *soul* of the Jewish People through the Torah. For this reason, we rejoice with the Torah on these day(s), since the Torah preserves the survival and rejuvenation of the soul of the Jewish nation for all time.

---

21   *Yalkut Shimoni, Tehillim* 682.
22   Ibid.
23   Rabbi Hirsch Dachowitz, *Pri Shlomo*, p. 130.
24   Rabbi Shimshon Raphael Hirsch, *Horeb, Edoth* 23:165–169.

Detaching from the Temporal World

A person who experiences discomfort is absolved from the *sukkah*.[25] Why does *sukkah* differ, in this aspect, from all other mitzvos in the Torah? Generally, there is no such dispensation for mitzvos, and a person must fulfill them despite discomfort!

Rabbi Moshe Feinstein answers that the mitzvah of *sukkah* impresses upon a person that the physical world is transitory and of no intrinsic value. This message must be absorbed gradually and cannot be forcibly thrust upon a person. Therefore, one who is in discomfort is absolved from *sukkah* to demonstrate that one should not abstain from this world in an extreme manner but rather in a gradual and healthy way.[26]

There are two cities named Sukkos mentioned in the Torah:

1. One Sukkos was located east of the Jordan River and was the location where Yaakov built huts (*sukkos*) for his cattle.
2. The other Sukkos was the place of Israel's first encampment upon leaving Egypt.

The *Rokeach* says that the two cities sharing the same name hint that the Jews left Egypt in the merit of Yaakov who journeyed to the city of Sukkos.[27]

What was the great significance of Yaakov's traveling to Sukkos? Secondly, why was the city only named after the huts Yaakov built for his cattle instead of the house he built for the members of his household?

We may suggest that Sukkos represents the manner in which Yaakov viewed his temporal belongings. His material possessions

---

25   *Sukkah* 25b.
26   Rabbi Moshe Feinstein, *Derash Moshe*, p. 343.
27   *Rokeach, Shemos* 12:37.

were placed in temporary huts, which can be readily transported from place to place at a moment's notice. This was a necessary trait for the Jewish People to possess, both in their leaving Egypt as well as in their moving from encampment to encampment in the wilderness, in accordance with Hashem's command.

The "Transjordan" Sukkos later became part of the inheritance of the tribe of Gad. Rabbi Aharon Kotler says that the reason the tribe of Gad requested that specific territory is because they wished to acquire Yaakov's attitude towards materialism, one which his actions embedded into that particular place.[28]

"You shall dwell in *sukkos* for a seven-day period; every native in Israel shall dwell in *sukkos*."[29] Why does the Torah reiterate the obligation of sitting in the *sukkah* twice in the same verse?

The *Arizal* answers that this verse alludes to the Midrash that states that whoever fulfills the mitzvah of *sukkah* during his lifetime will merit to sit in the *sukkah* of the Leviathan in the World to Come.[30] A person who views this world as a temporal place, which is the underlying message of the mitzvah of *sukkah*, becomes deserving of permanent residency in the *sukkah* of the World to Come. While the first part of the verse addresses a person's obligation in this world, the latter part of the verse is an assurance of one's eternal reward in the next world.[31]

In the Shechinah's Shade

"You shall make *sukkos* [from matter] that you gather in from your threshing floor and from your wine vat."[32] The Gemara

---

28   See *Peninim M'Shulchan Gavoah, Bamidbar* 32:1.
29   *Vayikra* 23:42.
30   *Yalkut Shimoni, Emor* 653.
31   Cited in *Shalmei Todah, Sukkos*, p. 936.
32   See *Devarim* 16:13.

derives from this verse that only detached vegetation may be used for *schach*.[33] Why was this crucial information only first mentioned at the end of Israel's forty-year sojourn in the desert instead of in the Torah's original command of the mitzvah of *sukkah* in the book of *Vayikra*?

The *Binyan Shlomo* answers that *sukkos* commemorate the Clouds of Glory, and *Bnei Yisrael* fulfilled the mitzvah of *sukkah* by sitting directly beneath the Clouds of Glory themselves for the duration of their forty years in the desert. (The Clouds of Glory also fulfill the criteria of kosher *schach* since they were not susceptible to impurity and grew from the ground.[34]) Only when they were ready to enter the Land of Israel, where the Clouds of Glory would no longer accompany them, were they commanded to substitute cut vegetation to recall the Clouds of Glory of the desert.[35]

The *Sifri* addresses two seemingly contradictory verses regarding the nature of the mitzvah of sitting in the *sukkah*:

> One verse states that *"The festival of Sukkos; a seven-day period **for Hashem**."*[36] *Based on this verse alone, one would conclude that the sukkah should be devoted solely to sanctified purposes.*
>
> *The Torah therefore writes, "The festival of Sukkos you shall make **for yourself**,"*[37] *to demonstrate that the sukkah should be used for one's own physical pleasure, just as one would use their own home.*

---

33   *Sukkah* 12a.
34   See *Sukkah* 11b; *Bereishis* 2:6.
35   Rabbi Shlomo HaKohen (author of *Cheshek Shlomo*), *Binyan Shlomo*, vol. 1, *Devarim* 16:13.
36   *Vayikra* 23:34.
37   *Devarim* 16:13.

If that is the case, why then does the Torah write that the
sukkah should be made "for Hashem?" To teach that when
you make the sukkah for yourself, Hashem considers it as if
it has been made solely for His sake.[38]

This *Sifri* requires clarification. How could one have thought that
the *sukkah* be devoted solely to sanctified purposes if the Torah
writes explicitly that the *sukkah* is to be used as a human dwelling?[39]

The *Binyan Shlomo* explains that since one who dwells in a *sukkah*
sits in the shade of the Divine Presence,[40] he is thus required to
maintain a spiritual level worthy of such a distinction. In fact, the
reason Sukkos immediately follows Yom Kippur is because we are
only capable of dwelling under Hashem's canopy when we have been
totally cleansed from sin.

Since dwelling in the *sukkah* is akin to sitting at the entrance of
the Sanctuary, one would think that he would be prohibited from
eating or sleeping in the *sukkah* and must instead utilize it to sit
and meditate about Hashem and the spiritual messages of the
festival. The second verse therefore comes to modify the first; the
Torah desires us to eat and live in the *sukkah* in an enjoyable manner while at the same time remain cognizant of Hashem's loving
presence. When we do so, Hashem rewards us for living enjoyably
in the *sukkah* as if we lived in it in an ascetic manner of total physical deprivation.[41]

Taste of the World to Come

"Satiated with joy — in Your Presence."[42] Commentators apply
this verse to the reward awaiting the righteous in the World to Come,

---

38   *Sifri* 140, acc. to text of Vilna Gaon.
39   *Vayikra* 23:42.
40   *Zohar* 3:103a.
41   *Binyan Shlomo*, vol. 1, *Devarim* 16:13.
42   *Tehillim* 16:11.

where they enjoy the bliss of beholding the splendor of the Divine Presence.[43] The Midrash homiletically reads the word שׂבַע (*sova*) — satiated, as שֶׁבַע (*sheva*) — seven, and applies this verse to the festival of Sukkos, which is filled with seven joyous commandments:

- the four species (4)
- the *sukkah* (1)
- the *Chagigah* sacrifice (1)
- the mitzvah of rejoicing (1)[44]

Rabbi Aharon Kotler comments that on all three pilgrimage festivals Hashem invites His children to sit at "the table of the King," in His palace, to behold His presence. One can achieve an even higher level of closeness to Hashem during Sukkos, though, because of the numerous (seven) mitzvos associated with this festival, and thereby attain a level of joy that surpasses that of the other festivals.[45]

"Whoever fulfills the mitzvah of *sukkah* in this world, Hashem will seat him in the future that is to come in the *sukkah* of the Leviathan."[46] Rabbi Hirsch explains that the word *leviathan* comes from the word *loveh*, which connotes attachment or joining.[47] Consequently, "leviathan" connotes a society or company, and is a metaphor for a powerful society in the midst of mankind. In *Yeshayah* we encounter two primary forces in human society: Leviathan the straight serpent, which symbolizes a society based on brute force (which shoots like a straight arrow), and Leviathan the coiled serpent, which represents a society that attains its objectives through cunning.[48]

---

43   Ibn Ezra, *Tehillim* ibid.; *Metzudas Dovid* there.
44   *Vayikra Rabbah* 30:2.
45   Cf. *Mishnas Rebbi Aharon*, *Tehillim* 16:11.
46   *Yalkut Shimoni*, *Emor* 654.
47   Rabbi Shimshon Raphael Hirsch, *Collected Writings*, vol. 2, *Tishrei* 5.
48   *Yeshayah* 27:1.

In the end of days, Hashem will slay the world order of Leviathan (both of its forms) and from amid this chaos will emerge a new world order predicated on the service of Hashem. Those who dwell in *sukkos*, which represent living in a manner of peace and unity, will merit a seat in *"the hut of the union of nations"* in the world that is to come.[49]

SUKKOS IN THE TORAH

Dual Perspectives

After the Torah finishes its discussion of the festivals of the year, including Sukkos, and concludes, "These are the appointed festivals of Hashem,"[50] the next verse begins to discuss the festival of Sukkos anew. Why does the Torah seemingly end the section on Sukkos and then begin a new section on the same topic?

Rabbi Zalman Sorotzkin explains that it separates between the two seemingly contradictory elements inherent in the festival of Sukkos:[51]

1. One aspect of Sukkos is that it serves as a continuation of Rosh Hashanah and Yom Kippur, as the Midrash says: "Why do we observe Sukkos after Yom Kippur?...In case Israel have been sentenced to exile...they exile themselves from their homes into the *sukkah*, and Hashem considers it as if they had been exiled."[52] The first section refers to the festival of Sukkos in its aspect of exile, completing the atonement of Rosh Hashanah and Yom Kippur. "Joy" is therefore not mentioned in the first section because it is a continuation of the Days of Awe.

---

49   Rabbi Hirsch, *Collected Writings* ibid.; *Michtav M'Eliyahu, Teshuvah, Sukkos*, p. 681.
50   *Vayikra* 23:37, 38.
51   *Oznayim L'Torah, Vayikra* 23:39.
52   *Yalkut Shimoni* 1:653.

2. The second aspect of Sukkos is that it is a time for thanksgiving and rejoicing, since it is a time when one gathers in the crop of the land. It is this second aspect that transforms the festival from one of sighing to rejoicing.

Alternatively, one can understand the dual nature of Sukkos as follows. In one respect, Sukkos is an exclusively Jewish national festival: "So that your generations will know that I caused the Children of Israel to dwell in booths when I took them from the land of Egypt." However, there is also a universal aspect of Sukkos, since Sukkos is the time when the world is judged regarding the amount of water that will be provided during the coming year. From this vantage point, Sukkos is also an "international" festival. This is why Zechariah prophesized that after the coming of Mashiach, "All the remnants of all the nations...will go up every year to bow down to the King, God of hosts, and to celebrate the festival of Sukkos. And if one [nation] does not go up...the rain will not be upon them."[53] The Torah divides its discussion of Sukkos into two sections to differentiate between the unique Jewish aspect of the festival from its more universal themes.[54]

Sukkos and the Exodus

"So that your generations will know that I caused the Children of Israel to dwell in *sukkos* when I took them from the land of Egypt; I am Hashem, your God."[55]

Seeing as Hashem provided *sukkos* for Israel throughout their forty-year sojourn in the wilderness, why does the Torah specifically associate Sukkos with the Exodus?[56] Secondly, the Torah concludes the commandment to dwell in *sukkos* with the words, "I am Hashem,

---

53   *Zechariah* 14:16–17.
54   *Oznayim L'Torah* ibid.
55   *Vayikra* 23:43.
56   See *Tur, Orach Chaim* 625.

your God." This particular appellation, when mentioned in connection with the Exodus, is generally reserved for those mitzvos that only Hashem can tell whether one is honestly performing. An example of this is brought in the Gemara:

> Why does the Torah mention the Exodus in connection with the laws of interest, honest weights, and tzitzis? Says the Holy One, Blessed is He: "I am He who discerned in Egypt between a drop that brought forth a firstborn and a drop that did not bring forth a firstborn. I am the One who will exact punishment from one who lends money to a Jew with interest and attributes the money to a gentile, and from whoever buries his weights in salt so they do not reflect their true weight, and from whoever hangs imitation techeles on his tzitzis and claims that it is techeles."[57]

The *Binyan Shlomo* explains that this term is equally appropriate for the mitzvah of *sukkah*. Since a person can evade sitting in the *sukkah* by pretending that he is *mitztaer* — in pain — and thereby exempt himself from the mitzvah, the Torah attests that Hashem will ultimately exact justice from such an individual.[58]

Avraham's Sukkah

According to some opinions, the Torah's narrative of Avraham and the wayfarers transpired on Sukkos.[59] One may ask: since Avraham fulfilled the entire Torah, why did Avraham sit at the entrance of his tent[60] instead of inside his *sukkah*?

It is to answer this very question that the verse concludes that the event took place "in the heat of the day." The halachah is that

---

57   *Bava Metzia* 61b.
58   *Binyan Shlomo*, vol. 1, *Vayikra* 23.
59   *Rosh Hashanah* 11a; *Bamidbar Rabbah* 14:2.
60   *Bereishis* 18:1.

a person who is in pain is exempt from sitting in the *sukkah*. Since Avraham was in pain as a result of the extreme heat and from his recently performed *bris milah*, he was absolved from the mitzvah of *sukkah* and instead chose to sit under the shade of his tent where the heat was less oppressive.[61]

The Midrash states that the reason Avraham told the wayfarers to "recline beneath the tree" was so that they could fulfill the mitzvah of *sukkah*.[62] Several questions arise:

1. Since a tree is attached to the ground, it is disqualified for use as *schach*.
2. Although Avraham personally fulfilled the mitzvos that would be given to his descendants in the future, why was he concerned that non-Jews should also fulfill those commandments?
3. Since the halachah is that wayfarers are exempt from *sukkah*, why did he insist that they sit in the *sukkah*?

Rabbi Chaim Kanievsky answers these questions as follows:

1. We must say that Avraham's tree was detached from the ground, and it therefore served as a kosher *sukkah*.
2. Since Avraham was intent on converting people to Judaism, he wanted to accustom them to the performance of mitzvos.
3. The halachah is that if wayfarers chance upon a *sukkah* during their travels and are not inconvenienced by sitting in the *sukkah*, they are obligated to dwell in the *sukkah*. Since the travellers were anyway stopping at Avraham's tent to rest, they were not exempt from *sukkah*.[63]

---

61 *Ta'ama D'kra, Bereishis* 18:1.
62 *Bamidbar Rabbah* 14:2.
63 *Derech Sichah; Ta'ama D'kra, Bereishis* 18:4.

Leaving Eisav

On Yom Kippur, Satan is not vanquished but merely distracted from opposing Israel. The *Zohar* writes that this is hinted to in the verse, "And Eisav returned on his way back to Seir."[64] This alludes to the goat (*seir*) offering that is brought to Azazel — the repository of evil and abode of Eisav — on Yom Kippur. This offering appeases Satan who then (temporarily) takes leave of us. The verse continues, "and Yaakov journeyed to Sukkos."[65] At this time, Yaakov departs from Eisav/Satan's company and goes to fulfill the mitzvah of *sukkah*. When the Jewish People fulfill the mitzvah of *sukkah* with joy, Satan's power becomes completely neutralized.[66]

Neutralizing Curses with Joy

The Midrash states that the ninety-eight lambs brought during the festival of Sukkos are to counteract the ninety-eight curses contained in the book of *Devarim*.[67] What is the connection between the two?

The *Avnei Nezer* answers that the ultimate cause of all curses is: "Because you didn't serve Hashem with joy."[68] Sukkos is called "the festival of joy." Since it is particularly during Sukkos that Israel serves Hashem with joy, their joyful service succeeds in nullifying the ninety-eight curses they may have previously deserved.[69]

Tikun Olam

The seventy bulls brought on Sukkos correspond to the seventy nations of the world.[70] Rashi explains that they offer atonement

---

64　*Bereishis* 33:16.

65　Ibid. v. 17.

66　*Chasam Sofer, Drashos*, vol. 1, Sukkos 581, s.v. *"v'hayisa."*

67　Cited in Rashi, *Bamidbar* 29:18.

68　*Devarim* 28:47.

69　Cited in *Shem M'Shmuel, Sukkos*, p. 169.

70　*Sukkah* 55b.

for the nations so that rain will fall throughout the world. Since the world is judged regarding rainfall on Sukkos, these sacrifices were brought particularly at this time.[71]

This concept can be understood on a deeper level as well.

When a person is in a happy frame of mind, he feels expansive and generous. This explains why Pharaoh freed the wine butler on his birthday and Achashverosh lowered the countries' taxes to celebrate his marriage to Esther. The Ramban says that all blessing comes to the world via Eretz Yisrael; similarly, the Jewish nation is the original channel for receiving Divine blessing, whereupon it then flows to the other nations.[72] Since the nations persecute Israel, this should prevent them from receiving rain or other physical bounty. However, on Sukkos the Jewish People are in a happy frame of mind and they overlook their mistreatment. Thus, Sukkos is a propitious time for Hashem to judge the nations favorably for rain, and therefore the sacrifices brought on their behalf are specifically brought during this time.[73]

Mah Nishtanah on Sukkos?

Commentators wonder why *Mah Nishtanah* is only asked on Pesach night? Why don't the children ask why is this night different than all other nights on the first night of Sukkos?[74]

According to the *Rabbeinu Ephraim*, the question-and-answer format is indeed implemented during the festival of Sukkos. When a child sees his father building a hut for no apparent purpose, it arouses the child's curiosity to inquire, "What is this service to you?" The Torah provides us with the answer to his query: "So that your generations will know that I caused the Children of Israel to dwell in booths when I took them from the land of Egypt." We inform the children that the

---

71   Ibid.

72   Ramban, *Devarim* 11:12.

73   *Mishnas Rebbi Aharon, Nach, Zechariah* 14:16.

74   See Rabbi Tzadok HaKohen, *Likutei Ma'amarim* 7:64.

reason we sit in *sukkos* is to recall the *sukkos* Hashem provided for our ancestors after they left Egypt.[75]

Sukkos-Menorah Connection

The Torah juxtaposes the command to light the Menorah to the mitzvah of Sukkos.[76] *Rabbeinu Ephraim* explains the connection between these two mitzvos: It is to hint to one of the outstanding aspects of the *Simchas Beis HaShoevah* celebration on Sukkos when numerous large candelabras were lit in the Temple courtyard.[77] It also hints that Chanukah, the festival of lights, should share some similarities to Sukkos in that both Sukkos and Chanukah are eight-day holidays and that the entire *Hallel* is recited for the entire duration of both festivals.

A Mitzvah for Natives

"Every native (אזרח) in Israel shall dwell in *sukkos*."[78] Why does the Torah employ the unusual description of "native" particularly in respect to the mitzvah of *sukkah*?

Rabbi Avigdor Miller comments that the purpose of living in temporary dwellings on Sukkos is to engender an awareness of the transient nature of the physical world. The Torah therefore addresses this mitzvah particularly to those people who feel smugly entrenched in this world, such as natives in the land.[79]

In a similar vein, Rabbi Shimshon Raphael Hirsch observes that generally only homeless strangers live in temporary huts. Here it is emphasized that even those full-born citizens who have full rights of domicile are to dwell in a *sukkah*. To emphasize that it is not out of necessity (e.g., due to a lack of home or space) that we are driven to the protection of a leafy-roofed dwelling, the *pasuk* concludes with

---

75   Rabbeinu Ephraim, *Vayikra* 23:43.

76   Ibid. 23:33–44, 24:1–4.

77   *Rabbeinu Ephraim, Vayikra* 24:2.

78   Ibid. 23:42.

79   Rabbi Avigdor Miller, *Ohr Olam*, vol. 6, p. 105.

the word *teishvu*, which teaches that one must dwell as comfortably in the *sukkah* as one lives in one's home.[80]

To the Letter of the Law

"Go out...to make *sukkos* as written in the Torah. And they made *sukkos*, each man on his roof...and they dwelt in *sukkos* as they had not done from the days of Yehoshua Ben Nun."[81] How did the *sukkos* built during the time of Nechemiah differ from those built since the time of Yehoshua Ben Nun?

The Chasam Sofer answers that although it is preferable to build a *sukkah* with four complete walls (as it is more beautiful), *Chazal* derive from how the Torah wrote the word *sukkos* in the diminutive singular tense (בסכת without the letter ו) that a *sukkah* is kosher even if it is lacking four full walls.[82] After the time of Yehoshua, people generally built the ideal four-walled *sukkos*.[83] However during the time of Nechemiah, there was a spiritual backsliding among the populace as many were influenced by the deviant sects who did not believe in the Oral Law. To refute the prevalent mistaken belief, they intentionally built three-walled *sukkos* "as it is *written* in the Torah" (i.e., בסכת in the diminutive written form, in contrast to its plural pronunciation) to demonstrate the authenticity of the Sages' interpretation of the verse.[84]

THE SUKKAH

Symbolism of Sukkah

The *sukkah* serves as a portal between the present physical world and the World to Come. Our sages teach that this world was created

---

80   Hirsch Chumash, *Vayikra* 23:42.

81   *Nechemiah* 8:15–17.

82   As elaborated in *Sukkos* 6b.

83   Perhaps the reason why minimalistic *sukkos* were also used during the days of Yehoshua was because of the limited resources available to them in battle while conquering the land of Israel from the Caananite nations.

84   *Chasam Sofer, Devarim, Ha'azinu*, s.v. "asu sukkos"; *Minchas Yitzchak* 5:1, 18.

with the letter ה. The letter ה is shaped like a doorway, which is why a *sukkah* also requires a doorway.[85] The numerical value of ה is five, since the physical world can only be perceived through the five senses. When a person builds a physical *sukkah* with his five senses and enters through the portal of the *sukkah*, which is in the shape of the letter ה, he is then enveloped within the inner domain of the *sukkah*, which represents the World to Come.

The Sages say that the World to Come is created with the letter י, whose numerical value is ten. The minimum height of a *sukkah* is ten handbreadths, since the domain of the physical world extends ten handbreadths above the ground, after which the realm of the heavenly spiritual sphere begins.[86] The protective shade of the *sukkah* represents the Divine Presence, which will act like a crown of glory above the heads of the righteous in the World to Come.

In short, the mitzvah of *sukkah* symbolizes that through the physical efforts one exerts in performing mitzvos in this world, one merits to bask in the light of the *Shechinah* in the World to Come.[87]

Since the *sukkah* represents the World to Come, which can only be attained through the Torah, the *sukkah* is also compared to the Torah in numerous ways:[88]

- *Sukkah* in Aramaic means "to see," and it is a metaphor for the Torah that gives a person the ability to properly view the world.
- Just as the *sukkah* requires shade, so must a person seek shelter in the shade of the Torah.

---

85   Rambam, *Mishnah Torah, Sukkah* 4:2. While a doorway is only required in a minimalistic *sukkah* to comprise its incomplete wall, it is customary for all *sukkos* to have doorways for beauty (*Shulchan Aruch, Orach Chaim* 630:2–3).

86   See *Sukkah* 5a.

87   This section is based on Rabbeinu Bachya, *Kad HaKemech, Sukkah*.

88   Ibid.

- The *sukkah* requires a minimum of three walls, and the Torah also has three parts: Torah, *Nevi'im*, and *Kesuvim*.
- The minimum height of the *sukkah* is ten *tefachim*, which alludes to the Ten Commandments.
- The minimum width of a *sukkah* is seven *tefachim*, which hints to the seven branches of worldly wisdom included in the Torah.
- The dimensions of the width and height of a *sukkah* wall equals seventy (10 x 7), which hints to the seventy facets of Torah.
- One must dwell in a *sukkah* by day and by night, and so too a person must study the Torah both by day and by night.
- Women are exempt from Torah study and are likewise absolved from the mitzvah of dwelling in the *sukkah*.

Clouds of Glory

Hashem surrounded the Jewish People in the desert with seven Clouds of Glory. These clouds encompassed them from above, below, and on all four sides, as well as there being another cloud that traveled before them. Our Sages say that there are also seven Clouds of Glory that surround Hashem's presence like a *sukkah*.[89]

The mitzvah of *sukkah* commemorates these clouds, which symbolizes that while dwelling in the *sukkah* we are in close proximity to Hashem's presence — as if within His abode comprised of seven clouds.

Since there are *seven* clouds, we are commanded to perform this mitzvah during the *seventh* month for *seven* days. As these Clouds of Glory are associated with Hashem's purity, the *schach* for the *sukkah* must also be taken from matter that does not accept ritual impurity. (According to the view that one may use matter that accepts ritual

---

89   *Pirkei D'Rebbi Eliezer* 4; *Radal* ibid., 30; *Tehillim* 18:12.

impurity for *schach*, it is in accordance with the concept that even when the Jewish People are in a state of impurity the *Shechinah* dwells amid them).[90]

The *schach* — foliage covering of the *sukkah* commemorates the seven Clouds of Glory that accompanied the Jewish People throughout their journey in the wilderness. The *Re'em* asks: since the clouds surrounded them from above, below, and on all four sides, why are we only commanded to place *schach* on the roof of the *sukkah*? Why aren't we obligated to also use *schach* on the floor and the four walls of the *sukkah* as well?[91]

The Maharal answers that since the Clouds of Glory were of a spiritual and miraculous nature, they are best commemorated by recognizing that they come from Above. Everything miraculous is considered as coming from heaven above, even if it be physically in front or even underneath us. For this reason, the verses describe the heavens as being above man, even though the heavens are actually underneath man as well (since the earth is suspended in space and is surrounded by heaven from all sides).[92]

Why Only Clouds of Glory?

When the Jewish People left Egypt, Hashem miraculously provided them with water (through a well that accompanied them on their journeys through the desert), manna, and Clouds of Glory.

The mitzvah of *sukkah* only commemorates the Clouds of Glory.[93] Why didn't Hashem also command us to commemorate the miracles of the well and the manna?

---

90   The section is also based on Rabbeinu Bachya, *Vayikra* 16:16, and on *Kad HaKemach*, *Sukkah*.

91   Rabbi Eliyahu Mizrachi, *Bamidbar* 10:34.

92   *Gur Aryeh, Bamidbar* 10:31.

93   *Sukkah* 11b.

We will present a number of explanations:

- The Jewish nation is called *tzivaos Hashem* — the army of Hashem. Therefore, there is nothing wondrous in the fact that Hashem provided food and water to the Jewish People in the desert, since it is incumbent for a king to sustain his army. However, a king is not obliged to present a soldier with a medal of honor. If the king does so, it leaves an indelible impression on the recipient and he forever cherishes the badge of honor and lovingly bequeaths it to his future descendants. Similarly, Hashem gave the Clouds of Glory to show honor to the Jewish People, and it is therefore endearingly recalled for all future generations.[94]

- The miraculous well and manna were given to the Jewish People as a result of their complaining for food and water. Since the Clouds of Glory were not precipitated by any ignoble behavior on their part, Hashem wished to memorialize this miracle. (Regardless, it would have been pointless for the Jews to request the Clouds of Glory, since the Clouds of Glory were provided to give honor to *Bnei Yisrael*, and a requested honor is not an honor.)[95]

- The nations of the world were unaware that the Jews were miraculously provided with manna and water, which is why the nations of Ammon and Moav were faulted for not taking the initiative of providing Israel with food provisions even though Israel actually had no need for them.[96] Accordingly, we may suggest that the reason we celebrate the miracle of the Clouds of Glory is because it created a greater sanctification of Hashem's name, since the nations were also cognizant of this miracle.

---

94   *Oznayim L'Torah, Vayikra* 23:43.
95   *Oznayim L'Torah*, ibid.
96   Maharal, *Gur Aryeh, Devarim* 2:29.

- Upon leaving Egypt, the *Bnei Yisrael* first encamped in a city named Sukkos.[97] The *Mechiltah* says that the city was given that name because Hashem gave them the Clouds of Glory at that time.[98] Since the Clouds of Glory were given immediately upon leaving Egypt, while the manna and the well were only given later in the wilderness, we commemorate the first miraculous gift bestowed upon the nation.[99]

In Whose Merit?

A *sukkah* protects a person against the elements and represents Hashem's protection over the Jewish People, both physically as well as spiritually. In what merit did we earn this protection?

1. The Midrash states that in the merit of Avraham telling his guests to rest under the tree, Hashem rewarded his descendants with the protection of *sukkos* in the desert, in the Land of Israel, and in the World to Come.[100]

2. The Gemara says that the Clouds of Glory in the desert existed in the merit of Aharon HaKohen.[101] Because Aharon loved people, pursued peace, and sought to bring them under the protective canopy of the Torah,[102] Hashem also lovingly enveloped Israel with the protective Clouds of Glory.[103]

3. The *Rabbeinu Ephraim* comments that it was a result of the actions of our ancestor Shem, the son of Noach. When Noach lay uncovered in his tent, Shem covered his father with a garment to protect him from the disgrace of being exposed. Measure

---

97   *Shemos* 12:37.
98   Ibid.
99   Rabbi David Keviat, *Sukkas Dovid, Moadim, Sukkos*, p. 245.
100 *Bereishis Rabbah* 48:10.
101 *Ta'anis* 9a.
102 *Avos* 1:12.
103 Mabit, *Beis Elokim Shaar HaYesodos* 37.

for measure, Hashem covers our inadequacies and protects us against exposure from the elements through the *sukkah*.[104]

Sukkos in Autumn

The mitzvah to sit in a *sukkah* is to commemorate the *sukkos* (lit. "huts") in which Hashem sheltered Israel upon leaving Egypt. According to one opinion in the Gemara, these *sukkos* refer to actual huts the Jews built for themselves in the wilderness.[105] According to another opinion, the *sukkos* commemorate the Clouds of Glory that surrounded Israel for the duration of their travels in the wilderness.[106] According to either opinion, the question arises: why is the festival celebrated on the fifteenth of Tishrei? It would seem to make more sense for the festival to occur during the month of Nissan to coincide with the time the Jewish People first left Egypt.

The *Tur* famously answers that Nissan occurs when the seasons begin getting warmer, and it is natural for people to build huts at that time to protect themselves from the sun. Had the mitzvah of *sukkah* been commanded at that time, it would not be discernible whether one is dwelling in a *sukkah* to fulfill the mitzvah or out of personal comfort.[107]

In the view of the Ibn Ezra,[108] the mitzvah of *sukkah* commemorates the actual huts the Jews built in the wilderness. When the Jewish nation left Egypt during Nissan, the protection offered by a *sukkah* was unnecessary, as the weather was pleasant and people naturally sit outdoors under the sun during that time. However, in the month of Tishrei, the weather becomes cooler, so the Jewish People in the wilderness then began to erect *sukkos* to protect themselves from the cold. We therefore celebrate Sukkos in Tishrei to commemorate the *sukkos* that were first built during this season.

---

104 Rabbeinu Ephraim, *Bereishis* 9:23.
105 *Sukkah* 11b.
106 Ibid.
107 *Tur, Orach Chaim* 625.
108 Ibn Ezra, *Vayikra* 23:43.

According to the Vilna Gaon, the *sukkah* commemorates the Clouds of Glory. However, it does not commemorate the *initial* appearance of the Clouds of Glory when they first accompanied the Children of Israel upon leaving Egypt during the month of Nissan. Rather it commemorates the *return* of the clouds that temporarily abandoned the Jewish nation after they sinned with the Golden Calf.

When Moshe successfully attained Hashem's forgiveness for the sin of the Golden Calf on Yom Kippur (on the tenth of Tishrei), he commanded the Jewish nation to bring material for the construction of the Mishkan the following day (the eleventh of Tishrei). The *Bnei Yisrael* brought the materials for the next two days (the twelfth and thirteenth of Tishrei),[109] and the material was given to the artisans the following day (the fourteenth of Tishrei). When the construction of the Mishkan began on the fifteenth of Tishrei, the Clouds of Glory returned. Just as the Mishkan symbolizes the return of Hashem's presence to Israel after their state of sin, so too does the Festival of Sukkos embody the same idea.[110]

It is peculiar that when the Torah mentions the festival of Sukkos in the book of *Shemos*,[111] it is merely called *Chag Ha'Asif* — the Festival of the Ingathering. Later, in *Vayikra* and in *Devarim*, the Torah calls the festival by its more commonly known name — the Festival of Sukkos.

The *Meshech Chochmah* resolves this difficulty based on the principle posited by the Vilna Gaon mentioned above: When the Tishrei festival was initially given at Sinai, the festival's primary function was to praise Hashem for the bountiful harvest. Only after the Sin of the Golden Calf did the nature of the festival change to an emphasis on the *sukkah* dwelling to stress the loving return of Hashem's presence, which was demonstrated

---

109   See *Shemos* 36:3.
110   *Biur HaGra, Shir HaShirim* 1:4.
111   *Shemos* 23:16, 34:22.

by the return of the Clouds of Glory at that time. Therefore, after the sin, Moshe called the festival "Sukkos" to reflect its current reality.[112]

Love for the Mitzvah

During the second Pesach in the desert, there were several righteous individuals who were unable to bring the *Korban Pesach* because they became spiritually impure while performing the mitzvah of tending to the dead. They asked Moshe, "Why should we be left out from offering the *korban [Pesach]*?"[113] Since they were aware that an impure person may not partake of the *Korban Pesach*, they suggested to Moshe that perhaps they could be counted among the participants of the *korban*, even though the actual eating would only be done by those who were pure.

What did these impure individuals hope to accomplish by being appointed together as participants in the Pesach lamb if they would be unable to fulfill the mitzvah as they were not allowed to eat it?

Rabbi Moshe Feinstein deduces from this a remarkable principle: Even when circumstances beyond one's control prevent a person from fulfilling a mitzvah, someone who loves mitzvos will nonetheless strive to be connected to the mitzvah in any way possible. Among the examples he gives is a person whom the doctors forbade to sit in a *sukkah*. Although he is unable to fulfill the actual mitzvah, he can still demonstrate his love for the mitzvah by constructing a *sukkah*, which he can do.[114]

Ushpizin

Seforim write that the day of the week on which Aharon HaKohen's *yahrtzeit* falls (Rosh Chodesh Av) always coincides with the same day of the week as the fifth day of Sukkos (during that upcoming Sukkos), which is the *ushpizin* of Aharon. Likewise, Shavuos, which is the *yahrtzeit* of Dovid HaMelech, always falls out on the same day of the week as Hoshanah Rabbah, whose

---

112   Rabbi Meir Simchah HaKohen M'Dvinsk, *Meshech Chochmah, Shemos* 23:16.

113   *Bamidbar* 9:7.

114   *Derash Moshe, Bamidbar* 9:7.

ushpizin is Dovid. Finally, Lag B'Omer, which is the *yahrtzeit* of Rabbi Shimon Bar Yochai, falls out on the same day of the week as the *ushpizin* of Moshe, since Rabbi Shimon Bar Yochai had the same root soul as Moshe.[115]

THE FOUR SPECIES

The Esrog

There is no mitzvah in the Torah upon which people willingly spend as lavishly as they do when acquiring a beautiful *esrog* for Sukkos. It is also common for people to show off their perfect *esrog* and "brag" of their prized trophy to their friends. Why is the *esrog* the source of man's arrogance?

There is an opinion that the forbidden fruit that Adam and Chava ate of was the *esrog*. The root of Adam and Chava's sin was haughtiness, since they believed the ruse of the snake that by eating from the Tree of Knowledge they would become like gods. Since the nature of the beautiful *esrog* fruit is to arouse feelings of haughtiness, we are commanded to elevate that primeval urge by bringing glory to Hashem through beautifying His commandments.[116]

The Aravah

The requirements for a kosher *aravah* are that its branches be red and that its leaves be smooth-edged, long, narrow, and moist.[117] As the *aravah* symbolizes the lowly Jew who has neither Torah nor good deeds, these attributes allude to the positive qualities that the *aravah*-Jew possesses:[118]

---

115 Rabbi Yechiel Michel Stern, *Peninei Kedem, Vayikra* 23:43.

116 *Oznayim L'Torah, Vayikra* 23:40.

117 *Sukkah* 34a.

118 *Derash Moshe*, pp. 220–221.

- Sin is associated with the color red,[119] and the *aravah*'s overtly red branch represents a person who is aware of his sins and is full of regret over them.
- The *aravah* leaf is shaped liked a closed mouth; although he may be personally wicked, he is quiet and does not influence others to sin.
- Its elongated leaves evoke a flowing river, which symbolizes that he is open to accepting the flow of G-dliness.
- If such a person is moist — meaning, he inwardly desires to be spiritually nourished — we bring him close and thereby elevate his level.

The custom of beating the *aravah* on Hoshanah Rabbah demonstrates that ultimately all the deficiencies of the *aravah* Jew will fall away and that he will return in complete *teshuvah*.[120]

There is a species of willow called *tzaftzafah* that superficially resembles the kosher *aravah* but is nonetheless invalid. Its non-kosher signs are that its branch is white and that its leaves are round with sharp saw-like edges. After the destruction of the Temple, people began confusing the kosher *aravah* with its non-kosher imposter.

Homiletically, Rabbi Moshe Feinstein explains that the *tzaftzafah* represents the lowest "class" of Jews who lack the saving graces of the kosher *aravah*:[121]

- The *tzaftzafah*'s branch is white — totally dead and lacking all life-giving moisture. White is the color that represents purity. Ironically, despite his copious sins, the *tzaftzafah* individual deludes himself that he is pure and righteous.

---

119 *Yeshayah* 1:18.
120 *Derash Moshe* ibid.
121 Ibid.

- Its leaves are also round instead of drawn, which demonstrates that he is closed off from bettering himself.
- Finally, its leaves are sharp like a saw, which represents the harmful influence he has on others.

Despite their seeming similarities, the *tzaftzafah* and *aravah* are two entirely different species, and unlike the *aravah*, the *tzaftzafah* Jew may not be joined together with the Jewish community.

"...With one *lulav* and one *esrog* for Hashem Who is One and His Name that is One. With the two *aravos* like the two *imahos* — matriarchs, and the three *hadasim* like the three *avos* — patriarchs."[122] How are Rachel and Leah comparable to *aravos*?

The leaves of the willow are elongated as lips and are therefore compared to the mouth. The destinies of both Rachel and Leah were transformed through their lips, albeit in opposite ways:

- Leah was destined to marry Eisav, but she reversed the decree in merit of her constant heartfelt prayers that she uttered with her lips.
- Rachel merited to give birth to children because she gave over the signs to Leah and because she remained silent and did not tell Yaakov about Lavan's intent to switch her with Leah under the *chupah*.[123] It was Rachel's great power in being able to control her lips that enabled her to be a mother of the Jewish People.

---

122 Quoted from the liturgy *Ekcha B'rishon*, which some have the custom to recite during the chazzan's repetition of *Shacharis* on Sukkos.

123 Rashi, *Bereishis* 30:22; Rashash, *Megillah* 13b.

Bringing It All Together

To hold the *lulav* and *esrog* together while shaking them during the recitation of *Hallel* is not explicitly discussed in the Gemara. The *Beis Yosef* cites Kabbalistic references that shed light on this practice.[124]

The Rekanti relates that once, on the first night of Sukkos, he dreamt that a pious man by the name of Rav Yitzchak Ashkenazi, who was then a guest at his home, wrote the four-letter name of Hashem, leaving a large gap between the third and fourth letters. When the Rekanti questioned this peculiar behavior, the pious guest responded that this was how it was customarily written in his homeland. In his dream, the Rekanti admonished him that it was proper for the letters of Hashem's name to be written together. Upon awakening, he was perplexed as to the meaning of his strange dream. The following day, the Rekanti observed how during *Hallel* Rav Yitzchak shook only the *lulav*, which was bound together with the *aravos* and the *hadasim*, without the *esrog*. He then understood the meaning of his dream.

In Kabbalistic literature, the four species correspond to the four-letter name of Hashem, with each letter corresponding to one of the species. The same way it is necessary for all the letters in Hashems name to be closely adjacent to each other in order for Hashem's name to be written properly, so must the four species be held together when shaken during *Hallel*.[125] Based on the Rekanti, the *Shulchan Aruch* rules that the *lulav* and *esrog* should be joined and shaken together during the *nanuim* of *Hallel*.[126]

This Kabbalistic concept is also hinted to in the following Midrash:[127]

- The beautiful (*hadar*) *esrog* alludes to Hashem, about whom it is written, "Majesty and splendor (*hadar*) are before Him."[128]

---

124 *Tur, Orach Chaim* 651:11.
125 *Rekanti*, as cited in *Beis Yosef* ibid.
126 *Shulchan Aruch, Orach Chaim* 651:11.
127 *Vayikra Rabbah* 30:9, cited in *Beis Yosef* ibid.
128 *Tehillim* 96:6.

- The *lulav* palm also refers to Hashem, as it is written, "The Righteous One [i.e., Hashem] will flourish like a date palm."[129]
- The *hadas* alludes to Hashem, as the *pasuk* states, "And He was standing among the *hadas* bushes."[130]
- The *aravos* also allude to Hashem, as it is written, "Extol He Who rides upon the highest heavens (רכב בערבות)."[131]

Shaking the Lulav

Part of the mitzvah in taking the four species is to shake the leaves of the *lulav*.[132] What is the significance of this?

- The Midrash says that Hashem commanded that we shake the *lulav* in order to recall Hashem's kindness at the time of the Exodus when He "shook away" the mountains that lay in the path of the Children of Israel,[133] and He assured us that He will do the same at the time of the final redemption.[134]
- One of the names for a tree is *siach*,[135] a word that also means "to speak." The reason a tree is called *siach* is because the swaying movement of trees gives the appearance that they are "speaking" to each other and to mankind.[136] The *Rabbeinu Ephraim* comments that the trees are in fact communicating in a language known as *sichas dekalim*.[137] Our shaking of the *lulav* demonstrates that we are identifying and joining in the "song" of the trees and together giving praise to Hashem.[138]

---

129 Ibid. 92:13.
130 *Zechariah* 1:8.
131 *Tehillim* 68:5.
132 *Yerushalmi, Sukkah* 3:8; Rama, *Orach Chaim* 651:9.
133 *Tehillim* 114:4.
134 *Yeshayah* 55:12. See *Yalkut Shimoni, Emor* 653.
135 Rashbam, *Bereishis* 24:62.
136 *Bereishis Rabbah* 13:2.
137 *Sukkah* 28a.
138 *Rabbeinu Ephraim, Bereishis* 2:5. See *Vayikra Rabbah* 30:4.

Waving the Four Species

The four species are waved during various points of the *Hallel* recital on Sukkos. The Gemara explains that they are waved upward and downward to demonstrate that Hashem is the Master of heaven and earth, and are moved outward and inward for the sake of the One whom the four directions of the world are His.[139] What does this waving represent?

- These actions constitute a form of accepting Hashem's Kingship upon oneself, similar to the recital of the first verse of *Shema*, when one extends the pronunciation of the letter *daled* in the word *echad* — one — to contemplate Hashem's Oneness, encompassing above, below, and the four directions of the world.[140]
- The four species correspond to the human body. We wave them in a manner that demonstrates that "I am for my Beloved" and pursue Him lovingly without reservation.[141]

THE SUKKOS WATER LIBATION

Most Joyous Mitzvah

The Rambam calls *Simchas Beis HaShoevah*, the water libation celebration in the Beis HaMikdash, *simchah yeseirah* — an extreme *simchah*.[142] Although this expression is found in the Gemara in relation to the *Simchas Beis HaShoevah*,[143] Rabbi Aharon Kotler maintains that this *simchah* essentially draws from the general mitzvah to rejoice during Yom Tov (notwithstanding that there is a greater mitzvah to rejoice on Sukkos more so than on other Yomim Tovim).[144] The rabbis emphasized

---

139　*Sukkah* 37b.

140　Rabbi Aharon Kotler, *Mishnas Rebbi Aharon*, vol. 3, p. 58.

141　Rabbi Shlomo Zalman Auerbach, *Halichos Shlomo*, Moadim, p. 229, footnote 81.

142　Rambam, *Mishnah Torah*, Lulav 8:12.

143　*Sukkah* 51a.

144　*Mishnas Rebbi Aharon*, *Orach Chaim* 13.

the extreme *simchah* of the mitzvah of the *Simchas Beis HaShoevah* merely to counter the view of the *Tzidukim* — Sadducees — who did not believe in that celebration, as it did not have an explicit Torah source.

Rabbi Moshe Feinstein maintains that the one mitzvah in the Torah that was celebrated with the most joy and fanfare was the *Nisuch HaMayim* — the water libation in the Temple on Sukkos.[145]

Unlike all the other offerings in the Temple, the water libation did not involve any monetary expense. Still, its merit was so great that through its performance the Jewish People merited bountiful rain for the upcoming year.[146] This taught that even the humblest pauper who is not blessed with money or talent should joyously serve Hashem with the meager gifts at his disposal. When brought with sincerity, even a little water finds as much favor with Hashem as the most expensive offering.[147]

The Hinted Service

In connection with the offerings brought on each day of Sukkos, the Torah generally writes ונסכה — "and its [wine] libation" (that accompanied the offering). An exception is made for the following three days:

- the second day of Sukkos, where it says ונסכיהם with an extra letter מ
- the sixth day, which states ונסכיה with an extra letter י
- the seventh day, which states כמשפטם with an extra letter ם

The Gemara expounds that these extra letters spell the word מים — water, and that this is a Scriptural allusion to the water libation service performed on Sukkos.[148]

Why did the Torah embed its hint on these specific days?

---

145   *Derash Moshe*, p. 221, 344.
146   *Rosh Hashanah* 16a.
147   *Derash Moshe* ibid.
148   *Ta'anis* 2b.

The *Rokeach* explains that these particular days all have a connection with water:[149]

- On the second day of creation, Hashem divided between the upper and lower waters.
- On the sixth day of creation, a cloud ascended from the earth and gave rain for the first time.
- Rain on Friday night is a sign of blessing, since it is at a time when the world is at rest.

It is understandable that the plural tense for the word "libation," ונסכיה/ונסכיהם, is employed to hint to the additional water libation on Sukkos, but what connection does the word כמשפטם — "in accordance with their law," have with water?

The Mishnah teaches that the world is judged for water on Sukkos.[150] Hashem therefore commanded the water libation be brought in the Temple in order to bring blessing to the annual rainfall.[151] Since the climax for the judgment on water is on Hoshanah Rabbah, the seventh day of the festival, the word כמשפטם, which can also be translated as "according to their judgment," is used for this day.[152]

The mitzvah of *Nisuch HaMayim* is alluded to by the extra letters *mem*, *yud*, and *mem*, which spell the word *mayim* — water — and which are written in the verses that deal with the offerings brought on Sukkos.[153] Why did the Torah not write this mitzvah explicitly?

---

149 *Rokeach, Bamidbar* 29:12, *Sha'ar Shinui.*
150 *Rosh Hashanah* 16a.
151 Ibid.
152 Maharshah, *Ta'anis* 2b.
153 *Ta'anis* 2b.

Rabbi Mendel Kaplan answers that Sukkos connects with the whole of creation, just as the seventy sacrificial bulls brought on Sukkos correspond to the seventy nations of the world. The water libation, however, expresses Hashem's private connection to the Jewish People,[154] and is therefore only hinted to in the Torah.[155]

Washing Away Sin

During the *Simchas Beis HaShoevah* celebration in the Temple, the pious men would dance and sing words of praises before Hashem. The Gemara quotes their praises: "Those who were penitents would say, 'Happy is our old age that has atoned for our errant youth' ... all would say, 'Happy is he who never sinned; but as for he who has sinned, let him repent and be forgiven.'"[156]

Why did their songs and praises focus on their forgiven sins? Rabbi Yosef Ber Soleveitchik answers that the verse likens a sinner cleansed from his sin to a sick person healed from his illness:[157] Just as there is an obligation for a healed person to offer thanks and praise to Hashem, so is a pardoned sinner obligated to offer praises to Hashem.[158] When the prophet Shmuel gathered the Jewish nation in a demonstration of repentance, they drew water and poured it out before Hashem.[159] The Radak says that the poured water symbolized that all their sins were cleansed and forgiven.[160] It is likely that the water libation ceremony at the *Simchas Beis HaShoevah* also conveyed this message.[161]

---

154 The *Yerushalmi* (*Sukkah* 5:1) states that the area in the Temple courtyard where the water libation ceremony was celebrated was called בית שואבה — the "place of the [water] drawing," — even though, in fact, the water was drawn in the Shilo'ach spring outside the Temple because those present at the festivities would "draw" *ruach HaKodesh* — the Divine spirit.

155 Rabbi Mendel Kaplan, *Reb Mendel and His Wisdom*, p. 72.

156 *Sukkah* 53a.

157 *Tehillim* 103:3.

158 *Hararei Kedem*, vol. 1, 165:2.

159 *Shmuel I* 7:6.

160 Ibid.

161 *Hararei Kedem* ibid.

HOSHANOS

The Mystical Hoshanah Prayer

Ani V'ho Hoshi'ah Na.[162] The words *Ani* and *V'ho* both refer to Hashem and are taken from the seventy-two-letter name of Hashem.[163] Tosfos further explains that *Ani* refers to the verse in *Yechezkel* that says, "*Ani* — I [Hashem] am in the exile,"[164] and *V'ho* refers to the verse in *Yirmiyah* that says, "*V'ho* — And He [Hashem] is bound in chains [in exile]."[165] Both verses demonstrate that Hashem, so to speak, is suffering in exile with us. We therefore beseech Hashem to save us for the sake of His Great Name that is now desecrated in exile.

The *Derashas HaRamban* says that the seventy-two-letter name of Hashem was used by the pious of Israel "to kill and to give life, to destroy and to build." Since this name has extreme spiritual power, we invoke it during *Hoshanos* in order to arouse Hashem's mercy to redeem us from exile in a miraculous manner.[166] As it states regarding the future redemption,[167] Hashem will deliver us from exile using His seventy-two-letter name.

The source of the seventy-two-letter Name of Hashem is derived from three verses taken from the narrative of the splitting of the *Yam Suf*, each containing seventy-two letters.[168] The Radvaz says that the seventy-two-letter name of Hashem specifically relates to Hashem being the Master of water.[169] Since the great spiritual energies inherent in these verses enabled Moshe to achieve *Krias Yam Suf*, this name is

---

162 *Hoshanah* prayers.
163 Rashi, *Sukkah* 45a.
164 *Yechezkel* 1:1.
165 *Yirmiyah* 40:1. See Tosfos, *Sukkah* ibid.
166 Cited in footnote to Chizkuni, *Shemos* 14:21 (Rabbi M.M. Aharon edition).
167 *Bereishis Rabbah* 44:19.
168 *Shemos* 14:19–21.
169 Radvaz 4:257.

especially auspicious to recite on Sukkos, since we are judged regarding water at this time.[170]

HOSHANAH RABBAH

The Judgment of Hoshanah Rabbah

The *Rokeach* points out that the word כמשפט, which denotes משפט — judgment — is used in only two places in the Torah:[171]

- in reference to Rosh Hashanah[172]
- on the seventh day of Sukkos[173]

This teaches that just as Rosh Hashanah is a day of judgment, so too is the seventh day of Sukkos a day of judgment.

According to the revealed Oral Law, the judgment on the seventh day of Sukkos is limited to how much rainfall will be supplied in the upcoming year.[174] However, the secret works of Kabbalah teach that the judgment of this day encompasses a much greater scope. They say that the seventh day of Sukkos, more commonly known as Hoshanah Rabbah, is the culmination of the judgment of Rosh Hashanah and the time the Heavenly judgments are sent forth to be carried out in the world.[175]

There are many similarities between the Days of Judgment and Hoshanah Rabbah:

- The chazzan wears a *kittel* and sings the *davening* of Hoshanah Rabbah in the same tune as during the Yomim Noraim.

---

170   Chizkuni, *Shemos* 14:21.
171   *Bamidbar* 29:6.
172   Ibid.
173   Ibid., v. 33.
174   *Rosh Hashanah* 16a.
175   *Zohar* 3:31.

- We greet each other with *gmar chasimah tovah*.
- Some have the custom to light the remainder of the candles of Yom Kippur.
- Some communities would even blow the shofar during the *Hoshanos* on Hoshanah Rabbah.[176]

All this is to demonstrate that Hoshanah Rabbah is also part of the days of judgment.[177]

The Hidden Day of Judgment

Why isn't it mentioned anywhere in the revealed Oral Law — neither the *Talmud Bavli* nor *Yerushalmi* — that Hoshanah Rabbah is the conclusion of the judgment on Rosh Hashanah? Secondly, what is meant that Hoshanah Rabbah is the conclusion of the judgment on Rosh Hashanah if Yom Kippur is the time when one's judgment is sealed?

Rabbi Yaakov Kamenetsky explains that the heavenly kingdom parallels the earthly monarchy system. Just as it is a sign of a king's sovereignty to be able to pardon criminals from their sentence, the same is true with Hashem. Even when a person's fate is sealed on Yom Kippur, Hashem grants an additional ten-day amnesty period that concludes on Hoshanah Rabbah.

Had the Sages openly revealed this secret, the masses would have treated the festival of Sukkos as another ten days of repentance and would spend the entire festival crying and davening, thereby refraining from properly rejoicing on the festival.

Therefore, this information was only made privy to a select few great and holy individuals who would be able to properly rejoice on Sukkos despite being aware of the magnitude of this time. As the piety of the masses lapsed in later generations and they were no longer fearful of judgment as in earlier times, the rabbis decided to publicly reveal this

---

176   Rabbi Yaakov Yitzchak **Ruderman**, *Sichos Levi*, p. 7.
177   *Oznayim L'Torah, Vayikra* 23:34; *Sichos Levi* ibid.

information. They even incorporated some customs of the Days of Awe into the Hoshanah Rabbah service, since they realized that this newfound awareness would not detract from the joy of Yom Tov.[178]

Repentance through Joy

The *Zohar* states that Hoshanah Rabbah is the culmination of Hashem's judgment of the world and on this day the transcript of one's decree is sent out from before the King.[179] Rabbi Zalman Sorotzkin explains that Hashem, in His mercy, wishes to give another chance to those who did not merit a good judgment during Rosh Hashanah and Yom Kippur.[180] The festival of Sukkos immediately follows Yom Kippur so that one who did not achieve full repentance through fasting and crying can still rectify his situation by joyously celebrating Sukkos and thereby attain the level of *teshuvah me'ahavah* — repentance through love of Hashem. This is why the *pasuk* uses the same word "*hazeh* — this" in reference to Yom Kippur and Sukkos,[181] since they both accomplish the same goal of repentance — only that on Yom Kippur it is achieved with fear and on Sukkos through love.

Day of Forgiveness

> *Said HaKadosh Baruch Hu to Avraham: "I am One and you are one; I will give your descendants one day to atone for their sins. If your children will not attain atonement on Rosh Hashanah, they will attain it on Yom Kippur. If they still won't achieve it on Yom Kippur, they will achieve it on Hoshanah Rabbah."*[182]

Why did Hashem grant this promise specifically to Avraham? The *Mateh Moshe* explains that just as Avraham began to spread the light

---

178   *B'mechitzas Rabbeinu*, p. 135; *Emes L'Yaakov, Vayikra* 23:24.
179   *Zohar* 3:31.
180   *Oznayim L'Torah, Vayikra* 23:34.
181   *Vayikra* 23:27, 34.
182   Midrash, quoted in *Mateh Moshe* 957.

of Hashem's Oneness after twenty-one generations from Creation, so too will the light of atonement not tarry for his descendants more than twenty-one days, which are the number of days between Rosh Hashanah and Hoshanah Rabbah.[183]

The Poor Chazzan

On Hoshanah Rabbah and Shemini Atzeres, we pray for abundant rain so that the crops will be blessed. In *Yirmiyah*, the verse describes how the officers of Yehudah sent out their youngsters to obtain water during a time of drought.[184] The word used for "youngsters" (צעיריהם) is spelled with the letter *vav* (צעוריהם) which means "those in pain." The *Sefer Chasidim* derives from this that one should choose a chazzan for Hoshanah Rabbah and Shemini Atzeres who is impoverished and pained by rising food prices, and not a food merchant who is happy when the price of produce rises.[185]

Climax of Joy

Even though there is a mitzvah to be joyous on all the festivals, and even more so during the festival of Sukkos,[186] a still greater expression of joy was displayed on Hoshanah Rabbah. The following are some examples of these extreme expressions of joy performed exclusively on Hoshanah Rabbah:

- On Hoshanah Rabbah, the adults would grab the *lulavim* from the hands of the children and would eat the children's *esrogim*.[187] Rashi explains that doing this wasn't an act of theft since this custom was practiced as an expression of joy.[188]

---

183 Ibid.

184 *Yirmiyah* 14:3.

185 *Sefer Chasidim* 248.

186 Rambam, *Mishnah Torah*, Lulav 8:12.

187 *Sukkah* 45a.

188 Ibid.

- It was customary to extinguish candles with the *hoshanos* because of joy.[189]
- All the customs of Hoshanah Rabbah, such as encircling the *bimah* seven times and beating the *aravos* on the floor, were all instituted to express joy.[190]
- Some say that the reason for the custom of throwing the beaten *hoshanos* on top of the Torah-ark on Hoshanah Rabbah is in order to increase joy.

Removing the Lulav's Rings

There is a custom to remove the rings from the *lulav* on Hoshanah Rabbah before shaking it for the final time. (The *Kaf HaChaim* points out that if the *lulav* will later be used by others, one should not remove them, since the vigorous shaking of the *lulav* may cause its middle leaf to split and thereby disqualify it.[191])

There are several reasons for this custom:

- The Torah describes the *lulav* as כפת תמרים — "branches of date palms."[192] Since the first word can be vowelized *kafus*, which means "tied up," the Gemara derives that the *lulav* should be bound together.[193] In the Torah, the word כפת is spelled without the letter *vav*, which has the numerical value of six. This hints that the *lulav* should be bound for only six days of Sukkos. Therefore, during the seventh day of Hoshanah Rabbah, it is proper for the *lulav* to be untied.[194]
- The *Levush* writes that the primary reason for the custom

---

189 Maharil, cited in *Darkei Moshe, Orach Chaim* 664.

190 *Levush, Orach Chaim* 664:3.

191 *Kaf HaChaim* 664:25.

192 *Vayikra* 23:40.

193 *Sukkah* 31a.

194 *Tur, Orach Chaim* 664.

is to increase joy. This is because one experiences more joy while shaking the *lulav* without its rings.[195]

- The reason for shaking the *lulav* is to ward off harmful winds and damaging dews.[196] Removing the rings from the *lulav* enhances its movement, since the leaves can then move more freely in an unrestricted manner. Since Hoshanah Rabbah is the climax of the judgment on water, we remove the rings at this time so that the *lulav* can be shaken in the best possible manner.[197]

Beating the Aravah

There is a custom to beat the *aravah* branches (*chibut aravah*) on the ground on Hoshanah Rabbah. There are numerous reasons given for the source of this custom:

- The *aravah*, which is a willow branch, comprises one of the four species of the *lulav*. Its long and narrow leaves correspond to a person's lips and atone for sins committed through utterances of the lips. After having attained atonement on Sukkos, we henceforth commit ourselves to refrain from misusing the gift of speech. We therefore touch the *aravah* on the ground to remind us to be careful with our words, as the verse states,[198] "Let him put his mouth to the dust — there may yet be hope."[199]
- The *aravah* looks like the lips of a mouth. Since the Jewish People have attained complete atonement on this day against the prosecuting angels, our actions symbolize that any mouth that will now attempt to raise accusations against Israel will be cast to the ground.[200]

---

195 *Levush, Orach Chaim* 664:1.
196 *Sukkah* 37b.
197 Bach, commentary on *Tur, Orach Chaim* 664.
198 *Eichah* 3:29.
199 *Teshuvas HaGaonim, Sha'arei Teshuvah* 340.
200 Ibid.

- If you remove the covering of the *aravah* seed, you will find the form of a flayed beheaded snake. In the Torah, the snake represents the evil inclination. The reason we hit the *aravah* on the floor on Hoshanah Rabbah is to symbolize that the forces of evil have been rendered impotent.[201]
- The Jewish People in *galus* are bent and beaten just like a beaten *hoshanah*. The numerous beatings, however, do not destroy us, but rather they purify us and make us worthy of the redemption. According to the custom of the *Arizal*, the *aravos* are beaten only five times. This symbolizes the five exiles (Mitzrayim, Bavel, Madai, Yavan, Edom) that we will ultimately be redeemed from.[202]

READING OF KOHELES

Why Koheles?

It is customary to read the book of *Koheles* on Sukkos. There are several reasons given for this:

- King Shlomo composed *Koheles* and recited it at the *Hakhel* ceremony during which the king read parts of the Torah to the entire Jewish People just after the *Shemitah* year on Sukkos.[203]
- It says in *Koheles*, "Distribute portions to seven or even to eight,"[204] which hints to the seven days of Sukkos and the eighth day of Shemini Atzeres.[205] This serves as a reminder that one should finish distributing his tithes and pay all his outstanding vows at this time so as not to come to transgress the prohibition of delaying one's vows.[206]

---

201   *Asarah Ma'amaros*, cited in *Ruach Chaim*, introduction to *Avos*.
202   *Otzer Kol Minhagei Yeshurun*, p. 116.
203   *Avudraham, Krias HaMegilos B'Moadim*, p. 240.
204   *Koheles* 11:2.
205   *Eruvin* 40b.
206   *Avudraham* ibid.

- The Midrash says that King Shlomo wrote Song of Songs in his youth and *Koheles* in his old age. We therefore read the Song of Songs on Pesach in the spring, which hints to the springtime of life, and *Koheles* during the Feast of the Ingathering, which hints to the period of old age, the time when Shlomo looked back at his life and saw that all is vanity.[207]

- Sukkos is the season of our rejoicing. *Koheles* urges people to rejoice in their portion and not to excessively pursue increasing one's wealth, as it states in *Koheles*, a person who enjoys what he has, "It is a gift from God."[208]

- On Sukkos, we are commanded to be extremely joyous. A person who is entrenched in the pleasures of the physical world is unable to be truly joyous since his joy is marred by tinges of jealousy and the relentless pursuit for pleasure and honor. By internalizing the message of *Koheles*, which belittles the vanities of the physical world, one can achieve a state of true joy.[209]

LAWS

Conversing in the Sukkah

Generally, it is prohibited to talk during the performance of a mitzvah — such as while searching for *chametz* before Pesach or during the shofar blowing on Rosh Hashanah — so as not to interrupt between the blessing and the completion of the mitzvah. If so, why is it permissible to talk during the meal while fulfilling the mitzvah of sitting in a *sukkah*?

The *Taz* answers that one may interrupt any mitzvah that is in one's power to conclude whenever he wishes. Since one may conclude his meal at any time, it is therefore permissible to talk during the *sukkah*

---

207   *Keser Shem Tov*.
208   *Koheles* 3:13. Idea found in *Levush, Orach Chaim* 663:2.
209   Rabbi Yaakov Naiman, *Darkei Mussar*, p. 284.

meal.[210] We may also suggest that since the mitzvah of dwelling in the *sukkah* is to be in the same manner as one lives in one's home, talking during the meal is not considered an interruption.

Buying from a Non-Jew

The *SMaG* rules that when purchasing an *esrog* or any mitzvah item from a non-Jew, one should not haggle over the price but should rather pay slightly above its actual value.[211] This is so that non-Jews should not get the impression that Jews lack the proper respect for mitzvos.[212] In addition, if non-Jews see that it is not profitable for them to supply Jews with their religious obligations, they will refrain from providing them with these items in the future.[213]

Hiddur Mitzvah on Esrog Boxes?

There is a mitzvah to beautify mitzvah objects (*hiddur mitzvah*), such as by obtaining a beautiful *lulav* or a nice *sukkah*. One may ask, though, whether *hiddur mitzvah* applies only to the actual object used for the mitzvah or if it also extends to the peripheral items associated with a mitzvah, such as placing the *esrog* in a silver *esrog* box?

The *Chavos Yair* says that even the container for a mitzvah object should be beautiful.[214] As the *Sefer Chasidim* notes, just as a person places his valuables in a dignified chest, even more so should one place all his objects of mitzvah, such as a *lulav* and *esrog*, in beautiful containers according to his means.[215]

Hoshanos during Mourning

There is a debate whether a mourner should circle the *bimah* together with the congregation during the *Hoshanos* ceremony on Sukkos.

---

210   *Taz, Orach Chaim* 592:2.
211   *Sefer Mitzvos HaGadol*, positive commandment 44.
212   *Aruch HaShulchan, Orach Chaim* 651:3.
213   *Mishnah Berurah* 649, introduction.
214   *Mekor Chaim* 28. See *Sotah* 14b.
215   *Sefer Chasidim* 129. See also *Kaf HaChaim* 297:12.

The rationale of those forbidding it is based on the verse: "You shall rejoice before Hashem, your G-d, for a seven-day period."[216] This verse alludes to the ceremony when the *Kohanim* encircled the Temple Altar on Sukkos, which is presently reenacted by encircling the shul *bimah* during *Hoshanos*. Since this ceremony represented the pinnacle of joy of the festival, it is not appropriate that it be represented by a mourner, who is lacking a state of joy.[217]

Those who permit the participation of a mourner argue that unlike the *Hoshanos* ceremony performed in the Temple, the *Hoshanos* circles we currently conduct in exile are not a service of joy. On the contrary, that we recite supplications during the recital of *Hoshanos* demonstrates that the ceremony is one of longing and prayer, rather than one of joy.[218]

The *Aruch HaShulchan* presents another rationale for the exclusion of mourners from the *Hoshanos* service. Since a mourner is in state of experiencing Divine judgment, he is not in a suitable position to request Divine mercy at this time.[219]

Time of Hoshanos

There are differing customs whether the *Hoshanos* service is practiced immediately after *Hallel* or deferred until after *Musaf*.

The reason for those who give precedence to the Torah reading and *Musaf* is because the reading of the Torah and the *Musaf* prayer are true Rabbinic obligations, while *Hoshanos* were instituted as a custom, which is also why a blessing is not recited over it.[220]

In the view of those who perform *Hoshanos* immediately after *Hallel*, since we are already holding the *lulav* and *esrog* during *Hallel*, we wish to continue immediately with *Hoshanos* where the four

---

216 *Vayikra* 23:40.
217 *Biur HaGra, Orach Chaim* 660:2.
218 Rabbi Moshe Feinstein, *Igros Moshe, Yoreh Deah* 4:61:11.
219 *Aruch HaShulchan, Orach Chaim* 660:4.
220 *Igros Moshe, Orach Chaim* 3:99.

species are also grasped. If we were to put down the *lulav* at the conclusion of *Hallel*, it would be a slight to the *lulav*.[221]

SHEMINI ATZERES

Hints of the Festivals

The Vilna Gaon comments that the first four verses in *Shir HaShirim* correspond to each of the four festivals in order:[222]

1. "Song of Songs" corresponds to Pesach, when the Jews sang songs of praise to Hashem for their redemption from slavery.
2. "Let Him kiss me with the kisses of His mouth" corresponds to Shavuos, when Hashem spoke to the Jewish People in a direct manner upon giving the Torah on Sinai.
3. "Your fragrant oils [of the Temple offerings]...therefore do the young maidens love you" corresponds to Sukkos, when the seventy bull-offerings were brought in the Temple on behalf of the seventy nations.
4. "The King has brought me into His chambers" corresponds to Shemini Atzeres, which is the consummation of the yearly festival cycle.[223]

Why Only Sukkos?

Shemini Atzeres derives its name from the word *atzar* — restraining — as Hashem holds us back next to Him for another day. Rashi famously explains that it is like a king who invited his sons to a banquet for a certain number of days. Once their time to depart arrived, the king said, "My sons, I request of you, linger with me one more day. Your departure is difficult for me."[224]

---

221   Ibid.
222   *Gra, Shir HaShirim* 1:4.
223   *Ma'amarei Rama M'Panu*, p. 224.
224   *Vayikra* 23:36.

The question arises, why isn't there also a day of *atzeres* for the festivals of Pesach and Shavuos?

The Chizkuni answers that it is comparable to a king who invites his children to his palace at several times in the year. At the end of their first visit, the king inquires, "When will you return?" The children respond, "in fifty days," and the king sends them home in peace. When they arrive the second time, the king again asks them when will they return and the children answer, "in four months." This time as well the king sends them home in peace. On their third visit, when the king asks them when will they be returning, the children reply that they will not be able to return for another six months. This time the father tells them, "It is difficult to be away from you for so long. Please stay another day."[225]

Similarly, after Pesach there is only a fifty-day lapse until the next holiday, and again between Shavuos and Sukkos there is only a period of four months, which is also tolerable. Between Sukkos and Pesach, however, where there is a span of six months, Hashem finds the long separation unbearable.

Epicenter of the Festivals

In the Torah, the festivals are termed *chag*, which derives from the word *chugah* — a circle. All the festivals are like concentric circles. What is the center core that all the festivals revolve around?

According to the works of Kabbalah, Shemini Atzeres is the epicenter of all the festivals. Unlike Rosh Hashanah which has shofar, Pesach which has matzah, Sukkos which has *sukkah* and the four species, and Shavuos which has the *Sh'tei Halechem* offering, Shemini Atzeres is so sublime that it does not require any unique mitzvos. The great sanctity of Shemini Atzeres does not come through action but solely via a person attaining joy and pleasure with Hashem.[226]

---

225 Ibid.
226 *Rama M'Panu*, cited in *Chasam Sofer, Drashos*, vol. 1, Sukkos 581, s.v. "*v'hayisa.*"

In some respects, Shemini Atzeres is similar to Yom Kippur, which is why the *Musaf* sacrifices of both days are exactly the same. But in fact, the holiness of Shemini Atzeres surpasses even that of Yom Kippur. This is because the sanctity of Yom Kippur comes about by afflicting one's body, while the sanctity of Shemini Atzeres comes from rejoicing with Hashem.[227]

Sukkah on Shemini Atzeres

Why does the Torah exempt one from sitting in the *sukkah* on Shemini Atzeres?

The *Chizkuni* answers that since we begin praying for rain on this day, Hashem wished that our prayers be recited wholeheartedly. If we were commanded to sit in the *sukkah* on Shemini Atzeres as well, we would pray in a half-hearted manner, since we would not want the rain to disrupt and ruin our festive meals.[228]

Korbanos of Shemini Atzeres

On all festivals, a minimum of two bulls are brought for the *korban Musaf*. An exception to this is the *korban Musaf* brought on Shemini Atzeres, when only one bull is brought. There are many reasons for this:

- On Rosh Hashanah and Yom Kippur, only one bull was brought for the *korban Musaf*. This alludes to the fact that Shemini Atzeres is the culmination of the Days of Judgment, as on this day our sins from the previous year are completely exonerated.[229]
- It is comparable to a king who makes an elaborate formal banquet for his countrymen. At the end of the seven-day feast, he calls over his good friend and tells him, "We fulfilled our official obligation for our country. Let us now enjoy each

---

227 *Chasam Sofer* ibid.
228 Chizkuni, *Bamidbar* 29:35.
229 *Sefer HaToda'ah*, p. 125.

other's company with whatever we can find — be it a bit of meat, fish, or vegetables."

Similarly, the seventy bulls brought over Sukkos correspond to the seventy nations of the world. Shemini Atzeres represents the informal, familial relationship Hashem has with the Jewish People. So while the royal state dinner is an elaborate affair, our relationship with Hashem is more *heimishe* — homey, and even leftovers will suffice.[230]

- The two *Musaf* bulls brought on Pesach, Shavous, and Rosh Chodesh represent the dual nature of our Divine service through love and awe (*ahavah* and *yirah*). On Rosh Hashanah and Yom Kippur, only one bull is brought, since the primary service of these days is *yirah* alone. Shemini Atzeres alludes to the epoch of the future redemption, when our relationship with Hashem will be primarily one of love. Therefore, only one bull, representing *ahavah*, is brought.[231]

SIMCHAS TORAH

Chassan Torah and Chassan Bereishis

When calling up the *Chassan Torah* for his *aliyah* on Simchas Torah, a unique introduction is recited. In it we announce three times, "*Amod, amod, amod* — Stand, stand, stand," calling upon the *Chassan Torah* to arise to the Torah. The *Hararei Kedem* explains the basis for this custom as follows: when a person is called to *daven* for the *amud*, it is correct to demure until asked three times.[232] When a person receives an *aliyah*, the halachah is the opposite; one should go up to the Torah without delay.[233] Why?

---

230 *Bamidbar Rabbah* 21:24.
231 Seforno, *Kavanas HaTorah* 12.
232 *Berachos* 34a.
233 Ibid. 55a.

The distinction is that a chazzan is a position of honor and authority, and it is not proper for a person to accept honor eagerly. However, since receiving an *aliyah* is not a matter of honor, there is therefore no reason to hesitate.

An exception to this is the final *aliyah* of the Torah, the *aliyah* of *Chassan Torah*. Since the outstanding Torah figure of the community is chosen to receive *Chassan Torah*,[234] the *aliyah* is one of great honor. Therefore, it is similar to the appointment of a chazzan, where it is proper for the one receiving the honor to initially decline. By calling the *Chassan Torah* three times, we allow him to accept the honor without delay.[235]

There is a slight variation in the way we call up the *Chassan Torah* and *Chassan Bereishis* for their *aliyos*. When introducing the *Chassan Bereishis*, we add: "**Maher**, *amod amod amod* — **Quickly**, arise, arise, arise."

Based on the explanation above, it would appear inappropriate to request that the *Chassan Bereishis* arise quickly, since that would give the appearance that he is pursuing honor!

We may suggest that there is a fundamental difference between *Chassan Torah* and *Chassan Bereishis*. The Radvaz writes that the reason we read *Bereishis* immediately upon completing the Torah is in order that Satan should not raise accusation against us. If we were to stop upon completion of the Torah, the Accuser may claim, "Now that the Jews have finished the Torah and completed their mission, allow me to take them from this world." However, since we immediately return and begin the Torah anew, we demonstrate that we view our mission as perpetual.[236] That is why we urge the

---

234   *Darkei Moshe, Orach Chaim* 669.
235   *Hararei Kedem* 1:155.
236   Radvaz 1:288.

Chassan Bereishis to speedily arise — to show our eagerness to begin the Torah once again without the slightest delay.

From End to Beginning

Various commentators explain the connection between the end of the Torah, "And all the great sights that Moshe displayed before the eyes of all Israel,"[237] and the beginning of the Torah, "In the beginning Hashem created heaven and earth."[238] The *Ha'amek Davar* explains that the "great sights" refer to the revelation of the *Shechinah* that Moshe made accessible before the eyes of the entire nation, such as at the splitting of the *Yam Suf* and the giving of the Torah at Sinai. These great visions elevated the Jewish nation and infused them with the firm belief that Hashem was the Creator of heaven and earth, which is the purpose of creation.[239]

---

237 *Devarim* 34:12.
238 *Bereishis* 1:1.
239 Rabbi Naftali Tzvi Berlin, *Ha'amek Davar*, *Devarim* 34:12.

The Rabbinic Festival

Chanukah is the only festival that has no basis in *Tanach*, only in *Torah Sheba'al Peh* — the Oral Law. When the Chashmonaim desperately sought a flask of pure oil for the Menorah, their zealousness was to preserve a Rabbinic injunction, since using impure oil for communal use is permissible according to the Torah. Hashem rewarded their self-sacrifice to uphold a Rabbinic mitzvah with a miracle of pure oil and the commemoration of the Chanukah miracle through the establishment of a Rabbinic festival.

The Unwritten Miracle

Unlike the story of Purim, which is written in the *Megillah*, the miracle of Chanukah was not permitted to be written.[1] Additionally, virtually all the laws of Chanukah were also not written in the Mishnah. Why?

The Greeks regarded the Written Torah in great esteem and even had it translated into Greek. It was specifically the Oral Law that the

---

1   *Yomah* 29a.

Greeks sought to eradicate. Since the festival of Chanukah is a celebration of the Oral Law, the rabbis instituted that Chanukah retain its oral nature as much as possible and refrained from committing it to writing in any way.[2]

Is Creating Rabbinic Festivals Permissible?

There is a Torah prohibition of *ba'al tosif* — that one may not add to the mitzvos of the Torah. If so, why aren't the Rabbinic holidays of Chanukah and Purim included in this prohibition, since they are not commanded in the Torah?

According to some opinions, *ba'al tosif* only applies to adding on to a pre-existing mitzvah, such as adding an additional *parashah* in one's *tefillin*. To create an entirely new mitzvah, such as the Rabbinic festivals of Chanukah and Purim, is not included in this prohibition.[3]

Others, however, are of the opinion that even adding an entirely new mitzvah would be included in the prohibition of *ba'al tosif*.[4] (For this reason, the rabbis were initially hesitant in instituting the mitzvah of reading the *Megillah*, were it not for the fact that it was hinted to in the Torah.)[5] According to this opinion, how then was it permissible for the rabbis to institute the festivals of Chanukah and Purim?

The Chasam Sofer answers that there is a general Torah obligation to commemorate the day of one's miraculous salvation by offering praise (*hallel v'hoda'ah*) to Hashem.[6] Therefore, to celebrate Chanukah and Purim as a festival is essentially a mitzvah in the Torah, since it is a form of thanking and praising Hashem for miraculously saving us during those times.

---

2   Rabbi Shlomo Zalman Auerbach, *Halichos Shlomo*, Chanukah 16:42.
3   Rabbi Moshe Feinstein, *Shemaitsah D'Moshe*, Chanukah 670:1.
4   Ramban, *Devarim* 4:2.
5   Ibid.; *Yerushalmi, Megillah* 1:7.
6   Chasam Sofer, *Shabbos* 22a, s.v. *"pesulo,"* ad loc.

The *Rokeach* presents a totally different approach. Although a prophet does not have the authority to enact a new mitzvah,[7] *Chazal* may institute a new Yom Tov if it is hinted to in the Torah.[8] The *Pesiktah* says that the hint to Chanukah in the Torah can be found in the *parashah* listing all the festivals, which is immediately followed with the mitzvah of lighting the Menorah with pure oil.[9] The juxtaposition teaches that the *Bnei Yisrael* will someday create a new Yom Tov that involves the oil of the Menorah.[10] In addition, the Midrash says that the reason the *parashah* of the *Chanukas HaMizbei'ach* is immediately followed by the *parashah* of lighting the Menorah in the Mishkan,[11] is to hint that in the future the Menorah will also have a **Chanukah** festival of its own.[12]

TORAH HINTS

Early commentators present additional hints for Chanukah in the Torah:

The *Ba'al HaTurim* adds that the verse in the beginning of *parashas Beha'aloscha* not only hints to the Chanukah Menorah, but also hints to the mitzvah of *pirsumei nisah*, the obligation to perform the lighting of the Chanukah Menorah in a publicized manner.[13]

How does the verse hint to this idea? Rabbi Yaakov Rainetz, in his commentary to *Ba'al HaTurim*, explains that the wording of the verse, "When you cause the flame to rise," demonstrates that the lights should be lit in a manner that is highly visible.[14]

---

7   *Shabbos* 104a.

8   *Rokeach, Vayikra* 27:34.

9   *Vayikra* 23, 24:1–4.

10   *Pesikta Zeirta, parashas Beha'aloscha.*

11   *Bamidbar* 7, 8:1–4.

12   See Ramban, *Bamidbar* 8:2.

13   *Ba'al HaTurim, Bamidbar* 8:2.

14   Rabbi Ya'akov Reinitz, *Ba'al HaTurim* ibid., footnote 2.

זאת חנוכת המזבח ביום המשח אתו מאת — "This was the dedication (*Chanukas*) of the Altar, on the day it was anointed."[15] The *Rabbeinu Ephraim* writes that this verse contains numerous hints for the festival of Chanukah:[16]

- זאת חנוכת המזבח is the numerical value of:
  (אז) בשמונת ימי חנוכה — "Then, during the eight days of Chanukah," and
  זאת יהיה בימי חשמונים — "This will be during the days of the Chashmonaim."
- אתו מאת (ביום המשח) — is the numerical value of:
  חנוכה ביום ה' ועשרים בכסלו — "Chanukah is on the twenty-fifth day of Kislev."

This *parashah* directly precedes the Torah portion that deals with the lighting of the Menorah and the consecration of the Levites,[17] further hinting to the role of the Levites in the miracle of Chanukah and of the obligation to light the menorah on Chanukah.

Fruitful Well

The *Rokeach* writes that the Torah's account of how the Pelishtim fought over several wells that Yitzchak dug corresponds to the different exiles of his future progeny. The third well he dug, over which there was no quarrel, he called Rechovos, saying, "For now Hashem has granted us wide spaces and we can be fruitful in the land."[18] The third well of Rechovos corresponds to the third exile — that of Yavan — which concluded with the victory of the Jewish People over the Greeks, enabling us to keep the Torah in peace.[19]

---

15 *Bamidbar* 7:84.
16 *Rabbeinu Ephraim, Bamidbar* ibid.
17 *Bamidbar* 8.
18 *Bereishis* 26:22.
19 *Rokeach, Bereishis* ibid.

Aside from the general miracle that transpired for the entire nation, the *Rokeach* adds that the specific reference of being fruitful in the land alludes to an additional miracle that occurred specifically for women at that time. The Midrash Chanukah records that the Greeks decreed that the Jewish women were prohibited from going to the *mikvah*. The intention of their decree was to thereby diminish the population of the observant Jews. However, Hashem made a miracle and springs miraculously sprung up in each person's home, allowing the women to purify themselves and be with their husbands, thereby enabling them to be fruitful and multiply.

Yaakov and the Chanukah Oil

The patterns of Jewish history follow the principle of *maaseh avos siman l'banim* — the experiences of the *Avos* are a portent for their descendants. We may therefore inquire: Where can we find a precedent for the Chanukah miracle in the lives of the *Avos*?

When Yaakov fled from his brother Eisav, he was caught by Eisav's son Elifaz, who summarily robbed him of all his physical possessions. Yet we find that immediately after his dream of the ladder, Yaakov erected a stone monument and anointed it with oil. From where did Yaakov obtain the oil? The Midrash says that the oil miraculously came down from heaven.[20]

The *Birchas Shmuel* cites the Shach who writes that when Yaakov took a jug of oil and anointed a stone after awakening from his dream, Hashem revealed to him all the miracles that would later transpire with that jug of oil: that oil would be used to anoint the vessels of the Temple, the future kings of Israel, and eventually be used after the coming of Mashiach.[21] The author then adds, "It is

---

20   *Midrash Tehillim* 91.
21   Rabbi M. Cohen, a student of the school of the Arizal, not to be confused with a commentary of the *Shulchan Aruch* with the same name.

simple in my eyes, that this was this very same jug that was revealed to the Chashmonaim. The seal of the *Kohen Gadol* with which the jug was imprinted was the seal belonging to Aharon HaKohen."[22]

While this explanation of the *Shach* is rather amazing, the Chidah raises numerous difficulties with this assertion:[23]

1. Firstly, the Chidah was unable to locate the source of the Shach's statement, and "it is incredulous and wondrous. If [the Shach] had a direct tradition [for his claim], then we will accept it."

2. Secondly, only the vessels of the Mishkan were consecrated with oil, but the Temple vessels were consecrated through its service.[24]

3. Thirdly, the Chashmonaim would be unable to rely on the seal of the *Kohen Gadol* to ascertain the oil's purity, since the seal had already been broken in order to consecrate the Temple vessels and the kings of Israel.

CHANUKAH — THE INAUGURATION OF THE TEMPLE

Inauguration of the Altar

The word "*chanukah*" derives from the word "*chinuch*" — inauguration. The Midrash relates that the construction of the Mishkan was completed on the twenty-fifth of Kislev. Moshe kept the Mishkan folded in storage until the month of Nissan, since he wanted the inauguration of the Mishkan to coincide with the month in which Yitzchak was born.[25] (A similar event occurred with the construction

---

22   Rabbi Aharon Shmuel Kaydanbor, *parashas Miketz*, s.v. "*v'agav.*"
23   Chidah, *Devarim Achadim* 32, s.v. "*v'od kosav.*"
24   *Shavuos* 15a.
25   *Pesikta Rabasi* 6; *Yalkut Melachim* 184; see also Maharshah, *Shabbos* 21b.

of the first Beis HaMikdash, which was completed during the month of Cheshvan but remained locked for nearly a year because Shlomo HaMelech wanted the inauguration to be in Tishrei, the month in which Avraham was born.)

Hashem "repaid" the month of Kislev for losing the opportunity of inaugurating the Mishkan by orchestrating the rededication of the *Mizbei'ach* by the Chashmonaim (over a thousand years later!) to transpire on precisely the twenty-fifth of Kislev. When the Chashmonaim reclaimed the Temple in the month of Kislev, they reinaugurated the Altar that had been defiled by the Greeks.

However, if someone takes away an item from another, the victim is only appeased if he is repaid with something of equal or greater value. How then was the month of Kislev appeased for foregoing the dedication of the Mishkan by the hands of Moshe, with the dedication of the Altar in later generations by men of lower spiritual caliber?

We must therefore conclude that the Chashmonaim's dedication of the *Mizbei'ach* matched or even surpassed the Mishkan's initial inauguration. On Chanukah, the Chashmonaim fought the Greeks with *mesiras nefesh* and were willing to sacrifice their very lives for Hashem. Such an inauguration was even greater than the original inauguration of the Mishkan through Moshe and the other spiritual giants of his generation.

As mentioned above, Chanukah commemorates the inauguration of the defiled Temple Altar. This is one of the reasons Chanukah is celebrated for eight days, as it took eight days to construct the Altar and the other Temple vessels that were destroyed by the Greeks and required replacement.[26] In addition, when the Greeks conquered the Temple, they abolished the sacrifices during Sukkos and Shemini Atzeres — a total of eight days. Therefore, when the Chashmonaim

---

26   *Sefer HaToda'ah*, p. 173; *Megillas Ta'anis* 9.

rededicated the Temple, they did so for eight days as well.[27] The dedication of the Altar also relates to the lighting of the Menorah since the light for the Menorah was kindled from the fire of the Altar.

Why "Chanukah"?

What was so important about the inauguration of the Temple's Altar that the festival of Chanukah is named after this particular event? Indeed, when the Chashmonaim entered the Temple they also found the Menorah unfit for use and they had to reconstruct that as well.

The *Bach* says that the sin that triggered the Greeks' persecution of the Jews was their laxity in their Divine service.[28] The Gemara highlights the Hellenist influence upon the Jews of that era by recounting how Miriam, a daughter from the Kohanite watch of Bilgah, became an apostate and married a Greek officer. When the Greeks entered the sanctuary, she scornfully kicked the Altar of the Temple and exclaimed, "Wolf! Wolf! How long will you consume the money of Israel, and you do not stand by them during their time of need!"[29]

According to another opinion in the Gemara, the entire family of Bilgah was tardy in performing its Temple duties. Because the Jewish People did not sufficiently respect the Altar and Temple service, the Greeks were able to not only defile the oil of the Menorah but to abolish the daily *Tamid* sacrifice as well.[30] Since their laxity in the Divine service manifested itself by disdaining the altar, the altar was also the focus of their rededication.

Another aspect of the Temple service was *hallel v'hodoah* — singing praises and thanksgiving to Hashem, which accompanied the *korbanos*. (Similarly, in our *tefilah*, which is in place of *korbanos*, we also praise Hashem at the commencement and offer thanks at the

---

27   *Sefer Chashmonai*, quoted in *Aruch HaShulchan, Orach Chaim* 670:5.
28   Bach, *Tur, Orach Chaim* 670.
29   *Sukkah* 56b.
30   Bach ibid.

conclusion of *Shemoneh Esrei*.) Chanukah contains this aspect of Temple service as well, since the essence of the festival of Chanukah is to offer *hallel v'hodoah* to Hashem.

Inauguration of the Menorah

In the restoration of the Beis HaMikdash from its defilement at the hands of the Greeks, the Chashmonaim were required to reconstruct the Menorah. Due to their extreme poverty, they could not afford to make it out of gold, so they made it from iron instead.

Rabbi Moshe Feinstein explains that since that generation did not value mitzvahs properly, they were not worthy to construct the Menorah from gold but only from an ordinary metal. Nevertheless, the righteous of the generation did not become discouraged, for when the small pure light of the Menorah miraculously burned for eight days, it conveyed to them the message that from a little pure light can eventually become a great bright flame that can shine forth in a wondrous fashion. This lesson was taken to heart and within a short time the Jews fully repented, became wealthy, and were once again able to make the Menorah out of gold.[31]

The Menorah was just one of the numerous items in the Temple that had been defiled by the Greeks and required rededication. So why does the festival of Chanukah seem to focus specifically on the inauguration of the Menorah?

The underlying idea of *chinuch* — inaugurating an item to a level of holiness, is to purge it from its previous mundane state. During the period of the Chanukah story, the *Yevanim's* secular influence penetrated even areas of the Temple itself. The six branches of the Menorah symbolize six branches of secular knowledge, but the *ner maaravi* — the seventh branch closest to the Holy of Holies,

---

31 *Derash Moshe*, p. 379.

represents the pure wisdom of Torah,[32] which was untainted by the *Yevanim*. According to the *Tzafnas Paneach*,[33] the miracle of Chanukah occurred only with the *ner maaravi*. This demonstrated that the wisdom of Torah is eternal and transcends all physical laws of the natural world. This realization purged them from the secular influences the *Yevanim* attempted to infiltrate them with. Since these messages were conveyed via the Menorah, it served as the focal point of the inauguration.

PHILOSOPHY OF THE GREEKS

Message on an Ox's Horn

The Greeks decreed that the Jews must write on the horn of their oxen: "We do not have any portion in the G-d of Israel."[34] While the decree itself requires explanation, it's interesting to note why the Greeks specifically chose the ox's horn as the subject of their decree?

We present a number of possible solutions:

- The ox is a symbol of power and achievement.[35] By writing on the ox's crown of glory that they are not in Hashem's hand, they would be showing that they believe solely in the might of their own prowess.
- Rabbi Leib Gurwitz relates that he once visited a museum containing ancient artifacts and among the items he saw were baby bottles that were fashioned from the hollowed-out horns of oxen. The *Yevanim* wished to brainwash the Jewish children with their vapid message from infancy, like the Communists who also emblazoned their atheistic beliefs on the cribs of babies.

---

32 *Ya'aros Devash*, vol. 2, 7, p. 688–689, s.v. *"zehu mah."*
33 Rambam, *Mishnah Torah*, Chanukah 3:2.
34 *Bereishis Rabbah* 2:4.
35 *Devarim* 33:17; *Mishlei* 14:4.

- Some suggest that since it was common for oxen to travel in public thoroughfares, the Greeks wished to spread their message in a very public manner. (Rabbi Hanoch Teller wryly observes that this was the precursor to the concept of "bumper stickers.")

On the Ox and Donkey's Forehead

As mentioned above, one of the decrees the Greeks promulgated was that the Jewish People must inscribe on the horn of an ox that they denounce their portion in the God of Israel. The *Megillas Taanis* has a slightly different text that reads that the Jews had to write that inscription upon the forehead of an ox and a donkey.[36]

Why did the Greeks particularly choose an ox and donkey as the object for their decree?

The *Nachalas Dovid* says that the marriage of Eisav to Mochalas, the daughter of Yishmael,[37] was to achieve a united entity comprised of these two primary nations.[38] In Kabbalistic literature, Eisav is represented by the ox; therefore, his nemesis on the "side of holiness" is Yosef, who is also compared to an ox. Yishmael is compared to a wild donkey; his combatant is Mashiach ben Dovid, who is characterized by a donkey rider.[39] With this, we can understand Yaakov's message in his confrontation with Eisav: "And I have acquired an ox and a donkey."[40] Yaakov hinted that his "ox and donkey of holiness" would ultimately prevail against the "ox and donkey" of the forces of impurity. The Greeks, recognizing that the Jews believed in their predestined victory over the nations, wanted to smash their hopes with this decree.

---

36   *Megillas Ta'anis* 2.
37   *Bereishis* 28:9.
38   *Nachalas Dovid*, as cited in *Talalei Oros*, end of *parashas Toldos*.
39   *Zechariah* 9:9.
40   *Bereishis* 32:6.

Abolishing Milah, Chodesh, and Shabbos

The mitzvos of *bris milah*, *kiddush hachodesh*, and Shabbos demonstrate the spiritual qualities that are to be infused in the physical body and within the physical realm of time. Since the Greeks renounced the spiritual dimension of the physical world, they therefore attempted to abolish the institutions of these three mitzvos. Hence, every Chanukah has a Shabbos and a Rosh Chodesh. This is also why the Sages instituted eight days of Chanukah — to hint to the mitzvah of *bris milah*, which takes place on the eighth day.[41]

FESTIVAL OF LIGHT

Hidden Light of the Menorah

When Hashem created the world, He originally created a very sublime light. Hashem saw that it was not fitting for the wicked to benefit from this intense spiritual light, so he concealed it for the righteous in the World to Come.[42] The twenty-fifth word in the Torah is *ohr* — light, and is the first time "light" is mentioned in the Torah. This hints that the light of Chanukah that we begin to kindle from the twenty-fifth of Kislev derives from this original hidden light. The *Rokeach* says further that the thirty-six lights we light during the duration of Chanukah correspond to the thirty-six hours that the original light shone during the first days of creation before it was concealed.[43]

Light to Counteract the Darkness

The Torah's description of the chaotic primeval state of the world hints to the four future exiles of the Jewish People.[44] The Midrash says that the Greek exile is hinted in the word *v'choshech* — "and

---

41   Chidah, *Chadrei Beten, Miketz* 1:15.
42   Rashi, *Bereishis* 1:4.
43   Quoted in *Ohr Gedalyahu, Moadim*, p. 25.
44   *Bereishis Rabbah* 2:4.

darkness," since the Greeks darkened the eyes of the Jews with their decrees. To counteract the darkness of this exile, Hashem made a miracle specifically with the Menorah, since the Menorah embodies the light of Torah and Divine wisdom.[45] The Midrash expounds the conclusion of the *pasuk*, "And the spirit of Hashem hovered upon the surface of the waters," to refer to the spirit of Mashiach. Since the next verse discusses the creation of light,[46] the juxtaposition of these verses hints that the merit of elevated Torah study will help herald the spirit of Mashiach and bring an end to our exile.

The Maharal explains that the physical is compared to darkness and the spiritual to light.[47] The Sages compare the exile of Greece to darkness since they worshiped physicality and denied the existence of all things spiritual.[48] The Chanukah miracle that demonstrated the victory of spirituality over physicality therefore occurred with the light of the Menorah in the Beis HaMikdash. The Menorah, as well as the Beis HaMikdash itself, is compared to light, as the Midrash relates that the primeval light was created from the site of the Beis HaMikdash.[49]

It is not coincidental that the date of Chanukah begins on the twenty-fifth of Kislev. Hashem first created light on the twenty-fifth

---

45   See for example *Ha'amek Davar*, *Shemos* 27:20, 37:19.

46   *Bereishis* 1:3.

47   Maharal, *Ner Mitzvah*, pp. 90–96.

48   Although the Greeks had "gods," the gods they invented lived in human-like bodies and possessed human vices such as infidelity, anger, and cruelty. One way in which they honored their gods was with religious festivals that centered on athletic activity (the forerunner of the Olympics) and theatrical performances (Greek tragedies and comedies).

Just as Pharaoh made the Nile River his god, and yet the Torah says that he "stood over his river," meaning that his god was enslaved to him, similarly the Greeks' gods existed only to allow them do what they pleased.

49   *Bereishis Rabbah* 3:4.

of Elul, the time in the year at which day and night are of equal duration. During the following three months of winter, the duration of the darkness of night becomes progressively longer each day. It is therefore fitting that Chanukah falls out on the twenty-fifth of Kislev, since it is on this day that the daylight hours begin increasing, while the darkness of night begins to gradually diminish.[50]

Spiritual Victory

When the Sages instituted the Yom Tov of Chanukah, they did not incorporate any specific action to commemorate the military victory over the Greeks. Rather, the mitzvos of Chanukah pertain solely to the miracle of the flask of oil. This is to demonstrate that true victory is not achieved through battle but with peace. The warm, illuminating glow of the Menorah's lights signifies that the ultimate victory of the Jewish nation will be achieved only through the light of Torah. Although in exile we have only small lights to brighten the dark night of *galus*, we are confident that this small light will eventually become a mighty torch that will spread infinite light to the entire world, at which time the entire earth will be filled with the knowledge of Hashem.[51]

Sign of Divine Love

"Even when they are in their enemies' land, I will not have been revolted by them, nor will I have rejected them."[52] The Gemara expounds the latter part of the verse to refer to the period of the Greeks, when Hashem brought salvation to Israel through Shimon

---

50   *Ner Mitzvah* ibid. Although the length of day is dependant on the solar year, with the shortest day in the year being December 21, *Chazal* superimpose numerous aspects of the solar year on the lunar calander. An example of this is that our Sages say that the strength of the summer sun begins waning from the fifteenth of Av (cf. *Kovetz Shiurim, Bava Basra* 369).

51   Rabbi Moshe Feinstein, *Derash Moshe*, p. 377.

52   *Vayikra* 26:44.

HaTzadik and Matisyahu Kohen Gadol.[53] What connection is there between Shimon HaTzadik and Matisyahu Kohen Gadol, as they lived in two entirely different time periods? Furthermore, Shimon HaTzadik lived during the time of Alexander the Great, who respected the autonomy of the Jewish People and allowed them to uphold the Torah without fear of persecution!

On a simple level, we may say that both Shimon HaTzadik and Matisyahu Kohen Gadol successfully dealt with the threat posed by the Greek Empire. During the period of Alexander, Hashem sent Shimon HaTzadik, who was best-suited to deal with the Greek ruler with respect and diplomacy. During the era of the Chashmonaim, Hashem sent Matisyahu Kohen Gadol and the Chashmonaim, who were best suited in confronting the Greeks with forceful resistance, which was the appropriate response for that era.

We may also present a deeper explanation: The Gemara says that one of the constant miracles in the Beis HaMikdash, which demonstrated Hashem's open love to His people, was that the western lamp of the Menorah burned continuously, twenty-four hours a day.[54] This miracle ceased after the death of Shimon HaTzadik.[55] Hashem performed a similar miracle in the time of Matisyahu Kohen Gadol with the miraculous burning of the oil for eight whole days. The Gemara equates both figures as they both demonstrated Hashem's love to His people in a similar fashion.

THE MILITARY MIRACLE OF CHANUKAH

Service of Blood and Water

From where did the Chashmonaim know that they were obligated to risk their lives in order to maintain the Temple service?

---

53   *Megillah* 11a.
54   *Shabbos* 22b.
55   Rashi, *Shabbos* ibid.

The *Meshech Chochmah* derives this from the fact that initially blood was used to initiate the *Kohanim* into the performance of the Divine service in the Mishkan.[56] This conveys the message that a Kohen must be willing to sacrifice his life for the *avodah* when necessary.

In future generations, water was used to consecrate the *Kohanim* instead of blood.[57] This symbolized that at times when *mesiras nefesh* is not required, the ideal is to be humble and able to pour out one's heart like water before Hashem.[58]

Power of the Spirit

The Midrash says that the Greek Empire is compared to a bow. Unlike the crude sword, which can only strike a blow by using crushing force at close range, a bow is a more sophisticated form of weaponry in that it can destroy an enemy from afar through the aid of a spiritual element, namely wind (*ruach*).[59]

Similarly, the Syrian Greeks utilized the most spiritual tool they had — i.e., secular knowledge — to subdue the Jewish nation.

The Chashmonaim, who dwelt in the land of Yehudah, were also compared to a bow, as it states: "For I will draw Yehudah as a bow for Me, against your children, O Greece."[60] The Chashmonaim were able to overpower the *Yevanim* through the spirit of Hashem that stirred within them. This may explain why the *Haftorah* for Shabbos Chanukah contains the verse: "'Not through armies and not through might, but through My spirit (*ruchi*),' says Hashem."[61]

---

56   *Mechech Chochmah, Devarim* 7:12.

57   *Yomah* 4a.

58   See *Eichah* 2:19; *Meshech Chochmah* ibid.

59   *Bereishis Rabbah* 65:13.

60   *Zechariah* 9:13; *Bereishis Rabbah* ibid.

61   *Zechariah* 4:6.

Victory over the Greeks

"...And to make you supreme over all the nations that He made."[62] The *Rabbeinu Ephraim* says that the word "supreme" — עֶלְיוֹן — can be read עַל יָוָן — "upon Yavan."[63] This hints that in the merit of the *Bnei Yisrael* keeping the mitzvos during the time of the Chashmonaim, they were able to be victorious over the Greeks.

This victory runs counter to the expected cause-and-effect relationship of nature. One would think that the survival of the Jews would come from subordinating themselves to their powerful overlords. The Chanukah miracle demonstrated otherwise; it was their commitment to Hashem that brought them victory. One may have also thought that the Gentiles would disdain the Jews for rebuffing the arts and culture of the Greeks, which at the time was internationally in vogue. The *pasuk* therefore continues: "for praise, for renown, and for splendor." This is what actually came to pass, for after the Chanukah miracle, the enlightened among the nations came to recognize and praise the Jewish People for the superlative qualities they possessed.

Celebrating the Military Miracle

The Rabbis instituted the mitzvah to light the menorah on Chanukah to commemorate the miracle of the jug of oil that burned for eight days. Why didn't the Sages also institute that we observe an additional ritual to celebrate the military victory over the Greeks?

The *Meshech Chochmah* observes that the Jewish People never rejoice over the downfall of their enemies.[64] That's why the Torah doesn't mention *simchah* — joy, regarding the festival of Pesach, since our redemption caused death to the Egyptians.[65] On Purim,

---

62   *Devarim* 26:19.
63   Ibid.
64   Rabbi Meir Simchah of Dvinsk, *Meshech Chochmah, Shemos* 12:16.
65   *Yalkut Shimoni, Emor* 654.

too, we do not celebrate the day Haman was hanged or the day the Jews killed their enemies, for this is not a cause of celebration for a Jew. Rather we celebrate the day, "we rested from our enemies."[66] Similarly, Chanukah is observed only through kindling the Menorah to demonstrate that our joy in the victory over the Greeks was solely that it enabled us to devote ourselves to serving Hashem without hindrance.

The *Meshech Chochmah* also suggests an alternative approach.[67] The primary miracle we celebrate on Chanukah is indeed Israel's miraculous military victory, which allowed Israel to have autonomy over their sovereignty for over a century. To commemorate this alone, the rabbis would have instituted the mitzvah of lighting candles (not necessarily oil) on Chanukah, as monarchy is compared to a burning lamp.[68] The rabbis, however, would have been unable to institute a blessing to commemorate this miracle, since a military victory falls under the category of a concealed miracle and a blessing is only recited for open miracles that clearly contradict the laws of nature. [69] Therefore, the rabbis instituted that the blessing we recite on Chanukah — "Who has performed miracles for our ancestors" — refers to the open miracle with the jug of oil that lasted eight days. Since the blessing relates specifically to the miracle of the oil, the rabbis instituted that the mitzvah of lighting the menorah ideally be performed with oil.

---

66   *Esther* 9:22.

67   *Bereishis* 37:24.

68   *Tehillim* 132:17.

69   *Avudraham*, gate 8, p. 340. One may ask why then we make a blessing on Purim to commemorate the miracle of being saved from Haman if that too was a concealed miracle. The Avudraham answers that Purim was indeed an open miracle, because 1) the king changed the law to save the Jews, which was illegal to do according to Persian law, and 2) that Achashverosh allowed tens of thousands of his countrymen to perish because of his love for a woman.

EIGHT-DAY MIRACLE

Why Celebrate Eight Days?

There is a famous question asked by the *Beis Yosef*: why do we celebrate Chanukah for eight days? Since there was enough oil to burn for one day, the miracle itself only lasted seven days![70]

Many answers have been offered. Following is a sample:

- After the *Kohanim* filled all the cups of the Menorah on the first day, they found that the jug was miraculously refilled with oil.[71]
- In the *Al HaNisim* prayer, it states: "And they kindled lights in the courtyards of Your sanctuary." How could the Menorah be kindled in the *courtyard* of the Beis HaMikdash if its correct location was *inside* the structure of the *Heichal*, opposite the *Shulchan*? The Chasam Sofer answers that when the Chashmonaim entered the Sanctuary, they found that the Greeks had defiled it by filling it with idols. They therefore took the Menorah out into the courtyard and lit it there until the *Heichal* was properly cleansed. Since the Menorah of the Chanukah miracle was kindled in the courtyard in full view of everyone, we also light the Menorah by the outer doorway of our homes at the entrance of our courtyard.[72]

  It is now understandable why the Chanukah miracle is celebrated for eight days rather than seven even though there was enough oil to burn for one night. The amount of oil was only sufficient to burn for one night when lit indoors. However, when the Menorah was lit outdoors in windy conditions, the quantity of oil was diminished and the fact that it still burned for one full night was in itself a miracle.[73]

---

70   *Beis Yosef, Orach Chaim* 670.
71   *Beis Yosef* ibid.
72   *Chasam Sofer, Derashos, Chanukah* p. 67.
73   Ibid.

- Most authorities are of the opinion that the Chashmonaim were victorious over the Greeks on the twenty-fourth of Kislev and lit the Menorah in the Beis HaMikdash on the eve of the twenty-fifth. Rambam, however, states that they were victorious on the twenty-fifth and that accordingly they must have first lit the Menorah on the eve of the twenty-sixth.[74] This poses a difficulty: if the Chashmonaim lit the Menorah on the twenty-sixth, why do we light the Menorah on the twenty-fifth? The *Pri Chadash* answers that the kindling on the night of the twenty-fifth is to commemorate the military victory over the Greeks.[75] This resolves the question of why the Menorah is kindled for eight days even though the miracle of the oil was only seven days. Since according to the Rambam the Chashmonaim did not light the Menorah on the twenty-fifth of Kislev, our lighting on this night clearly does not reflect the miracle of the oil but solely the miracle of the war.

Significance of Eight

Why did the miracle of the oil occur specifically for eight days? There are a number of answers found in the *Rishonim*:

- The location of the facility used to produce the oil used for the Menorah was a distance of four-days' travel. Therefore, eight days were required in order to return with new pure oil.[76]
- Since the miracle of the oil occurred in the Beis HaMikdash, it was fitting that the miracle lasted eight days, as most things pertaining to the Temple contain the number eight. For example, the *Kohen Gadol* wore eight garments, the Levites

---

74 Rambam, *Mishnah Torah*, Chanukah 3:2.
75 *Pri Chadash, Orach Chaim* 670:1.
76 Ran, *Shabbos* 21b; also Meiri there.

songs were accompanied with eight musical instruments, and there were eight fragrant spices used in the *ketores* and *shemen hamishchah*.[77]

- The number seven corresponds to the natural world, and eight corresponds to the supernatural world that will exist during the time of Mashiach. The Menorah in the Beis HaMikdash had seven branches since it represented our current earthly existence. However, the oil of the Chanukah miracle hints to the ultimate victory that will usher in the epoch of Mashiach, at which time all the nations of the world will become enlightened to recognize and serve Hashem.[78]

Seal of the Kohen Gadol

Why was it necessary for the flask of oil found in the Beis HaMikdash to have the seal of the *Kohen Gadol* to ensure its purity?

Simply, we may answer that since the light of the Chanukah miracle derives from the supernal hidden light,[79] it is no wonder that it was sealed by the holiest representative of the nation. Rabbi Isaac Bernstein cites a Midrash that says that just as the oil in the Mishkan had to be brought to Moshe so he could inspect it for impurities, so too in future generations it was the responsibility of the *Kohen Gadol* to inspect the Temple oil.[80] That being the case, it is likely that the *Kohen Gadol* would affix his own seal on the flasks that passed his inspection.

Other commentators explain that the reason the jug was found to have the seal of the *Kohen Gadol* on it was because it was his personal

---

77   Rabbeinu Bachya, *Kad HaKemach*, *Ner Chanukah*, p. 268 (MHK edition). The *Kad HaKemach* explains that the *ketores* and the *shemen hamishchah* were comprised of four spices each, totaling eight spices. Although the Rabbis taught that eleven different spices were used in the incense mixture, we are presently counting only the four spices that are listed explicitly in the Torah (נטף, שחלת, חלבנה, לבנה).

78   Ibid.

79   See above, "Festival of Light."

80   Rabbi Isaac Bernstein, audio lecture series, *parashas Tetzaveh*.

oil that he had prepared for his daily *Minchas Chavitin* offering. The *Minchas Chavitin* required three *lug* of oil (one-and-a-half *lug* in the morning and one-and-a-half in the evening). However, the Menorah required three-and-a-half *lug* per day.[81] Therefore, even on the first day there was a miracle for the oil to burn for the full-prescribed time (since it was deficient by one-half *lug*).[82] This view also resolves the *Beis Yosef's* question why the miracle was for eight and not seven days.

Shemen zayis zach — pure olive oil — was a requirement for the Menorah but was not a requirement for *menachos*. Because the *Kohen Gadol* beautified his *minchah* offering by using pure olive oil, (even though it was not required), it later became possible for the Chashmonaim to fulfill the mitzvah of Menorah during the time of Chanukah. Therefore, the rabbis also made a special requirement of *hiddur mitvzah* — beautifying the mitzvah — with respect to lighting the Menorah on Chanukah.

LIGHTING THE MENORAH

In a Beautiful Manner

Why was the mitzvah of Menorah instituted to be performed in the most beautiful manner (*mehadrin min hamihadrin*), something that we do not find by other mitvzvos?

The *Beis HaLevi* answers that if the Chashmonaim wanted the jug of pure oil to last for eight days, they could have simply made the wicks thinner. However, since that would diminish the beauty of the flame, they chose to fashion the wicks so that it would burn in the most preferable manner and relied on Hashem that more oil would be found. Since they were so careful in performing the mitzvah of Menorah in the most beautiful manner, we have unique

---

81   This is consistent with the text of the *Sheiltos* (26) that reads, "*velo haya lehadlik afilu yom echad*," that there was not enough oil to burn for even one day.

82   See *P'nei Aryeh* 40; *Higyonei Halachah*, pp. 210–211.

stringencies of *hiddur mitzvah* specifically in regard to the mitzvah of Menorah.[83]

Preference of Olive Oil

Some authorities explain the reason why olive oil should ideally be used for the Menorah is because the Chanukah miracle occurred with olive oil. The *Binyan Olam* says that the Gemara relates that Abaye originally used sesame seed oil on Chanukah since it radiates a bright light. Once he heard the statement of Rabbi Yehoshua ben Levi that one should ideally use olive oil, he switched to olive oil and exclaimed that indeed olive oil gives forth a clearer light.[84] From this Gemara, we see that the superiority of olive oil is only in that it gives off a better light and not because the miracle occurred with olive oil.[85]

Rabbi Moshe Feinstein explains that this is because the miracle in the Temple was performed with *shemen zayis zach* — "pure" olive oil.[86] Since our olive oil does not have that degree of purity, our olive oil is not considered the same type of oil that was used in the Temple. As such, the only advantage of our olive oil is that it provides a better light.[87]

Oil or Wax?

Although one should ideally use olive oil for the Chanukah Menorah, if olive oil is not readily available one may substitute other oils that give a pure, clear light.[88] If one must choose between using an oil that does not give a clear flame, and wax that burns brightly as oil, *Sefer Minhagim* rules that one should use the wax since it gives a clear

---

83   *Beis HaLevi al HaTorah, Chanukah* p. 78.

84   *Shabbos* 23a.

85   Rabbi Yitzchak Izak Chaver, *Binyan Olam* 34, cf. *Darkei Moshe* 673:1.

86   See *Menachos* 86a.

87   *Shemaitsah D'Moshe, Orach Chaim* 673:1.

88   Rama, *Orach Chaim* 673:1.

flame.[89] The Maharal disagrees and rules that one should nonetheless use the inferior oil since the Chanukah miracle occurred with oil.[90]

What is the basis for their disagreement?

Perhaps their disagreement hinges on the following question: what is the essential aspect of Chanukah lights — the fuel or its flame? If it is the fuel, the fuel used should then be similar to the one with which the miracle occurred, despite its inferior light. If, however, the salient aspect of Chanukah lights is the light they produce, then the fuel that gives the brightest flame should be sought.

Increasing or Decreasing the Lights?

According to Beis Shammai, one lights eight wicks on the first night of Chanukah and gradually decreases one candle each night, while according to Beis Hillel one begins with one candle on the first night and adds an additional candle each progressive night.

The Maharal explains their debate as follows:[91]

According to Beis Shammai, the Chanukah lighting follows the general principle that the sum of a matter is contained in its onset. This is why there were more sacrifices brought on the first day of Sukkos, as the first day of a Yom Tov is the main source of its holiness, and from there it spreads to the remainder of the festival. Since the first day of Chanukah is the most elevated and the source of holiness for the duration of the festival, it is fitting to light the most candles on that night.

Beis Hillel, however, focuses on the effect of Chanukah on the person. In matters of holiness, a person only acquires holiness by beginning at the lowest rung and gradually ascending. Since a person absorbs holiness in a gradually ascending manner, one should light only one candle on the first night and gradually increase the number of lights each subsequent night.

---

89 Cited in *Darkei Moshe* 673:1.
90 Cited in *Sha'ar HaTzion* 673:4.
91 Maharal, *Ner Mitzvah*, s.v. "*tanu rabbanan*," pp. 77–79 (Machon Yerushalayim ed.).

The Beis Hillel Approach

The Rambam writes that when there is a Torah reading of ten verses to divide among three people, any one of them may receive the larger Torah portion comprised of four verses.[92] This seems to contradict the principle we apply to Chanukah of *ma'alin bakodesh*, where we "increase holiness" by adding additional lights each night.

The *Magen Avraham* answers that the rule of increasing holiness only applies when one person is doing a mitzvah, but not when a mitzvah is divided among three different people.[93]

The *Ma'asei Rokeach* answers that only on Chanukah are we concerned to perform the *mitvzah* in an ascending order. Firstly, because we wish the number of Chanukah lights to correspond to the current night of the Chanukah festival, and secondly, so that the blessing be recited on the additional light on each night.[94]

The Beis Shammai Approach

According to Beis Shammai, one kindles eight lights the first night of Chanukah and continues in a gradually descending order until the last night when only one candle is lit. This approach seems to contradict the principle of *ma'alin bakodesh* — that we perform spiritual matters in an ascending and not a descending manner.

According to Beis Shammai, the Chanukah lights follow the pattern of the Temple sacrifices brought on the festival of Sukkos, during which seventy bull-offerings were brought in a progressively diminishing fashion.[95]

What is the connection between lighting the menorah and the Sukkos offerings?

Rabbi Moshe Feinstein answers that *Chazal* explain that the seventy bulls sacrificed on Sukkos represent the seventy nations of the

---

92   Rambam, *Mishnah Torah, Tefilah* 12:4.

93   *Magen Avraham, Orach Chaim* 137:2.

94   *Ma'asei Rokeach* to Rambam ibid.

95   *Shabbos* 21b.

world.[96] Ideally, all of mankind should be united, and this utopian state would herald world-peace as it would eliminate wars among nations. The descending order thus demonstrates the increase of unity, the epitome of which will be achieved with the coming of the redemption.

The same principle applies to the spiritual realm as well. The light of the Menorah represents Torah. In *galus* we have many such "lights" and each group thinks that only its Torah is correct. The ideal state will be achieved when there will be only one light that will not only guide the Jewish People but the entire world, as it states: "And the nations will walk to Your light."[97] The singular usage of *l'orach* — "to Your light" signifies that ultimately there will be only one light.[98]

Rabbi Eliezer Ginzburg suggests an entirely different approach. The Midrash relates that the Jewish People complained before Hashem: "We are sacrificing these seventy bull-offerings [on Sukkos] for the benefit of the nations, but instead of showing gratitude, they display hatred toward us." The Torah therefore says that the sacrifices should steadily diminish to demonstrate the decline and eventual destruction of the (ancient) seventy nations.[99]

A similar scenario plays out on Chanukah as well: the Greeks should have appreciated the blessings the Temple brought them, but instead their jealousy led them to defile the Temple. The diminishing lights therefore represent our victory over the Greeks and how the light of the Greeks will also disappear in the course of time.[100]

---

96   *Derash Moshe* 30.
97   *Yeshayah* 60:3.
98   *Derash Moshe* ibid.
99   *Bamidbar Rabbah* 21:24.
100 *Mesilas Maharshah, Bamidbar* 29:18.

One Menorah per Household

Why is the mitzvah of *ner Chanukah* different than other mitzvos, in that other mitzvos must generally be performed by each individual whereas on Chanukah only one menorah has to be lit per household?

The *Aruch HaShulchan* answers that the main mitzvah of *ner Chanukah* is not to *light* the menorah, but rather to *see the lit candles*, i.e., so that the miracle of Chanukah be publicized (*pirsumei nisah*) before all.[101] Since this can practically only be achieved by someone first lighting the menorah, the rabbis delegated this task to the master of the home.

Alternatively, since the Greeks issued decrees against the home, such as prohibiting the Jews from locking their doors, and against the mainstay of the home, such as by prohibiting women from immersing themselves in the *mikvah*, the rabbis instituted that the menorah be a requirement on the home in a similar fashion to the mitzvah of *mezuzah*. In addition, since the Chanukah miracle occurred with the Menorah in the Beis HaMikdash, we light the menorah in our homes, which is a *mikdash me'at* — a miniature sanctuary. Just as the Beis HaMikdash only had one Menorah, so too do our houses only have one menorah.

Lighting through an Agent

Mishnah Berurah cites the view of the *Magen Avraham* that an agent who lights the menorah for another person may only recite the blessings if the owner of the house is present at the time of the lighting.[102] Why is Chanukah lighting different than other mitzvos — such as affixing a *mezuzah*, building a fence around a roof, or checking for *chametz* — when the agent makes a blessing regardless of whether the owner is present?

Rabbi Shlomo Zalman Auerbach explains the distinction between Chanukah lights and other mitzvos. The essential aspect of

---

101 *Aruch HaShulchan, Orach Chaim* 671:17.
102 *Mishnah Berurah* 675:9.

the mitzvah of Chanukah lights is that the *owner's* home should be illuminated by the light of the menorah. As such, the agent is not viewed as performing a complete mitzvah but merely assisting as an accessory to the performance of a mitzvah. This would be comparable to where an agent puts *tefillin* on another person's head. Since the mitzvah is that the *wearer's* head should be adorned with *tefillin*, the agent's act is considered incomplete and he therefore does not recite a blessing.

However, in cases where an agent independently performs a complete mitzvah, such as checking for *chametz* or affixing a *mezuzah*, where the mitzvah is that one's *home* be rid of *chametz* or affixed with a *mezuzah*, the agent would recite the blessings regardless of whether the owner is present.[103]

Benefiting from the Menorah's Light

It is prohibited for a person to derive benefit from the light of the menorah, such as to count one's coins by its light. The *Mishnah Berurah* gives two reasons for this:[104]

1. So that it should be recognizable that the light was lit for the purpose of the mitzvah.
2. Since the miracle occurred with the Menorah of the Beis HaMikdash, which one was prohibited to benefit from because of its sanctity, so too our menorah must also be treated with the same level of sanctity.

The *Beis HaLevi* says that a practical distinction between these two reasons would be in a case where a passerby wishes to count his money. If the concern is that people may say that the menorah was lit for utilitarian purposes, since the passerby did not light the menorah, in this case there is no concern of people thinking this

---

103 Rabbi Shlomo Zalman Auerbach, *Halichos Shlomo*, Tishrei–Adar 16:5, 9.
104 *Mishnah Berurah* 673:8.

way. However, if the menorah was given the status of the Menorah of the Temple, which no one may benefit from due to its sanctified status, the prohibition would apply even to a passerby.[105]

Chanukah Lights vs. Shabbos Lights

There is a fundamental difference between the mitzvos of lighting the menorah and kindling Shabbos lights. A guest who visits someone's home during Chanukah must contribute a minimal amount toward the cost of the oil in order to include himself in his host's menorah lighting.[106] This is unlike the law of candle-lighting on Shabbos, where it is unnecessary for a guest to contribute a token amount to be included in the host's lighting of the Shabbos candles.

What therefore is the difference between Shabbos and Chanukah lights?

The distinction between these two mitzvos is that the obligation of Shabbos candles is dependent on the place where one eats one's Friday night meal. Since the guest is eating the Friday night meal at the host's home, he is included in the host's Shabbos candles. Regarding the lighting of the menorah, the mitzvah is *ish u'beiso* — a man and his household. Since the guest is not a permanent resident of the home, he is not included in the host's lighting unless he actively becomes a partner in the oil.[107]

Eternally Sanctified Oil

On Sukkos, *sukkah* decorations are *muktzah* — designated only for the mitzvah of beautifying one's *sukkah* — and are thus prohibited for personal use during the duration of the festival. Still, after Sukkos, the decorations no longer retain any holiness and are permissible for consumption and other mundane use. Similarly,

---

105 Cited in footnote *Oz Vehadar* edition of the *Mishnah Berurah* ibid.
106 *Shulchan Aruch, Orach Chaim* 677:1.
107 See Rabbi Yehoshua Neuwirth, *Shemiras Shabbos K'hilchasoh* 45:1.

although the oil used for candle lighting on Shabbos also becomes *muktzah*, it reverts to its mundane permissible state after Shabbos.

This is not the case regarding the excess oil placed in the menorah, which maintains its holiness even after the mitzvah is performed and must be burned after the eighth night of Chanukah.

What gives the oil of the Chanukah menorah its distinction that it remains holy even after the festival?

Rabbi Moshe Feinstein explains that the mitzvah of *sukkah* is limited to the duration of Sukkos; there is no mitzvah to sit in a *sukkah* after Sukkos is over. This applies to Shabbos, as well. However, the underlying message of the menorah is to give praise and thanks to Hashem for His miraculous salvation. Since thanking Hashem is just as relevant after Chanukah as during the Chanukah festival, the oil of the menorah still retains the sanctity of its mitzvah even after the conclusion of the mitzvah.[108]

Menorah at the Doorpost

Ideally, the menorah should be placed at the doorway of one's home. Why is this so?

The significance of the doorway may relate to another mitzvah that pertains to a doorway — the law of a Jewish servant who wishes to extend his servitude beyond the prescribed time. The Torah requires that the slave be brought to the doorway and his ear bored against the door since he was a witness when the Jews placed the blood of the Pesach-offering on their doorposts prior to leaving Egypt. When Hashem took the Jews out of Egypt, He acted so that they may be servants unto Hashem, and not "servants to servants." Since the slave prefers a human master over Hashem, it is fitting that his ear be bored in the presence of the "witnesses," i.e., the door and the doorposts.

Just as the ceremony for the bonded slave serves as a message of his degradation for accepting a human ruler over Hashem's

---

108 *Shemaitsah D'Moshe, Chanukah* 677:4.

sovereignty, the menorah presents the opposite message: that the *Bnei Yisrael* spurned the servitude of the Greeks and instead chose to hear the Divine call to remain servants solely to Hashem. The doorway is therefore a fitting testimony of our loyalty to Hashem during this period.[109]

Ideally, the menorah is placed on the left side of the doorpost opposite the *mezuzah* in order that when entering one's home he will be surrounded by mitzvos on all sides and will thereby be protected from sin.[110] Rabbi Avraham Yaffin comments that the menorah at one's doorway seems to be an unnecessary safeguard, for the Gemara assures that it is sufficient to be saved from sin by merely entering the doorway of one's home, which is affixed with a *mezuzah*, while wearing *tallis* and *tefillin*![111]

He suggests that initially a person was protected from sin by being surrounded by the mitzvos of *mezuzah*, *tallis*, and *tefillin* alone. This may be compared to clothing; it is sufficient for a healthy person to dress moderately, while a sickly person needs to wrap himself with additional garments to protect him from the cold. Similarly, as a result of the chilly heretical winds brought about by the Greeks, the extra protection of being surrounded with the menorah was also required in order to counteract the negative influences unleashed in the world.[112]

"Blessed shall you be when you come in and blessed shall you be when you go out."[113] The *Rabbeinu Ephraim* explains that the bless-

---

109   Rabbi Yechiel Stern, *Mo'adei HaShanah*, p. 267.

110   *Shabbos* 22a; *Sheiltos, Vayishlach* 26; Maharil, end ch. 40. In practice, whether it is preferable to light at the doorpost or the window of one's home, see *Mishnah Berurah* 671:7, 38 and *Igros Moshe* 4:125.

111   *Menachos* 43b.

112   *Chachmas HaMitzfon, Moadim*, pp. 51–52.

113   *Devarim* 28:6.

ing of "coming in" is in reward for the mitzvah of *mezuzah*, which is placed at the entrance of one's home, and the blessing of "going out" is in reward for the mitzvah of the Chanukah lights.[114] On a simple level, this could be understood as a reference to the *mezuzah* being on one's right side when entering one's home and the menorah being on one's right when exiting. However, it seems to imply a deeper message as well. An aspect of *pirsumei nisah* — publicizing the miracle of Chanukah — also entails that a person fortify his commitments before stepping out into the world so that he may be a "blessing and light unto the nations."

Wearing a Tallis

According to the *Sheiltos*, the head of the household should wear a *tallis gadol* while lighting the menorah.[115] This can be understood in light of the *Meshech Chochmah* who comments that the mitzvah of *tzitzis* is to demonstrate that the world is like a garment — it is well-developed and intertwined, yet it camouflages a Creator.[116] We put strings on the corners to demonstrate our recognition of this and that the Creator left "unfinished strings" for us to perfect ourselves. This belief diametrically opposes the Hellenistic philosophy that man is naturally perfect and in total control of the world.

The *Sheiltos* says that the *mezuzah* should be on the right side of the doorway, the menorah on the left, and the homeowner wearing his *tallis* with *tzitzis* in the center. What is the significance of the last statement, a point that is omitted in the nearly identical text of the Gemara?[117]

The miracle of Chanukah demonstrates that the descendants of Shem can overpower the descendants of Yefes through their deeper spiritual

---

114   Ibid.
115   *Sheiltos, parashas Vayishlach* 26.
116   *Bamidbar* 15:40.
117   *Shabbos* 22a.

connection to Hashem. This first manifested itself when Shem took the initiative to cover the nakedness of his father, Noach, with a garment, and as a result was rewarded with the mitzvah of *tzitzis.*[118]

Erev Shabbos Chanukah

Based on the principle that a regularly performed mitzvah takes precedence over a sporadic one (*tadir kodem*), Tosfos rules that on Erev Shabbos Chanukah one should first light Shabbos candles (with the intention not to accept Shabbos at that point) and then afterwards light the Chanukah candles.[119] Although this is not the halachicaly accepted opinion,[120] the *Pri Megadim* advises that one should ideally prepare and light the Chanukah menorah before even preparing the Shabbos candles.[121] In this manner, one avoids "embarrassing" the Shabbos candles by bypassing them, and the principle of *tadir kodem* is not applicable since the Shabbos candles are not present when lighting the menorah.

According to the Rambam, one has to beg for alms in order to have candles for Shabbos, but one is not obligated to sell one's clothes.[122] Chanukah is stricter, though, in that one is required to even sell one's clothing to obtain candles to light the menorah.[123] There is a third halachah that says that if one only has enough money to either buy candles for Shabbos or to light the menorah, the lights for Shabbos have precedence.[124]

The combination of these two laws presents the following dilemma: if on Erev Shabbos Chanukah a person doesn't have money for

---

118   *Bereishis Rabbah* 36:6.
119   See *Tur, Darkei Moshe, Orach Chaim* 679.
120   *Shulchan Aruch, Orach Chaim* 679:1.
121   *Pri Megadim, Shulchan Aruch* ibid.
122   Rambam, *Mishnah Torah, Shabbos* 5:1.
123   Ibid., *Chanukah* 4:12.
124   Ibid. 14:4.

either Shabbos candles or the menorah, is he required to sell his clothing in order to obtain candles? Secondly, if one is required to sell his clothing to obtain candles, should the candles be then used for lighting the Chanukah menorah or for the honor of the Shabbos?

According to some opinions, one is obligated to sell his clothing to obtain candles for Chanukah, but once he obtains the candles he must use them for Shabbos, as the lights for Shabbos take precedence over Chanukah. Rabbi Shlomo Zalman Auerbach disagrees; since the person only sold his clothing in order to obtain candles for Chanukah, in respect to his obligations towards Shabbos, those candles have the status of clothing. He must therefore only use the money to buy candles to light the menorah.[125]

One may light the menorah from *plag haminchah* (one-and-a-quarter hours before nightfall) in extenuating circumstances. It is understandable why one can bring in Shabbos from *plag haminchah* on Friday, since there is a mitzvah to extend the holiness of Shabbos into the mundane weekday (a principle known as *mosifin mechol al HaKodesh*). However, Chanukah lights were instituted to be kindled at night, so how may one light the menorah at this earlier time?

Rabbi Moshe Feinstein explains that the rabbis were compelled to make an exception for Erev Shabbos Chanukah and allow lighting the menorah before nightfall, since it is prohibited to kindle a flame after the onset of Shabbos.[126] Once the rabbis made an exception for Erev Shabbos Chanukah, they did not wish to differentiate the permissible time frame for the mitzvah for the other nights of Chanukah.[127] They therefore instituted that Chanukah lights may always be lit from *plag haminchah* onwards.[128]

---

125   *Halichos Shlomo, Chanukah* 13:35.
126   *Shemaitsah D'Moshe* 672:4.
127   This is based on the halachic principle known as לא פלוג — *lo ploog.*
128   See, however, *Meorei Shearim, Divrei Halachah, hosafah* 3.

Reward for Chanukah Lights

The Gemara says that one who is accustomed to performing the mitzvah of candle-lighting will merit children who are Torah scholars.[129] While this Gemara is generally understood to be referring to the mitzvah of lighting candles prior to the onset of Shabbos, it actually applies to the mitzvah of lighting the menorah on Chanukah as well.[130] Rabbi Shlomo Zalman Auerbach explains that since lighting the menorah is incumbent upon all members of the household, it is fitting that both parents be rewarded equally, namely by deserving to produce children who are Torah scholars. Additionally, since the Greeks attempted to make the Jews forget the Torah, measure-for-measure lighting the menorah creates more Torah to be brought into the world and those who are careful in this mitzvah will merit offspring who will be Torah scholars.[131]

BLESSINGS

Shehechiyanu Blessing

The *Biur Halachah* cites the view of Rabbi Yaakov Emden that one should recite a *Shehechiyanu* on Purim for the day itself just like on all the other Yomim Tovim.[132] In support of his view, the *Biur Halachah* cites the view of the Meiri that if one is unable to light the menorah on Chanukah, he should still recite *Shehechiyanu* to commemorate the day. Rabbi Moshe Feinstein, though, argues that one should not recite *Shehechiyanu* on these festivals since Purim and Chanukah do not have the status of a Yom Tov.[133] According to

---

129   *Shabbos* 23b.

130   Rashi ibid.

131   Rabbi Shlomo Zalman Auerbach, *Shulchan Shlomo, Orach Chaim* 263:1,1.

132   *Biur Halachah, Orach Chaim* 692:1.

133   Rabbi Moshe Feinstein, *Igros Moshe, Orach Chaim* 5:20, 5:43. Regarding the source of the Meiri, Rav Moshe contends that our present text is corrupted and the Meiri should actually read that one does *not* recite *Shehechiyanu*.

this view, the *Shehechiyanu* one recites the first night of Chanukah is not for the festival itself but rather for the mitzvah of lighting the menorah.[134]

Blessing after Lighting

If one forgot to make a *berachah* prior to lighting the menorah and only realized his mistake after having finished lighting all the candles, he can no longer recite the blessing of *l'hadlik ner shel Chanukah* — "to kindle the Chanukah light."[135] However, in regard to Shabbos candles, the halachah is different; one recites the blessing for lighting the Shabbos candles after the candles are lit. Since both mitzvos involve kindling, why does the placement of the two blessings differ?

Rabbi Yehoshua Neuwirth explains the distinction as follows: regarding the Chanukah menorah, the *mitzvah* is the **act** of lighting, which explains why if the flame became extinguished after one lit the candles he is not required to relight them. Once the mitzvah is completed with the act of lighting, one may no longer make a *berachah* since *berachos* must be recited prior to completion of the mitzvah. But regarding Shabbos candles, the mitzvah is that the candles **remain** lit so that the household may benefit from the light. Being that the mitzvah continues even after the act of lighting, one may recite the blessing the entire time the candles are burning.[136]

"Singular" Blessing

The blessing on Chanukah lights is expressed in the singular: "to kindle the Chanukah *light*." Since many candles are lit throughout the duration of Chanukah, why don't we instead use the plural form: "to kindle the Chanukah *lights*?"

---

134 *Shemaitsah D'Moshe* 676:1:1.
135 *Mishnah Berurah* 676:4.
136 *Shemiras Shabbos K'hilchasoh* 43:164.

The *Pri Megadim* answers that since on the first night only one light is lit, the rabbis didn't alter the structure of the blessing for the rest of Chanukah.[137]

Another answer given is that the rabbis did not institute a blessing for *hiddur mitzvah* — a non-obligatory enhancement of the mitzvah.[138] Since one fulfills one's primary obligation by lighting only one candle each night of Chanukah, the blessing does not reflect the additional non-compulsory lights.

Lighting in Isolation

There is a debate among the *poskim* whether a person who lights the menorah alone in an isolated area is required to make a blessing. Some compare it to a situation when one returns home late at night after his household is sleeping, where the *Magen Avraham* rules that one does not make a blessing since there is no *pirsumei nisah* — publicizing of the miracle — under those circumstances.[139]

Rabbi Moshe Feinstein, though, makes a distinction between these two cases. Just as the rabbis revoked one's right to recite the *Shema* after midnight so that people should not be lax in the performance of the mitzvah, so too did the rabbis wish that people should hurry home to light the menorah early in the evening and revoked the blessing for those who lit at a tardy hour. However, one who lights in the proper time is required to make a blessing even when the aspect of *pirsumei nisah* does not apply. This is likened to the case where one would recite the blessing for reading the *Megillah*, which was also instituted for *pirsumei nisah*, even in situations where one reads the *Megillah* in private.[140]

---

137   *Pri Megadim, Orach Chaim* 263:11.
138   *Pri Chadash*, end 672; *Mishnah Berurah* 676 (*Oz Vehadar* ed.), footnote 2.
139   *Magen Avraham, Orach Chaim* 672:6.
140   *Shemaitsah D'Moshe, Orach Chaim* 672:5.

HANEROS HALALU

In *Haneros Halalu*, we say: הנרות הללו קדש הם — "These lights are holy." The term *holy* means that since the oil was set aside for the mitzvah of Chanukah light, it becomes sanctified and may not be used for mundane purposes. However, the last word הם — "them", appears superfluous. In fact, according to the version of *Haneros Halalu* found in *Meseches Sofrim*, the word הם does not appear.[141]

The *Binyan Shlomo* explains that the word הם is meant to limit the extent of the prohibition, in that if one were to add an extra amount of oil, the additional non-required amount of oil is permitted for personal use. The text that omits the word הם is of the opinion that even the additional measure of oil is also prohibited.[142]

MAOZ TZUR

Unfinished Dedication

In the first stanza of *Maoz Tzur*, we say: "Restore my House of prayer...then I will *complete* the dedication of the Altar." In other words, with the coming of Mashiach and the rebuilding of the Beis HaMikdash, we will *complete* the *Chanukas HaMizbei'ach* — the inauguration of the Beis HaMikdash. This clearly implies that the inauguration of the Third Temple had already begun!

Rabbi Yaakov Kamenetsky explains that the era of the second Beis HaMikdash was not a proper redemption and the *Bnei Yisrael* were still deserving to remain in exile as a result of their sins. Hashem, in His mercy, built the second Beis HaMikdash so that they should not fall into despair and to help prepare them for the long exile that awaited them. It is therefore fitting to describe the second Beis HaMikdash as only the first step in the inauguration of the true Beis HaMikdash that will only be completed

---

141 *Sofrim* 5:6, cited by the Rosh, *Shabbos* 2:8.
142 *Binyan Shlomo*, vol. 2, *Orach Chaim* 62, p. 187.

after the coming of Mashiach, with the building of the third Beis HaMikdash.[143]

Praise for Every Occasion

In the song *Maoz Tzur*, we praise Hashem for the exodus from Egypt, the redemption from the Babylonian exile, as well as for the miracle of Purim.

While in the midst of celebrating the miracle that transpired during Chanukah, why do we mention miracles that occurred on other occasions?

We can derive from here that while one is praising Hashem for a present miracle or blessing, it is proper to also offer thanksgiving for other acts of kindness He performs for us. We find this idea in the blessing of *Hagomel*. The blessing not only expresses thanks to Hashem for one's current salvation, but also thanks Hashem *shegmalani kol tov* — "Who has bestowed *every* goodness upon me." Similarly in *Birchas Hamazon*, not only do we give thanks to Hashem for the food we ate, but we also thank Him for other blessings, such as for giving us the Torah and the Land of Israel.

The Thirteen Breaches

In *Maoz Tzur* we say: "[The Greeks] breached the walls of my towers," a reference to the thirteen breaches the *Yevanim* made in the walls of the Beis HaMikdash. Why did the Greeks make specifically that number of breaches?

1. The numerical value of *echad* — one — is thirteen. The *Yevanim* were trying to breach the unity of Hashem that was manifest in the Beis HaMikdash. When the Chashmonaim were victorious over the Greeks and the breaches were repaired, the Sages instituted bowing in honor of Hashem every time someone passed the place of those former

---

143   Rabbi Yaakov Kamenetsky, *Emes L'Yaakov*, Avos 1:1.

breaches.[144] This served to counteract the pernicious effect the *Yevanim* attempted to accomplish.

2. The Greeks opposed the Divine sanctity of the Oral Torah. The thirteen breaches were created to negate the thirteen principles with which the Oral Torah is expounded.[145]

3. It was to counteract the thirteen *middos harachamim* — traits of Divine mercy. A human being is created to emulate the compassionate attributes of Hashem by which we perfect our *neshamah*. This philosophy ran contrary to the animalistic worldview held by the Greeks.

War against the Oil

In *Maoz Tzur*, we say further that the Greeks defiled all the oil. Why were they so focused on defiling the oil?

Some say that the objective of the Greeks was to demonstrate that the wisdom of the Torah is not superior to their secular wisdom. In their attempt to defile the sanctity of the Torah, they also set out to defile the oil found in the Temple since oil is a metaphor for wisdom.[146]

AL HANISIM

...And for the Battles

In *Al HaNisim*, we thank Hashem *al hamilchamos* — for the battles. We can understand that there is a need to give praise for the military victory, but why for the battle itself?

Here are some approaches:

1. The *Beis HaLevi* says that when *Bnei Yisrael* sang after the splitting of the *Yam Suf*, they not only rejoiced in Hashem's

---

144 Mishnah, *Middos* 2:3.
145 *Nitei Gavriel*, introduction to laws of Chanukah.
146 See *Berachos* 57a.

salvation, but also in their earlier servitude.[147] This is because they then came to the realization that their prior suffering was the prerequisite for Hashem's honor to become elevated when He vanquished Pharaoh's army at the sea. The same applies with the battles leading up to the Chanukah miracle, as it says: *ulecha asisa Shem gadol vekadosh be'olamecha* — "For Yourself You made a great and holy Name in Your world."[148]

2. The Maharal explains that just as black and white are most clearly visible when contrasted next to each other, so too is the relationship between exile and redemption. Salvation is most highlighted when contrasted to a period of misfortune, such as during a time of war.

3. The Rabbeinu Yonah answers that we thank Hashem for the afflictions because salvation only comes as result of prior suffering.[149]

Was Matisyahu a Kohen Gadol?

"In the days of Matisyahu the son of Yochanan Kohen Gadol." The terminology is unclear; does the description *"Kohen Gadol"* apply to Matisyahu himself, or was Matisyahu a *Kohen Hediot* (ordinary *Kohen*), and it was only his father, Yochanan, who was a *Kohen Gadol*?

The *Iyun Tefilah* is of the view that Matisyahu was a *Kohen Hediot* and it was only his father Yochanan, the youngest son of Shimon HaTzadik, who was the *Kohen Gadol*.[150]

However, the Gemara says explicitly that Matisyahu was a *Kohen Gadol*![151] In addition, there are a number of Midrashim that state that the miracle of Chanukah was brought about by a *Kohen Gadol*.[152]

---

147 *Shemos* 15:1.

148 *Al HaNisim* prayer.

149 Rabbeinu Yonah, *Sha'arei Teshuvah* 2:5; cf. Malbim, *Tehillim* 118:21.

150 *Siddur Otzer HaTefilos, Al HaNisim*.

151 *Megillah* 11a.

152 Cited in *Siddur Tzalusah D'Avraham, Al HaNisim* prayer.

Perhaps this is why *Al HaNisim* singles out Matisyahu with credit for the victory of the Chashmonaim, since he was the *Kohen Gadol* and spiritual leader of his people.

In defense of the approach of the *Iyun Tefilah*, the *Siddur Tzalusah D'Avraham* cites an alternative text of the Gemara that does not explicitly state that Matisyahu was a *Kohen Gadol*.[153] He also reconciles the other Midrashic sources that state that Matisyahu was a *Kohen Gadol* by proposing that the Sages loosely employed the terminology *Kohen Gadol* when they meant to say a "great *Kohen*," even though he did not technically serve in the Temple in the capacity of the *Kohen Gadol*.[154]

Greece or Rome — Which Was Worse?

"When the wicked Greek empire rose up against Your nation." Rabbeinu Yakov bar Yakar writes that the Greek Empire was not as evil as the Roman Empire. Although in *Al HaNisim* we refer to the Greek Empire as "wicked," as in "*Malchus Yavan Haresho'oh*," the Roman Empire is termed *Malchus Hazadon* — the empire of intentional wickedness — which is a more malevolent form of evil.[155] Although both nations persecuted the Jews, the Midrash says that when the word *tzor* — persecutor — is written without a *vav*, it is a reference to Greece, and when written with a *vav*, it refers to Rome.[156] The missing letter *vav* demonstrates that the persecution of the Greeks was also diminished and incomplete.

One can bring proof that the Greeks were better than the Romans from the fact that unlike the Romans, the Greeks did not attempt to destroy the Beis HaMikdash. However, it can be argued that since Noach's gift to Yavan (Greece) was an appreciation of the arts,[157] they did not desire to destroy the Beis HaMikdash only because of its architectural beauty.

---

153 *Dikdukei Sofrim, Megillah* 11a.
154 *Tzalusah D'Avraham*, ibid.
155 *Perush al Tefilah*, ibid.
156 *Midrash Tanchumah, Shemos* 13.
157 *Bereishis* 9:27.

From Study to Fulfillment

"*Lehashkicham Torasechah ulehaaviram mechukei retzonechah* — When the wicked Greek kingdom rose up against Your people Israel to make them forget Your Torah and compel them to stray from the statutes of Your Will." The *Aruch HaShulchan* says that these two phrases are juxtaposed since by making the Jewish People forget the Torah, the Greeks intended that they would forsake all of Judaism.[158]

...Into the Hands of the Weak

When Bar Kochba led a revolt against Roman rule, he prayed merely that Hashem should not come to the aid of the Romans. The *Yerushalmi* relates that Bar Kochba was punished for refraining from asking Hashem to grant his army success in battle.[159] Rabbi Moshe Feinstein questions: What was deficient about Bar Kochba's prayer? Since his army was militarily superior to the Romans, it would require a miracle for the Romans to be victorious. Bar Kochba simply asked Hashem not to perform miracles for the sake of the Romans — so what did he do wrong? Rav Moshe answers that when it comes to war, there is no such thing as a natural outcome, as we can never predict with certainty whether it will be the weak underdog or the mighty warrior that will emerge victorious.[160]

If so, why do we praise Hashem in *Al HaNisim* for miraculously delivering "the mighty in the hands of the weak and the many in the hands of the few"? If there is no natural order to war and one can never be certain whether victory will go to the weak or the strong, there should be nothing supernatural in the Chashmonaim's victory! We must therefore qualify the above statement and say that when a superior army so vastly outnumbers and outpowers the weaker side, as was in the case with the Chashmonaim against the Greeks, it does require an open miracle for the weak to win.

---

158   *Aruch HaShulchan, Yoreh Deah* 246:6.
159   *Ta'anis* 4:5.
160   *Derash Moshe, Shemos* 15:3.

...Into the Hands of the Pure

"You delivered...the impure into the hands of the pure." What is the significance that the pure Chashmonaim were victorious over the impure Greeks? Rabbi Shlomo Zalman Auerbach explains that the Greeks were extremely knowledgeable in the worldly sciences and they fiercely opposed the Jews whose source of wisdom — the Torah — was diametrically different from the wisdom of the Greeks in one important respect. The secular wisdom of the Greeks did not require its adherents to become spiritually elevated; one could be impure and still be a great secular scholar. With Torah, though, Hashem only grants its wisdom to one who aspires to personal purity.

The Greeks primarily sought to defile the sanctity of the Torah and the Temple, as Antiochus exhorted his soldiers: "They have one mitzvah: the Menorah (which symbolized the Divine source of the Torah's wisdom). If you are able to abolish it, then they are lost."[161] The victory of the Chashmonaim therefore demonstrates the ultimate triumph of purity over the forces of darkness and impurity.[162]

The Greek Advantage

The Chasam Sofer says that each of the corresponding terms used in *Al HaNisim* to contrast the Jews with the Greeks describes an advantage the Greeks had:[163]

- *Temayim* — impure, allows for greater proliferation (since they are not concerned with ritual impurity of *niddah*), and therefore they were greater in number than the Jews.
- *Reshaim* — lit. evil, in this instance means uncircumcised, who are stronger than those who have a *bris milah*.[164]

---

161 Cited in Bach, intro. laws of Chanukah.
162 *Halichos Shlomo*, Chanukah 16:46.
163 Rabbi Moshe Sofer, *Toras Moshe*, beginning *Divrei Aggadah* on Chanukah (after *parashas Vayeshev*).
164 Rabbeinu Bachya, *Bereishis* 17:1.

- *Zaidim* — lit. deliberate ones, are cunning individuals who shrewdly calculate how to outsmart their opponents. This would imply that *Yiddin* are not inherently sharp enough to win their opponents in a battle of wits. The Chasam Sofer rejects such a position outright, as it is clearly untrue. He therefore says this phrase must be understood that the *oskei haTorah* are so absorbed in their commitment to Torah study that they do not have the luxury to indulge in battles of wits against their enemies. They instead cast their burden unto Hashem, having complete trust that Hashem will save them from the machinations of their enemies.
- The fact that the Greeks were *Rabim* — many, and *Giborim* — mighty, are obvious benefits and require no further elaboration.

Praise to Your Great Name

"And they established these eight days of Chanukah to express thanks and praise to Your Great Name." What is the distinction between Hashem's "Great Name" and the other names of Hashem?

Based on the Gemara, the *Binyan Shlomo* says that the "Great Name" refers to the *Shem HaMeforash* — the Ineffable Name that was only permitted to be uttered in the Beis HaMikdash.[165] Therefore, it was only when the Chashmonaim reclaimed the Beis HaMikdash from the *Yevanim*, that Hashem's "Great Name" could be praised once again.[166]

A TIME FOR GIVING PRAISE

Hallel on Chanukah

Why do we recite the entire *Hallel* each day of Chanukah, unlike Pesach where the entire *Hallel* is recited only on the first day?

---

165   *Yomah* 69b.
166   *Binyan Shlomo*, vol. 2, *Orach Chaim*, chap. 8.

There are a number of reasons given:

1. Since on each night of Chanukah a different number of candles are lit, it becomes more like Sukkos when the entire *Hallel* is recited each day because the Temple sacrifices that were brought on Sukkos varied on each day of the festival.[167]
2. The miracle of Chanukah increasingly progressed each day. Therefore, each day is considered a new miracle and it is appropriate to recite a complete *Hallel* each day.[168]
3. The Torah reading for each day of Chanukah delineates the sacrifices each *nasi* — prince — brought during the inauguration of the Mishkan. Since each *nasi* said *Hallel* to accompany his sacrifice, it would not be befitting to read about his offerings without also reciting a complete *Hallel* on that day.[169]
4. Since Chanukah was instituted as a festival *l'hodos ul'hallel* — for giving praise — the fulfillment of this specific objective inherently requires that the full *Hallel* be recited each day.[170]

CHANUKAH CUSTOMS

Doughnuts

Rabbi Maimon Ben Yosef (the father of the Rambam) writes regarding the festival of Chanukah:

> One should not make light of any custom, even one that appears insignificant...such as the prevalent custom to make *sufganiyos* (doughnuts) [on Chanukah], since they are fried in oil and recall Hashem's blessing [of the Chanukah miracle that transpired with oil]...One should not belittle these

---

167 *Shibolei HaLeket*, cited by *Beis Yosef, Orach Chaim* 683:1.
168 Tosfos, *Ta'anis* 28b.
169 *Beis Yosef* ibid.
170 Rabbi Shlomo Zalman Auerbach, *Minchas Shlomo*, vol. 2, 54.

> *customs for they were made as fundamental institutions,*
> *as the prophet states, "Do not stray from the Torah of your*
> *mother"—do not forsake the insightfulness of your nation.*[171]

Rabbi Shlomo Zalman Auerbach provides another rationale for the custom of eating doughnuts on Chanukah: when the Chashmonaim reclaimed the Temple, they rebuilt the Altar that the Greeks had destroyed. When one eats a doughnut, he recites *al hamichyah* as an after-blessing, which contains a specific reference to the Altar (unlike the Grace after Meals, which makes no explicit mention of the Altar).[172]

Women Refraining from Work

The *Kol Bo* discourages the custom some women have to refrain from work throughout the duration of Chanukah, as excessive idleness leads to mental instability.[173] However, he maintains that this custom may be sufficiently fulfilled by merely refraining from work on the first and last day of Chanukah.[174]

A precedent for refraining from work on specifically these two days is that it parallels the festivals of Pesach and Sukkos on which the Torah obligates the cessation of work on the first and last day of the Yom Tov.[175] An additional significance of these two days is that the first day of Chanukah marks the miracle of the military victory over the Greeks and the last day coincides with the completion of the rededication of the Temple by the Chashmonaim.

Dairy Products

The custom to eat dairy on Chanukah is based on the story of Yehudis who brought about a great victory over the Greeks. When

---

171   Cited in *Halichos Shlomo*, Chanukah 17:20.
172   *Halichos Shlomo* ibid.
173   *Kesuvos* 59b.
174   *Kol Bo*, laws of Chanukah.
175   Ibid.

she was brought into the private chambers of the Greek general, she first gave him salty cheese that made him thirsty, after which she poured him strong wine that made him fall into a deep sleep. After he fell asleep, she stealthily beheaded him and escaped from the Greek camp. Upon returning to Yerushalayim, the Chashmonaim displayed the general's severed head from above the walls of the city. When the Greek army saw what had befallen their general, the soldiers fled in fright.[176]

The question is: why do we only commemorate this miracle by eating dairy products? Why do we not also drink wine, since Yehudis gave the general wine as well?

One answer given is that such an enactment would be unnecessary, as there is already a mitzvah in place to drink wine and eat meat on Chanukah as is the case on other Yomim Tovim.[177] Rabbi Nissim Karelitz disagrees.[178] In his view, there is no obligation to eat meat or drink wine on Chanukah. The intention of the *Mishnah Berurah* is merely to convey that one may not refrain from eating these foods as a form of self-affliction to atone for one's sins. Such behavior would be similar to fasting, which is forbidden on Chanukah. As to why the rabbis did not institute a custom to drink wine on Chanukah, perhaps it is to differentiate between the tone of Chanukah, which was instituted primarily for giving praise to Hashem, and the other festivals, for which the manner of celebration is primarily feasting and drinking.

Collecting Tzedakah for Poor Scholars

There was a custom for young Torah scholars to go collecting from door-to-door on Chanukah while singing songs.[179] The reason for this is that the word Chanukah (חנוכה), in the exegesis system of

---

176 Ibid.
177 See *Mishnah Berurah* 529:20.
178 *Chut Shani*, Shabbos 4, pp. 358–359.
179 See *Magen Avraham* in his introduction to *Orach Chaim* 670.

א"ת ב"ש, corresponds to סוד צדקה — "the secret is *tzedakah*," which hints that one should give *tzedakah* on Chanukah especially to young Torah scholars who are comparable to a small flask of pure olive oil.[180] The *Kitzur Shulchan Aruch* adds that supporting Torah scholars on Chanukah rectifies the blemishes of one's soul.[181]

Why is there a specific mitzvah on Chanukah to give *tzedakah* to poor Torah scholars?

- In the *Al HaNisim* prayer, it states: "You delivered...the wanton into the hands of the diligent students of Your Torah." Since the festival of Chanukah would not have occurred if not for the merit of the students of Torah, we recall the Chanukah miracle by supporting those who study Torah.[182]
- On Purim, Haman attempted to destroy the physical bodies of the Jewish People; the rabbis therefore instituted that we support the bodies of the poor through *matanos l'evyonim*. On Chanukah, the Greeks desired to uproot the soul of the Jewish People by preventing them from studying the Torah. We therefore commemorate this miracle by supporting the class of people who were saved during the Chanukah miracle, which are those who are wholly dedicated to Torah study.[183]

Chanukah Gelt

Rabbi Yaakov Kamenetsky was once asked whether it is prohibited to give children Chanukah gelt, since it mimics the custom of non-Jews who also give gifts to their children during their winter holiday. He answered that on the contrary, it is more likely that the non-Jews derived their custom from us. The source of giving out Chanukah gelt to children derived from the custom of giving *tzedakah* to poor

---

180   *Chanukas HaBayis*, p. 72, as cited in *Magen Avraham* ibid.
181   Rabbi Shlomo Ganzfried, *Kitzur Shulchan Aruch* 139:1.
182   Rabbi Menashe Klein, cited in *Rivevos Ephraim, Orach Chaim* 440:3.
183   *Rivevos Ephraim* ibid.

Torah scholars on Chanukah. Since the father would give money to his children to give to their *rebbi*, he would also give some money for the children themselves.

Reb Yaakov was accustomed to giving his children Chanukah gelt on the fifth night of Chanukah. Rabbi Chaim Kanievsky did likewise and explained that the reason for this is because the fifth day of Chanukah never falls on Shabbos.[184]

---

184 *Emes L'Yaakov, Orach Chaim* 670:583; *Derech Sichah*, p. 187; story about Reb Chaim found in the biography of Rebbetzin Kanievsky (Brooklyn, NY: Artscroll Publications), p. 220.

THE MONTH OF ADAR

The Great Month of Adar

As we said above, although the names of the Hebrew months of the year are of Babylonian origin, the Sages adopted their use since they expounded the names in a manner that conveyed Jewish themes. There are several interpretations of the significance of the name *Adar*:

- *Adar* means "mighty," as in the verse: "You are mighty (*adir*) on high, Hashem."[1] In this month, Hashem's greatness was manifested through the miracle of Purim.[2]
- Alternatively, "mighty" is a reference to the great master Moshe, who was born in this month.[3] The Gemara says that *adir* is a reference to monarchy.[4] Moshe had the status of being the spiritual king in disseminating Torah to Israel.

---

1   *Tehillim* 93:4.
2   See *Kiddush Yerachim D'Rav Pinchus*, cited in *Torah Sheleimah, Bo, Miluim*, p. 178.
3   *Midrash HaChefetz*, cited in *Torah Sheleimah, Bo, Miluim*, p. 177.
4   *Gittin* 56b.

- Some suggest that Adar is related to *hadar* — return, since the Jewish People "returned" to renew their commitment to Torah during the days of Achashverosh.

The Small Month of Adar

The Jewish months are based on the lunar cycle, which requires a rotation alternating between a thirty-day and a twenty-nine-day month. The "distinguished" full (*malei*) thirty-day month is called *melech* — king — and the incomplete (*chasser*) twenty-nine-day month is called *meshores* — the helper.[5]

The months chosen to be *melech* are those that have special qualities to them: Nissan — Pesach; Sivan — Shavuos; Av — in this month, the yearly supply of wood used for the Temple Altar was prepared; Tishrei — Yomim Noraim and Sukkos; Kislev — Chanukah; and Shevat — the Rosh Hashanah for trees.[6]

Surprisingly, although the festival of Purim falls in Adar, this month is generally a *meshores* (except for a leap year in which there are two Adars, and the first Adar has thirty days and the second has twenty-nine days). Why isn't Adar a *melech* month?

Possibly, since Purim commemorates the miracles Hashem performs in a concealed manner, it is appropriate for it to be celebrated in a *meshores* month.

Increasing Joy

"Just as when Av begins we curtail joy, so too when Adar begins we increase joy."[7] The first part of this statement is brought by the halachic codifiers, but surprisingly, the second part — "When Adar begins we increase joy" — is not mentioned in the Rambam or in the *Shulchan Aruch*. What is the difference between the two?

---

5   *Levush, Orach Chaim* 428:1.
6   Ibid.
7   *Ta'anis* 29a.

Rabbi Chaim Kanievsky answers that unlike the laws pertaining to the month of Av, which are actual halachic requirements, the increasing of joy in Adar was not intended as a law, but merely as good advice.[8]

How can we increase joy in Adar?

- Rabbi Shlomo Zalman Auerbach explains that the best way one can fulfill the dictum of "when Adar begins we increase joy" is by not allowing oneself to dwell on any worries or concerns that may cause one to become despondent.[9]

- According to Rabbi Chaim Kanievsky, if one is making a *siyum* or a *simchah*, he should try to celebrate it during the month of Adar. Even if someone is not celebrating a *simchah*, he can increase his joy by drinking a bit of wine at the onset of Adar. Reb Chaim relates that his father, the Steipler Gaon, was accustomed to drink a little wine every Rosh Chodesh. On Rosh Chodesh Adar, he would drink a little more than he did the other months.[10]

PURIM INSIGHTS

Why "Purim"?

The holiday of Purim is named after the *purim* — lots — that Haman cast to help him determine the most opportune day to destroy the Jews. Why should this relatively minor act become the name for the festival?

Rabbi Moshe Feinstein answers that the name *Purim* conveys one of the major themes of Purim — the power of prayer. Often a person

---

8   *Derech Sichah*, p. 188.
9   *Halichos Shlomo*, Purim 18:36.
10   *Derech Sichah*, p. 187.

prays to Hashem in times of need, but when fortune smiles upon him, he mistakenly thinks that success is already his and he no longer needs to pray. The story of Purim teaches otherwise. Even when a person strikes upon good *mazal* — as was the case with Haman when he cast the lots against the Jews — one's "lucky stars" do not guarantee one's success, just as Haman's *purim* did not help him in any way to achieve his ends.[11]

From Dust to Stars

The Chofetz Chaim writes that the story of Purim is a paradigm for the Jewish People in exile. During the time of Haman, the Jews lived in trepidation that they would be annihilated on the thirteenth of Adar, and yet it turned out exactly the opposite — it became a day of destruction of their enemies. Similarly, at a time when we see the Jewish nation trampled by our enemies, we should not despair but take it as a sign of Hashem's imminent salvation.[12]

The Gemara says that the Jewish People are compared to the dust and the stars — when they fall, they fall till the dust, and when they rise, they rise till the stars.[13] The two extremes are closely connected; when Hashem sees how the Jews are downtrodden and despised like dirt by their enemies, Hashem then has mercy on them and speedily lifts them up to the stars.[14]

Miracles in Exile

"Where in the Torah is there an allusion to Esther? From the verse, 'And I will surely *astir* — conceal My countenance from them.'"[15] Why does the Talmud only seek a source in the Torah for the epic story of Queen Esther and not for the miracles that were performed to

---

11   *Derash Moshe*, p. 67.
12   *Shem Olam*, vol. 2, ch. 14.
13   *Megillah* 16a.
14   *Shem Olam* ibid.
15   *Devarim* 31:18; *Chulin* 139a.

countless other righteous people, such as the Chashmonaim during the time of Chanukah?

The Vilna Gaon answers that as great as the miracle of Chanukah was, it was still not such a surprising occurrence, since the children of Israel dwelled in their land and the Temple still stood. The Torah wishes to bring a proof that Hashem brings salvation to His people, albeit in a concealed manner, even during the darkest periods of exile.[16]

A Time for Public Works

"On the fifteenth day [of Adar], the *Megillah* is read in the fortified cities and we begin repairing paths and roads, *mikvaos*, and all public works."[17] What is the connection between reading the *Megillah* and the maintenance of public works in that they should both commence on the same day?

We may answer that since Purim arouses our deep love and concern for our fellowman, through our giving *matanos l'evyonim* and *mishloach manos*, it is fitting that we utilize the impetus of this day to initiate further projects to benefit the community.

The Eternal Festival

The Midrash says that all the Yomim Tovim, except Purim, will cease in the future.[18] The *Sefer Chasidim* explains that during the time of Haman, the existence of the entire Jewish people was in threat of extinction (unlike the servitude in Egypt in which only the males were in danger of being destroyed). Since the eternity of the Jewish People was threatened in the time of Haman, this Yom Tov is also celebrated for eternity.[19]

The Rashba, however, states that this Midrash cannot be understood at face value. How can one think that Pesach will be abolished

---

16   *Chumash HaGra, Devarim* 31:18.
17   *Shekalim* 1:1.
18   *Midrash Mishlei* 9:2.
19   *Sefer Chasidim* 369.

in the future if the Torah explicitly states in numerous places that Pesach is a *chukas olam* — a statute for all time?[20] Rather, the point the Midrash is conveying is that in future times the Jews may sin and may be unable to practice some festivals for a limited period.[21] However, Hashem promises that the festival of Purim will be observed for all time. The verse that states, "and these days of Purim will never cease among the Jews,"[22] is therefore to be taken not as a commandment but as an assurance.[23]

The Radvaz understands the Midrash as follows: Although all the festivals will continue to be observed, after the arrival of Mashiach we will be in a constant state of joy and happiness and the joy of the Torah festivals will no longer be discernible. However, since the Purim miracle transpired later in Jewish history, its joy is fresher in the collective conscious of the nation and is therefore celebrated with more intense joy.[24]

AL HANISIM

An Aramaic Insertion

The prayers were generally formulated in *Lashon HaKodesh*. It is therefore peculiar that in *Al HaNisim*, the Aramaic word *purkon* is used instead of the more common Hebrew word for redemption — *geulah*.

Rabbi Yosef Ber Soloveitchik explains that since human beings played an active role in the Chanukah and Purim saga, there is a danger that one may mistakenly attribute the salvation to the work of man. We therefore use the weaker terminology for salvation — *purkon* — which can also mean to lessen one's burden, rather than the more encompassing word for redemption — *geulah* — to describe

---

20   *Shemos* 12:14, 17.
21   See *Eichah* 2:6.
22   *Esther* 9:28.
23   *Teshuvos HaRashba* 1:93.
24   *Teshuvos* Radvaz 2:828.

the deliverance in that time.[25] We may add that since the redemption of Chanukah and Purim was incomplete, insofar as the Jewish People did not achieve self-governance, the weaker terminology for salvation is a more appropriate choice.

"For the Wars"

There are diverging opinions whether one should insert the phrase *"al hamilchamos* — for the wars" in the *Al HaNisim* prayer on Purim.[26] The idea in favor of mentioning the praise is that the Jewish People's victory in battle against their enemies was one of the prominent miracles of the Purim story. The opinions that hold not to mention this miracle explain that *Al HaNisim's* focus is to praise Hashem's salvation from danger, while the war after Haman's downfall was primarily to fulfill the mitzvah of eradicating the Amalekite nation.

"For the Wonders"

There are various opinions as to whether one should say *"al hiniflaos* — for the wonders" on Purim. The *Aruch HaShulchan* is of the opinion that on Chanukah one should recite *"al hamilchamos,"* since the military victory over the Greeks was an integral component of the Chanukah miracle, but on Purim one should recite *"al haniflaos."*[27]

Hararei Kedem cites an opposing view, saying that *niflaos* signifies a supernatural miracle that defies the laws of nature, such as a flask of oil burning for eight days. One would therefore not classify the miracle of Purim in that category since the miracle of Purim transpired in a concealed, superficially natural manner.[28]

However, we may counter this position and say that in the story of Purim, the string of "coincidental" phenomena was of such

---

25   *Hararei Kedem*, vol. 1, 179:1.

26   *Aruch HaShulchan, Orach Chaim* 682:2.

27   Ibid.

28   See *Hararei Kedem* 1:179:3.

magnitude, culminating in a complete turnabout (*v'nahapoch hu*) of all human expectations, that this too can also be classified as an act of Hashem's *niflaos*.

"To Plunder Their Possessions"

The *Al HaNisim* prayer includes these words: "When Haman the wicked arose against them he sought to destroy, slay, and to exterminate all the Jews...and to plunder their possessions."

If the Jews had already been decreed for death, what does it matter whether Haman also decreed that their possessions be plundered? Isn't death bad enough?!

1. The Chofetz Chaim used to say that Eisav constantly wants to destroy the Jews and has the means to do so. The only reason the nations don't is because they are too lazy to bother. Haman therefore decreed that the populace be allowed to plunder the Jews' property as an incentive to overcome their laziness.
2. Had the Jews' property gone to the Crown, it would have been possible to bribe the murderers to allow them to live. However, if the estates of the Jews were free for the taking, bribery would be futile, since the murderers would be able to seize whatever they wanted in any case.[29]

THE FAST OF ESTHER

Source of the Fast

There is no mention in the Talmud of the requirement to fast on Taanis Esther. *Mishnah Berurah* writes that it can be derived from the behavior of Moshe, who decreed a fast on the day *Bnei Yisrael* went to war against Amalek.[30] Since the Jewish People battled their enemies on

---

29 Chasam Sofer, *Toras Moshe*, end of *parashas Tetzaveh*, s.v. "*hakesef nasun*."
30 *Mechiltah, Beshalach.*

the thirteenth of Adar in the days Mordechai and Esther, they most certainly fasted to beseech Divine mercy for success on that day, as well.[31]

A story in *Sefer Shmuel* seems to contradict this principle. Once, when Shaul HaMelech waged war against the Plishtim, he adjured the people not to eat the entire day. When Shaul's son, Yonasan, unwittingly transgressed the oath, he defended his position by arguing that had the army eaten, they would have had the strength to strike the Plishtim an even greater blow.[32] The *Sefer Chasidim* sides with the position of Yonasan and rules that if enemies lay siege to a city, it is proper for the inhabitants to eat so they can properly defend themselves.[33]

Which approach is correct?

Rabbi Yisrael Reisman differentiates between the two situations: regarding the war with the Plishtim, Shaul HaMelech did not establish a proper public fast day, and as such he was merely calling for personal self-affliction, which can be outweighed by the consideration of having strength to fight properly. Moshe and Mordechai, however, instituted a communal fast day, and therefore fasting is appropriate to attain Heavenly success in battle.

Fasting before a Festival

Megillas Taanis records numerous minor festivals on which one is not permitted to fast. It states there further that one is also not permitted to fast on the day prior to those minor festival days. Numerous *Rishonim* ask how it is then permissible to fast on Taanis Esther, since it is the day prior to Purim on which fasting is prohibited. There are several answers given:

1. The later Sages saw fit to abolish *Megillas Taanis* in order to minimize the number of festival days in exile. Therefore,

---

31   *Mishnah Berurah* 686:2. See, however, Rashba to *Megillah* 2a, footnote 161 (MRK ed.); and *Maharitz Chiyos*, *Megillah* 2a, s.v. "*zman*," who cite explicit sources for the basis of Ta'anis Esther.

32   *Shmuel I*, 14:24–45.

33   *Sefer Chasidim* 618.

in respect to Purim, we follow the opinions that hold that fasting is only prohibited on the day of the festival, but is permissible on the day prior to it.[34]

2. The rabbis only prohibited fasting on the day prior to a minor Rabbinic festival in order to strengthen the acceptance of that holiday. Since Purim was universally accepted by the Jewish nation, it does not require strengthening and has the status of a Torah festival on which fasting is permissible on the day prior.[35]

3. Most fast days are instituted for crying and mourning, but Taanis Esther recalls the miraculous victory of the Jews against their enemies. As such, it is a joyful fast day and is not included in the general prohibition of fasting prior to a festival.[36]

LAWS AND CUSTOMS OF PURIM

Torah Reading

On a day the Torah is read publicly in shul, we generally read a minimum of ten verses. The Gemara presents numerous explanations for the significance of the number ten, such as corresponding to the *Aseres HaDibros* and the Ten Utterances through which Hashem created the world.[37]

An exception is made for the Torah reading on Purim, when only nine verses are read. Why is this so?

The Torah reading on Purim relates the episode of Amalek's war against Israel in the wilderness. The *parashah* concludes with Hashem making an oath by His throne of glory that there will be war and animosity against Amalek for all time. In that verse, the words for

---

34   Ritva, *Ta'anis* 10a.
35   Ra'avya 2:559.
36   Meiri, *Ta'anis* 18a.
37   *Megillah* 21b.

"throne" — כסא, and Hashem's Name — י-ה-ו-ה, are spelled deficient (כס, י-ה).[38] This is because Hashem swore that neither His Name nor His throne are complete until Amalek will be completely eradicated.[39] Just as Amalek caused Hashem's name and His throne to be diminished, the Sages instituted that the *parashah* dealing with Amalek should also be diminished and therefore only nine verses are read.[40]

V'Atah Kadosh

After the evening *Megillah* reading, we recite *V'Atah Kadosh*. We would think that it would be more fitting to begin with *Uva LeTzion*, since those verses deal with the redemption and Purim is a time of redemption (indeed, the *Siddur Rav Amram* writes that one should start with *Uva LeTzion*). The *Tur* explains our custom in that the main redemption occurs only by day.[41]

But why is *V'Atah Kadosh* recited on Purim as well as on Tishah b'Av? The *Aruch HaShulchan* answers that *V'Atah Kadosh* begins as follows: "And you are the Holy One, enthroned upon the praises of Israel." This means that Hashem's sole desire, so to speak, is the praises of Israel and that His primary involvement is in the affairs of the Jewish People. When we are joyous, Hashem rejoices, and when the Jewish People are suffering, Hashem suffers as well. It is therefore appropriate to recite *V'Atah Kadosh* both at times of great joy for the Jewish People such as Purim, as well as on Tishah b'Av, which is the day of great pain and calamity for the Jewish nation.[42]

No "Thank You"

Some have a custom not to say thank you when receiving *mishloach manos* because the sender had a mitzvah obligation to give it.[43] This

---

38   *Shemos* 17:16.
39   Rashi ibid.
40   *Orchos Chaim*, cited in *Mishnah Berurah* 137:3.
41   *Tur, Orach Chaim* 693.
42   *Aruch HaShulchan, Orach Chaim* 693:1.
43   See *Leket Yosher*, p. 158 (he was a student of the *Terumas HaDeshen*).

does not appear to be a unanimously held view. The Rashash brings a proof from the fact that one can thank the landowner when taking the fruits of his field during *Shemitah*, even though Hashem gave them to the recipient.[44] Similarly, one can say *yashar kochachah* — thank you to the *Kohanim* for blessing us, even though they are commanded to do so by Hashem.

The Purim Meal

Poskim say that one must have intention to fulfill the mitzvah of eating the *seudah* on Purim in order to discharge his obligation, which is not the case regarding the mitzvah of eating matzah on Pesach in which a person fulfills the mitzvah even without intent.

Why is the mitzvah of eating the Purim meal different than eating matzah?

The *Pri Megadim* answers that there is a general principle that a mitzvah that entails pleasure, such as eating matzah, can be fulfilled merely by doing the pleasurable act even when unaccompanied by any intention. The mitzvah of *seudah* on Purim is different because the essential aspect of the mitzvah is to recall the miracle that occurred because of Achashverosh's feast, and that requires intent.[45]

Hamantaschen

Rabbi Yaakov Kamenetsky suggests that the custom of eating *hamantaschen* on Purim is because eating is a form of destruction. By eating *hamantashen*, one fulfills the mitzvah of obliterating Amalek, since we are destroying the food that carries Haman's name. In addition, since eating is also used as a metaphor for easily destroying a nation,[46] it also a sign that we would should easily prevail over Amalek.[47]

---

44   *Shevi'is* 4:2.
45   *Mishpetei Zahav, Orach Chaim* 695:1; *Mishnah Berurah* 695:4.
46   As in *Bamidbar* 14:9 and *Tehillim* 79:7.
47   *B'mechitzas Rabbeinu*, p. 142.

Eating Seeds

The Rema cites a custom to eat seeds on Purim to recall the seeds Daniel and his company ate while serving in King Nevuchadnetzar's palace.[48] The *Aruch HaShulchan* wonders why the Rema bases the custom on Daniel's diet, which has no connection to Purim. Instead, he maintains that the custom commemorates the behavior of Queen Esther, who also observed a "seed diet" at Achashverosh's palace.[49]

Perhaps we can understand the view of the Rema in the following way:

While Esther ate seeds in order to refrain from eating non-kosher food,[50] Daniel and his friends ate certain seeds that cause bad breath in order to distance themselves from interacting with non-Jews.[51] This relates to the story of Purim, for the Jews were threatened with destruction because of their sin of partaking of the king's feast, the prohibition stemming from the possibility of social interaction with non-Jews.[52] Our eating of seeds "in the spirit of Daniel" expresses the commitment to refrain from repeating the same errors of those who partook of the king's feast.

Custom-Made Purim

During various periods in history, Jewish communities around the world would institute the day on which they experienced a life-saving miracle as a perennial Yom Tov (such as Purim Frankfurt, Purim Cairo, and Purim Saragossa). While the *Pri Chadash* strongly condemned this practice,[53] the Chasam Sofer justifies the custom.[54] The Gemara states that the basis for the establishment of the festival of Purim is a *kal v'chomer* reasoning: if the Jewish People praised

---

48   Rama, *Orach Chaim* 695:2.
49   *Megillah* 13a. *Aruch HaShulchan, Orach Chaim* 695:9.
50   Rashi, *Megillah* ibid.
51   Rabbi Saadiah Gaon, *Daniel* 1:12.
52   *Megillah* 12a; cf. Rambam, *Mishnah Torah*, Ma'achalos Asuros 17:9–10.
53   *Pri Chadash, Orach Chaim* 496:14. See *Rosh Hashanah* 18b (end).
54   Chasam Sofer, *Shulchan Aruch, Orach Chaim* 191.

Hashem when they left Egypt and were freed from slavery, all the more so one should commemorate deliverance from death to life during the time of Haman.[55] This logic would equally apply to any community that wishes to institute an annual Yom Tov to celebrate a life-saving miracle that they experienced.

The Netziv disagrees and argues that the *kal v'chomer* reasoning is limited only to the obligation of reciting *Hallel* at the time at which the miracle occurred, just as when the Jewish People sang *shirah* when they left Egypt. But the *kal v'chomer* does not obligate a person to praise Hashem in the future on the anniversary of the event, nor does it pertain to establishing the date of the miracle as a festival in future years.[56]

DRINKING ON PURIM

Why Drink?

Why should there be an obligation on Purim to get drunk until one is no longer capable of thinking clearly? Normally the Torah discourages drinking for that very reason![57]

A possible explanation is that when a person is drunk, one's mind recedes to the background, while his physical body becomes prominent. This becomes a fitting way to celebrate Hashem's salvation on Purim, a time when our bodies, rather than our minds, were in danger.

No Zecher L'Churban

As a reminder of the destruction of Jerusalem, the Sages decreed that when one prepares a feast one should not serve all the dishes that would ordinarily be served at such a feast.[58] The *Shaarei Teshuvah* writes that this law does not apply to the *seudah* on Purim. Since one

---

55   *Megillah* 14a.
56   *Ha'amek Shailah, Vayishlach.* See *Shevet HaLevi* 3:89.
57   *Mishlei* 23:31, Rashi *ad loc.*; Chofetz Chaim, *Machaneh Yisrael* 2:7.
58   *Shulchan Aruch, Orach Chaim* 560:2.

will be drunk during the meal *ad delo yada*, making a rememberence for the *Churban* would be pointless at such a time.[59]

Ad Delo Yada

A person is obligated to drink on Purim *ad delo yada* — until he can no longer distinguish between *Arur Haman* — cursed is Haman, and *Baruch Mordechai* — blessed is Mordechai. What does this mean?

Rabbi Moshe Feinstein explains that there are two methods in serving Hashem: There are some who are only motivated to repent in times of danger, as was the case during the time of the cursed Haman. Although this method works for most people, there is a danger that one will return to his old ways the moment the danger passes. A loftier level is to emulate the righteous Mordechai, who was constantly motivated to self-improvement. Although fewer people follow this approach, it lasts longer. When one can no longer discern which approach is more beneficial — i.e., short-term effectiveness for many people or a stronger and long-lasting effect for a few — one is exempt from drinking further.[60]

Permissible Purim Lie

The Gemara states that in three areas a Torah scholar may deviate from the truth.[61] One of them is *puryah*. The common translation of *puryah* is "bed," and Rashi and Tosfos both understand the Gemara to be dealing with matters pertaining to sleeping on a bed.

The Maharshah presents an alternative explanation. Since *puryah* is also the Aramaic word for Purim, he therefore explains that the Gemara is teaching that a Torah scholar may decline intoxicating drink on Purim by claiming that he can no longer distinguish between *Arur Haman* and *Baruch Mordechai*, even when that is not actually the case![62]

---

59 *Sha'arei Teshuvah, Orach Chaim* 695:1.

60 *Derash Moshe*, end of *parashas Tetzaveh*.

61 *Bava Metzia* 23b.

62 Ibid.

How Much Wine?

The obligation to drink on Purim is until one reaches the point where he can no longer differentiate between *Arur Haman* and *Baruch Mordechai*. Halachic authorities rule that it is sufficient to drink more than one is accustomed and then to go to sleep.[63] The simple explanation of this idea is that one's obligation is fulfilled through the combination of wine and sleep.

Rabbi Moshe Heineman, however, is of the opinion that one need not actually go to sleep in order to fulfill *ad delo yada*. In his view, the obligation to drink wine *ad delo yada* is not an obligation to obtain a certain state but is rather a measurement of how much wine one must drink. Since a person who drinks more than he is generally accustomed to tends to feel like going to sleep, one fulfills his obligation merely by drinking that specific amount.[64]

KLAPPING HAMAN

Source of the Custom

There is a custom to bang when hearing Haman's name mentioned during the *Megillah* reading,[65] of which the *Beis Yosef* adds that the custom should not be disregarded or made light of because it was instituted for good reason. The *Mateh Moshe* says that a hint to this custom can be found in the verse, והיה אם בן הכות הרשע — "And it will be that if the wicked one is liable to lashes,"[66] in which the last letters of the words והיה אם בן spell Haman.[67]

The Chasam Sofer comments that banging upon hearing the name of Haman demonstrates our eagerness to obliterate the memory of Amalek. Just as when a prophet performed an action associated with

---

63   Rama, *Orach Chaim* 695:2.

64   Heard from the Rav.

65   *Shulchan Aruch, Orach Chaim* 690:17.

66   *Devarim* 25:2.

67   *Mateh Moshe* 1006; *Siddur Rabbi Yaakov Emden*, introduction to *Megillas Esther*.

his prophecy it helped materialize the fulfillment of the prophecy, so too does our banging, which echoes the sounds of warfare, help actualize the ultimate downfall of Amalek in battle.[68]

Banging with One's Feet

There are some authorities who maintain that the custom of banging when hearing Haman's name should be specifically performed by banging one's feet on the ground.[69] I once heard the following explanation for this custom:

Kabbalists write that a person should wear shoes to separate between one's feet and the ground, as the ground was cursed as a result of Adam's sin.[70] (This is why Hashem told Moshe to remove his shoes at the burning bush since the ground was holy,[71] and shoes were therefore inappropriate on hallowed ground.) Since the essence of Haman is hinted to in the Tree of Knowledge that led to Adam's sin,[72] we bang with our shoes on the ground to demonstrate that it was because of Haman, who caused us to sin, that we are required to wear shoes to separate between our feet and the ground.

MEGILLAS ESTHER

All-Night Mitzvah

According to the Torah, one may fulfill the mitzvah of reading *Shema* the entire night. However, the rabbis instituted that one may only read *Shema* until midnight as a precaution lest one become lax and push off the mitzvah and later forget about it altogether.

Regarding reading the *Megillah* at night, the halachah is that one may read it the entire night. Why didn't the rabbis impose the same

---

68   Cited in *Yemei HaPurim*, p.110.
69   *Ben Ish Chai, parashas Tetzaveh; Kaf HaChaim* 690:96.
70   See *Shemiras HaGuf V'Hanefesh*, vol. 1, p. 336.
71   *Shemos* 3:5.
72   *Chulin* 139b.

safeguard for the *Megillah* as they did for *Shema*? The *Magen Avraham* offers two answers:[73]

1. Since the mitzvah of reading the *Megillah* comes only once a year, it is precious in a person's eyes and one will not be lax in its fulfilment.
2. Since the primary obligation of reading the *Megillah* is during the day, the rabbis were not stringent regarding the evening reading.

After Torah Reading

On all Yomim Tovim, we read the *Megillah* before *krias haTorah*, with the exception of Purim when the *Megillah* is read after *krias haTorah*. Why is this so?

Some explain that this is because reading the Torah portion regarding the war against Amalek is considered *zechirah* — a remembrance. However, the positive mitzvah obligations on Purim, such as reading the *Megillah*, are deemed *asiyah* — an action. The general principle is that *zechirah* always precedes *asiyah*.[74]

Female Sofer for Megillah

A woman is disqualified from writing a *sefer Torah*, but may write a *get*. There is a dispute among the *poskim* whether a woman may write a *Megillah*.[75] An interesting source permitting a woman to write a *Megillah* is based on the Gemara that derives the laws of writing the *Megillah* from the verse, "And Queen Esther wrote...the letter of Purim."[76]

The *Har Tzvi* rejects this proof, since the verse may simply mean that she had someone write the *Megillah* on her behalf.[77] This is like

---

73 *Magen Avraham, Orach Chaim* 687:1.
74 See *Megillah* 30a; *Hararei Kedem*, vol. 1 (second edition), p. 368.
75 *Keses HaSofer* 28:3; *Hamoadim B'halachah* p. 203.
76 *Esther* 9:29; *Megillah* 19a.
77 *Avodah Zarah* 27a.

the Gemara that interprets the verse, "And Tziporah took a sharp stone and circumcised her son,"[78] to mean that she appointed a man to circumcise her son.[79]

Mispronouncing the Megillah

The *Yerushalmi* rules a unique leniency regarding the reading of the *Megillah* (which does not apply to *Hallel*, *Shema*, or Torah readings) in that one fulfills his obligation even if he was not particular with the correct pronunciation.[80] The *Aruch HaShulchan* explains that this is because the *Megillah* is referred to as an *igeres* — a letter — in which one is not so careful regarding reading it with the exact pronunciation.[81]

While the view of the *Yerushalmi* is the accepted halachic opinion,[82] one can take exception with the *Aruch HaShulchan's* proof and argue that the term *igeres* is not referring to the manner of reading, but rather to the scroll itself. Unlike the pages of a *sefer Torah*, which is termed a *sefer* — a book — and therefore requires stitches along almost the entire length,[83] the *Megillah* is comparable to a letter in that its pages require only minimal stitching to connect the pages together.[84]

Dual Aspects of Megillah

The *Megillah* is unique in that it is also a form of *Hallel*, as well as a prayer. There are a number of proofs to support this idea:[85]

The Gemara says that *Hallel* is not read on Purim since the reading of the *Megillah* is itself deemed a recital of *Hallel*.[86]

---

78   *Shemos* 4:25.
79   *Avodah Zarah* ibid.
80   *Yerushalmi, Megillah* 2:2.
81   *Aruch HaShulchan, Orach Chaim* 690:20.
82   *Shulchan Aruch, Orach Chaim* 690:14.
83   *Shulchan Aruch, Yoreh Deah* 278:1.
84   *Yerushalmi* ibid.; *Shulchan Aruch, Orach Chaim* 691:6.
85   *Hararei Kedem*, Moadim 192.
86   *Megillah* 14a.

The *Megillah* is also considered a prayer,[87] since it recalls how the Jews gathered to fast and pray to Hashem to annul Haman's decree. When reading the *Megillah*, we are also praying to Hashem — by way of intimation — that just as He saved the Jewish nation in the days of Mordechai and Esther, so too should He come to our salvation as well.

The Gemara derives the obligation to read the *Megillah* at night and to repeat it during the day from the verse, "O my Hashem, I call out by day and You do not answer; by night and there is no respite for me,"[88] for the Jews cried day and night for Hashem's salvation during the time of Purim.[89] This demonstrates that the *Megillah* is also a form of prayer for which it is proper to entreat Hashem again and again until one's prayers are answered.[90]

BLESSING BEFORE AND AFTER MEGILLAH READING

Obligatory Blessing

The *Taz* maintains that if one omits the blessing prior to reading the *Megillah*, he does not fulfill his obligation.[91] This opinion appears difficult since it contradicts the general principle that one nonetheless fulfills a mitzvah even if he neglected to recite the appropriate blessing over it.[92]

Rabbi Yaakov Kamenetsky answers that we find a similar opinion regarding the laws of *shechitah*; if a person properly slaughters an animal without reciting the blessing on *shechitah*, the *shechitah* is invalid. This is because the act of *shechitah* requires the positive intent of permitting the animal in accordance with the manner prescribed

---

87   See *Magen Avraham, Orach Chaim* 689:10.
88   *Tehillim* 22:3.
89   *Megillah* 4a; Rashi there.
90   *Berachos* 32b.
91   *Taz, Orach Chaim* 688:9.
92   *Tur, Orach Chaim* 60.

by the Torah.[93] Similarly, the isolated events leading to the episode of Purim are not unique in the annals of history. Similar stories of kings, queens, and palace intrigues also transpired in the courts and palaces of the kings of Poland or Austria. If one does not recite the blessing over the *Megillah*, it is therefore unclear whether his intention is to fulfill the mitzvah or merely to read an interesting royal chronicle.[94]

Two Equals One

There is a general principle that when one is required to make two blessings (such as upon seeing a Jewish king who is also a sage, where each distinguishing attribute requires its own distinct blessing), one is required to make two separate blessings and not combine them into one blessing.[95]

Why, then, does the blessing after reading the *Megillah* conclude with a double-blessing: "Who exacts vengeance for His people Israel from all their foes, the G-d who brings salvation"?

The Meiri answers that both praises are actually stating the same idea. In the course of war, it is normal for both sides to suffer casualties. With the miracle of Purim, the enemies were so petrified of the Jews that not one of them attempted to strike back in self-defense. Hashem miraculously wreaked revenge against the enemy in a manner that simultaneously saved the Jewish nation from even a single loss.[96]

Five Expressions of Praise

The blessing recited upon the conclusion of reading the *Megillah* contains numerous expressions of praise:

1. Who takes up our grievance
2. Judges our claim

---

93   Rosh, *Chulin* 1:2.
94   *B'mechitzas Rabbeinu*, pp. 141–142.
95   See Tosfos, *Moed Katan* 8b; *Halichos Shlomo, Tefilah* 23:42.
96   *Megillah* 21b.

3. Avenges our wrong
4. Who brings retribution upon all enemies of our soul
5. Exacts vengeance for us from our foes

Rishonim comment that these five expressions of praise correspond to the five times in Jewish history when Amalek fell into the hands of Israel:[97]

1. Immediately following the exodus from Egypt[98]
2. After the death of Aharon[99]
3. During the reign of Shaul HaMelech[100]
4. During the reign of Dovid HaMelech[101]
5. In the days of Mordechai

Double Miracle

The blessing of *She'asah Nisim* — "that He performed miracles" is recited once a day on Chanukah, since there was a separate miracle each day in that the oil continued to burn for each of the eight days.[102]

Why is the festival of Purim different in that we recite the blessing twice — once at night and once during the day — if we only celebrate one Purim miracle?

We may suggest that on Purim we actually celebrate not one but two distinct miracles — the downfall of the wicked Haman and the elevation of the righteous Mordechai. The Gemara derives the obligation to read the *Megillah* at night and again during the day from the verse: "So that my soul might sing to You and not be stilled, Hashem

---

97   Meiri, *Megillah* 21b; cf. *Avudraham*, s.v. *"harav es riveinu."*
98   *Shemos* 17:8–16.
99   *Bamidbar* 21:1–3. The Midrash explains that the "Canaanites" mentioned in the verse were actually Amalekites in disguise.
100   *Shmuel I*, 15.
101   *Shmuel II*, 1:1.
102   See Rashi, *Shabbos* 23a.

my G-d, forever will I thank You."[103] The first part of the verse pertains to the *Megillah* read at night, for which we praise Hashem for destroying Haman who sought to still our souls by annihilating the Jews. The latter part of the verse relates to a more positive aspect of praise — as a result of the ascension of the righteous.[104]

Since the focus of our celebration is never on the downfall of the wicked,[105] we do not make a separate Yom Tov for the day Haman was hanged, and so the primary mitzvos of Purim, such as the Purim feast and *mishloach manos*, may only be performed during the day. Neverthless, we make reference to the two aspects of the Purim miracle by reading the *Megillah* at night and by day and by proclaiming the blessing *She'asah Nisim* each time the *Megillah* is read.

HINTS IN THE TORAH

Source of Megillas Esther

Esther asked the Sages to canonize the story of the *Megillah* by incorporating it into the body of *Tanach*. The Sages resisted elevating *Megillas Esther* to that status until they found a support from the verse: *Ksov zos zikaron basefer* — "Write this for a memorial in a book."[106]

Why were the Sages initially hesistant in incorporating *Megillas Esther* into the books of *Tanach* and what made them change their minds?

The Sages' original opinion was based on the fact that the word *kesivah* — writing — appears only twenty-three times in the book of *Devarim*, which corresponds to the twenty-three books of *Tanach*. But afterwards they felt that the verse *Ksov zos* — "write this," which deals with the perpetual war against Amalek of whom Haman was a descendant, is a fitting allusion to the story of Purim

---

103 *Tehillim* 30:13.
104 *Megillah* 4a, Rashi there.
105 *Meshech Chochmah, Shemos* 12:16.
106 *Shemos* 17:14. See *Megillah* 7a.

and it is therefore appropriate for *Megillas Esther* to be written and included among the other books of *Tanach*.[107] That *Megillas Esther* is not grouped together with the other books of *Tanach*, but rather is hidden in *Sefer Shemos*, is fitting because the theme of Esther is also hidden.[108]

Portent for His Descendants

Yaakov endured four major misfortunes during his lifetime:

1. The difficulties he encountered with Eisav
2. Lavan
3. The violation of his daughter Dinah
4. The separation from his beloved son Yosef.

The *Shelah* writes that these four tribulations correspond to the four future exiles:[109]

1. The selling of Yosef corresponds to the Babylonian exile, since the Temple's destruction was an outgrowth of the split between the house of Yosef and the house of Yehudah in the days of King Rechavoam.
2. The adversity with Lavan corresponds to the exile of Paras/Madai: just as Lavan desired to uproot the entire family of Yaakov, so did Haman wish to decimate the entire Jewish nation.
3. The story of Dinah corresponds to the exile of Yavan, since the harshest decree promulgated by the Greeks was directed at the Jewish maidens.[110]
4. Yaakov's encounter with Eisav corresponds to the present exile of Edom, as Edom is another name for Eisav.

---

107 *Rokeach, Shemos* 17:14.
108 See *Chulin* 139b.
109 *Tzon Yosef, parashas Vayeshev–Vayigash* (Oz Vehadar edition), p. 171.
110 See *Kesuvos* 3b.

Personalities in the Megillah

MORDECHAI AND ESTHER

Fragrant Tzadik

"Where is there an allusion to Mordechai in the Torah? As it is written [in the ingredients of the anointment oil], '*mor dror* — pure myrrh,'[111] which the *Targum* translates as *merah dachyah* [which sounds similar to *Mordechai*]."[112] According to the Rambam,[113] *mor* is musk, an odorous glandular secretion from a non-kosher animal. Other *Rishonim* contest this view, since the Torah would not allow a substance from a non-kosher animal to be used in the Temple service, and therefore conclude that *mor* derives from a plant origin.

Commentaries defend the Rambam's view and explain that since the animal substance first deteriorates before it is used, it becomes permissible. In light of this explanation, we can understand the Midrash that expounds the verse, "Who gives forth purity from impurity, if not the One [Hashem]?"[114] to be referring to the righteous Mordechai who descended from the wicked Shimi ben Geirah.[115] Mordechai is analogous to the musk; although the original source is of impure origin, it is able to produce an entirely new pure entity that emits a beautiful fragrance.[116]

---

111   *Shemos* 30:23.
112   *Chulin* 139b.
113   Rambam, *Mishnah Torah*, Klei HaMikdash 2:4.
114   *Iyov* 14:4.
115   *Bamidbar Rabbah* 19:1.
116   Heard from Rabbi Chaim Kaufman.

Freedom for Prophecy

Esther is alluded to in the verse: *"V'anochi haster astir panai bayom hahu — I will surely conceal My face on that day."*[117] The Gemara deduces from the words "on that day" that only prophecy itself, which is comparable to the clarity of daylight, will be concealed from the Jews in exile. However, Hashem will still communicate with the righteous via dreams at night.[118] The Midrash says that Hashem revealed to Mordechai in a dream about Haman's impending decree.

Why did Hashem reveal Himself only to Mordechai in a dream but not to Esther?

The Chasam Sofer explains that the reason Esther was not worthy of receiving a prophetic dream was because she was lacking *simchah* — joy — which is a prerequisite for obtaining a prophetic vision. Although she lived in luxury and comfort, Esther's confinement to the palace dampened her happiness. Mordechai, however, although living a simple existence, was free to go as he pleased; this is an integral component in obtaining happiness.[119] In fact, we can perhaps enhance this with the explanation we just brought about Mordechai's name hinted to in the words *mor dror*. The Ramban says that *mor* is a substance taken from a wild animal that roams free (*dror*).[120] This highlights that it was specifically Mordechai's freedom that elevated his spirit and enabled him to attain prophecy.[121]

Role Reversal

In the beginning of the *Megillah*, we see that the relationship between Mordechai and Esther was that of a teacher to a disciple. We find that Mordechai instructed Esther not to divulge her past to Achashverosh, and exhorted her to go before the king unannounced. However, immediately

---

117 *Devarim* 31:18. See *Chulin* 139b. The word *astir* is similar to the word *Esther*.
118 *Chagigah* 5b.
119 *Chulin* 139b.
120 *Shemos* 30:23.
121 *Chasam Sofer* ibid.

after, their roles reverse, and we find Esther becoming the "teacher" and Mordechai the "student." Esther tells Mordechai to gather the Jews and have them fast on her behalf, and the verse states, "And Mordechai did all that Esther commanded him."[122] In addition, it was Esther who was instrumental in having *Megillas Esther* canonized as a *sefer* in *Tanach*.[123]

What caused this dramatic shift in their relationship?

Rabbi Nosson Wachtfogel explains that in the beginning of the *Megillah*, it is Mordechai who serves Hashem with *mesiras nefesh* by risking his life by refusing to bow to Haman. He therefore merited becoming the "Rebbi" of the Jewish People during that period.[124]

However, at the moment that Esther agreed to risk her life in order to save the Jewish People by coming before the king unannounced, she rose higher than Mordechai, merited prophecy, and became the leader of the Jewish People — to the extent that even Mordechai and the Sanhedrin heeded her requests.[125]

Why Not Megillas Mordechai?

Why is the *Megillah* called *Megillas Esther* and not *Megillas Mordechai*?

The *Megillah* concludes with the words, "and [Mordechai] was accepted by the majority of his brothers,"[126] from which the Sages derive that he was no longer considered the preeminent sage of the generation.[127] This diminished spiritual stature was due to his (albeit necessary) worldly involvement in saving the Jewish People, which detracted from his Torah study. Rabbi Shlomo Brevda writes that the reason the *Megillah* concludes with these words is to highlight the high level of commitment to Torah that generation achieved as a result of the Purim miracle. They reached a level whereby they would

---

122 *Esther* 4:17.
123 Ibid. 9:32.
124 Quoted in *Tehilah L'Yonah*, p. 521.
125 *Tehilah L'Yonah* ibid.
126 *Esther* 10:3.
127 *Megillah* 16b.

not accord the greatest distinction to someone who was not the greatest Torah sage, even if he was the physical savior of the Jewish nation, the one to whom they owed their existence.[128]

Strong, Silent Type

Our Sages say that because Rachel remained silent when she gave over Yaakov's signs to Leah, she merited that the kingship of Yosef (who was the viceroy of Egypt) and of Shaul would descend from her.[129] What is the connection between possessing the quality of silence to becoming a monarch?

A primary quality required of a monarch is inner strength. A person who is able to control his speech is also able to withstand the test of being a monarch, with all the temptations that go with it, and is therefore deserving of monarchy.[130]

In Yosef's dream about the sheaves, it says: "And behold, my sheaf arose and also remained standing; then behold — your sheaves gathered around and bowed down to my sheaf."[131] The Hebrew word for sheaf is אלם, which can also mean "mute." The *Rokeach* writes that the reason Yosef merited to be king over his brethren was in the merit that he made himself as a mute and did not reveal to anyone the secret teachings that his father Yaakov taught him.[132] Perhaps the reason the Torah uses the same word for "sheaf" and "mute" is because the strength required to remain silent is comparable to a strong and unbending sheaf of grain.

The *Rokeach* adds that the words "and also remained standing" allude to Queen Esther. Esther also shared Rachel's trait of silence by not revealing her identity to Achashverosh.[133]

---

128   Rabbi Shlomo Brevda, *Kimu V'kiblu*, p. 151.
129   *Megillah* 13b.
130   See also *Rokeach, Bamidbar* 26:39.
131   *Bereishis* 37:7.
132   *Rokeach, Bereishis* ibid., p. 280.
133   *Esther* 2:20.

"And it was on the third day and Esther donned royalty."[134] The
Zohar notes that the *pasuk* doesn't say that Esther wore *clothes* of
royalty, but rather that she donned royalty itself. This teaches that
as a result of her body becoming weakened from her three-day fast,
she attained an elevated spiritual state that enabled her to receive
ruach HaKodesh, which is termed "royalty." Nevertheless, the specific
merit that made her deserving of the Divine spirit was a result of
her heeding Mordechai's admonition and remaining silent about her
family background. The *Zohar* concludes by saying: "And we learn
from this that whoever guards one's mouth and tongue merits to be
donned with *ruach HaKodesh*."[135]

End of Era of Miracles...

The Gemara asks, "Why is Esther compared to the morning? To
tell you that just as morning is the end of the entire night, so was
the redemption brought by Esther the end of all the miracles."[136] The
Maharshah notes that night is symbolic of exile, while day symbolizes
redemption.[137] Accordingly, why is Esther compared to the morning?
It would seem to make more sense for Esther to be compared to "evening," which comes at the end of the "day" of redemptive miracles.

The Maharshah answers that most miracles in Jewish history occurred at night, as we recite on Seder night: *Az rov nisim
hifleisah balailah* — Then you performed abundant miracles
wondrously at night." Among the miracles enumerated in that
ode is: "The Agagite [Haman] nursed hatred and wrote decrees
at night. You began your triumph over him when You disturbed
[Achashverosh's] sleep at night." Since *Megillas Esther* marks the
end of the era of miracles that were performed at night, she is
therefore compared to the morning.

---

134 *Esther* 5:1.
135 *Chukas* 183b.
136 *Yomah* 29a.
137 Maharshah, *Yomah* ibid.

...Beginning of Era of Greatness

The Jewish People unanimously accepted the Torah on two occasions: first at *Har Sinai* and a second time during the days of Achashverosh.[138] The *Cheishev HaEfod* points out that this does not appear correct, as we find the Jewish People willingly accepted the Torah during the days of Yehoshua as well.[139]

The *Ya'aros Devash* comments that the generations of the wilderness (as well as those of during the First Temple period) often doubted Divine providence.[140] Hashem therefore performed open miracles for them to dispel their doubts. Even so, their righteousness was short-lived, as they quickly forgot the miracles Hashem performed and returned to their former ways.[141] During the time of Achashverosh, the Jewish People came to recognize that Hashem's presence was always with them, even in the natural course of life and history and was not contingent upon their observing open miracles. The reacceptance of the Torah at that juncture was therefore unparalleled to all the earlier acceptances in Jewish history.

YAAKOV AND RACHEL VS. EISAV, AMALEK, AND HAMAN

Yaakov, Eisav, and Haman

The *Rokeach* points out several striking similarities between Eisav and his descendant Haman:[142]

1. Eisav despised (*vayivez*) the birthright,[143] and Haman despised striking Mordechai alone (*vayivez b'einav*).[144] The

---

138 *Shabbos* 88a.
139 *Yehoshua* 24:22. *Cheishev HaEfod*, end of chapter 62.
140 *Ya'aros Devash*, vol. 2, pp. 48–49.
141 See *Tehillim* 106:13.
142 *Rokeach, Bereishis* 25:34, *sha'ar choyver.*
143 *Bereishis* 25:34.
144 *Esther* 3:6.

Midrash states: "'*Bozi ben Bozi* — Despised one son of the despised one; I [Hashem] am unable to destroy the Jewish People,[145] and you think you will succeed in destroying them?' It is comparable to a bird that built its nest at the seashore and a wave came and destroyed it. The bird called out angrily, 'You destroyed my nest, and I will wreak revenge by turning your ocean into dry land.' He began to draw water with his beak and throw it on the shore, when another bird inquired about his bizarre behavior. After the angry bird informed him of his plans, the other bird laughingly replied, 'You poor fool. How can you think you will be successful in your plans?'"[146]

2. The first letters in Eisav's request for the lentil stew — נא מן האדום — spell out the name Haman.[147] This further demonstrates that the source of Eisav's, as well as Haman's wickedness, was their excessive *ta'avah* — desire.

3. Yaakov purchased the birthright from Eisav with bread and drink; Mordechai acquired Haman as his slave with bread,[148] and Haman was hung because of a feast of drink.

4. Yaakov made a feast for Yitzchak on Pesach in order to obtain the blessings. Esther therefore chose the date of Pesach to make a feast for Achashverosh and Haman so that Yitzchak's merit would help in achieving the downfall of Eisav's descendant, Haman.

The *Rokeach* says that when Yaakov prepared to meet his brother Eisav, he foresaw the future clash between his descendants and

---

145 *Tehillim* 106:23.
146 Quoted in *Derashos Ri Even Shoav, parashas Tetzaveh.*
147 *Bereishis* 25:30.
148 *Megillah* 15b.

Eisav's descendant, Haman.[149] The last letters in the words, וילן שם בלילה — "he slept there that night,"[150] spell המן, and Yaakov's fear "lest he (Eisav) come and strike me down, mother and children,"[151] became a reality when Haman plotted to destroy the entire Jewish people. In addition, the word "night" appears three times in that episode. As night is symbolic of hardship, this hints to the three difficult days on which the Jewish People fasted and prayed for deliverance in the days of Mordechai, which culminated with Haman's downfall on the third night.

The *Rokeach* states that in the merit of Yaakov strengthening himself to sit up on his bed when Yosef came to visit him with his children, Haman would meet his downfall as a result of his falling on Esther's bed.[152] What is the connection between these two seemingly disparate events?

Perhaps it is because despite the fact that Yaakov was deathly ill, and both older and spiritually superior to his son, he mustered his last bit of strength to show honor to Yosef. This was because he knew that Eisav would fall by the hands of Yosef,[153] and he was therefore deserving of this great sign of respect.[154] Since Yaakov demonstrated *mesiras nefesh* in his desire to see Amalek's destruction by forcing himself to sit up on his bed, his descendants merited to experience Haman's downfall, which resulted from Haman falling on Esther's bed.

---

149   *Rokeach, Esther* 7:8, and ch. 235.
150   *Bereishis* 32:14.
151   Ibid., v. 12.
152   *Rokeach, Esther* 7:8.
153   Rashi, *Bereishis* 37:1.
154   Rabbi Shlomo Kluger, *Chachmas HaTorah*, p. 291.

Haman the Snake

The *Rabbeinu Ephraim* says that Haman is comparable to the snake of the story of Adam and Chava as they both share numerous salient features:[155]

- There are seventy verses from the beginning of the Torah until the curse of the snake, and there are seventy verses in the *Megillah* between the hangings of Bigsan and Seresh to the hanging of Haman (as stated at the end of *yotzros* for *Parashas Zachor*: "*Tachlis shivim nislah al chamishim* — at the end of seventy [verses], he was hanged on [gallows] fifty [*amos* high]").

- The snake was cursed for speaking *lashon hara* against Hashem. So too, was Haman punished for speaking *lashon hara* to Achashverosh against the Jews.[156]

- Just as the snake brought death to the seventy nations of mankind, so did Haman cause the death of the Jew-haters among the seventy nations by inciting them to battle against the Jews.

- According to one opinion, the Tree of Knowledge was a grapevine. Just as the snake's downfall was a result of the fruits of the vine, so was Haman's downfall brought about through a repast of wine.

- According to another opinion, the Tree of Knowledge was wheat. The Sages say that the roots of a wheat stalk descend fifty cubits;[157] so, too, the vehicle of Haman's downfall was a gallows measuring fifty cubits.

- Perhaps we may add another connection between Haman and the primeval snake. Eisav, and Amalek in particular, are referred to as the empire of זדון — malicious wickedness.[158] The word זדון has the same numerical value as גחון — stomach.

---

155   *Bereishis* 3:11.
156   See *Megillah* 13b.
157   *Yerushalmi, Berachos* 9:2.
158   See *Yalkut Shimoni, Mishlei* 947.

The first mention of "stomach" in the Torah deals with Hashem cursing the snake to travel on its stomach. It was the snake's insatiable desire that led to his punishment of being condemned to slither on his stomach — the organ associated with the desire for food. Similarly, the Sages say that Haman is alluded to in the verse that deals with eating from the forbidden Tree of Knowledge.[159] This demonstrates that Haman's irrepressible desire to harm the Jews was similar to the unrestrained desire of the primeval snake.

Construction via Destruction

Rabbi Aharon Kotler observes that there is a direct correlation between the mitzvos of destroying Amalek and building the Beis HaMikdash. As long as Amalek exists, it clouds the perception of Hashem's presence in this world; therefore, before one can create a space for the Divine presence to rest, one must first vanquish the forces of evil.[160] This is why the blessing of *V'lamalshinim* in *Shemoneh Esrei*, which speaks about the downfall of the wicked, precedes the blessing requesting the rebuilding of Yerushalayim.[161]

Throughout history, we find this principle repeated:

- Before the Mishkan could be built, Moshe first commanded Yehoshua to wage war against Amalak.
- As a prerequisite for the construction of the First Temple, Shaul HaMelech was commanded by the prophet Shmuel to first destroy Amalek.
- In the episode of Purim, as well, Mordechai's victory over Haman was a prelude to the building of the second Beis HaMikdash.

---

159 *Chulin* 139b.
160 *Sanhedrin* 20b.
161 *Mishnas Rebbi Aharon*, vol. 3, pp. 172, 180–181.

Since the tribe of Binyamin played such a crucial role in prelude to the construction of the Beis HaMikdash, as both Shaul and Mordechai descended from Binyamin, the tribe of Binyamin was rewarded in that a section of the Beis HaMikdash was constructed on their territory.[162]

Seeds of Contention

The Midrash states:[163]

> *Whoever says that Hashem is not so particular with his pious ones deserves to have his innards torn out. His forbearance grants long credit, but the debt must eventually be paid. The one cry that Yaakov caused Eisav to make [when Yaakov took Eisav's blessing][164] was eventually repaid in Shushan when Eisav's descendant caused Yaakov's descendant "to cry with a loud and bitter cry."[165]*

Why was Yaakov only punished for causing pain to Eisav? Why wasn't Yaakov also punished for causing his father, Yitzchak, to be filled with dreadful fear because of his taking the blessings through trickery?[166]

The Netziv answers that in regard to his father, Yaakov's deed was performed with entirely pure motives. As such, Yaakov was not penalized for any pain he inadvertently caused his father. However, his feelings towards his brother were not entirely free of tinges of comeuppance, and for that he was punished. (Rabbi Chaim Kanievsky once related this insight and added that only someone of the caliber of the Netziv may attempt to analyze the motivations of the holy *Avos*.)[167]

---

162   Ibid.
163   *Bereishis Rabbah* 67:4.
164   *Bereishis* 27:34.
165   *Esther* 4:1.
166   *Bereishis* 27:33.
167   *Derech Sichah, Bereishis* 27:33.

Welcoming Converts

Why didn't Mordechai hide Esther or send her away so that she would not be taken by Achashverosh?

The *Yaaros Devash* answers that Amalek possesses a redeeming quality that grants him power over the Jews. Amalek's mother, Timna, was a princess who sought to convert to Judaism but was rebuffed by Yaakov. She left and became a concubine of Elifaz, the son of Eisav, saying, "It is better to be a maidservant of this nation than to be a princess to any other nation," and from her, Amalek was born.[168] To rectify this misdeed, it is necessary to welcome converts into Israel. For this reason, Yehoshua, who was entrusted with battling Amalek, saw fit to marry the righteous convert Rachav. Similarly, Mordechai allowed Esther to be taken by Achashverosh so that she may be a positive influence on him and his people — and, as a result of the Purim miracle, many converted to Judaism.[169]

Mistaken Identity

Why didn't Mordechai flee from Shushan to avoid an open confrontation with Haman?

There is a tradition that Eisav can only be defeated through the descendants of Rachel. Since Mordechai descended from the tribe of Binyamin, he knew that he would be able to vanquish Eisav's descendant, Haman. Although Haman was also aware of this axiom, he did not desist from provoking Mordechai, since he mistakenly thought that Mordechai descended from the tribe of Yehudah. His error was a result of Mordechai being commonly known as Mordechai HaYehudi (from the tribe of Yehudah), when in fact the reason for this name was, as the verse goes on to explain,[170] that he had been exiled together with the King of Yehudah and the remnants of that tribe.[171]

---

168   *Sanhedrin* 99b.
169   *Yaaros Devash*, vol. 2, 2, p. 542 (p. 35 in the Machon Even Yisrael edition).
170   *Esther* 2:6.
171   *Yaaros Devash*, vol. 1, 8, p. 262 (vol. 1, p. 239 in the Machon Even Yisrael ed.).

Love Defeats Eisav

What is the rationale for the principle that Eisav can only be defeated through the descendants of Rachel?

Hashem's primary accusation against Eisav is that he wrongfully oppressed his brother Yaakov.[172] The Midrash says that if the sons of Yaakov will call Eisav to task for unjustly persecuting the children of his brother, Eisav has a ready reply: "Are you any better than me? You also unjustly persecuted your brother, Yosef, by selling him into slavery." Yosef will then confront Eisav with the aforementioned claim and Eisav will be unable to respond, for if Eisav will claim that Yaakov is deserving of oppression for the treacherous way Yaakov treated him (by cheating him of his birthright and his father's blessings), Yosef may respond: "My brothers, too, wronged me by selling me into slavery, but I did not take revenge against them. Instead, I repaid their evil with goodness." Immediately, Eisav will fall silent.[173] Although the Midrash singles out Yosef, all Rachel's descendants have similar sufficient merit against Eisav, since they were not involved in the sale of Yosef.[174]

There is another powerful message that can be learned from this insight. The Midrash says that the reason Achashverosh and Haman sat together to feast upon promulgating their decree against the Jews was because Yaakov's children also sat down to eat and drink upon selling their brother, Yosef.[175] The point the Midrash is conveying is that since Eisav's primary flaw was his unjustified persecution of his brother, to the extent that Bnei Yisrael share that same flaw, they lose their moral superiority and become subjugated to the power of Eisav.[176] It is now understandable why specifically Edom destroyed the Second Temple and sent the Jewish nation into exile.

---

172   *Ovadiah* 1:10.
173   *Yalkut Shimoni, Shoftim* 51.
174   *Yaaros Devash* ibid.
175   *Esther Rabbah* 7:25.
176   *Mishnas Rebbi Aharon*, vol. 4, pp. 138–139.

The Temple was destroyed as a result of the sin of baseless hatred for one's fellow Jew. When Israel's behavior mirrors Eisav's, they are given over into his hands.[177]

Rachel and Esther

Rabbeinu Yoel comments that the reason Yaakov especially loved Rachel was because he foresaw through *ruach HaKodesh* that Esther, who would save the Jewish nation, would descend from Rachel. It is therefore not surprising that the verses that describe Yaakov's initial encounter with Rachel contain numerous allusions to Esther:[178]

- Just as Rachel was beautiful and beloved by Yaakov, so was Esther beautiful and beloved by King Achashverosh.
- "Rachel was of beautiful form (יפת תאר)."[179] The numerical value of יפת תאר is equal to that of זה מרדכי היהודי ואסתר המלכה — this is Mordechai the Jew and Queen Esther.
- The reason Yaakov offered to work seven years for Rachel is because he foresaw that Esther would be taken into the palace of Achashverosh in the seventh year of his reign.
- "Rachel, your daughter (רחל בתך),"[180] has the same numerical value as Esther (אסתר).
- "Lavan said, 'It is better that I give her to you than I give her to another man.'"[181] This hints that Rachel's descendant, Esther, would not fall in the hands of another "man," which is an allusion to Haman.[182]

---

177   Rabbi Yisroel Greenwald.
178   *Rimzei Rabbeinu Yoel*, Bereishis 29:17–18.
179   *Bereishis* 29:17.
180   Ibid., v. 18.
181   Ibid., v. 19.
182   *Esther* 7:6; *Megillah* 12a.

Insights on Megillas Esther

THE FEAST

Cheap Atonement

"When he displayed the riches of his glorious kingdom."[183] This teaches that Achashverosh donned the garments of the *Kohen Gadol*.[184]

The *Kli Yakar* comments that Achashverosh's intention in wearing the clothing of the *Kohen Gadol* during the feast was because he was cognizant of how the clothing of the *Kohen Gadol* achieves atonement for eight cardinal sins,[185] and thus he wished that the clothing would atone for his personal sins as well. In addition, he named his advisors during the feast after the various Temple offerings to achieve the same result. His plan backfired, however, as the angels of mercy argued before Hashem that his fantastical intentions were merely flights of fancy, and unlike the Jewish nation he did not offer any concrete service to Hashem.[186]

Clothing Doesn't Make the Man

The Gemara expounds the names of Achashverosh's advisors to refer to aspects of the Temple service, which Achashverosh and his cohorts lacked. Regarding Tarshish, the Gemara says: "Said the

---

183   *Esther* 1:4.
184   *Megillah* 12a.
185   *Erachin* 16a.
186   *Kli Yakar, Shemos* 28:39. See *Megillah* 12b.

ministering angels before the Holy One, Blessed be He, 'Did they ever minister you with priestly garments, [of which one of the stones of the breastplate was] Tarshish?'"[187]

Why was this particular stone singled out for mention? According to the *Targum Yerushalmi*,[188] Tarshish was the stone that corresponded to the tribe of Asher. The daughters of Asher were extremely beautiful, as well as modest, and were therefore worthy of marrying the *Kohen Gadol*. This contrasted the actions of Achashverosh, who despite actually wearing the breastplate of the *Kohen Gadol* during his party, behaved immodestly by requesting Vashti to appear before him unclothed.[189]

The "Great" Guest

The Midrash expounds the verse, "Avraham made a 'great feast' (*mishteh gadol*) on the day Yitzchak was weaned,"[190] to mean that *Gadol Olamim* — the "Great One of all Worlds" (i.e., Hashem) was present. The Midrash similarly expounds the verse in *Megillas Esther*, "And the king made a 'great feast' (*mishteh gadol*),"[191] saying that at Achashverosh's feast Hashem was also present and was as joyous there as He was during the feast during the time of Avraham and Yitzchak.[192]

The *Binyan Shlomo* explains that the reason Hashem was so joyous at Achashverosh's feast is because the feast led to Esther being taken by Achashverosh, which in turn resulted in the salvation of the descendants of Avraham and Yitzchak — i.e., the entire Jewish nation.[193]

---

187 *Shemos* 28:20; *Megillah* 12b.
188 On *Shemos* 28:20.
189 *Meshech Chochmah, Shemos* 28:20.
190 *Bereishis* 21:8.
191 *Esther* 2:18.
192 *Bereishis Rabbah* 53.
193 *Binyan Shlomo*, vol. 2, p. 562. This insight is truly amazing. Although the feast caused the Jews to sin, which in turn led to Haman's decree, we see that Hashem can be simultaneously happy about an eventual positive outcome, even while angry at the sins

Unsavory Feast

The Gemara says that the sin that brought about Haman's decree was that the Jews partook of (literally, "for deriving pleasure from") Achashverosh's feast.[194] Why were they so severely punished when refusing the king's invitation would have put their lives in danger, since Achashverosh threatened death to all who didn't attend?

- Some say that they were not punished for partaking, but rather for *enjoying* the compulsory feast.
- The *Sifsei Chachamim* answers that since one of the purposes of the feast was to celebrate Achashverosh's erroneous calculation that Yirmiyah's prophecy regarding the rebuilding of the Beis HaMikdash was unfulfilled, their attendance at the feast demonstrated a lack of belief in the redemption.[195]
- The *Ya'aros Devash* says that their sin was that they drank non-Jewish wine and ate food cooked by gentiles, which, although is permissible according to the Torah, was prohibited by Rabbinic decree.[196]

His Wife Was a Cow

The Midrash relates a story about a pious Jew who sold his cow to a Persian gentile. The following week, the gentile returned to the seller and complained that his cow refused to do any work on Saturday. The Jew understood that the cow's peculiar behavior was a result of it having become accustomed to not working on Shabbos when it was owned by the Jew. The Jew whispered into the ear of the cow, "While I owned you, you were prohibited from doing work on Shabbos, but now that your owner is a non-Jew, it is permissible for you to work." The cow immediately stood up and began plowing the

---

Israel is presently commiting.

194   *Megillah* 12a.

195   Rabbi Avraham Herzl, *Sifsei Chachamim* to *Megillah* ibid.

196   *Ya'aros Devash*, 3, Adar 7, p. 86.

gentile's field. The gentile was very moved by the sight of his "pious" cow and said to himself, "If a cow that cannot talk or think is able to recognize its Creator, I, who am created in the image of my Maker, all the more so!"[197]

The gentile converted to Judaism and became known as Rabbi Chanina ben Torosa (the son of the cow). The *Rama M'Panu* reveals that the cow was a reincarnation of Vashti, who was punished in this manner for forcing the Jewish maidens to work on Shabbos, and the Persian convert was a reincarnation of Achashverosh.[198] Through this episode, they both achieved their rectification.

SEARCH FOR A NEW QUEEN

Quest for Inner Beauty

According to Rabbi Yehoshua ben Levi, Iyov lived during the days of Achashverosh and his daughter was the most beautiful woman in her generation.[199] If so, asks the Maharshah, why was Iyov's daughter not taken by Achashverosh? The *Iyun Yaakov* answers that Rabbi Yehoshua ben Levi is consistent with his reasoning in that he is of the opinion that Esther was not inherently beautiful. On the contrary, she had a green complexion and was beautiful in virtue of "a thread of grace that was drawn upon her." One may ask, what compelled Rabbi Yehoshua ben Levi to think that Esther was not physically beautiful? The answer is that were Achashverosh to choose a queen based on physical beauty alone, he would have chosen the daughter of Iyov.[200]

Sarah-Esther Connection

"Why did Esther merit ruling over 127 provinces? Said Hashem, 'Let Esther come, the descendant of Sarah who lived for 127 years,

---

197   *Pesikta Rabasi* 14.
198   *Rama M'Panu, Gilgulei Neshamos, Vav.*
199   *Bava Basra* 15b.
200   Rabbi Yaakov Reisher, *Iyun Yaakov,* ibid.

and rule over 127 provinces.'"[201] The *Be'er Yosef* comments that the reason the Midrash equates Esther with Sarah is because they both shared the same qualities:[202]

- Sarah was extremely modest,[203] and so was Esther.[204]
- Just as Sarah did not become vain despite her extraordinary beauty and instead focused on her spiritual essence and thus merited to become a prophetess, so did Esther.
- The *Rokeach* cites another connection between Sarah and Esther in that both went to the king's palace, but each nonetheless maintained her moral integrity.[205]

THE ASSASSINATION PLOT

For Redemption's Sake

The Gemara states that whoever reports something in the name of the one who said it brings redemption to the world. The Gemara derives this from Esther's behavior of crediting Mordechai with uncovering the assassination plot against the king.[206]

How can we derive the correct way to act from Esther's behavior? Perhaps Esther's sole intention of informing the king of Mordechai's role was in order that he find favor by the king and be handsomely rewarded as a result.

The Chasam Sofer answers that since it is not advisable to be overly familiar with the government,[207] Mordechai had no desire to court the king's favor. (Indeed, Mordechai's spiritual stature declined after

---

201 *Bereishis Rabbah* 58:3.
202 Rabbi Yosef Salant, *Be'er Yosef*, end of *sefer Shemos*.
203 *Bava Metzia* 87a.
204 *Targum Rishon*, Esther 2:7.
205 *Rokeach*, *Bereishis* 23:1.
206 *Megillah* 15a.
207 See *Avos* 1:10.

he was appointed as the king's prime minister.)[208] The only reason why Esther informed the king of the plot in Mordechai's name was solely because it was a great mitzvah to do so — and this overrode all other considerations.[209]

Redemptions Great and Small

"Whoever relates a saying in the name of the one who said it brings redemption to the world, as it states, 'And Esther said to the king in the name of Mordechai.'"[210]

The *She'arim Metzuyanim B'Halachah* asks: Many people have been careful to attribute sayings to their sources, and yet the redemption still has not come! What did *Chazal* therefore mean?

He quotes the Chozeh M'Lublin, who says that the Sages did not necessarily mean that this trait will automatically bring the *ultimate* redemption. Rather, the redemption may be a personal one or for one's individual community. This is why the blessing in *Shemoneh Esrei* concludes with the present tense, "the One Who Redeems Israel," even though we are still in exile. This is because this praise refers to Hashem's constant deliverance of the Jewish People, and not necessarily the final redemption.[211]

HAMAN'S LOTS

The Power of Lots

The *Geonei Kadmonai* write that a *goral* — lottery — that is done correctly has Divine significance, and a person who transgresses a lottery is as if he transgressed the *Aseres HaDibros*.[212] The *Chavos Yair* adds that even non-Jews were aware that a lottery is under Divine

---

208   *Megillah* 16b.

209   *Chasam Sofer, Megillah* 15a.

210   *Esther* 2:22; *Megillah* 15a.

211   Rabbi Shlomo Zalman Braun, *She'arim Metzuyanim B'Halachah, Megillah* 15a. See Rashi, *Megillah* 17a, s.v. *"milchamah."*

212   *Geonei Kadmoai* 60.

providence and cites Haman casting lots as an example. (He also brings proof from the story of Yonah, in which the Gentile sailors drew lots to determine the person responsible for the storm that endangered their ship.)[213]

Adar the Thirteenth

Haman planned to kill the Jews on the thirteenth of Adar. The reason why this day was a particularly auspicious day to destroy the Jews is because the majority of the Jewish population in Egypt died on this specific day. During the plague of darkness, the Jews who did not believe in the redemption perished. The *Rabbeinu Ephraim* writes that all those deaths occurred on the thirteenth of Adar. He explains that this is why we fast on this day — to commemorate their deaths and to cry about this tragic event.[214]

The *Rokeach* adds that although Haman was aware of the tragedies that befell the Jews on this day, he was unaware that on this very same day, during the plague of darkness, there was light in all the Jewish homes.[215] This miraculous light, which gave them the ability to see things that were concealed in barrels and chests,[216] demonstrated that Hashem's loving presence was with them even during this period of darkness and sadness.

HAMAN'S PLOT

Finding a Fifty-Amos Gallows

Haman built the gallows for Mordechai from a beam that was fifty *amos* high. From where did Haman obtain such a large wooden beam?

---

213   *Chavos Yair* 61. See, however, *Sefer Chasidim* 679 and 701 as to under what circumstances casting lots is permissible.
214   *Rabbeinu Ephraim, Shemos* 10:22.
215   *Rokeach, Shemos* 10:23.
216   See *Shemos Rabbah* 14:3.

According to the *Yalkut*, one of Haman's sons governed the area of Mount Ararat, the place where Noach's ark had grounded, and provided his father with a beam from Noach's ark, which was fifty *amos* long.[217] According to the *Pirkei D'Rebbi Eliezer*, Haman seized the beam from a wall of the Holy of Holies (which was fifty *amos* high) after the destruction of the First Temple.[218] Haman first built the beam into his own home and afterwards removed it in order to hang Mordechai on it.[219]

THE PLAN TO SAVE THE JEWS

The Right to Exist

Mordechai warned Esther that if she would refuse to go before the king at this opportune time, salvation would come to the Jewish People from another source, but she and her father's household [the tribe of Binyamin] would be destroyed. The question arises: if Esther would be at fault for refusing to come before the king, why should other members of her tribe deserve to be punished so severely?

Rabbi Aharon Kotler answers that only descendants of Rachel are capable of destroying Amalek.[220] At this crucial moment in history, Esther was given the ability to accomplish this task. Were she to decline and not accept her mission, then she and her entire tribe would lose the justification for their existence.[221]

Deliverance from "Another Place"

One of the names of Hashem is *Makom*, which literally means "the Place." This appellation expresses that Hashem's presence is everywhere and He reveals Himself in the most unexpected and unnatural

---

217 *Yalkut Shimoni, Esther* 1:056.
218 *Pirkei D'Rebbi Eliezer*, chap. 3.
219 *Binyan Shlomo*, vol. 2, 26:2.
220 *Bereishis Rabbah* 73:7.
221 *Mishnas Rebbi Aharon*, vol. 4, pp. 136–139.

manner, even in the darkest and most difficult periods of His concealment (*hester panim*). This explains why Mordechai told Esther, "Relief and deliverance will come to the Jews *mimakom acher*" (lit. "from another place").[222] This means that from the place of Amalek's dominion, which superficially appears out of the realm of Hashem's control, Hashem will arise and miraculously demonstrate His complete sovereignty by saving the Jews.[223]

Angelic Assistance

When Esther appeared unannounced before Achashverosh, she cried to Hashem: "I am a worm and not a man,"[224] which the *Yalkut* explains as meaning that she said, "I am not a man, but rather a woman. Woe to the generation whose leader is a woman."[225] What difference does it make whether the salvation is brought about by a man or woman?

The Chasam Sofer explains that "a man" refers specifically to Moshe,[226] who was so great that he was able to be a direct emissary between Hashem and the Jewish People and therefore spurned all angelic assistance. Esther's salvation, on the other hand, came through a concealment of Divine Providence, which necessitated Heavenly emissaries to come to her aid. The name of the angel who "cloaked" Esther to assist her in her mission was אכתריא-ל. The Gemara expounds the verse, "For an everlasting sign that shall not be cut off (לא יכרת)," as referring to the festival of Purim.[227] The letters לא יכרת spell the name of this angel and have the same numerical value as אסתר.[228]

---

222   *Esther* 4:14.
223   *Hararei Kedem*, vol. 2, p. 215.
224   *Tehillim* 22:7.
225   *Yalkut Shimoni, Tehillim* ibid.
226   *Bamidbar* 12:3.
227   *Megillah* 10b.
228   *Chasam Sofer, Vayikra*, p. 137.

Slightly Tipping the Scales

One of the reasons Esther invited Haman to her banquet was to arouse Divine mercy when Hashem saw how she had to demean herself by flattering the wicked Haman.[229] Israel's situation at that time was so precarious that the nation's prayers and fasting, the combined merits of Mordechai and Esther, and the heavenly efforts of the three *Avos* with Moshe Rabbeinu may have all been insufficient to rescind Haman's evil decree. Would, then, an insignificant slight to Esther's honor be sufficient to tip the scales to save the Jews?

From this episode, Rabbi Chaim Shmulevitz derives how Hashem's judgment takes even the minutest details into consideration. If the impending annihilation would cause even one individual to receive a minor, undeserved slight to his honor, that would be enough of a reason for Hashem to avert a potential national catastrophe.[230]

THE NATION REPENTS

A Nation of Heroes

One of the minor personalities in the Purim story is Hasach, who faithfully relayed messages between Mordechai and Esther. *Chazal* say that Hasach was actually the famous Daniel, who was called Hasach "because his greatness was cut down" (התך is related to the Hebrew word, חתך, which means "cut").[231]

Daniel's greatness is immortalized in the book of Daniel for his willingness to sacrifice his life and be thrown in a lion's den to fulfill the Rabbinic ordinance of praying three times a day. During the episode of the Purim story, there was a dramatic arousal of repentance among the entire populace. The Jews fasted for three days, studied Torah, and reaccepted the Torah upon themselves in an unparalleled

---

229 Rashi, *Megillah* 15b.

230 Rabbi Chaim Shmuelevitz, *Chachmas Chaim*, p. 192.

231 *Megillah* 15a.

manner. The point of the Sages' statement was not that Daniel's personal greatness was diminished, but rather that the greatness of the entire nation became so elevated that Daniel no longer stood out as a unique role model for the nation.[232]

Three-Day Fast

"Go gather for me all the Jews that are found in Shushan, and fast for me...for three days, day and night."[233] The Midrash asks how it was humanly possible for them to fast for three days and not die from starvation, and answers that on the first day they only fasted for one hour before nightfall, the second day they fasted the entire day, and on the third day they only fasted for one hour into the day. The Chasam Sofer brings a proof from this that a *taanis sha'os* — a fast for only several hours — is considered a proper fast.[234]

The *Teshuvos Rivosh* points out that this Midrash is contradicted by the Gemara that derives from the above verse that it is humanly possible for a person to fast for three consecutive days and that was, in fact, what Ester commanded the inhabitants of Shushan to do.[235]

Mourning a Life Lost

During the time of Haman, the Jews' repentance consisted of "fasting and weeping and eulogy."[236] Fasting and weeping are self-explanatory, but what do eulogies have to do with repentance? Furthermore, a eulogy is said over someone who is dead and gone, but they were still alive!

Rabbi Isser Zalman Meltzer answers that the eulogies were for the precious days that had gone to waste — i.e., days without Torah and mitzvos — and were gone forever.[237]

---

232 *Meshech Chochmah, Esther* 4:5.
233 *Esther* 4:16.
234 *Chasam Sofer, Avodah Zarah* 34a, s.v. *"b'mah shimeish."*
235 *Yevamos* 121b, *Teshuvos Rivosh* 416.
236 *Esther* 4:3.
237 Rabbi Isser Zalman Meltzer, as quoted in *The Rosh Yeshivah Remembers,* p. 264.

HAMAN'S MIDNIGHT MEETING WITH THE KING

A Night of Miracles

"On that night, the sleep of the king was disturbed."[238] The Midrash says that the reason the *pasuk* emphasizes "that night" was because numerous miracles for the Jewish People occurred on that specific night. As the *Targum* explains, that night fell out on the first night of Pesach, which is the night Hashem smote the firstborn in Egypt. This raises a contradiction, since the *Targum* comments on an earlier verse, "And it was on the third day,"[239] that the third day occurred on the third day of Pesach. The Radvaz answers that both calculations are correct; while according to the lunar year it was several days into Pesach, according to the solar year it was the night the firstborn of the Egyptians were killed.[240]

To Arouse a Sleeping Ruler

"And Haman said to King Achashverosh, '*Yeshno am echad* — There is one nation.'"[241] The Midrash interprets this as, "Hashem Who is One, is sleeping [and is no longer protecting His] nation."[242] (*Yeshno* is akin to the word *sheinah* — sleep). Hashem responded, "You claim that I who never sleeps and slumbers [from] protecting Israel is sleeping! By your life, I will appear that I am arising from slumber in order to destroy you."

Where do we find that Hashem (figuratively) arose from His slumber to kill Haman?

The *pasuk* says: "That night the sleep of the king was disturbed."[243] The Gemara expounds this to mean that the sleep of the King of the universe was disturbed.[244] This can be understood to mean that

---

238   *Esther* 6:1.
239   Ibid. 5:1.
240   Radvaz 2:818.
241   *Esther* 3:8.
242   *Esther Rabbah* 7:12.
243   *Esther* 6:1.
244   *Megillah* 15b.

the pivotal, miraculous events of that night, which ultimately led to the death of Haman, made the events of the earlier nights look, G-d forbid, as if Hashem was sleeping.

Miracle behind the Madness

Haman came to Achashverosh in the middle of the night to request permission to hang Mordechai on the gallows that he had built. It seems absurd, even for a minister of Haman's stature, to file such a request with the king after the king has retired for the night — particularly a king whose own queen is afraid that her improper entry in the king's chambers may have cost her her life. In addition, Haman's wife also advised him that his request should wait until the morning. For an otherwise shrewd and calculating person such as Haman to behave in such an insane and impulsive manner is another example of Hashem's hidden miracles to save the Jewish People at that time.

Name-Dropping

When Achashverosh was reminded that Mordechai saved his life, he asked his pages what reward was bestowed upon Mordechai. They answered the king, "Nothing has been done for him."[245]

On this, the Sages comment that they did not say this out of their love for Mordechai but out of their hatred for Haman.[246] How did *Chazal* know this?

The *Chidah* answers that when one likes a person, he takes pleasure in saying his name,[247] and the opposite holds true for a person one hates. Since the pages could have answered, "Nothing has been done for Mordechai" and instead referred to him in the pronoun form, this demonstrated their disregard for Mordechai.[248]

---

245 *Esther* 6:3.
246 *Megillah* 16a.
247 See *Yirmiyah* 31:19.
248 Cited in *She'arim Metzuyanim B'Halachah, Megillah* ibid.

HAMAN'S DOWNFALL

Falling into the Hands of Yehudah

Zeresh told Haman that if Mordechai descended from the tribes of Ephraim, Menashe, Binyamin, or Yehudah, he would not be able to prevail against Mordechai.[249] It is understandable why Zeresh feared the tribes of Ephraim and Menashe, for the Sages say that the offspring of Eisav will not be delivered into the hands of anyone but the offspring of Rachel.[250] But why was she concerned if Mordechai descended from the tribe of Yehudah?

Rabbi Aharon Kotler answers that the tribe of Yehudah also shares a role in the destruction of Amalek. The offspring of Rachel start the initial strike against Amalek, while afterwards the tribe of Yehudah succeeds in delivering the final blow. Yaakov blessed Yehudah, saying, "Your hand will be on the back of the neck of your enemies."[251] This means that after your brothers begin routing your enemies, you will succeed in pursuing them to annihilate them. As the Sages state, the reason Dovid was successful in smiting Amalek was because his officers on the front were from the tribe of Menashe.[252] This is why Zeresh told Haman, "If Mordechai, before whom you have begun to fall, is of the tribe of Yehudah, you will not prevail against him."[253] Since Haman had started to fall, the tribe of Yehudah would succeed in completing his downfall.[254]

Dirty Mourner

"Haman hurried home, mourning and with his head covered (with refuse)."[255] *Chazal* explain that when Haman's daughter realized

---

249   *Megillah* 16a.
250   *Midrash Tanchumah, parashas Vayechi.*
251   *Bereishis* 49:8.
252   *Shmuel I*, 30:17. See *Bava Basra* 123b.
253   *Esther* 6:13.
254   *Mishnas Rebbi Aharon* vol. 3, pp. 172, 180–181, citing *Amudei Ohr* 121:1.
255   *Esther* 6:12.

that she accidentally threw the contents of a chamber pot over her father's head, she fell out the window and died. If so, the order of the *pasuk* should have been reversed, "with his head covered and mourning," since that was the sequence of events.

Rabbi Chaim Shmulevitz answers, in the name of his father, that the Gemara discusses an opinion that states that when a vessel falls off a roof, it is considered as if it was already broken from the moment it begins its descent.[256] Therefore, although Haman's daughter fell out the window after having thrown the garbage, if the beginning of her descent was before the contents actually reached her father, at that moment she would be considered halachically dead and Haman would have been a mourner even before becoming dirty.

To answer this question using a more basic approach, we may say that the sequence is based on significance — that losing his daughter was far more tragic than becoming soiled.

A Fitting End

It is ironic that Hashem orchestrated Haman's downfall under false pretenses. Haman never intended to fall on Esther's bed or to harm her in any way. Similarly, Charvonah's statement insinuating that Haman intended the gallows for Achashverosh was also entirely untrue.

The Vilna Gaon says that this is how Hashem operates. If a person is straight and honest, Hashem punishes him in a straightforward manner as well. Since Haman utilized slanderous lies to convince Achashverosh to kill the Jews,[257] so did Hashem devise that his own demise should transpire in an unfounded manner as well.[258]

---

256 *Bava Kama* 17b.
257 *Megillah* 13b.
258 Rabbi Shlomo Brevda, *Kimu V'kiblu*, pp. 109–110; *Tehillim* 18:27.

Who Was Charvonah?

"And Charvonah, too, be remembered for good."[259] Who was Charvonah, and why should he be remembered for good?

- Charvonah was originally one of Haman's cronies, but upon seeing Haman fall into disfavor in the eyes of the king, he quickly switched allegiance to Mordechai. The *Sefer Chasidim* derives from this event that when one mentions a favorable deed a non-Jew performed on behalf of a Jew, he should add *zichronah livrachah* — may his name be remembered for blessing.[260]
- According to some opinions,[261] Eliyahu Hanavi appeared in the guise of Charvonah to intercede on behalf of the Jews. Rabbi Reuven Margolis suggests that the reason we always mention Eliyahu's name for the good[262] is because of a specific episode that transpired during his lifetime. When the son of the widow in whose home Eliyahu lodged became deathly ill, she said to the prophet, "Why have you come to me to *cause my sins to be remembered* [in Heaven], and cause my son to die?"[263] Since in that particular story Eliyahu was faulted for arousing strict justice, we therefore pray that Eliyahu's memory be remembered only for the good.[264]

Haman's Eternal Merit

The Talmud records that the descendants of Haman studied Torah in Bnei Brak.[265] In what merit did the despicable archenemy of the Jewish People merit such great distinction?

---

259 From *Shoshanas Yaakov*, sung at the end of the *Megillah* reading.
260 *Sefer Chasidim* 746.
261 *Esther Rabbah* 10:9.
262 *Berachos* 3a and elsewhere.
263 *Melachim* I, 17:18.
264 Rabbi Reuven Margolis, *Mekor Chesed; Sefer Chasidim* 746.
265 *Gittin* 57b.

- Rabbi Chaim Pinchas Scheinberg answers that although he was thoroughly wicked, he once proclaimed his recognition of Divine providence when forced to lead Mordechai on horseback.[266] In the merit of becoming momentarily aware that his success and suffering lay in the hands of Hashem, he was worthy of having such noble descendants.

- Rabbi Yaakov Kamenetsky derives a remarkable principle from this Talmudic statement: a person is rewarded for generating a *kiddush Hashem* irrespective of his personal motives. Since Haman's miraculous downfall resulted in a great sanctification of Hashem's honor, that alone deserves tremendous reward.[267] The Alter from Kelm draws a corollary to this lesson: if Hashem rewards so greatly even a despicable individual as Haman for the *kiddush Hashem* that resulted against his will, all the more so will Hashem infinitely reward a person who willingly strives to sanctify the Name of Hashem.[268]

THE NATION IS SAVED

Reprogramming the Prosecutor

The Gemara relates that when Haman came to dress Mordechai in the king's robes and ride the king's horse, Haman found him learning the sacrificial laws of *kemitzah* with his students.[269] The Chofetz Chaim asks that since Mordechai was aware that Haman was out to kill him, shouldn't he have attempted to flee rather than to publicly study the laws of *korbanos* at that time?

Based on the *Zohar*, he explains that someone who learns the laws of *korbanos* with the proper intentions (i.e., that the study of the *korban*

---

266   *Esther Rabbah* 10:4.

267   *Emes L'Yaakov, Bereishis* 27:40.

268   In a letter to Baron Rothschild, printed in *Chochmah U'Mussar* 2, p. 345.

269   *Megillah* 13b.

should atone for the sins that *korban* rectified), even the prosecuting angels are unable to harm him but rather do him only good.[270] Haman was akin to a prosecuting angel, for as the Gemara says, no one knew how to find fault against others as expertly as Haman.[271] Mordechai's study was indeed effective, for precisely at the time of his study of *kemitzah*, Haman was compelled to go serve and honor Mordechai.[272]

The Ludicrous Law

When Achashverosh accepted Esther's supplication to save her people, he granted the Jews the right to defend themselves against their enemies. This edict seems ludicrous, for even if it were illegal to defend oneself, only a fool would abide by such a law. Since the enactment would not provide the Jews with any concrete military advantage, what did Mordechai and Esther hope to accomplish with this decree?

The Ibn Ezra answers that Mordechai's objective in sending the second letters was to give the impression that the king originally instructed Haman to issue a decree allowing the Jews to kill their enemies. Otherwise, why would the king issue a second decree diametrically opposed to his first? The populace would therefore draw the conclusion that it was Haman, due to his hatred for the Jews, who inverted the king's decree without authorization. People would then assume that Haman's punishment of hanging was due to his tampering with the king's edict.[273]

Eradicating Amalek's Possessions

The mitzvah to destroy Amalek applies not only to the members of the nation but extends to their property as well. If so, how was it possible for Mordechai to accept the house of Haman after he was killed, since he was a descendant of Amalek?

---

270 Chofetz Chaim, *Torah Ohr* 3.
271 *Megilah* 13b.
272 *Torah Ohr* ibid.
273 Ibn Ezra, *Esther* 8:8.

The *Oneg Yom Tov* explains that the mitzvah to destroy the property of Amalek is given so that we will eradicate the last vestiges of that nation, so people shouldn't be able to point and say that "this ox belonged to an Amaleki." Therefore, until the nation of Amalek is totally wiped out, it would be futile to destroy their property. Since at the time of *Megillas Esther* there were survivors of Amalek still extant, the mitzvah to destroy their property did not yet apply.[274]

Lesson of Restraint

"And to the booty they did not stretch forth their hands."[275] Why didn't the Jews seize the booty of their enemies? The *Rokeach* says that they learned this from the behavior of their forefathers in Egypt, who did not take any of the Egyptian's property during the plague of darkness.[276]

THE HANGING OF HAMAN'S TEN SONS

Ten as One

"*Aseres Bnei Haman* — The ten sons of Haman."[277] The *Rokeach* says that while the Hebrew words *asarah* and *aseres* both mean "ten," the difference between them is that *asarah* denotes separate entities that add up to that particular number, whereas *aseres* is used to express a single unit, as in the *Aseres Yemei Teshuvah* — the Ten Days of Repentance.[278] Why then does it say **aseres** *b'nei Haman* rather than **asarah**? The *Rokeach* answers that they were considered a unit in the manner they died — namely, that they expired *b'neshimah achas*, i.e., in (the timespan of) one breath.

---

274   Rabbi Raphael Yom Tov Lipman, *Oneg Yom Tov, Derush L'parashas Zachor*.

275   *Esther* 9:15–16.

276   *Rokeach, Shemos* 10:22.

277   *Esther* 9:10.

278   *Rokeach, Vayikra* 27:1.

A UNIQUE FESTIVAL

First of All Festivals

"As the first (lit. 'head') of all festivals, You elevated Pesach."[1] Why is Pesach considered the "head" of all the festivals? We may suggest that just as the head encapsulates the essence of a person, so are all the festivals included in the "head" festival, namely Pesach. Shavous was the culmination of the exodus from Egypt, Sukkos was the result of leaving Egypt, and Rosh Hashanah and Yom Kippur materialize the lessons of reward and punishment that were learned at *Yetzias Mitzrayim*. For this reason, all festivals are considered *zecher l'yetzias Mitzrayim* — in remembrance of the exodus from Egypt.

Name of the Festival

Why do we call the festival Pesach, when the Torah refers to it as *Chag HaMatzos* — the Festival of Matzos?

The song of *Shir HaShirim* describes the reciprocal loving relationship between Hashem and *Bnei Yisrael*. In it, *Bnei Yisrael*

---

1   From the Seder night liturgy, *Ve'amartem Zevach Pesach*.

focuses on Hashem's superlative qualities, and Hashem in turn focuses on ours. We therefore call the Yom Tov after what Hashem does for us while the Torah names it after what we do for Him. We call the festival "*Pesach*" to recall how Hashem had mercy on us by skipping over our houses while killing the Egyptian firstborn. The Torah, on the other hand, calls the festival *Chag HaMatzos* to recall how the *Bnei Yisrael* quickly left Egypt without preparing any proper provisions.[2]

Rendezvous with the Master

"Three times during the year shall all your males appear before the Master, Hashem."[3] Why does the Torah refer to Hashem as the "Master," specifically in respect to the mitzvah of *oleh regel* — making the pilgrimage to the Beis HaMikdash three times a year?

The *Oznayim L'Torah* explains that the three pilgrimage festivals are *zecher l'Yetzias Mitzrayim* — a reminder of the Exodus from Egypt. Since Hashem released us from the servitude of Pharaoh to become servants of Hashem, we demonstrate our subordination to Hashem and our recognition that He is our Master at these particular times.[4]

Naturally Joyous

Why doesn't the Torah give a mitzvah to be happy and to gladden the poor on Pesach as it does on the other festivals? Rabbi Moshe Feinstein explains that an explicit command is unnecessary for Pesach, since even without an obligation we would naturally rejoice on Pesach since it is the time of our freedom and the beginning of our nationhood. We also experienced on Pesach the way Hashem lowered the mighty Egyptians while simultaneously elevating the poor, downtrodden children of Israel. It would therefore be superfluous to

---

2   Rabbi Shimshon Chasid, *Tosfos Chadashim*, *Pesachim* 1:1.
3   *Shemos* 23:17.
4   *Oznayim L'Torah*, *Shemos* ibid.

command us to care for the poor on Pesach, since it is obvious that wealth and power are meaningless unless used to help the needy — and one would be embarrassed to act otherwise at this time.[5]

Erev Pesach

Why does the Torah include the day before Pesach in its list of festival days?[6] The Vilna Gaon explains that since the Pesach sacrifice was brought on this day, it is considered a day of joy on par with the intermediary days of the festival.[7] For this reason, a mourner may cut his hair on Erev Pesach, since it is already considered the onset of the festival during which the laws of mourning do not apply.

First Night of Pesach

In the *Haggadah*, we say: *"Ta'ir k'or yom cheshchas laylah* — The darkness of the night will illuminate like the light of day." This was originally fulfilled during the night of *Yetzias Mitzrayim* when the clarity of Hashem's power was illuminated so brightly that the night was comparable to the day. This unique aspect of Pesach explains several anomalies:

- We can now understand why *Bnei Yisrael* performed *bris milah* the night of *Yetzias Mitzrayim* (in order to be able to partake of the *Korban Pesach*), even though in general *bris milah* should be performed during the day.
- Also, *korbanos* are generally primarily eaten during the day, with the exception of the *Korban Pesach*, which is eaten only at night.
- Finally, we generally recite *Hallel* only during the day, with the exception of the *Hallel* recited on the first nights of Pesach.

---

5   Rabbi Moshe Feinstein, *Derash Moshe*, p. 80.
6   *Vayikra* 23.
7   *Biur HaGra, Yoreh Deah* 399:9; see also *Ha'amek Shailah* 171:10.

The reason for all these exceptions is that the night of *Yetzias Mitzrayim* is considered to be like day.

The Chizkuni says that Yitzchak wanted to bless Eisav specifically on the first night of Pesach since the celestial beings sing a special *shirah* at this time and the heavenly storage houses of dew are also opened.[8] Therefore, this is an auspicious time for a person's blessing to take effect.

Last Day of Pesach

The last day of the Sukkos and Pesach festival are both called *Atzeres*,[9] which literally means "gathering in." On the last day of Sukkos, we are meant to absorb the lessons of the festival to maintain a level of holiness before returning to everyday life, and we are to utilize the last day of Pesach to reflect on the lessons of Pesach to cleave to Hashem with love. For this reason, Shlomo HaMelech would publicly read *Koheles* on Sukkos, which discusses the vanity of materialism, and *Shir HaShirim* on Pesach, which bespeaks of our love of Hashem, in order to arouse the assembled with the particular message of each Yom Tov.[10]

CHAMETZ AND MATZAH

The Strict Prohibition

Why is the Torah so strict regarding *chametz* on Pesach that it must be totally eliminated from one's home? Ordinarily, foods that are forbidden to be consumed — even those carrying the penalty of *kares*, such as blood and forbidden fats — are permitted to remain in one's possession. The Vilna Gaon answers that since *chametz* may

---

8   *Bereishis* 27:4.

9   *Vayikra* 23:36; *Devarim* 16:8.

10   Rabbi Naftali Tzvi Yehudah Berlin, *Ha'amek Davar, Devarim* 16:8.

be eaten all year round, the Torah instituted this precaution in order that one may not unintentionally come to eat it on Pesach.[11]

With this introduction, we can now understand the verse that commands the removal of *chametz* on Pesach: "By the first day, you must have your homes cleared of all leaven. *Because* whoever eats leaven from the first day until the seventh day will have his soul cut off from Israel."[12] What is the meaning of the word "because" (כִּי) in this verse? The Vilna Gaon explains that the verse is giving the reasoning why the Torah is so strict regarding *chametz* in that one must remove it from one's possession. Since the prohibition of eating *chametz* is limited to a short seven-day period, after which the prohibition is lifted, the Torah therefore deals with it in such a strict manner.[13]

Soul Food

The Maharal says that *chametz* corresponds to the body, while matzah corresponds to the *neshamah*. On Pesach we eat matzah since only our souls came to recognize Hashem and desired to cleave to Him. (The three matzos on the Seder plate corresponding to the three levels of the soul — *nefesh*, *ruach*, and *neshamah*.) Pesach can therefore be compared to *kiddushin* — the initial betrothal to Hashem. During the period of *sefirah* leading to receiving the Torah on Sinai, the Jewish People worked on elevating their bodies as well. When they received the Torah on Shavuos, their bodies also achieved perfection and they became completely wedded to Hashem (*nisuin*). Since there was no dichotomy between the body and the soul at this time, the *korban* on Shavous consists of both *chametz* and matzah.[14]

---

11   See Tosfos, *Pesachim* 2a, s.v. *"ohr."*
12   *Shemos* 12:15.
13   *Chumash HaGRa, Shemos* ibid.
14   Maharal, *Derashas Shabbos HaGadol* 244b.

Return to the Source

Chametz symbolizes the evil inclination,[15] while matzah represents the forces of holiness and purity. The words *chametz* and *matzah* both contain the letters *mem* and *tzadi*, which using the *gematriah* (numerical substitution) of *a"t b"ash*, are the letters *yud* and *hei*, which together comprise the name of Hashem. Since the name of Hashem is concealed within the *mem* and *tzadi* of both the words *chametz* and *matzah*, this hints to a person who has sinned and has obscured his Divine holiness.

The difference between *chametz* and matzah are the letters *hei* and *ches*, which appear almost identical and take the shape of a pavilion that opens widely at the bottom. The sages compare this world to a pavilion where anyone who wishes to leave the Divine service may do so.[16] The distinction between the two letters is the tiny opening in the upper left side of the *hei*:

- The letter *hei* is the letter of *teshuvah*, as the penitent climbs back inside through that small opening to return to Hashem.
- The letter *ches* represents the unrepentant sinner, who retains the barrier blocking between himself and Hashem.

Eating matzah on Pesach helps return us to our spiritually elevated source, akin to the *Kohanim* who would eat the *korban minchah*, which consisted of matzah, as part of their Temple service.[17]

Mercy Matzah

Chametz symbolizes *midas hadin* — the trait of strict justice, while matzah represents the trait of Divine mercy.[18] The Jewish People needed Divine mercy to leave Egypt to counteract the challenge of the accusing angels who said, "These [Egyptians] are idolaters, and

---

15   *Berachos* 17a.
16   *Menachos* 29b.
17   Maharshah, *Pesachim* 116b.
18   See Ramban, *Vayikra* 23:17.

these [Jews] are idolaters,"[19] so we are therefore commanded to eat matzah upon leaving Egypt.

Based on the above, we can now resolve a difficulty the commentators pose on the Rambam's ruling that the matzah must also be dipped into *charoses* prior to eating it.[20] This appears difficult to understand, seeing that matzah represents our freedom from slavery while *charoses* reminds us of the mortar we made while slaves in Egypt. We may answer that since matzah represents redemption through mercy, this was only achieved because of the harsh slavery we endured. Therefore, *charoses* is appropriate for the matzah as well.

Matzah's Protective Power

The name for *matzah* is derived from the word *matzusa* — a fight.[21] Just as a *mezuzah* protects a person's home by driving away the *mazikim* — forces of evil — so does matzah have equivalent protective powers. Perhaps this may explain why the matzah symbolizes the redemption. Pesach night is called *leil shimurim* — "the night guarded [against the forces of evil]" — and it is the matzah that offers this protection. Since the matzah protects like a *mezuzah*, some have the custom to break off a small piece of the *afikomen* and hang it in one's home.[22]

---

19   See Rashi, *Shemos* 12:13.

20   Rambam, *Mishnah Torah, Chametz U'Matzah* 8:8.

21   *Zohar, Pinchas* 251b.

22   *Be'er Hetev, Orach Chaim* **477:4**; *Be'er Miriam* on the *Haggadah*.

The Pesach Story

IN THE DAYS OF AVRAHAM

The Cookie King

The Midrash relates that when Og came to inform Avraham that Lot had been captured in war, he found Avraham baking matzos for Pesach. Og's real name was Palit, since he was saved (פליט) from the flood during the time of Noach, but he changed his name to Og after the עוגות — the thin wafers that Avraham baked.[23] It is understandable why he was named for being the sole survivor of the Great Deluge (aside from Noach's family), but why should he name himself after Avraham's matzos?

We see from this that merely witnessing a *tzadik* perform a mitzvah with great devotion leaves a life-altering impact on a person's life, even greater than surviving the cataclysmic flood.[24] Nonetheless, that his name was not changed to "Matzos", but rather to "Cookie," indicates a degree of superficiality on his part, similar to Eisav being called Edom ("Red") after his attraction to the external color of the lentil porridge he requested from Yaakov.

Mitigated Years of Slavery

Hashem decreed that the Jewish People be exiled for four hundred years. The *Rabbeinu Ephraim* comments that in the merit that Avraham was one hundred years old and Sarah ninety at the time of

---

23   *Devarim Rabbah* 1:25.
24   Rabbi Chaim Zaytchik, *Mayanei HaChaim* 2:18–19.

the birth of Yitzchak, 190 years was deducted from the four hundred years of exile.[25] (The four hundred years therefore began from the birth of Yitzchak, and the exile in Egypt lasted only two hundred and ten years.) Why was the age of Avraham and Sarah a determining factor in diminishing the years of exile?

In the liturgy for *Parashas HaChodesh*, it reads: "Thanks to the many prayers of [Avraham and Sarah] who were buried in Machpelah, Hashem skipped 190 years of slavery and this calmed Israel." Since the purpose of exile is to bring out one's trust in Hashem and the quality of prayer, all the prayers during the many years of Avraham and Sarah's childlessness were carried over to their descendants, thereby sparing them the need to pray and trust in Hashem for 190 additional years in exile.

DOWN TO EGYPT

The Enslaved Prince

When Hashem promised the Land of Israel to Avraham's descendants, Avraham was concerned that his children may lose their rights to the Land because of their sins. Hashem's response was that his children will go into exile in a strange land [Egypt], and Hashem will ultimately punish the nation who persecuted them.[26] How did Hashem's reply assuage Avraham's fears?

The *Devar Avraham* answers that Hashem was conveying to Avraham that He considers the Jewish People as His children and not just His servants. It is comparable to a king who sent his son and one of his slaves to prison for a crime they committed. How can one tell which prisoner is the prince and which is the slave? Suppose the warden of the prison was a cruel person and mistreated both the slave and the prince. The king would ignore the excesses the warden

---

25 *Bereishis* 15:13.
26 *Bereishis* 15:7–14.

committed against the slave, but would be enraged and severely punish the warden for the unwarranted harm inflicted upon his son. Hashem thus told Avraham likewise: the fact that I will harshly judge the Egyptians for mistreating your descendants is a sign that I consider them My children, and therefore — despite their inadequacies — I will keep the Land of Israel for them forever.[27]

Yehudah — Builder of Torah

Yaakov sent Yehudah ahead to Egypt in advance of his family's arrival to establish a house of Torah study. Why was Yehudah specifically chosen to build a yeshivah over Levi or Yissachar, both of whom were paragons of Torah scholarship?

Rabbi Eliezer Ginzburg maintains that Yehudah's exceptional quality was that he excelled in taking responsibility. Yehudah took responsibility in the affair with Tamar, in saving Yosef from the pit, and in fighting for the return of Binyamin. Only one possessing the quality of responsibility is qualified to build Torah.

Out of Egypt

One of the reasons Yaakov did not want to be buried in Egypt was that he foresaw the Ten Plagues that would someday afflict the Egyptians. Yaakov feared that the Egyptians would descend upon his grave and beseech him to intervene on their behalf to bring the plagues to an end, just as he had saved them during his lifetime during the great famine. This was a no-win situation: he had no desire to spare the enemies of Hashem and the oppressors of his children from their rightful punishment, but at the same time, if he would not come to their aid it would bring about a desecration of Hashem's name, as the Egyptians would say that the righteous Yaakov had no power to help them.[28] Therefore, he wanted to be buried outside of Egypt to eliminate both possibilities.

---

27   Rabbi Avraham Dov Kahan Shapiro, quoted in *Peninim M'Shulchan Gavoah, Bereishis* 15:17.

28   *Otzer HaMidrashim, Bereishis* 47:29.

Falling to Depths of Depravity...

A great contemporary of the Chazon Ish once wrote that the Jews in Egypt had achieved the highest level of Torah study and mitzvah observance and had scaled the peaks of faith and piety.

The Chazon Ish found his approach objectionable and wrote an uncharacteristically lengthy letter to prove otherwise.[29] In it, he demonstrates that the Jewish People were in a spiritually dismal state, and quotes numerous sources stating that the vast majority were sinners unworthy of redemption, as the Rambam writes:[30]

> As their sojourn in Egypt lengthened, the Children of Israel began to learn from the ways of the Egyptians and to worship idols as they did...The trunk planted by Avraham was very close to being uprooted, and the sons of Yaakov would be returned to the errors of the world and their straying. And out of Hashem's great love for us, and as a result of keeping His promise to our father Avraham, He sent Moshe [to redeem the Jewish People].

...With Radiant Purity

"Like the practice of the Land of Egypt in which you have lived you shall not do."[31] Rashi comments that the superfluous words "in which you have lived" tell us that the practices of the Egyptians were the most corrupt of all the nations. This interpretation is difficult, as one may mistakenly infer from this that one is only exhorted to abstain from the immoral practices of Egypt since they were the most depraved of the nations, but need not refrain from imitating the other nations who were not as wicked.

The Maharal therefore understands that the intent of the phrase "in which you have lived" is to reveal the purity of the Jewish People and to

---

29   See *Chazon Ish Haggadah*, pp. 12–19.
30   Rambam, *Mishnah Torah*, *Avodas Kochavim* 1:3.
31   *Vayikra* 18:3.

explain why immorality is so unbecoming for them. Hashem specifically placed the Jewish People in Egypt since they were the complete antithesis of each other. The beauty of our purity only emerged under those conditions as a result of the stark contrast between the two counter cultures.[32]

Abolishing Yosef's Decrees

"A new king arose over Egypt who did not know of Yosef."[33] The *Targum* translates the verse as meaning "a new king arose over Egypt who *did not fulfill the decrees* of Yosef." *Rimzei Rabbeinu Yoel* explains that Yosef instituted that the Jews keep the mitzvos of *bris milah* and Shabbos. Pharaoh sought to abolish Yosef's decree and prohibited the Jews from fulfilling these two mitzvos. When the children of Israel defied Pharaoh's edict, he enforced the abolishment of *bris milah* by decreeing that all male children be drowned in the Nile, and the abolishment of Shabbos by decreeing that the Jews do backbreaking labor seven days a week.[34]

SLAVERY

Punished for Their Plans

"All that the Egyptians *planned* to do against Israel, Hashem did to them."[35] Regardless of whether the Egyptians actually succeeded in carrying out their nefarious plans, they were punished for their evil designs alone.[36]

The Midrash elaborates:[37]

> *Since the Egyptians intended that the Jews draw their water, their water was turned to blood. They wanted the Jews to carry*

---

32   Maharal, *Gur Ayreh*, *Vayikra* ibid.; *Gevuras Hashem* ch. 4.
33   *Shemos* 1:8.
34   *Rizmei Rabbeinu Yoel*, *Shemos* ibid.
35   *Targum Onkelos*, *Shemos* 18:11.
36   See *Yerushalmi*, *Pe'ah* ch. 1, s.v. "*b'goyim*."
37   *Midrash Tanchumah*, *parashas Bo*.

their merchandise to load onto their ships, so Hashem sent frogs to destroy their merchandise. They intended for the Jews to clean their environment, so Hashem polluted their environment with lice. They wanted the Jews to tend their numerous children, so Hashem sent a horde of wild animals that snatched their children. They wanted the Jews to watch their livestock, so a plague decimated their animals. They intended for the Jews to heat their baths, so Hashem brought upon them boils that would be aggravated through bath water. They planned to stone the Jews, so Hashem stoned them with hail. They wanted the Jews to tend to their orchards, so Hashem brought the locusts to consume their crops. They wanted to imprison the Jews in dark pits, so Hashem brought darkness upon them. They planned to kill the Jews, so Hashem killed their firstborn. And just as they wanted to drown the Jews, so did Hashem drown them in the Yam Suf.

Reward for Devotion

The Midrash details the numerous rewards Moshe received for alleviating the suffering of his brethren in Egypt:[38]

- Moshe saw the shoulders of his brothers were bloodied from their heavy loads and bandaged them. In that merit, he lived to the age of 120 without the ailments and infirmities of old age.
- The dust from the cement would blow into the eyes of the Jews and Moshe would go rinse and cleanse their eyes. Since he healed the eyesight of the Jewish People, he was rewarded that his eyesight did not fail him in his old age.
- Because he would bury the Jews who died during their work, Hashem said, "You involved yourself with the burial of your brothers; I will personally involve Myself with your burial."
- Moshe left his royal entourage to personally assist his

---

38   *Otzer HaMidrashim, Shemos* 2:11.

brethren with their heavy loads. Hashem said, "You left your personal affairs to go out and see the suffering of Israel and dealt with them as brothers. I too will leave [My abode] in heaven to speak directly with you."

From Savior to Teacher

"They were the ones who spoke to Pharaoh, king of Egypt, to take the Children of Israel out of the land of Egypt; this is Moshe and Aharon."[39] The *Rabbeinu Ephraim* notes that the words משה ואהרן together have the numerical value of 613, since through both of them the 613 commandments were given.[40] Why is this hint alluded to specifically in this verse?

We may suggest that in the merit that they undertook the difficult responsibility of challenging the world's most mighty and dangerous monarch to demand that he free the Jewish People from slavery, for that they merited to become the transmitters of Torah to the Jewish nation.

Three-Day Sojourn

"Now we request that you allow us to take a three-day journey...to sacrifice to Hashem."[41] Why did Moshe specifically request a three-day journey into the wilderness to offer their sacrifices to Hashem?

The *Rokeach* observes that a precedent for this request may be derived from Avraham, who also traveled a three-day period to Har Moriah in order to offer a sacrifice at *Akeidas Yitzchak*.[42]

Alternatively, Rabbi Aharon Kotler says that the reason Yaakov distanced himself from Lavan an interval of three-days travel[43] was because the impure spirit that emanates from a wicked person spreads over the distance of three-day travel.[44] Therefore, Moshe

---

39 *Shemos* 6:27.
40 *Rabbeinu Ephraim, Shemos* ibid.
41 *Shemos* 3:18.
42 *Rokeach*, 8:23.
43 Rashi, *Bereishis* 31:22.
44 See *Yalkut Shimoni, Tehillim* 843.

requested from Pharaoh that the Jews be allowed to distance themselves from Egypt the necessary distance so that they would no
longer be negatively affected by the Egyptians.[45]

Israel — the Firstborn Son

"My firstborn son is Israel."[46] What is the special quality of a firstborn and how are the Jewish People comparable to this characteris-
tic? A number of answers are offered:

- The Jewish People are considered the first son since Hashem
  thought of creating Israel before the world was created.[47]
- The son with the greatest personal attributes is called the
  bechor — the firstborn.[48]
- The firstborn creates the status of the one who bore him as
  a father and a parent. Similarly, the Jewish People create the
  bridge for Hashem's relationship with mankind.[49]
- Since the firstborn is a child without siblings at one point,
  there is a special relationship between a father and his firstborn. As the relationship of a father to his *bechor* is especially
  close and independent of his other siblings, so is the relationship between Hashem and Israel.

THE TEN PLAGUES

Who Needs a Miracle?

There is a general principle about miracles: if a person is worthy of a
miracle on his own merit, he will merit to be aware of the miracle performed on his behalf. However, when a miracle is performed in the merit

---

45 Rabbi Aharon Kotler, *Haderech Hanechonah B'Hora'as Tanach*, p. 7.
46 *Shemos* 4:22.
47 *Rabbeinu Ephraim*, ibid.
48 *Rabbeinu Ephraim*; cf. *Tehillim* 89:28.
49 Rabbi Mordechai Elan, *Mikdash Mordechai*, *Bereishis* 31:43.

of others, such as his righteous ancestors, then the recipient will be oblivious to the miracle performed.[50] If so, how were the Jews in Egypt worthy of witnessing the wondrous miracles of the Ten Plagues and the splitting of the *Yam Suf* if they were at the forty-ninth level of impurity?

Rabbi Shlomo Zalman Auerbach answers that the purpose of the miracles was not to save the Jews, since this could have been equally achieved in a more natural manner. Rather, it was to implant *emunah* in *Bnei Yisrael*; to teach them of Hashem's power, kindness, and greatness, which was to last them for all future generations.[51]

In a similar vein, Rabbi Moshe Feinstein comments that had the Exodus occurred in a less miraculous fashion, one may have thought that it was merely an isolated and temporary event to save the Jewish People at that specific time. If in the future, the Jewish People will find themselves once again in exile, there will no longer be any lasting benefit from their original deliverance. Hashem therefore took the Jews out of Egypt "with a strong hand" in the most miraculous manner to demonstrate that the effects of redemption were everlasting and made the Jewish nation an intrinsically free people for all eternity.[52]

Three Great Tens

The ten *makkos*—plagues—correspond to the ten tests of Avraham,[53] as well as to the *Aseres HaDibros* — the Ten Commandments.[54] Here are several examples how this is so:[55]

- Avraham's first test was in coming to recognize the existence of Hashem. This corresponds to the first commandment, "I am Hashem." This also corresponds to the plague of blood,

---

50 Cited in *Halichos Shlomo*, pp. 519–520.

51 *Halichos Shlomo* ibid. See Ramban, end *parashas Bo*.

52 *Derash Moshe*, *Shemos* 13:14.

53 *Shemos Rabbah* 15:27.

54 Rashi, *Avos* 5:3.

55 Modzhitzer Rebbe, *Aish Tamid* (1989), p. 8; quoted in *Otzros Tzadikei v'Geonei HaDoros*, p. 151.

since before Hashem punishes idolaters He first destroys the idols they worship — in this case, the Nile.

- Avraham's second test was throwing himself into the fiery furnace in order not to bow to idols. This corresponds to the second commandment that one may not have strange gods. This also corresponds to the plague of frogs, who were willing to sacrifice their lives by jumping into the fiery ovens to fulfill the will of Hashem.

- The third commandment, that one may not utter Hashem's name in vain, corresponds to the plague of lice. *Chazal* say that witchcraft appears to undermine Divine providence. When the sorcerers were unable to duplicate the plague of lice, they came to recognize "the finger of G-d."

- The fourth commandment is the observance of Shabbos. This corresponds to the plague of beasts since the *pasuk* says specifically regarding this plague that it served to differentiate between the Egyptians and the children of Israel. A gentile is prohibited from observing the Shabbos, and the Sages say that a gentile who observes the Shabbos is punished by being devoured by wild beasts.

Duration of the Plagues

The Torah says that the plague of blood lasted for seven days. From this, *Chazal* derive a general principle (*binyan av*) that the remainder of the plagues lasted for seven days as well.[56]

This seems difficult, since the Death of the Firstborn certainly did not last seven days — it takes only a moment to die! The same can be said regarding the plague of pestilence, as the cattle's demise also occurred in a brief second. Furthermore, the verse says that the plague of darkness lasted only for six days!

---

56   Cf. Ibn Ezra, *Shemos* 7:25.

The Radvaz defends the position of the Sages as follows:[57]

- Death of the Firstborn: The general principle stated above only applies to plagues that were followed by an additional plague, similar to the plague of blood. Since the death of the firstborn was the final plague, after which no further plagues were necessary (since Pharaoh agreed to free the Jews), this principle does not apply.
- Pestilence: Regarding the plague of pestilence, though the animals contracted the plague on the first day, they continued dying throughout the remainder of the week.
- Darkness: The Torah records the plague of darkness in two units of three days each, as there was a distinct difference between the two stages.[58] On the seventh day of darkness, the plague began to wane and therefore was not recorded.

Did the Jews Experience the Plagues?

According to the Ibn Ezra,[59] the first three plagues (blood, frogs, lice) befell the Jewish People as well the Egyptians. He brings proof to his position from that the Torah only mentions how the plagues differentiated between the Egyptians and the Israelites from the plague of beasts onwards.

The Radvaz strongly challenges his view, as the Torah writes regarding the plague of blood that the *Egyptians* were unable to drink the water from the Nile and that the *Egyptians* dug in vain to find drinkable water.[60] From this we can infer that the Jews were not affected by the blood in any way. Moreover, Moshe warned Pharaoh that the plague of frogs will affect "you [Pharaoh] and your nation," implying that it did not affect the Jews. Furthermore, if the first

57   Radvaz, 2:813.
58   See Rashi, *Shemos* 10:22.
59   *Shemos* 7:24.
60   Ibid., v. 21, 24. Radvaz ibid.

few plagues affected the Jews as well, why would those plagues motivate Pharaoh to free them? While the Ibn Ezra's commentary addresses most of the points raised by the Radvaz,[61] the Radvaz concludes that it is nonetheless forbidden to accept Ibn Ezra's novel view, as it counters the traditionally accepted approach.[62]

The Midrash says that during each of the ten plagues that the Egyptians suffered, the Jewish People also suffered, albeit momentarily. One may ask how the Jews could experience the plague of the firstborn when the *Haggadah* explicitly says that the homes of the Jews were spared from death!

Rabbi Dovid Heinemann refers to a *Chazal* that says that the Egyptians were in the throes of death the entire night and only expired in the morning. Accordingly, the Jewish People momentarily experienced the death throes alone, after which they fully recovered.

Why should *Bnei Yisrael* have to suffer the affliction of the Ten Plagues, even for a moment? The Chidah answers that through this experience they would fully appreciate what Hashem did to the Egyptians. Additionally, since the Ten Plagues corresponded to the *Aseres HaDibros*,[63] Hashem wanted them to get a tangible feeling of the dire consequences for transgressing those laws.[64]

The Warning

The plagues were brought in cycles of three:

- Prior to the first plague, Moshe would meet Pharaoh at the Nile and warn him about the forthcoming plague.

---

61   Ibid. and *Shemos* 7:29.
62   Radvaz ibid.
63   *Pesikta Rabasi*, ch. 21.
64   Chidah, *Geulas Olam*, p. 9.

- Before the second plague, Moshe would warn Pharaoh at his palace.
- Finally, the third plague would come without any warning.

The Maharal comments that Moshe would first warn Pharaoh at the Nile in order not to invade his privacy by entering his home. If that did not succeed, he would then warn him in his palace, which was more intrusive. If even that failed to move him, he then deserved to be smitten even without warning.[65]

The Lingering Plague

When Moshe first went to Pharaoh to ask him to let the Jews out of Egypt, he said, "Let us now go...lest He strike us dead with the plague (*dever*) or the sword."[66] Rashi explains that Moshe's threat was actually intended for the Egyptians, but out of respect for the monarchy, Moshe did not say so directly. Why did Moshe specifically mention these two punishments? The "sword" is readily understandable as it represents the death of the firstborn, which was the climax of the Ten Plagues. But what is the special significance of the plague of *dever* — pestilence, that it was singled out?

The Midrash says that each plague was accompanied by pestilence.[67] Unlike the plague of pestilence itself that killed the cattle exclusively, the pestilence that accompanied each plague affected the Egyptians themselves.[68] It is specifically this plague of pestilence that is referred to in the *Haggadah*: "'With a strong hand' — this is [the plague of] pestilence." Since *dever* would accompany all ten plagues, Moshe therefore singled it out at the onset of his warnings.

Another reason why *dever* accompanied each of the Ten Plagues was to negate the Egyptian's polytheistic beliefs. The various plagues

---

65   *Gevuras Hashem* 57, p. 251.
66   *Shemos* 5:3.
67   *Shemos Rabbah* 10:2.
68   Rashi, *Tehillim* 78:50; *Orchos Chaim on the Haggadah*, s.v. "*b'yad chazakah*."

demonstrated Hashem's power and control over air, land, and sea. Lest they mistakenly believe that each plague was performed by a different power, Hashem stamped one plague to accompany each of the plagues to proclaim that there was one single God who was responsible for all the diverse plagues. This is why the *Haggadah* states, "'With a strong hand' — this is [referring to] *dever*." Just as a hand unites each separate finger, so did the pestilence establish Hashem as the sole Ruler over the whole world.

"Random" Order of Plagues

In *Tehillim* 105, the Ten Plagues are enumerated in a seemingly random order. Of course, the order isn't random at all. The *Rokeach* explains that the reason blood is mentioned there next to darkness is because as a result of both these plagues, the Jews became wealthy. (The Jews sold water to the Egyptians for profit during the plague of blood. During the plague of darkness, the Jews located the Egyptians' hidden treasures, and prior to their departure from Egypt they requested to borrow those items from their Egyptian neighbors.) Lice is mentioned next to wild animals since the lice also came in an assortment of species. Hail is mentioned adjacent to the locusts since as a result of both plagues, the Egyptian populace became impoverished.[69] This is why it says in reference to the plague of locust, "That He remove from me only this death,"[70] since a poor person is considered as dead.[71]

In *Tehillim* 105, Dovid HaMelech recaps the Ten Plagues that befell the Egyptians. Regarding the plagues of lice and wild beasts he writes, "He spoke and hordes of beast arrived, and lice throughout

---

69   *Rokeach, Shemos* 10:23.

70   *Shemos* 10:17.

71   *Nedarim* 64b.

their borders."[72] The order is problematic, since the actual order was in the reverse — the plague of lice preceded the plague of wild beasts.

The Dubno Maggid resolves this difficulty by way of a parable: It was the custom in pre-war Europe for people to set up a table for the poor when making a wedding for their children. The custom eventually evolved into a special meal prepared for the town's poor the night before the wedding. Once, some poor people who came to the pre-wedding feast also showed up to the wedding itself. The host approached them and requested an explanation. They responded that although they were poor and were thus entitled to attend the original repast, they were also distant relatives so they came the following day as well. Similarly, although the lice had a plague of their own, at the end of the day they are still animals, so they also came during the plague of wild beasts.

Calculating the Stroke of Midnight

There is an old question as to how it is possible for Hashem to kill the firstborn at precisely midnight. If you split the night into two equal parts, you have a period of "before midnight" and a period of "after midnight." But the exact moment of "midnight" cannot exist. Secondly, since time is constantly in motion it is impossible to define the precise moment of midnight, and the plague must have therefore occurred either before or after midnight.

The Radvaz presents two solutions: either Hashem stopped the passage of time at midnight, or that only human beings are unable to precisely pinpoint midnight, but Hashem is capable of doing that as well.[73] These two alternatives are, in fact, disputed by the sages of the Midrash. One opinion says that *Yotzro chalkoh* — the Creator divided the night [by stopping the passage of time and miraculously creating a moment called midnight], while the other opinion says

---

72   *Tehillim* 105:31.
73   Radvaz 2:814.

Yodaya itosav — [unlike man], Hashem knows the precise moments of time.[74]

The Future Ten Plagues

"For if you do not send out My people, behold, I shall incite (משליח) against you..."[75] The *Rabbeinu Ephraim* notes that the word משליח has the same letters as למשיח, hinting that in the days of Mashiach, Hashem will once again bring ten plagues upon the enemies of Israel.[76] This is a fulfillment of the verse, "As in the days when you left Egypt I will show them wonders."[77] The source of this idea is found in the Midrash that states: "The One who exacted payment against the earlier ones (i.e., Egypt), will exact payment against Edom [in the days prior to the coming of Mashiach]."[78]

The Midrash delineates the prophecies that detail how each of the Ten Plagues will be meted out to Edom in the End of Days:[79]

1. **Blood** — "I will set wonders in the heavens and earth...blood."[80]
2. **Frogs** — Made deafening noise. In the future: "The sound of tumult comes from the city...the sound of Hashem dealing retribution to His enemies."[81]
3. **Lice** — Ground became inhospitable mass of lice. In the future: "Its soil will turn to sulphur; its land will become burning tar."[82]

---

74 Ibid.
75 *Shemos* 8:17.
76 *Rabbeinu Ephraim, Shemos* ibid.
77 *Michah* 7:15.
78 *Midrash Tanchumah, Bo.*
79 Ibid.
80 *Yoel* 3:3.
81 *Yeshayah* 66:6.
82 Ibid. 34:9.

4. **Wild beasts** — "Owls and bitterns will occupy it..."[83]
5. **Plague** — "I will punish him (Edom) with pestilence."[84]
6. **Boils** — "Each one's flesh will melt away..."[85]
7. **Hail** — "Hailstones, fire, and sulphur will I rain down upon him."[86]
8. **Locusts** — "All winged creatures gather...a great feast."[87]
9. **Darkness** — "Behold, darkness will cover the earth..."[88]
10. **Death of firstborn** — "Princes of the North...will lie...with those slain."[89]

"AND AFTERWARDS THEY WILL LEAVE WITH GREAT WEALTH"

Deceptive Escape

Why was it necessary for the Jews to "borrow" gold and silver from their Egyptian neighbors before leaving Egypt; couldn't they have received it without having to resort to trickery? Similarly, the entire Exodus appears to have been predicated on deception, in that Moshe requested from Pharaoh to allow the Jews a three-day sojourn in the wilderness when he had no intention of them ever returning at the end of that period. Why were these "tricks" necessary?

The Vilna Gaon explains that Hashem repaid Pharaoh measure-for-measure. Pharaoh tricked the Jews into slavery by first offering them handsome compensation for their work. He also asked the Jewish midwives to kill the Jewish boys at birth and then

---

83   Ibid. v. 11.
84   *Yechezkel* 38:22.
85   *Zechariah* 14:12.
86   *Yechezkel* ibid.
87   Ibid. 39:17.
88   *Yeshayah* 60:2.
89   *Yechezkel* 32:30.

to feign that the death was a result of a miscarriage. It was there-fore fitting for Hashem to also fool Pharaoh upon Israel's departure from Egypt.[90]

Permanent Loan

Hashem commanded the Children of Israel to borrow gold and silver vessels from their Egyptian neighbors.[91] Since Hashem want-ed the *Bnei Yisrael* to acquire the Egyptians' wealth, why didn't He command them to request the vessels as an outright gift? Also, why did Hashem suggest that the *Bnei Yisrael* do something that may be perceived as a *chilul Hashem*, for there was no intention that the borrowed items would ever be returned?

Several answers are given:

- Hashem intended to trick the Egyptians into believing that they merely lent their valuables to the Jews so that the Egyptians would be motivated to pursue the Jews into the *Yam Suf* to retrieve their possessions. The Ran makes the point that since the Egyptians deserved drowning as a pun-ishment for drowning the Jewish babies in the Nile, it was proper for Hashem to contrive a means for them to receive the punishment they deserved.[92]
- The word *sha'al* sometimes means a request for a gift, as in *Tehillim* 2:8. Therefore, *v'yishalu* in this verse does not mean a loan but rather the Jews were actually instructed to request an outright gift from their Egyptian fellowmen.[93]
- Since the Egyptians were desperate to get the Jews out of their country, they told the Jews that they could keep the borrowed items as a gift.

---

90   *Chumash HaGra, Shemos* 11:2.
91   *Shemos* 11:2.
92   *Drashos HaRan*, quoted in *Ein Yaakov, Berachos* 9a. See *Tehillim* 18:27.
93   Chizkuni, *Shemos* 11:2; Rashbam, Rosh, Rabbeinu Chananel there.

- The *Yidden* turned back to Egypt at *Pi Hachiros* to fulfill their obligation to return to Egypt after a three-day period.[94] However, once the Egyptians pursued them in battle, they were no longer under any commitment to return to Egypt or to return the borrowed items.[95]
- The Jews left behind their fields and possessions because they were being pursued, and this compensated for the items borrowed.[96]

When lending money to a widow, it is prohibited to take a garment for collateral. This applies even if she is wealthy and even if the garment is returned to her daily.

The Torah presents the reasoning for this mitzvah: "You shall not take the garment of a widow as a pledge. You shall remember that you were a slave in Egypt, and Hashem, your God, redeemed you from there; therefore I commanded you to do this thing."[97] The *Rokeach* expounds the rationale of the mitzvah as follows: remember that when you left Egypt to go to an unfamiliar place, Hashem saw to it that you should not leave empty-handed and instructed that you receive garments and other valuables from your Egyptian neighbors. This helped minimize your discomfort and helped strengthen you for your journey into the wilderness. The widow also feels alone and emotionally insecure. Do not take away from her any of her possessions so as not to contribute to her loneliness and anxiety.[98]

---

94 *Shemos* 5:3.
95 Chizkuni, *Shemos* 14:2.
96 Ibid.
97 *Devarim* 24:18–19.
98 *Rokeach, Devarim* ibid.

BIRTH OF A NATION

To Merit Freedom

Commentators note that for Israel to be worthy of leaving Egypt, they required the merit of *mesiras nefesh* — self-sacrifice. Where do we find an example of this self-sacrifice?

It was extremely difficult for each adult male to undergo a *bris milah*, as well as for each family to take a lamb to be slaughtered as a *Korban Pesach*. They were actually risking their lives in the process, as Moshe told Pharaoh, "Behold, if we were to slaughter the deity of Egypt in their sight, will they not stone us?"[99] By the *Yam Suf* as well, the sea only split after Nachshon ben Aminadav leaped into the water, which nearly drowned him.[100]

In the *Haggadah* we read: "Then I passed you and saw you wallowing (מתבוססת) in your bloods (the blood of *bris milah* and of *Korban Pesach*), and I said to you, 'In your bloods shall you live.'"[101] מתבוססת derives from the word בסיס, a base. The willingness of the Jewish People to be *moser nefesh* in Egypt became the foundation — the base — for their freedom and an eternal merit for their descendants.[102]

This Nation I Have Created

All the nations of the world are essentially physical entities and as such are under the influence of *mazalos* — the physical heavenly spheres. When the Jewish People left Egypt, they became a spiritual entity and attained *ma'alah Elokis* — a quality akin to the Divine. The *Haggadah* states "And Hashem took us out of Egypt — not through an angel, not through a *seraph*, not through an agent, rather HaKadosh Baruch Hu in His glory, Himself." The Maharal explains

---

99   *Shemos* 8:22
100   *Sotah* 37a.
101   *Yechezkel* 16:6.
102   Rabbi Yechezkel Abramsky, *Chazon Yechezkel*, *Yehoshua* 3:15; Rabbi Chaim Kanievsky, *Derech Sichah*, p. 244.

that the reason it was an absolute necessity for Hashem to take us out of Egypt Himself is because every creation is similar to its creator. Just as only a human can give birth to a human, and only an ox to an ox, so too only Hashem Himself could bring a spiritual nation into existence.[103]

There are many ways to mend a torn garment. The easiest way is to simply take a needle and thread and sew up the hole. Better yet, though, is to take a piece of fabric and make a patch. But both of these methods are imperfect, as the garment will retain a ragged look. The best approach is to open the seams and reshape the entire garment. The perfection attained by the Jewish People in Egypt was similar to this latter method. Egypt is called *kur habarzel*; it was a refinery that melted down and reshaped the Jewish People. When the time came for them to leave Egypt, they transformed into a new creation — "A created nation to praise God."[104]

Leaving Egypt

There appears to be a contradiction between two verses that depict the day the children of Israel left Egypt:

- "It was on this very day that all the legions of Hashem *left* the land of Egypt."[105]
- "It happened on this very day, Hashem *took* the Children of Israel out of the land of Egypt."[106]

The passive tense in the former verse implies that the Exodus did not require much Divine intervention, in contrast to the active tense employed in verse 51, which conveys a more active role on Hashem's part.

---

103   Maharal, *Gevuras Hashem* ch. 52, p. 227; *Gur Aryeh, Bamidbar* 21:33, footnote 110.
104   *Tehillim* 102:19; Rabbi Shimshon Dovid Pincus, *Nefesh Shimshon*, Gates of Emunah, p. 55.
105   *Shemos* 12:41.
106   Ibid. 12:51.

Rabbi Yechezkel Abramsky reconciles the two verses as follows: the "legions of Hashem" describe those people who were steadfastly loyal and devoted to Hashem. Those people eagerly left Egypt at the first moment the opportunity arose. But those Jews who were not in "the army of Hashem" reasoned that after the plague of the first-born, the Egyptians would certainly improve their relations with the Jews and they would be able to continue living in Egypt in peace. It was for this group of Jews that it was necessary for Hashem to actively *take* them out of the land of Egypt.[107]

SPLITTING OF THE YAM SUF

Why All the Drama?

The Egyptians were drowned in the *Yam Suf* as a punishment for their drowning the Jewish newborn boys in the Nile. But why was it necessary for their punishment to occur in such a dramatic and public fashion? As *Chazal* say, fifty miracles occurred at *Krias Yam Suf* and Hashem publicized the miracle by making all bodies of water in the world split at the same time. The *Beis HaLevi* answers that this was done as a kindness to the Egyptians. Since *Krias Yam Suf* caused the name of Hashem to be sanctified in the eyes of all mankind, this mitigated the punishment due to the Egyptians for their myriad sins.[108]

Enamored by the Sea

It is unusual that Noach's son, Cham, named his son Mitzrayim using the plural form (i.e., the *yud-mem* suffix). Continuing that tradition, Mitzrayim also named his sons using the plural form: Ludim, Anomim, etc.[109] The Midrash explains that the letters *yud* and *mem* comprise the word *yam* — sea. The Egyptians were enamored by the sea and therefore

---

107 *Peninim M'Shulchan Gavoah, Shemos* 12:41.
108 *Beis HaLevi*, end of *parashas Vayigash*.
109 *Bereishis* 10:13.

named their descendants after it.[110] Little did they realize that the sea would also be the place where they would ultimately meet their demise!

Universal Miracle

"Yisro heard...everything that Hashem did to Moshe and Israel."[111] What tidings did Yisro hear that brought him to come? Rashi famously says it was the Splitting of the Sea and the war against Amalek. Why was Yisro more impressed with the miracles at the sea than with the Ten Plagues in Egypt?

We see that Pharaoh's sorcerers attributed the plagues to "the *finger* of God."[112] The reason they only compared it to a finger was because the Ten Plagues were limited in scope in that they were confined exclusively to the country of Egypt. An idolater may rationalize that Hashem's power is restricted to certain geographic locales and is no different than other deities to which they also attribute supernatural, but limited powers, r"l.

The Splitting of the Sea was different than the Ten Plagues in that it was an international miracle. As our Sages explain, when Hashem split the *Yam Suf*, all bodies of water in the world also split at that time. Since *Krias Yam Suf* demonstrated Hashem's universal power, it was only then that Yisro proclaimed: "Now I know that Hashem is greater than all the gods."[113]

Pharaoh's Repentance

When the Jewish People sang to Hashem at the parting of the *Yam Suf*, Pharaoh joined in their song and declared in Egyptian the verse, "Who is like you among the heavenly powers."[114] His statement was subsequently translated into the holy tongue and incorporated into

---

110   *Bereishis Rabbah* 37:4.
111   *Shemos* 18:1.
112   Ibid. 8:15.
113   Ibid. 18:11; Maharal, *Gur Aryeh*, *Shemos* 18:1; cf. Rav Saadiah Gaon, *Shemos* 18:11.
114   *Shemos* 15:11.

the Torah as part of *Az Yashir*.[115] It is ironic that the mouth that originally said, "*Who* is Hashem that I should listen to His voice,"[116] ultimately came to confess Hashem's righteousness and greatness using the same word, "Who." In the merit of expressing his belief in Hashem, Pharaoh and his people were greatly rewarded both at that time as well as for future generations.[117]

No matter how low a person has sunk, one can never know how he will turn out in the end. Rabbi Yaakov Yitzchak Ruderman derives this from the story of Pharaoh. Pharaoh was evil incarnate:[118] he subjugated the Jewish People to slavery in the most brutal fashion, killed their firstborn boys, and denied the existence of Hashem.

Yet, we find that he underwent a gradual spiritual metamorphosis. When Moshe first appeared before Pharaoh, Pharaoh said, "Who is Hashem?"[119] Later, he admitted "Hashem is the Righteous One."[120] Hashem considered his admission as an act of repentance and in that merit he was spared the fate of his countrymen during the plague of the firstborn, as well as being the sole Egyptian survivor at *Krias Yam Suf*. The Midrash says that Pharaoh lived a long, accomplished life and eventually became the king of Nineveh. When Yonah rebuked the inhabitants of Nineveh for their sins, the former Pharaoh got off his throne and led the people to repentance. So sincere was his repentance that our Sages learn many laws of proper *teshuvah* from his behavior. We see from here the great potential that is latent in every human being, and how a person can rise from the lowest depths to the greatest heights.[121]

115 *Pirkei D'Rebbi Eliezer* 42, and *Radal* 74.
116 *Shemos* 5:2.
117 *Mechiltah*, beginning *parashas Beshalach*.
118 Rambam, *Igeres HaMussar*.
119 *Shemos* 5:2.
120 Ibid. 9:27.
121 Rabbi Yaakov Yitzchak Ruderman, *Sichas Levi*, p. 76.

The Seder and Insights on the Haggadah

THE SEDER

Exodus as Torah Study

Rav Saadiah Gaon does not list the mitzvah to relate the story of the Exodus on Seder night among the 613 mitzvos. This is because he considers the mitzvah of relating the Exodus as a detail subsumed in the broader mitzvah of teaching Torah to one's children.[122] With this idea, it is understandable why the *Haggadah* instructs the father to teach his wise son the laws of eating the *afikomen*. Although the technicalities of these laws seem unrelated to the story of the Exodus, it nonetheless satisfies the ultimate criteria of Torah study. According to this approach, it also appears that the mitzvah of relating the Exodus is only incumbent upon fathers to their sons, as women are exempt from the mitzvah of Torah study.

Something New

There are several words in the Torah that mean "speaking." The mitzvah to recount the story of the Exodus on Seder night is termed *Sippur Yetzias Mitzrayim*. The Ramban points out that the word *sippur* denotes relating something new.[123] Accordingly, it would seem

---

122   Rabbi Yeruchem Perlow, *Sefer Hamitzvos L'Rav Saadiah Gaon* 33, s.v. "*ela.*"
123   Ramban, *Shemos* 24:1. See also Maharal, *Gur Ayreh, Shemos* 24:3.

that to properly fulfill the mitzvah of *Sippur Yetzias Mitzrayim*, one should relate something one has not known before.

Direct Transmission

Another term the Torah uses in connection to relating the Pesach story is *magid*, from the *pasuk*: "*Vehigadta levincha*... — And you shall relate to your son, etc."[124] *Magid* means to talk to someone directly, as opposed to *amirah* — saying — which can mean to convey a message through an emissary.[125] Hence, the mitzvah of *magid* is specifically for the father himself to relate the Pesach story to his son, as the *pasuk* concludes: "because of this Hashem did to *me* when I left Egypt."[126]

Blessing for Magid?

Why don't we make a *berachah* before reciting the *Haggadah*, as we generally do before fulfilling a mitzvah? There are a number of answers given:

- The blessing over mitzvos must be recited prior to fulfilling the mitzvah. We already fulfilled the minimal obligation of the mitzvah of relating the Exodus through the recital of *krias Shema* and *kiddush*.[127] *Maseh Nisim*, though, rejects this answer, since the mitzvah of *Sippur Yetzias Mitzrayim* requires a lengthy narrative of the story of the Exodus, and one would not fulfill his obligation with merely a brief mention of the event.[128]

- Some answer that relating the story of *Yetzias Mitzrayim* is a form of recounting Hashem's praises, and one does not make a blessing upon reciting the praises of Hashem.[129] This answer appears difficult, however, since we do make a

---

124   *Shemos* 13:8.

125   *Oznayim L'Torah, Bereishis* 48:2.

126   Ibid.

127   *Pri Chadash, Orach Chaim* 473; Meiri, end of the first chap. of *Berachos*.

128   Rabbi Yaakov M'Lisa, *Maseh Nisim, Haggadah Shel Pesach, Pesichah*.

129   *Besamim Rosh* 196.

blessing over *Hallel*, which consists of praises of Hashem. The Brisker Rav answers that *Hallel* can be read in two fashions: as a reading of text or as praise. When recited as a text, we make the blessing "to read the *Hallel*." When reciting *Hallel* as praise, as we do on Pesach night during the Seder, one does not make make a blessing.

- The *Shevilei HaLeket* answers that the blessing of *Asher G'olanu* constitutes the blessing for reciting the *Haggadah*. The reason why the blessing is said at the end of reading the *Haggadah* is because the blessing contains praises of Hashem's redemption. We are unable to make this blessing prior to reading the *Haggadah* since *Magid* begins with the period of subjugation and it would be inappropriate to mention the subjugation after we already blessed Hashem for the redemption.[130]

The Four Cups of Wine

The four cups of wine correspond to the four expressions of redemption the Torah mentions in reference to *Yetzias Mitzrayim*. Rashi enumerates them as:[131]

- *v'hotzeisi* — "I shall take you out"
- *v'hitzalti* — "I shall rescue you"
- *v'goalti* — "I shall redeem you"
- *v'lakachti* — "I shall take you."

The *Gra* argues that we are only to use the three expressions cited in *Shemos* 6:6, namely *v'hotzeisi*, *v'hitzalti*, and *v'goalti*. He reasons that if we are to include *v'lakachti* (verse 7), we should equally include *v'heveisi* — "I shall bring you" (verse 8). He therefore posits that we obtain four expressions since *v'goalti* — "I shall redeem you" is really divided into two expressions, as the *pasuk* says: "וגאלתי אתכם (א) בזרוע

---

130   *Shevilei HaLeket* 218.
131   *Pesachim* 99b, s.v. *"arba."*

נטויה (ב) ובשפטים גדלים — I shall redeem you (1) with an outstretched arm (2) and with great judgments." It is for this reason that one may not drink between the third and fourth cups of wine, since these two cups are inherently an expression of one idea.[132]

The Matzah

There is a custom to bake the three matzos used on Seder night from one *isaron* (a measurement of volume equal to approximately 5.5 pounds or 2.5 liters) of flour, since this was the amount of flour necessary to produce an equivalent number of matzos for the *korban todah* — the thanksgiving offering — brought in the Beis HaMikdash. Among those required to bring a *korban todah* was someone who was freed from prison. It is therefore fitting that the matzos eaten on Seder night are made from this measurement, since the entire Jewish nation was freed from the prison of Egypt on the night of Pesach.[133]

According to the Rambam, one may eat matzah the entire night.[134] The Rosh writes that one should be careful to finish before midnight to ensure that one does not procrastinate and come to forget to eat the matzah.[135] We can explain the rationale of the Rambam's view by saying that since the mitzvah of matzah comes only once a year, it is dear to a person and he will not be lax in its fulfillment. This is similar to a law regarding the reading of the *Megillah*: while in general a person cannot listen to two voices simultaneously, one may hear the *Megillah* being read from more than one person. The reason for this is that since the *Megillah* is an infrequent mitzvah, the listener will focus his full attention to hear it properly.

---

132 Vilna Gaon, *Haggadah, Ha Lachma Anya*, s.v. "*di acholo.*"
133 Rosh, cited in *Tur, Orach Chaim* 475; *Perishah* 15.
134 Rambam, *Mishnah Torah, Chametz U'Matzah* 6:1.
135 Rosh, *Pesachim* 10:38.

The Missing Mnemonic

Before beginning the Seder, many recite the fifteen *Simanim* (*Kadeish, Urchatz*, etc.), a mnemonic that highlights the order of the Seder in rhyme. Why isn't there a *siman* for the four cups of wine?

The *Meshech Chochmah* comments that the Jewish People were redeemed from Egypt in merit of their maintaining their purity by remaining separate from the Egyptians. Nothing signifies this separation more than the fact we do not drink the wine of other nations, and we commemorate this by drinking four cups of wine the night of Pesach.[136] Accordingly, we can say that the four cups are included in the sign of *Kadeish*, which derives from the word *kodesh* — holy.

Night of Protection

The reason *Ha Lachma Anya* (in which we invite guests to our Seder) is recited in Aramaic is in order that *mazikim* — demons — shouldn't hear our invitation, as spiritual beings do not understand Aramaic.

The question arises: since Pesach night is already protected against *mazikim*, why are we concerned if they hear our invitation? Also, wouldn't it make more sense if we would open the door at the beginning of the Seder to welcome guests, instead of first opening the door only after the meal is finished?

Rabbi Chaim Kanievsky answers that indeed *mazikim* have no power to harm us Pesach night. But, although they are harmless, we still do not desire their company at our table during the meal. We therefore refrain from opening the door until after the meal and we do not express our meal invitation in a language that they can understand.[137]

Since harmful spiritual forces hold no power on Pesach night, Rabbi Pinchus Epstein rules that (unlike the rest of the year) it is

---

136 *Shemos* 6:6.
137 Rabbi Chaim Kanievsky, *Kehilas Yaakov Haggadah*, pp. 55, 244.

permissible to place food under one's bed the first night of Pesach. In addition, he would also not recite the *al netilas yadayim* blessing on Pesach morning, since the reason a blessing was instituted for washing one's hand in the morning is to remove the impure spirit that rested upon one's hands while one slept during the night.[138]

Rabbi Nissim Karelitz argues that perhaps only certain forms of impure forces are inoperative on Pesach night, such as those mentioned specifically in the Gemara (namely, *zugos*). Since *poskim* do not address whether or not one is obligated to wash one's hands upon arising Pesach morning, or whether it is permissible to place food under one's bed Seder night, we cannot deduce such matters based on logic in the absence of an explicit tradition.[139]

This Is the Bread of Affliction — הא לחמיא עניא

What is the connection between the first part of *Ha Lachma Anya*, in which we invite the poor to join us for the Seder, to the latter part that concludes that this year we are in exile but next year we will be free men in Jerusalem?

Rabbi Moshe Feinstein explains that with this declaration, we are imploring Hashem to bring an end to the *galus*. Since the *Churban* was a result of baseless hatred, we are demonstrating that we have rectified this sin by showing love to our fellow man, as expressed by inviting the poor to our table. And while we admit that perhaps not all Jews are inviting the poor to their table, we claim that their behavior can still be viewed in a favorable manner. We therefore tell Hashem that those people who do not do kindliness to the poor are not acting that way out of mean-spiritedness, but rather as a result of *hashatah hachah* — they are suffering under the burden of exile. The hardships of exile cause them to become self-absorbed and to not have others in mind. But we express with certainty: "Next year

---

138 *Shemiras HaGuf V'Hanefesh* 14, end footnote 1; cf. *Mishnah Berurah* 4:1.
139 Rabbi Nissim Karelitz, *Nesivei HaMinhagim*, p. 181.

we will be in Jerusalem." When the exile will end and they will live in tranquility in Jerusalem, then they will certainly demonstrate their brotherly love in the proper manner.[140]

We Were Slaves — עבדים היינו

עבדים היינו לפרעה במצרים — "We were slaves *to* Pharaoh in Mitzrayim." This could have been stated more succinctly: עבדי פרעה היינו — "we were slaves *of* Pharaoh," which is the terminology the Torah always uses in reference to Pharaoh's non-Jewish slaves.[141] The *Hararei Kedem* comments that unlike the non-Jewish slaves who viewed their whole identity as being slaves of Pharaoh, the Jewish People did not share this slave mentality. The Jews considered only their bodies subjugated to work for Pharaoh, but their essence always remained independent.[142] As the Midrash relates, each Shabbos they would take comfort by reading from the scrolls in their possession that assured them of Hashem's ultimate redemption.[143]

"If Hashem would not have freed our forefathers from *Mitzrayim*, we, our children, and our children's children would still be subjugated to Pharaoh in *Mitzrayim*." Rabbi Yosef Breuer asks: would not one benevolent ruler in the course of history arise to emancipate the Jews?

- Some say that the answer is no, as history has sadly proven that the nations are typically loathe to come to the aid of the Jews.
- An alternative answer is that the *Haggadah* does not say, "We would still be slaves to Pharaoh," but rather, "We would be *subjugated* to Pharaoh." This means that if a later Pharaoh

---

140   *Derash Moshe*, derush 11.
141   *Shemos* 9:20, 10:7, 11:3, and elsewhere.
142   *Hararei Kedem*, vol. 2, p. 213.
143   *Shemos Rabbah* 5:22.

would have freed us out of the goodness of his heart, we would have been eternally indebted to him, which in turn would have mitigated our special relationship with Hashem.

Slaves to Kings

"We were slaves to Pharaoh in Egypt." The Midrash comments: "Slaves to kings, but not slaves to slaves."[144] What difference does it make whether one is a slave to a king or to a commoner?

When a person is a slave in a royal household, he becomes enlightened to the proper honor, service, and etiquette due to a king. Egypt was an important training ground for the Jewish nation, who left there to become servants of the King of all kings.

The Midrash relates that as a result of the Jews being under the direct authority of Pharaoh, when a Jewish slave would pick various expensive fruits in the field or go to the market and take bread, fish, and meat, the Egyptian overlords would be unable to protest, since they could very well have been acting upon the orders of their royal masters.[145] This point is mentioned at the onset of the *Haggadah* to praise Hashem for providing this significant consolation amid our servitude.[146]

Selling Yosef into Slavery

The Mishnah teaches that we should begin the narrative of the Exodus with Israel's disgrace, which is why the *Haggadah* opens with "We were slaves."[147] The Rashbatz explains that the disgrace is not the fact that we were slaves in Egypt, but rather that Yaakov's children sold their brother, Yosef, as a slave, which resulted in Israel's eventual bondage in Egypt,[148] as the Midrash relates: "You sold your

---

144 *Mechiltah, Yisro* 5.
145 *Mechiltah,* 16:3.
146 *Ta'ama D'kra,* p. 69.
147 *Pesachim* 116a.
148 Rashbatz, *Haggadah,* s.v. *"V'amar Rebbi Elazar Ben Azarya"* (end).

brother as a slave; by your life, every year you shall read, 'We were slaves to Pharaoh in Egypt.'"[149]

As this episode is such an integral aspect of the Pesach story, the Seder contains several other references to the sale of Yosef into slavery by his brothers:

- The dipping of *Karpas* (כרפס) in saltwater is to recall Yosef's special coat (כתונת פסים) that his brothers dipped in blood, which ultimately led to Israel's descent to slavery.[150]
- The Vilna Gaon explains that the *Chad Gadya* (lit. "One young kid") song also relates to the sale of Yosef. The cat, which is known for its jealous nature, represents Yosef's brothers who wished to snatch the blessing of the firstborn that Yaakov received from Yitzchak (upon preparing him a meal consisting of a young goat) and thereupon conferred upon Yosef.[151]

It Happened with...Rabbi Akiva and Rabbi Tarfon —
מעשה ברבי אליעזר

"There is a story with...Rabbi Akiva and Rabbi Tarfon." Why is Rabbi Akiva mentioned before Rabbi Tarfon, when in fact Rabbi Akiva was Rabbi Tarfon's student?

Tosfos cites this as proof that the order in which the Sages are cited in a statement of the Talmud is therefore of no particular significance.[152]

There is a debate whether one should or may recline while reading the *Haggadah*. According to the Meiri, the mitzvah of reclining is not limited

---

149 *Midrash Tehillim* 10:3.
150 Rabbeinu Manoach, Rambam, *Mishnah Torah*, Chametz U'Matzah 8:2.
151 *Perush HaGra al Chad Gadya.*
152 *Avodah Zarah* 45a, s.v. *"amar."*

to the drinking of the four cups of wine but extends to all aspects of the Seder, such as the recital of the *Haggadah*, *Hallel*, and *Birchas Hamazon*.[153] Rabbi Shlomo Kluger brings a support to this view from the *Haggadah*'s story of Rabbi Eliezer and his colleagues who were *reclining* while discussing the story of the Exodus the entire Seder night.[154]

The Shelah maintains an opposite approach: one should not recline during the recital of *Haggadah* but rather sit upright, with awe and respect.[155] According to this approach, one may challenge the proof from the story of Rabbi Eliezer and his colleagues by saying that the *Haggadah* is merely relating two separate activities the rabbis did: 1) reclining at times when one should recline, and 2) relating the *Haggadah*, without reclining, the rest of the time.[156]

The Wicked Son's Question — רשע מה הוא אומר

The wicked son says: "What is this service unto you?" The *Yerushalmi* elaborates his question to mean, "What is this bother that you burden us with every year?"[157] The Avudraham understands the wicked son's complaint as to why must we bother every Seder night to delay the meal with all this lengthy talking and thus curtail our enjoyment of the festive meal.

The *Rokeach* expounds the *Yerushalmi* differently. The wicked son's complaint deals with all the preparations prior to Pesach, such as thoroughly cleaning one's home to rid it from *chametz*. The *Rokeach* therefore advises that one should be careful not to complain that they find the preparation for Pesach difficult, since this sums up the attitude of the wicked son.[158]

153　*Pesachim* 108a.

154　Rabbi Shlomo Kluger, *Haggadah*, s.v. "ma'aseh."

155　This is also the accepted view cited by *Mishnah Berurah* 473:71.

156　*Derech Sichah*, p. 242.

157　*Pesachim* 10:4.

158　Cited in *Aruch HaShulchan*, *Orach Chaim* 469:5.

How does the wicked son's question differ from that of the wise son? After all, both sons use the word "you," which implies that they are excluding themselves from participating in the Pesach celebration. The Vilna Gaon answers that the son's wickedness is a combination of two factors:

1. his excluding himself by use of the word "you"
2. not mentioning Hashem's name

The *Haggadah* is to be thus understood: "Because he excluded himself from the community [in addition to] denying Hashem [as demonstrated by his omission of Hashem's name], we therefore blunt his teeth."[159]

Go and Learn — צא ולמד

"Go and learn what Lavan the Aramean attempted to do to our father Yaakov...and Lavan wanted to uproot everything." Where in the Torah do we find Lavan attempting to uproot the entire Jewish nation?

Rabbi Yaakov Kamenetsky finds the source in the final encounter between Lavan and Yaakov. Lavan wished to make a treaty with Yaakov and said, "May the God of Avraham and the god of Nachor judge between us — the god of their father."[160] Lavan wished that there should be a benevolent treaty between their two families, despite Yaakov believing in the God of Avraham and Lavan believing in the idols of his grandfather Nachor, being that they both shared the same ancestry.

Such a bond would have brought ruin to the purity of the Jewish faith and ultimately bring about the destruction of the entire nation. Yaakov spurned his overture by specifically swearing solely in the name of the God of his father, Yitzchak.[161]

---

159   *Chumash HaGra, Shemos* 12:26.
160   *Bereishis* 31:53.
161   *Emes L'Yaakov, Bereishis* ibid.

He Sojourned There — ויגר שם

"'And he sojourned there' — this teaches that our father Yaakov did not descend to Egypt to settle, but only to sojourn there." If Yaakov initially did not intend to settle permanently in Egypt, what changed that his children eventually did feel comfortable remaining in Egypt?

Perhaps we may suggest that Yosef instituted numerous decrees in Egypt that contributed to making the *Bnei Yisrael* feel comfortable in the land. Yosef instituted a law that no Egyptian owned their own land and even made them all relocate to different cities. Yosef's intention was to weaken the pride of the Egyptians and thus making their culture less alluring in the eyes of the Jews. The plan may have backfired, since by raising the status of the Jews to that of their Egyptians hosts, they began to view themselves as equals. Had they been treated as refugees, while they may have felt somewhat inferior, they would have felt socially distant from the Egyptians and uncomfortable in their presence.[162]

The Children of Israel Groaned — ויאנחו בני ישראל

ויאנחו בני ישראל מן העבדה ויזעקו
ותעל שועתם אל האלקים מן העבודה

And the children of Israel groaned because of the work and they cried out. Their outcry went up to Hashem on account of [lit. from] the work.[163]

What is meant that their outcry came "from" their work? The *Ohr HaChaim* offers several explanations:[164]

- Despite the fact that their cries were not prayers directed to Hashem but merely the cries of one who suffers and groans from pain, those cries rose before Hashem and were accepted by Him.

---

162 Cf. *Emes L'Yaakov*, *Bereishis* 47:4.
163 *Shemos* 2:23.
164 *Ohr HaChaim*, *Shemos* ibid.

- The word שועה — outcry, is a specific term for prayer uttered from pain and distress. Generally, people get depressed when in a dismal situation and find it hard to daven. The *pasuk* emphasizes that Hashem heard the extra effort and conviction in their prayers, which was especially difficult for them due to the harsh slavery.
- Generally, prayers rise to heaven via emissaries, such as angels. However the cries from pain are so potent that they rise directly before Hashem without any intermediaries.

Our Toil — ואת עמלנו

"'Our toil' — this refers to the sons." What is the connection between "toil" and "sons"? Some explain that since the Jews had to extend enormous planning and effort to protect their sons from being cast into the Nile (as was the case with baby Moshe), the decree was thus termed *amaleinu* — our toil.

Not through an Angel — לא על ידי מלאך

"Not by an angel, and not by a *seraph*, and not by an emissary, but HaKadosh Baruch Hu Himself." The truth is that Hashem does everything Himself, all the time. We say that an angel is Hashem's agent, but as Rabbi Shimshon Pincus explains, a glove would be a better comparison. The hand does everything, while the glove merely hides the hand.[165] When it is said that angels carry out His will, it is because Hashem's personal involvement is generally concealed from our perception. What is meant that the Exodus from Egypt was not performed through an angel is that Hashem's personal involvement became openly revealed.

"Hashem brought us out of Egypt — not through an angel." This statement appears to be contradicted by the verse, "He sent an

---

165 See *Nefesh Shimshon*, Gates of Emunah, p. 169.

angel and took us out of Egypt."[166] Commentators present a few explanations:

- According to Avudraham, the "angel" in the verse is referring to Moshe. (Scripture sometimes refers to prophets as angels, as in *Shoftim* 2:1). The verse therefore reads as follows: "He sent an angel [Moshe], and [Hashem] (who is the subject of the beginning of the verse) took us out of Egypt."[167]
- Rabbi Eliezer Ashkenazi rejects the Avudraham's approach. Since the verse is Moshe's own words while addressing the King of Edom, it is improbable that the humble Moshe would refer to himself as an angel. He therefore posits that the "angel" of the verse refers to the angel that appeared at the burning bush, which began the process of the Exodus.[168]
- An agent is entrusted with the means to act on behalf of the one who sent him and has the choice whether to carry out his mission. Generally, angels act as agents in fulfilling Hashem's will.[169] At the Exodus, however, Hashem utilized angels merely as tools, not unlike a person who takes a stick to accomplish a task. The *Haggadah* is conveying that when Hashem took us out of Egypt, the angels did not serve in their ordinary capacity as independent agents, but only as tools in Hashem's hand.[170]

---

166 *Bamidbar* 20:16.
167 *Avudraham*, p. 227.
168 *Haggadas Rabbi Eliezer Ashkenazi*, p. 156.
169 Of course, in a practical sense, an angel is never challenged as to whether to accept a mission that Hashem presents him. Angels are said to lack free will since they possess such extraordinary clarity of Hashem's sovereignty that it thoroughly dispels any thoughts or notions of disobedience.
170 *Haggadah, Masei Nisim.*

Plagues at the Sea — ועל הים לקו

There is a debate among the *poskim* whether one fulfills the daily mitzvah of remembering the Exodus by recalling the splitting of the *Yam Suf*, which transpired a week after they left Egypt.[171] Accordingly, one may also question whether one fulfills the mitzvah of relating the Exodus from Egypt on Pesach night by discussing the splitting of the *Yam Suf*. Rabbi Dovid Soleveitchik brings proof that one does from the *Haggadah*, which enumerates the number of miracles that transpired at the *Yam Suf*.[172] Why should the *Haggadah* delve into this point if it were not an integral component of the story of the Exodus? However, one may refute this proof by arguing that the *Haggadah* mentions the miracles at the *Yam Suf* only tangentially to its discussion of the number of miracles that occurred during the Ten Plagues in Egypt.

THE PESACH LAMB

Israel — the Lamb of Hashem

Rabbi Shimshon Raphael Hirsch expounds the symbolic significance as to why a young lamb or goat is specifically chosen to be used for the *Korban Pesach*. He says that it is to remind us that Divine Providence not only watches over us to save and protect us from all harm, but that Hashem is also our Shepherd; He will guide and lead us if we would only follow him. "Pesach is the call of the Shepherd to His flock and the greeting of the flock to its Shepherd. He alone knows the goal; He alone knows how to lead you. Over land and sea, through rivers and fire, He leads Israel, He leads you, if only you follow Him, to the most holy goal."[173] Just as a shepherd tenderly cares for its flock and gathers in the lambs with his arms,[174] so does Hashem lovingly guide us towards attaining our destiny.

---

171   *Magen Avraham, Rabbi Akiva Eiger, Orach Chaim* 67.
172   Rabbi Dovid Soloveitchik, *Meorei HaMoadim*, pp. 46–47.
173   Rabbi Shimshon Raphael Hirsch, *Collected Writings*, vol. 1, p. 7.
174   *Yeshayah* 40:11.

A Convert's Praise

The Mishnah in *Bikurim* says that a *ger tzedek* cannot recite the praise of thanksgiving that accompanies his bringing of *bikurim*,[175] since he is unable to say the phrase, "That Hashem promised our forefathers."[176] The *Yerushalmi* argues that a *ger* can indeed recite that phrase, since all converts are considered descendants of Avraham, the father of all *geirim*.

The *Torah Temimah* brings a proof that the halachah follows the *Yerushalmi* from the *Haggadah shel Pesach*, in which one says, "Pesach, which our forefathers ate to commemorate that HaKadosh Baruch Hu passed over the houses of our forefathers," in order to fulfill his obligation.[177] Since no distinction is made, in either the Talmud or the *poskim*, between the version recited by a *ger* to that of other Jews, we must conclude that the *Yerushalmi* is the halachically-accepted opinion.[178]

Microcosm of the Redemption

The three processes involved in offering the *Korban Pesach* correspond to the three expressions of redemption:

1. The tying of the lamb to the Jews' bedposts represents the subjugation of the Egyptians under the control of the Jews and corresponds to the expression of *v'hotzeisi* — I will remove you from under the burden of Egypt.
2. The slaughtering of the lamb corresponds to *v'hitzalti* — I will save you from their servitude, as the Egyptians would no longer be capable of enslaving the Jews. This was demonstrated by their powerlessness in preventing the Jews from sacrificing their deity.

---

175 *Bikurim* 1:4.
176 See *Devarim* 26:3.
177 Rabbi Baruch HaLevi Epstein, *Torah Temimah*, *Devarim* ibid., note 16.
178 See, however, the view of Rabbeinu Tam, cited in Tosfos, *Bava Basra* 81a, s.v. *"l'miuti."*

3. The eating of the *korban* represents *v'goalti* — the culmination of the Jews' redemption, as Pharaoh himself begged the Jewish People to immediately leave Egypt.

4. Afterwards, they were worthy of receiving the Torah, which corresponds to *v'lokachti* — I will take you for Me as a nation.[179]

Akeidas Yitzchak Connection

"The ram [lit. sheep] that was caught was offered on the *Akeidah*... He said that the Pesach lamb should be bound from the tenth of Nissan."[180] The liturgist compares the sheep that was bound on the altar at *Akeidas Yitzchak* to the binding of the *Korban Pesach* lambs to the bedposts prior to the Exodus. The connection may be that just as Yitzchak demonstrated *mesiras nefesh* by allowing himself to be bound to the altar at *Akeidas Yitzchak*, the Jewish nation demonstrated similar self-sacrifice by tying the Paschal lamb to their bedposts, despite the danger it posed to them, as the lamb was worshiped as the god of the Egyptians.

The Sages say that the erection of the Mishkan was delayed to the month of Nissan so that it would coincide with the month of Yitzchak's birth. We may add and say that the offering of the *Korban Pesach* also falls out on the day of Yitzchak's birth (as Yitzchak was born on the fifteenth of Nissan[181]), since his self-sacrifice instilled into *Bnei Yisrael* the quality of self-sacrifice that emerged through their offering of the *Korban Pesach*.

Eliminating the "Husk"

Yetzias Mitzrayim was a prerequisite for receiving the Torah, as the *pasuk* says, "When you take the nation out of Egypt, you shall serve Hashem on this mountain."[182] The *Zohar* explains that the

---

179   Rabbi Yitzchak Minkovski, *Keren Orah*, *Ta'anis* 30b.
180   *Yotzer*, *Parashas HaChodesh*.
181   *Mechiltah*; *Tosfos HaRosh*, *Rosh Hashanah* 11a.
182   *Shemos* 3:12.

klipah — husk — of *Mitzrayim* created a partition around their souls that prevented them from receiving the light of Torah. This "husk" was destroyed when *Bnei Yisrael* offered the *Korban Pesach*, consumed the lamb, and afterwards discarded its bones, effectively nullifying the deity of the Egyptians.[183]

No Satisfying Aroma

All Temple offerings provided "a satisfying aroma before Hashem," except for the *Korban Pesach*.[184] This results in many significant distinctions between the Pesach offering and other sacrifices:

- Unlike other sacrifices, the aroma of the *Korban Pesach* was not to bring satisfaction to Hashem, but to instill the Jewish People with faith in Hashem. The *Zohar* writes that since Egypt worshiped the lamb, the *Korban Pesach* served to eradicate all vestiges of idol worship from the hearts of the Jewish People. Since this was achieved specifically by the Jews absorbing the aroma of the offering, the Torah commanded that the offering be roasted — a cooking method that gives forth a strong, pleasing aroma — and not eaten raw or boiled. It was for this same reason the sacrifice was to be eaten after one was satiated — in order to underscore that the primary pleasure is to be derived from the fragrant smell of the *korban* and not through eating it.[185]
- When the Temple was destroyed, all Temple services ceased. An exception was made with the Pesach offering, which was the only sacrifice that continued to be offered upon a makeshift Altar built on the Temple site. The reason why other sacrifices were no longer brought is because the

---

183   *Keren Orah, Ta'anis* 30b.

184   *Chumash HaGra, Shemos* p. 107; *Emek Brachah* (Purmantzik), pp. 77–78; *Ha'amek Davar, Vayikra* 26:31, *Devarim* 16:3; *Ohr Sameach*, Rambam, *Mishnah Torah*, Chametz U'Matzah 6:1; *Rivavos Ephraim*, p. 264.

185   *Chumash HaGra, Shemos* p. 107; *Emek Brachah* (Purmantzik), pp. 77–78.

Torah writes that with the Temple's destruction, Hashem will no longer accept the appeasing fragrance of the sacrificial offerings.[186] Since the *Korban Pesach* does not entail "a pleasing aroma" to Hashem, it was therefore permitted to be offered.[187]

- Other sacrifices are primarily to bring satisfaction to Hashem, while the purpose of the Pesach offering was that it be eaten. As such, while there is a general obligation for a *korban* to be consumed in order to prevent it from being left over, there is no mitzvah incumbent on a specific individual to eat it. This is unlike the *Korban Pesach*, which entails a specific command that it be eaten by every member in Israel.[188]

MATZAH

Hasty Redemption

Rabbi Moshe Feinstein comments that the matzah is a symbol of redemption and offers encouragement even when a person's situation appears hopeless. Just as when the Jews left Egypt it happened so suddenly that they didn't even have enough time to allow their bread to rise, so too does all of Hashem's salvation come in a sudden, unexpected manner.[189] This can be seen in the verse regarding the future redemption, when the prophet declares: "And suddenly the Master will come to His sanctuary."[190]

---

186 *Vayikra* 26:31.
187 *Ha'amek Davar*, *Vayikra* 26:31, *Devarim* 16:3.
188 *Ohr Someach*, Rambam, *Mishnah Torah*, Chametz U'Matzah 6:1; *Rivavos Ephraim*, p. 264.
189 *Derash Moshe*, p. 82; also Seforno, *Bereishis* 41:14.
190 *Malachi* 3:1; Seforno ibid.

AFIKOMEN

A Taste of the Korban Pesach

The reason why the *afikomen* is represented by matzah may be because the mitzvah of eating matzah all seven days of Pesach also relates to the *Korban Pesach*, as the *pasuk* says, "You shall eat matzos seven days because of it."[191] The word *it* refers back to the *Korban Pesach* mentioned in the previous verse. This implies that the matzah serves as a continuation of the *Korban Pesach*.[192] Nevertheless, in order to demonstrate that the matzah does not have the actual holiness of a *korban*, we have the custom to hide the *afikomen*. If it were an actual *korban*, it would become disqualified because it was not properly watched.

A Lingering Taste

One may not eat anything after the *afikomen* in order that the taste of the matzah should linger in one's mouth. The *Orchos Chaim* states cryptically that the reason for this is "because we are obligated to relate the story of *Yetzias Mitzrayim* the entire night."[193] What is the connection between retaining the taste of the *afikomen* and relating the story of the Exodus?

The Avudraham explains that having the taste of matzah linger in one's mouth serves as a reminder of the rationales for the mitzvos of Pesach and will thus stimulate one to discuss them the entire night.[194]

Alternatively, we may suggest that this is like the requirement of having the matzah and *maror* placed before you while reciting the *Haggadah*. This may be to involve the senses — in this case the sense of sight — to help stimulate us in reciting the *Haggadah*. While this is not possible to fulfill once the matzah and *maror* are eaten, we

---

191   *Devarim* 16:3.
192   Heard in the name of Rabbi Nosson Gugenheim.
193   *Orchos Chaim, Hilchos Leil Pesach* 28.
194   *Avudraham, Haggadah,* s.v. *"chacham mah."*

then resort to enlisting the sense of taste. By retaining the taste of the *afikomen* in our mouths, it assists us to continue relating the Exodus story until we are overcome with sleep.

One may not eat anything after partaking of the *afikomen* so that the taste of the *afikomen* will linger in one's mouth. The Radvaz rules that after eating the *afikomen*, it is permissible to go elsewhere, wash, and eat another *afikomen* (for example, to conduct a Seder for those who are unknowledgeable in conducting one), since the taste of the second *afikomen* will remain.[195]

THE THIRD CUP OF WINE

One may not drink wine between the third and fourth cups of the *arbah kosos*. The *Yerushalmi* explains that the reason is because one may become drunk and be unable to say *Hallel* or complete the Seder.[196] If so, why is it permissible to drink between the first and second cups, as well as during the meal, and yet we are not concerned that a person will become drunk?

The Maharal answers that it is not customary to get drunk before eating one's meal, so the Sages were not concerned with drinking between the first and second cups. The reason why we are not concerned that a person will get drunk during the Seder meal is because wine consumed during a meal does not intoxicate. The Maharal suggests that since the *Talmud Bavli* does not cite the reason of the *Yerushalmi*, it therefore has another rationale for this law. He explains that since the third cup of wine symbolizes the redemption (*v'goalti*), the purpose of which was to bond with Hashem by accepting the Torah (*v'lokachti*), there may be no separation between those two cups.[197]

195   Radvaz 1:480.
196   *Yerushalmi*, *Pesachim* 10:6.
197   Maharal, *Gevuras Hashem*, end ch. 49 and p. 270.

THE CUP OF ELIYAHU

Why is the cup of wine placed on the table after *bentching* called "the cup of Eliyahu"?

The *Hararei Kedem* comments that the four cups of wine we drink at the Seder correspond to the four expressions of redemption. The fifth cup of wine corresponds to *v'heveisi* — "I shall bring you to the land," which is where the Jewish People can attain the highest level of closeness with Hashem.[198] Since this ultimate expression of redemption will only come to fruition with the coming of Mashiach, we do not drink this fifth cup, but just place it on the table to express our belief in Eliyahu's imminent arrival, which will herald our final redemption.[199]

There are different customs regarding what should be done with the *kos shel Eliyahu* — the fifth cup of wine. Some pour it into the participants' cups as the fourth cup of wine, while others leave it covered and use it the following day for *kiddush*. *Vayaged Moshe* explains that the rationale for not combining the fifth cup with the fourth is because the four cups of wine correspond to the redemption from *Mitzrayim*, while the fifth cup symbolizes the future redemption.[200]

Opening the Door

The night of Pesach is called *Leil Shimurim* — the night of protection. The Midrash explains it as "a night protected from harmful forces."[201] This may be the basis for the custom in some communities to leave the doors of their homes unlocked on the night of Pesach.

---

198   *Shemos* 6:8.
199   *Hararei Kedem*, vol. 2, 102:5.
200   Rabbi Moshe Yehudah Katz, *Vayaged Moshe* 30:5.
201   *Yalkut Shimoni, Bo.*

The *Orchos Chaim*, however, presents a different rationale for this custom. The Midrash presents an alternate translation for *Leil Shimurim. Shomer* can also mean to wait in anticipation.[202] From the beginning of creation, Hashem waited for the night of Pesach to bring the redemption from Egypt, and He also waits to bring the final redemption on this night.[203] The doors of one's home are therefore unlocked on this night so that when Eliyahu Hanavi arrives, he will find the doors to our homes open, and we will be ready to greet him without a moment's delay. Our eager anticipation for the arrival of Mashiach renders us worthy of redemption.[204]

The *Aruch HaShulchan* writes that our opening the door while reciting *Shefoch Chamascha* expresses this same idea. *Chazal* say that *Bnei Yisrael* merited leaving Egypt in merit of their *emunah*, and that the future redemption will also be brought in merit of our *emunah*. By opening the doors to our home at this time, we demonstrate our trust in Hashem that He will protect us from all external dangers, wreak revenge against the enemies of Israel, and speedily bring Eliyahu Hanavi to herald the redemption. In merit of this *emunah*, we will be deserving of the final redemption.[205]

Pour Your Wrath — שפך חמתך

Shefoch Chamascha is recited on the fourth cup of wine. Rabbeinu Bachya says that this symbolizes that the day will come when the nations who mistreated us will be forced to drink four bitter cups of retribution.[206]

---

202   See Rashi, *Bereishis* 37:11.

203   *Yalkut Shimoni, Yeshayah* 436.

204   Rabbeinu Aharon HaKohen M'Lunil, *Orchos Chaim, Leil Pesach* 37.

205   *Aruch HaShulchan, Orach Chaim* 480:1.

206   Rabbeinu Bachya, *Shemos* 6:8. Those verses describing the retribution are found in *Yirmiyah* 25:15, 51:7; *Tehillim* 11:6, 75:9.

Why is *Shefoch Chamascha* — "Pour your wrath upon the nations," recited at the end of the meal prior to pouring the fourth cup of wine?

- Generally we do not drink cups of wine in pairs because it incites the *mazikim* — demons, against us. On Pesach night, we specifically drink four cups of wine to demonstrate that it is *Leil Shimurim* — a night of protection against those dangerous forces.[207] We therefore recite *Shefoch Chamascha* at this point to highlight that on this night, not only do we not fear demons, but we order them around! In the *Shefoch Chamascha* prayer, we ask Hashem that He instruct the *mazikim* that they should leave us alone and that they should instead wreak their destruction upon the wicked nations."[208]

- Generally, a guest thanks his hosts at the end of the meal. The nations consume the Jewish nation as well as the earth's bounty and yet never express any praise to Hashem for all they eat.[209] We therefore use this opportunity when we are at the end of our Seder meal to call upon Hashem to destroy the nations who do not offer praise to Hashem after their meals.[210]

HALLEL

Why No Blessing?

Ordinarily when we recite *Hallel*, we preface and conclude the *Hallel* with a blessing. Why don't we recite these two blessings when we recite *Hallel* during the Seder?

---

207 *Pesachim* 109b.
208 *Chasam Sofer, Orach Chaim* 480:1.
209 *Tehillim* 14:4.
210 Meiri, *Pesachim* 99b.

The *Magen Avraham* explains that the blessings of *Asher G'olanu* and *Yishtabach* serve as the two blessings prior to and upon the conclusion of *Hallel*.[211]

Why Sitting?

Hallel is generally recited standing, since that is the proper manner for servants to praise their master.[212] If so, why on Seder night is the *Hallel* recited while sitting?

There are a number of reasons given for this custom:

- Since *Hallel* recited at the Seder is split up into two parts, the rabbis did not wish to burden people with the need to stand twice.[213]
- Since one is holding the cup of wine during *Hallel*, we are concerned that one may come to spill the wine were he to stand the entire duration of *Hallel*.[214]
- Since (in his opinion) one has already recited *Hallel* in shul while standing, one does not need to stand again.[215]
- Since at Seder night we are required to act in a reclining manner as befitting free men, the rabbis did not necessitate standing while reciting *Hallel*.[216]
- We may have become intoxicated from the wine drunk prior to *Hallel*, and thus may be unable to stand properly.[217]

---

211 *Magen Avraham, Orach Chaim* 422:6.
212 *Tehillim* 135:1, 2.
213 *Shebolei HaLeket*, cited in *Beis Yosef, Orach Chaim* 422:7.
214 *Shebolei HaLeket* ibid.
215 Ibid.
216 *Ra"M*, cited in *Beis Yosef* ibid.
217 *Pri Chadash* ibid., Chidah.

Chad Gadya — חד גדיא

According to the Vilna Gaon, the *Chad Gadya* song personifies the eternal struggle and interplay between the forces of good and evil:[218]

- The goat represents the right of the firstborn, which our forefather Yaakov bought from Eisav (who is compared to a goat) and gave to Yosef.
- The cat, which is known for its jealous nature, represents the brothers of Yosef who sold Yosef into slavery.
- Pharaoh, who subjugated the nation of Israel, is compared to a dog, which is finally hit by the staff of Moshe.
- The final stanza corresponds to the final redemption, at which time Hashem will destroy the Angel of Death.

The reason why we conclude the song with the repetition of all the earlier episodes of history is to indicate that in the end, all the blessings that were snatched from Israel when the forces of evil were in power will ultimately be restored to the Jewish People.

---

218   *Perush HaGra al Chad Gadya.*

SEFIRAS HAOMER — COUNTING THE OMER

...For a Bountiful Crop

Why does the Torah begin its discussion of Shavuos with the commandments regarding the *Omer* offering (and its accompanying animal sacrifices) and *sefirah* — the counting of the seven weeks?[1]

The Seforno explains that the purpose of each festival is to both give thanks for the past and to be a prayer for the future. Shavuos is referred to as חג הקציר — the Harvest Festival. The *korban Omer* is our manner of giving thanks for the early barley grain crop that is reaped at Pesach-time (similar to a sharecropper who gives the first fruits to the owner), and the animal offering is a prayer for the future grain crops. Since the success of the remainder of the harvest is dependent on the rainfall and optimal climate conditions during the following seven weeks, the mitzvah of counting *sefirah* is to remind Israel to pray daily during these critical weeks leading up to the wheat harvest. This seven-week

---

1   Seforno, *Vayikra* 23.

period culminates with Shavuos, at which time we give thanks for the bountiful wheat harvest.[2]

...For Fifty Gates of Enlightenment

"You shall count fifty days."[3] The *Rokeach* says that the fifty days correspond to the נ' שערי בינה — "fifty gates of understanding." The reason we count forty-nine days of *sefirah* is to unlock one of these gates each day.[4]

This is hinted to in the verse: וכמטמונים תחפשנה — "And search for her [the Torah] like hidden treasures,"[5] which can also be read: מ"ט מונים תחפשנה — "You shall search for her by counting forty-nine [days]."[6]

To remind us that each day of *sefirah* is to be utilized to unlock one of the gates of wisdom, some have the custom to bake a challah in the shape of a key (*shlissel challah*) on the first Shabbos following Pesach.[7]

...For the Jubilee Festival

The *Zohar* draws a parallel between Shavuos and *Yovel* — the Jubilee year, in that just as the sanctity of *Yovel* is only attained at the fiftieth year, so is the sanctity of Shavuos attained on the fiftieth day from Pesach. In addition, Shavuos is similar to *Yovel* in that just as the fiftieth year grants freedom to slaves, so too does the Torah, which is given on the fiftieth day, grant freedom from subjugation of the nations, freedom from suffering, and freedom from the Angel of Death.[8]

---

2   Ibid., v. 8.
3   *Vayikra* 23:16.
4   *Rokeach, Hilchos Pesach*, p. 162.
5   *Mishlei* 2:4.
6   *Rokeach* ibid.
7   *Haggadah shel Pesach, Ohev Yisrael*, p. 243.
8   Cited in *Meshech Chochmah, Vayikra* 25:2; cf. *Teshuvos Ohr Someach* 2:1.

Counting Fifty Days

Why do we only count forty-nine days of *sefirah* if the *pasuk* says, "You shall count fifty days"?[9]

The *Ha'amek Davar* explains that since it says the word *sefirah* twice in reference to the forty-nine days, while regarding the fiftieth day it is mentioned only once, the double usage signifies that the forty-nine days must be counted orally, while the fiftieth day has a diminutive form of counting in that it is sufficient to count the fiftieth day in one's thoughts alone.[10]

Rabbi Yitzchak of Volozhin answers that regarding the forty-nine days, it says, *u'sfartem lachem* — "you shall count for yourselves," from which we derive that every individual must count the *Omer*. However, since the word *lachem* is omitted in reference to the counting of the fiftieth day, the obligation of counting the fiftieth day is upon *Beis Din* and not on each individual.[11]

Complete Weeks

"You shall count…seven weeks; they should be complete (*temimos*)."[12] Why does the Torah add the seemingly superfluous word *temimos*?

The Midrash points out that whenever the Torah writes *tam* — complete, it denotes a number that it is divisible by seven. In reference to Avraham, it states, "You shall be *tamim* — complete"[13] and he lived 175 years (which is divisible by seven). Yaakov was called an *ish tam* and he lived 147 years. Iyov, who was also called *tam*, lived 140 years. Since Shavuos commences seven weeks after the bringing of the *korban Omer*, the Torah therefore utilizes the terminology *temimos*.[14]

---

9   *Vayikra* 23:16.
10   *Ha'amek Davar, Vayikra* 23:15.
11   Rabbi Yitzchak of Volozhin, *Peh Kodesh, parashas Emor*, cited in *Hararei Kedem* 2:113.
12   *Vayikra* 23:15.
13   *Bereishis* 17:1.
14   *Moshav Zekeinim, Bereishis* 25:27.

NAMES OF THE FESTIVAL

Shavuos

What is so important about the interim weeks between Pesach and Shavuos that we name the holiday after the *Shavuos* — weeks?

- The Seforno answers that it is to give praise to Hashem, "Who preserves for us *the weeks* appointed for the harvest,"[15] by providing the optimal climatic conditions throughout the weeks of the crops' growth, which thereby granted them a bountiful harvest.[16]

- Another approach focuses on preparation. The seven weeks between Pesach and Shavuos correspond to seven Divine attributes (such as *chesed* — kindness, *gevurah* — strength, etc.) that we strive to emulate during this period.[17] The festival is thus named after the preparatory weeks, and not the day we actually received the Torah, since one receives a portion in Torah to the degree one properly prepared for it in the weeks leading up to the Yom Tov.[18]

- Rabbi Shlomo Zalman Auerbach answers that it is to connect the significance of the *Minchas Omer* offering, which is brought at the beginning of the "weeks," to the *Shtei HaLechem* offering, which is brought at the end of the "weeks." The *Omer* permits the usage of the new crop for human consumption, and the *Shtei HaLechem* permits usage of the new wheat harvest for *korbanos*. These two offerings symbolize that when we offer the first of our monetary

---

15   *Yirmiyah* 5:24.

16   Seforno, *Vayikra* 23:8.

17   Rabbi Elya Lopian. In addition, there are forty-nine days between Pesach and Shavuos, and there are forty-eight ways (see *Avos* 6:5) through which the Torah is acquired. This is so that a person can utilize each day to internalize each of the traits and the forty-ninth day to review all forty-eight ways.

18   Rabbi Leib Gurwitz, *Kol HaTorah*, vol. 53, p. 140.

possessions to Hashem, it elevates our mundane objects and enables us to derive physical pleasure from them in a sanctified manner.[19]

ATZERES

Refraining from Work

In the Torah, the word *Atzeres* is used to describe the seventh day of Pesach,[20] as well as Shemini Atzeres.[21] It is ironic that the word *Atzeres* is not employed by the Torah in connection with Shavuos, and yet it is specifically this expression that is commonly associated with the Yom Tov of Shavuos.

The Rashbam and Ibn Ezra explain that the word *atzeres* means "refraining." The Torah utilizes the term *atzeres* to describe a festival day that has no specific mitzvah other than abstaining from work.[22] It is therefore an appropriate expression for the Yom Tov of Shavuos, which, unlike the festivals of Pesach and Sukkos, has no particular mitzvah associated with it.[23]

Climax of Pesach

Rabbeinu Bachya states a principle that the less explicit the Torah is about a certain mitzvah, the deeper and more spiritual it is. Thus the name *Atzeres*, which the Oral Torah uses to describe the holiday of Shavuos, but is not used in the written Torah, is a more hidden and more "more spiritual" name.[24]

According to Ramban, Shavuos is called *Atzeres* because it culminates the holiday of Pesach, just as Shemini Atzeres culminates the

---

19   *Halichos Shlomo, Shavuos* 11:15.
20   *Devarim* 16:8.
21   *Vayikra* 23:36.
22   Ibn Ezra, *Vayikra* ibid.; Rashbam there.
23   *Emes L'Yaakov, Devarim* 16:8.
24   Rabbeinu Bachya, *Vayikra* 23:24.

Yom Tov of Sukkos.[25] The period between Pesach and Shavuos — the days of *sefirah* — are comparable to the intermediate festival days of Chol Hamo'ed. (Accordingly, the days of *sefirah* are inherently a joyous period. It only changed into a time of mourning as a result of the death of Rabbi Akiva's students during this period.)

The Sukkos-Shavuos Connection

There is a connection between Shavuos and Sukkos in that both are called *Chag*,[26] as well as *Atzeres*.[27] The *Sefer HaToda'ah* makes a further connection — the Torah was originally given on *Atzeres* [Shavuos], and on Shemini Atzeres we celebrate our receiving of the Torah.[28]

The distinction between the two is that the first *Atzeres* [Shavuos] was accompanied with a *Bris HaYirah* — a covenant of fear (as *Bnei Yisrael* trembled with fear when receiving the Torah at Sinai) — while the second *Atzeres* [Shemini Atzeres and Simchas Torah] is accompanied with love and joy. The two complement each other, though; fear of Hashem alone is incomplete without love, and love of Hashem is incomplete if not accompanied by fear.

Reward for Holding Back

The *Bnei Yissachar* says that the reason the sages called Shavuos *Atzeres* is because *Atzeres* means holding back.[29] The only mitzvah incumbent upon the Jewish People during *Matan Torah* was to restrain themselves from ascending the mountain.[30] He explains that when a person is granted a spiritual revelation, in order to internalize that revelation, one must fulfill a mitzvah pertinent to that ideal. Thus, their *atzeres* — i.e., holding back from ascending the mountain — was the glue that bound the *Matan Torah* experience to the Jewish People.

---

25 Ramban, *Vayikra* 23:36.
26 *Eduyos* 7:6; see Bartenura there.
27 *Taanis* 12b; Rashi there.
28 *Sefer HaToda'ah*, p. 128.
29 *Bnei Yissachar, Sivan* 3,1.
30 *Shemos* 19:12.

One could offer a slightly different approach: As stated above, *atzeres* means holding back. We know that after *Matan Torah*, the Jewish People were overzealous in leaving Mount Sinai. Although they were faulted for this behavior, they obviously must have had their reasons; perhaps they were enthusiastic about leaving Har Sinai so that they could enter Eretz Yisrael as quickly as possible. Hence, since the Torah could have been equally given in Eretz Yisrael, their zeal to enter the land could have driven them to request delaying *Matan Torah* until they reached their ideal destination in the Land of Israel. However, to their great credit, they were instead *otzrim* — "holders-back," in order to receive the Torah at the earliest possible moment.

ZMAN MATAN TORASEINU

Given or Received?

Why is Shavuos called *Zman Matan Toraseinu* — the time the Torah was *given* to us, and not *Zman Kabalas Toraseinu* — the time we *received* the Torah?

- Out of our great love of Hashem, we wish to focus on praising Hashem for what He does for us, rather than for what we did for Hashem.[31] We therefore name the festival after Hashem giving us the Torah and not on our having accepted it.
- *Chazal* say that although *Bnei Yisrael* verbally accepted the Torah wholeheartedly, in their hearts they harbored ambivalence about it.[32] It would therefore be presumptuous for us to call the Yom Tov the *Zman Kabalas Toraseinu* — the time of our acceptance of the Torah.[33]

---

31 See *Tosfos Chadashim, Pesachim* 1:1.
32 *Tosefta, Bava Kama* 7:3; *Bamidbar Rabbah* 7:4.
33 Cf. *Halichos Shlomo*, Shavuos 12:1,1.

JUDGMENT OF SHAVUOS

Dual Judgment

The Torah calls all the Yomim Tovim *chagim* — joyous festivals, with the exception of Shavuos.[34] The *Rokeach* explains that on Shavuos, our joy is mitigated since Shavuos is a day of judgment for fruit trees,[35] as well as for our personal relationship with Torah, as Torah is also compared to a tree.[36]

The *Zohar* comments that this dual judgment is hinted to in the Mishnah that states: "*B'Atzeres al peros ha'ilan* — On Shavuos [is the judgment] on the fruit of the tree."[37] Why doesn't the Mishnah use the plural expression, *al peros ha'ilanos* — on fruit *trees*? The answer is that the singular "tree" is a hint to the Torah, which is compared to a tree.[38]

Although all festivals are also periods of judgment (e.g., Pesach on wheat, Sukkos on water), our joy is not mitigated on those days. The reason why only the judgment on Shavuos minimizes our joy is because the judgment on Shavuos parallels the judgment on Rosh Hashanah. Just as the world was created on Rosh Hashanah, so too was the world considered recreated anew at *Matan Torah*. Nevertheless, unlike Rosh Hashanah, where the focus is solely on the judgment of the day, the focus on Shavuos is also to rejoice exceedingly to celebrate our good fortune in meriting the crown of Torah.[39]

Shavuos Trees

There was an ancient custom to bedeck the shul on Shavuos with non-fruit-bearing trees. (The *Mishnah Berurah* writes that this custom was abolished when Gentiles adopted it during their holiday

---

34 *Bamidbar* chap. 28–29.
35 *Yalkut Shimoni, Emor* 654.
36 *Mishlei* 3:18. See *Rokeach, Bamidbar* 28:26.
37 *Rosh Hashanah* 16a.
38 *Zohar, Vayechi*, p. 226b.
39 *Shelah, Mesechtah Shavuos*, p. 252.

season).[40] Why were non-fruit trees specifically used if Shavuos is the Rosh Hashanah of fruit trees?

The primary reason is because of the prohibition of *ba'al taschis*, which forbids the wasteful destruction of fruit trees.

There could be a secondary reason as well. It says in the beginning of the blessings in *parashas Bechukosai* that if the Jewish People are worthy, even non-bearing trees will give forth fruit. Since this utopian state is attained as a reward for toiling in Torah study,[41] it is therefore fitting that this message be highlighted during the Yom Tov of Shavuos, which commemorates the giving of the Torah to the Jewish People.

Humble Vegetation

It is customary to decorate the shul with trees on Shavuos and to eat new fruits on Tu b'Shevat. It would seem more logical for these occasions to be commemorated in a reverse manner, as Shavuos is the time when the fruits are judged and Tu b'Shevat is the New Year for trees!

The Satmar Rav, Rabbi Yoel Teitelbaum, answers that the trees, in their humility, pray for their continued existence in the merit of their worthy fruit. The fruits, on the other hand, consider their own merits insufficient and attribute the tree as their sole source of merit.

JOY OF SHAVUOS

Most Joyous Festival

The ultimate *simchah* on Shavuos is to rejoice over the Torah. The Vilna Gaon would say that the mitzvah he found the most difficult to perform was to rejoice on Yom Tov, as it required him to be in a constant state of happiness for the duration of the festival. It is quoted that the Vilna Gaon was the happiest on Shavuos from all the festivals, as he used it to express his joy for Torah, which was his entire life.[42]

---

40   *Mishnah Berurah* 494:10.
41   See Rashi, *Vayikra* 26:3.
42   *Likutei HaGra, Ma'aseh Rav* 196.

Natural Joy

The Torah calls Shavuos the "Festival of the Harvest," and the obligation to be joyous at this time focuses exclusively on the happiness resulting from the bountiful harvest. Why doesn't the Torah command us to rejoice for having been given the Torah, whose value infinitely surpasses all material possessions?

The Chasam Sofer answers that Hashem wishes that our joy for the Torah be sincere and spontaneous. This would be impossible if we were compelled to rejoice over the Torah because of a sense of duty — i.e., because Hashem told us to.[43] The Torah therefore commands us to rejoice for the successful crop. Hashem's intent is that through this mundane joy, one will eventually ascend to rejoice over the Torah — whose goodness surpasses all physical fortune — on one's own accord.[44]

Joy beyond Logic

It is peculiar that when the Torah commands one to be joyous during the festival of Shavuos, it employs the terminology *chok* — a Divine fiat devoid of logic.[45] Rabbi Yisrael Salanter explains that this is because receiving the Torah is not without its risks. A person who neglects the Torah would be better off never having received it, and it was for this reason the nations declined the Torah — to avoid the risk of punishment for disobeying G-d's will. Although from a human perspective it may be difficult to appreciate why the acceptance of such a weighty responsibility is a cause for rejoicing, we nonetheless quash any personal apprehensions in order to fulfill Hashem's will.[46]

Considering the awesome responsibility inherent in accepting the Torah, how indeed is it possible for one to rejoice on Shavuos?

---

43 We can compare this to a parent who delegates chores to all family members. Would a parent command a child to buy him a present or to demonstrate other expressions of love? The parent desires that the child attains this aspect of the relationship on his own.

44 *Toras Moshe, Bereishis*, p. 246.

45 *Devarim* 16:11–12.

46 Rabbi Yisrael Salanter, *Ohr Yisrael* 23.

We may compare it to a poor groom from a simple background who is engaged to a beautiful princess. Even if he may have serious concerns as to how he will be able to support his wife, nevertheless, on the wedding day itself, he is completely focused on the joy of the moment and disregards the logical difficulties that lie in store for him in the future.

Worldly Enjoyment

Since on Shavuos we celebrate our receiving a spiritual Torah, why does the Torah require that we celebrate the festival specifically by partaking in physical enjoyment?

Rabbi Shlomo Zalman Auerbach offers two answers: Although we may personally enjoy the spiritual pleasures of Torah study, we are required to eat and drink to show others who are not familiar with such delights that we are happy on this day. In addition, we specifically enjoy the physical on Shavuos to demonstrate that Torah is not severe or austere, but that its ways are pleasurable even from a physical worldly perspective.[47]

A Perfect Combination

There is a debate among the Sages whether Yom Tov should be spent exclusively in Torah study, in physical enjoyments, or in a combination of the two. However, all authorities concede that Shavuos requires partaking of physical delights, since it was the day on which the Torah was given.[48] Rabbi Chaim Kanievsky explains that this is because the Torah was given on the morning of Shavuos, and prior to that time Bnei Yisrael were neither commanded in Torah study nor to rejoice on the festival. As the original Shavuos day was perforce not spent entirely in Torah study or through celebrating the festival with physical enjoyment, it was instituted that in the future Shavuos would also not be devoted entirely to either pursuit.[49]

---

47   Halichos Shlomo, Moadim, 12:51.
48   Pesachim 68b.
49   Ta'ama D'kra, p. 87.

TIME PERIODS OF SHAVUOS

Month of Sivan

The *Midrash Chefetz* says that the month of Sivan (סיון) derives from סיני (Sinai) and נס (miracle), since during this month the Jewish nation experienced miracles when they received the Torah at Sinai.[50]

The zodiac sign for the month of Sivan is the twins. This symbolizes that as a result of the giving of the Torah that occurred in the month of Sivan, the Jewish People and Hashem became, so-to-speak, similar to one another, as *Chazal* interpret Hashem's endearing description of the Jewish People in *Shir HaShirim*, יונתי תמתי — "My perfect dove," as תאומתי — "My twin."[51]

Date of Shavuos

On the fourth of Sivan, Hashem commanded the Jewish People to sanctify themselves for two days prior to receiving the Torah. (The day of instruction is counted as the first day of this preparation period.) According to Rabbi Yosi, Moshe was *hosif yom echad midato* — added an extra day on his own accord — in order for *Bnei Yisrael* to properly sanctify themselves for receiving the Torah.[52] Accordingly, *Bnei Yisrael* received the Torah on the seventh day of Sivan.

If so, asks the *Magen Avraham*,[53] why do we celebrate Shavuos on the sixth of Sivan, and how can that day be called *Zman Matan Toraseinu* — the Time of the Giving of Our Torah?

The *Beis HaLevi* answers that the sixth of Sivan is commemorated as the day of the giving of the Torah, since the the Torah also includes the right of the Sages to interpret the Torah according to their understanding. Since Hashem agreed to Moshe's decision to delay

---

50 *Torah Sheleimah, Bo, Miluim*, p. 177.
51 *Shir HaShirim Rabbah* 5:2.
52 *Shabbos* 87a.
53 *Magen Avraham*, in his introduction to *Orach Chaim* 494.

the giving of the Torah for one day,[54] the giving of the Torah actually began on the sixth of Sivan.[55]

The Disappearing Day

While the Torah says that Shavuos begins after fifty days of *sefirah*, the first Shavuos actually took place on the fifty-first day. This is because in the year of the Exodus the month of Iyar was *malei* (a thirty-day month), while in subsequent generations it is always *chasser* (twenty-nine days). That the original Shavuos occurred on the fifty-first day does not pose a difficulty in light of the Torah commandment to count fifty days of *sefirah*, since the Torah's obligation to count the fifty-day *sefirah* was not given prior to the original Shavuos but only took effect the following year, once Iyar would always have only twenty-nine days.[56]

Time Frame of Ten Commandments

"Save us in the merit of the three hours."[57] What is the explanation of "the three hours" and what "merit" transpired at that time?

The *Ayeles HaShachar* cites a *Pirkei D'Rebbi Eliezer* who says that *Bnei Yisrael* received the Torah at midday of the sixth of Sivan, and at the ninth hour of the day they went back to their tents.[58] Accordingly, *Kabbalas HaTorah* took three hours. The meritorious "three hours" is therefore a reference to the three hours during which *Bnei Yisrael* received the Torah on Mount Sinai.[59]

No Tosfos Yom Tov

On Shabbos and Yom Tov, there is a mitzvah of *Tosfos Yom Tov* — to voluntarily accept the onset of the festival prior to nightfall. An

---

54   *Shabbos* 87a.
55   *Parashas Yisro*, s.v. *"lehavin ha'inyan."*
56   Commentary of Rosh, *Shemos* 12:39.
57   *Hoshanos* liturgy, recited on Sukkos.
58   *Pirkei D'Rebbi Eliezer* 45.
59   Rabbi Aharon Yehudah Leib Shteinman, *Ayeles HaShachar*, *Shemos* 20:1.

exception to this general rule is the holiday of Shavuos, where there is no mitzvah of *Tosfos Yom Tov*. Therefore, the *Magen Avraham* rules that one should not make *kiddush* before nightfall,[60] and according to other views one should not even daven before that time.[61] Why is Shavuos different than Shabbos and the other festivals in this regard?

Although all Yomim Tovim are called *mikra'ei kodesh* — holy convocations, in the Torah, Shavuos is unique in that the Torah adds, "And you shall convoke *on this very day*, there shall be a holy convocation for yourselves."[62] Rabbi Yaakov Kamenetsky explains the distinction as follows:

Most festivals are fixed to a certain date in the month; for example, Pesach falls out on the fifteenth day of the month of Nissan. Thus, when *Beis Din* sanctifies Rosh Chodesh Nissan and the day of Pesach arrives later that month, the holiday has already been proclaimed sanctified as a result of *Beis Din*'s sanctification of Rosh Chodesh fifteen days earlier. The holiness of Shabbos is also considered preordained and set in place.

Shavuos is different to the other festivals in that it is not linked to a particular day in the month but is rather dependent on concluding the counting of the days of *sefirah*. Therefore, its convocation is not dependent on the *Beis Din*'s sanctification of the New Moon earlier that month; instead it comes when we proclaim the sanctity of Shavuos when we daven and recite *kiddush* on Shavuos night.

Tosfos Shabbos and *Tosfos Yom Tov* allow us the ability to extend the holiness of the festival into the previous day. This is only possible on Shabbos and on a festival in which there existed a certain degree of "pre-sanctity" prior to the onset of Shabbos and Yom Tov. *Tosfos Yom Tov* is therefore not applicable on Shavuos since it is only first sanctified with our acceptance of the festival at the time of the

---

60   *Magen Avraham*, in his introduction to *Orach Chaim* 494.
61   *Mashiv Davar* 18.
62   *Vayikra* 23:21.

festival itself. For this reason, we delay davening and making *kiddush* on Shavuos until after nightfall.[63]

One-day Festival

Why are Pesach and Sukkos celebrated for seven days while Shavuos is only celebrated for one?

The *Sifri* answers that Pesach and Sukkos fall out at the times of the year when the fields are fallow. Since there is no work to be done in the field, Hashem made those festivals last for seven days. Shavuos, however, coincides with the harvest season when everyone is busy in the field. Hashem was therefore considerate of the monetary needs of *Bnei Yisrael* and limited Shavuos to just one day.[64]

On a deeper level, the *Zohar* answers that since Hashem, the Torah, and the Jewish People are one, they are all joined together in a one-day festival.[65]

The *Zohar* explains that Pesach corresponds to the attribute of *chesed* — kindness — which is represented by the right side. Sukkos corresponds to the trait of *din* — justice — which corresponds to the left. Since each of those individual traits are incomplete, they are fragmented and divided into seven days. Shavuos falls out between Pesach and Sukkos, which represents the center trait of *tiferes* — splendor — which is a synthesis between the two extremes of *chesed* and *din*.[66]

Just as something that is in the center is on a higher level of perfection (as we find the Tree of Life was in the center of Gan Eden), so too is something singular also indicative of it being unique and perfect (as the verse says regarding the Jewish People, "Who is like Your nation, Israel, one nation on earth"). Since Shavuos is on a higher level than the other festivals, it is therefore celebrated for only one day.

---

63   *Emes L'Yaakov, Orach Chaim* 494:1.
64   *Sifri, parashas Re'eh.*
65   *Zohar, Emor* 96a.
66   *Zohar, Vayikra* 96a.

Second Day of Shavuos

During the Temple period when *Beis Din* sanctified the New Moon, messengers were sent out to the communities of Israel to inform them of the correct day to establish Yom Tov in that month. Since the messengers would not necessarily reach the distant communities in exile in time for Yom Tov (merely two weeks after Rosh Chodesh), a doubt would arise as to which was the correct day on which to observe Yom Tov. As a result, they kept two days *m'safek* — out of doubt. Eventually, the rabbis instituted that communities outside Israel would always observe two days of Yom Tov (called Yom Tov Sheni).

The *Yad HaMelech* believes we treat the second day of Shavuos with more leniencies than Yom Tov Sheni of the other festivals (for example, to allow a *get* to be written in cases of *agunah*). This is because a doubt would never arise as to which day Shavuos should be kept since the calculation to determine Shavuos is not dependent on the sanctification of the New Moon but rather by counting fifty days from Pesach (which allowed sufficient time for the residents of exile to establish the proper date of Shavuos). Since the rabbis only instituted Yom Tov Sheni on Shavuos in order not to differentiate between the festivals, it is therefore accorded more leniencies.[67]

Other *Acharonim* strongly disagree with the opinion of the *Yad HaMelech*. They argue that, on the contrary, since the second day of Shavuos was not instituted as a result of a doubt,[68] it would be more stringent than an ordinary second day of Yom Tov.[69]

---

67 *Yad HaMelech*, cited in *Halichos Shlomo* 12:76.
68 Rambam, *Mishnah Torah*, Kiddush HaChodesh 3:12.
69 See Rabbi Shlomo Kluger, *Sefer Shivas Enayim* p. 60a; *Chasam Sofer, Orach Chaim* end 145, *Yoreh Deah* 250; *Mishchas Shemen* 3:12.

KORBANOS OF SHAVUOS

Studying the "Laws" of Shavuos

"Moshe instituted that we study the laws of Pesach on Pesach, the laws of Shavuos on Shavuos and the laws of Sukkos on Sukkos."[70] This law is understandable regarding Pesach and Sukkos, since there are many laws pertaining to those festivals. But what practical halachos are pertinent specifically to Shavuos?

According to the *Magen Avraham*,[71] it appears that the word "laws" is not a precise terminology (*lav davka*) and one may fulfill this directive by studying the subject of *Matan Torah* or the laws of *korbanos* that were brought on Shavuos.

Rabbi Ben Tzion Blau derives the latter point from the story where Haman came to Mordechai's *beis medrash* and found him learning with his students the details of the laws of the *Omer* offering. Rashi explains that since this event transpired on the sixteenth of Nissan, he therefore studied the subject matter pertinent to that day.[72] Although this story occurred after the destruction of the Beis HaMikdash, we see that one fulfills the obligation to study the matters particular to that Yom Tov, even when those laws are no longer applicable.

THE OMER

Start of Shavuos

Why does the Torah begin its discussion of Shavuos with the mitzvos pertaining to the *Omer* offering?[73]

The Maharal says that when Hashem gave the Torah to the Jewish People on Mount Sinai, it was a time of great joy comparable to a

---

70   *Megillah* 32a.
71   *Magen Avraham, Orach Chaim* 429:1.
72   *Megillah* 16a, s.v. *"hilchos kemitzah."*
73   *Vayikra* 23.

marriage between a bride and groom.[74] This joy celebrating the marriage between Hashem and the Jewish People extended the entire time the Jewish People encamped at Har Sinai after receiving the Torah.[75]

In light of the above, we may offer an explanation why the Torah portion of Shavuos begins with the mitvzah of *Omer*. Just as we find that the spirit of Shavuos extended after the actual receiving of the Torah, perhaps the same applies prior to the festival of Shavuos as well. Since the purpose of the Exodus from Egypt was to receive the Torah, it is considered, in a certain sense, as if the festival of Shavuos begins from the day after they left Egypt, which in future generations corresponds to the time of the bringing of the *Omer*.[76]

From Start to Finish

Why does the Torah place the mitzvah of *pe'ah* (leaving the corner of one's field for the poor) in the *parashah* dealing with the *korban Omer*?

The Sefas Emes answers that the *Omer* offering coincides with the beginning of the harvest, while *pe'ah*, that which one leaves at the end of the field, transpires at the conclusion of the harvest. By sanctifying both the beginning and the end of one's crop, it brings sanctity and blessing to one's entire harvest.[77]

THE SHTEI HALECHEM MINCHAH OFFERING

Symbolism of Shtei HaLechem

The Seforno explains the symbolism of the *Shtei HaLechem* (two loaves of wheat bread) offering that was brought in the Beis HaMikdash on Shavuos. He says that it represents the revelation

---

74   See *Tashbetz* 467.

75   Maharal, *Gur Aryeh*, Vayikra 24:10. See *Ayeles HaShachar*, Vayikra 25:1.

76   Cf. Ramban, *Vayikra* 23:36.

77   Cited in *B'shem Omroh*, Vayikra 23:10.

of Hashem's greatness, akin to the wondrous experience at Mount Sinai, whose purpose was to instill awe of Hashem in the hearts of *Bnei Yisrael*.[78]

How does the *Shtei HaLechem* instill awe of Hashem like the wondrous miracles demonstrated at the giving of the Torah on Sinai?

We would like to suggest as follows:

In Psalm 136, Dovid HaMelech lists all the great miracles Hashem performed for the Jewish People, such as the creation of heaven and earth, the exodus from Egypt, and the defeat of the Gentile kings of Canaan. The final verse that serves as a climax to that chapter states: "He gives bread to all flesh, for His kindness is forever." This proves that an ordinary loaf of wheat bread is as great, if not a greater miracle, than the open miracles of the Splitting of the Sea or *Maamad Har Sinai*. The two loaves of wheat bread that are brought in the Temple on Shavuos therefore provide ample testimony of Hashem's wondrous grandeur, akin to the miraculous events surrounding the giving of the Torah on Mount Sinai.

(Reb Yeruchem Levovitz expressed a similar sentiment: "It was necessary for Yisro to see Hashem's miraculous splitting of water [at *Krias Yam Suf*] in order to see the greatness of Hashem.[79] A Jew should ideally come to the same recognition when beholding an ordinary glass of water.")

The Chametz Offering

Generally, it was prohibited to bring *chametz* as an offering in the Beis HaMikdash. Why, then, is the *minchah* offering on Shavuos made from *chametz*?

- The *Kli Yakar* answers that *chametz* corresponds to the *yetzer hara*. What makes humans worthy of receiving the Torah is, specifically, our evil inclination. If we lacked a *yetzer hara*, we

---

78   Seforno, *Kavanas HaTorah*, s.v. "*v'inyan korban shtei halechem.*" See *Shemos* 20:17.
79   See Rashi, *Shemos* 18:1.

would be no different than angels and be no more deserving of the Torah than they.[80]

- Aside from it being the time of the giving of the Torah, Shavuos also coincides with the harvest season. The only *korban* in the Beis HaMikdash that was permitted to be made from *chametz* was the *korban Todah* — the thanksgiving offering. The *minchah* on Shavuos is made from *chametz* like the *korban Todah* since we thank Hashem for giving us the Torah as well as for granting a bountiful harvest.[81]

- *Chametz* corresponds to the attribute of strict justice. Hashem originally intended to create the world through the trait of strict justice, but He saw that the world would be unable to exist through justice alone, and so He created the world via a synthesis of mercy and justice. Generally, we refrain from bringing *chametz* in the Temple, since the world cannot exist through pure strict justice. When *Bnei Yisrael* accepted the Torah on Shavuos, the world attained a state of balance and purity (*posku zuhamah*) as Hashem originally intended with creation. Since Shavuos reflects the recreation of the world, the offerings of the day include the two loaves made of *chametz*.[82]

No Sin Offering

Regarding all other festivals, the Torah describes the function of the *korban Chatas* brought on that day as *l'chatas* — "for a sin offering."[83] An exception is made for the *Chatas* of Shavuos, about which the Torah instead uses the terminology *l'chaper aleichem* — "to atone for you."[84]

The *Yerushalmi* explains the reason why the Torah doesn't call the Shavuos sacrifice a sin offering: "For since you have accepted upon

---

80   *Kli Yakar*, *Vayikra* 23:17.
81   Ramban, *Vayikra* 23:17.
82   Ramban ibid.; *Chachmas HaMitzfon*, *parashas Yisro*.
83   *Bamidbar*, chap. 29.
84   *Bamidbar* 28:30.

yourselves the yoke of Torah, I consider it as if you have never sinned in your life."[85] The *Rokeach* comments, in a similar vein, that the reason a sin offering is not required on Shavuos is because the Torah, which was given on Shavuos, atones for those who study it.[86]

Initially Imperfect

The *Rokeach* comments that the Torah generally stresses that the lambs of the festival offerings are *temimim* — perfect — to hint that the Jewish People also share that same quality, as Hashem describes the Jewish nation as "My perfect dove." [87] It is therefore suprising that regarding all the festival offerings, the Torah immediately writes that the lambs must be *temimim* — complete (without blemish)[88] — with an exception made for Shavuos, where the Torah does not say that the lambs were *temimim* until the end of the *parashah*.[89]

Why is the word *temimim* only mentioned at the end of the *parashah* in regard to the festival of Shavuos? We would think that, on the contrary, this quality of *temimus* should have been especially applicable on Shavuos, since the Torah, which was given on Shavuos, is also called *temimah* — perfect![90]

The answer is that unfortunately, because of the Sin of the Golden Calf, the Jewish People did not retain their quality of perfection. Since the Jewish People did not wait with simplicity (*temimus*) for Moshe's return with the Torah at Sinai, the word *temimim* is initially omitted when discussing the *korbanos* of Shavuos. However since the Jewish People eventually repented for their sin and reclaimed their title of *temimus*, the Torah does write *temimim* at the end of the *parashah*.[91]

---

85   *Yerushalmi, Rosh Hashanah* 4:8.
86   *Rokeach, Bamidbar* 28:30. See also *Mishnah Berurah* 615:3.
87   *Shir HaShirim* 6:9.
88   *Bamidbar*, chap. 28–29.
89   *Rokeach, Bamidbar* 28:27.
90   *Tehillim* 19:8.
91   *Rokeach* ibid.

INSIGHTS INTO SHAVUOS

Epoch of Torah

World history is broken up into three segments of two thousand years each:

1. The first two thousand years are called "nothingness" because they lacked Torah.
2. The second two thousand years are the years of "Torah."
3. The third two thousand years are the epoch of Mashiach.

The Gemara states that the two thousand years of Torah began when Avraham started spreading Torah in the world,[92] as the *Targum* translates the verse, "the people they made in Charan,"[93] as "the people [Avraham and Sarah] subjugated to the Torah."

Rabbi Moshe Feinstein observes that although there were righteous individuals before Avraham, they were inferior to him in the respect that they were overly smug in their piety. Avraham, in his great humility, attained the prerequisite quality for acquiring Torah — namely that one must always make safeguards to ensure one's righteousness and to accept Hashem's conduct without question. Through these traits, which he was able to successfully transmit to his descendants, he became worthy of becoming the progenitor of the Torah nation.[94]

Why the Delay?

As we saw, the two thousand year era of Torah began with the advent of Avraham. If so, why didn't the revelation of Sinai transpire during his lifetime?

The *Rabbeinu Ephraim* says that Hashem initially intended for *Matan Torah* to be given during the days of Avraham. However, when

---

92 *Avodah Zarah* 9a.
93 *Bereishis* 12:5.
94 *Derash Moshe*, pp. 302–303.

Avraham asked Hashem, "How shall I know that I am to inherit it?"[95] his question necessitated for his descendants to go into exile.[96] As a result, *Matan Torah* was postponed until after the exodus from Egypt.[97]

Why wasn't the Torah given to Adam, Noach, or the holy *Avos*? In the liturgy recited on the morning of the second day of Shavuos, the author enumerates the minor sins that each of them committed that disqualified them from being able to receive the Torah:

- Adam — for eating from the Tree of Knowledge
- Noach — for planting a grapevine upon leaving the Ark and becoming inebriated as a result
- Avraham — for asking Hashem for a sign that his descendants will inherit the Land of Israel
- Yitzchak — for countenancing his wicked son, Eisav
- Yaakov — for not accepting his travails with equanimity.[98]

Festival of Yitzchak

The *Tur* writes that the three festivals correspond to the three *Avos*:[99]

- Pesach corresponds to Avraham, as we find Avraham instructed Sarah to bake matzos for their angelic guests, whose visit occurred on Pesach.[100]
- Shavuos corresponds to Yitzchak, as the shofar taken from the ram that was offered in the place of Yitzchak at the *Akeidah* was the one blown at the giving of the Torah on Mount Sinai.

---

95   *Bereishis* 15:8.
96   *Nedarim* 32a.
97   *Rabbeinu Ephraim, Vayikra* 11:42.
98   *Chachmas Chaim*, p. 214.
99   *Tur, Orach Chaim* 417.
100 *Bereishis* 18:6, according to the interpretation of the Midrash.

- Yaakov corresponds to Sukkos, as it is written, "And for his livestock he made Sukkos."[101]

Yitzchak represents Torah, since the salient trait of Yitzchak was *gevurah* — strength, and Torah similarly necessitates strength and self-sacrifice as well.[102] Therefore, the *Aseres HaDibros* begin with "And *Elokim* spoke,"[103] because Elokim is the name of Hashem that connotes His trait of strength and strict justice.

The Midrash relates that when Avraham's knife reached Yitzchak's throat during *Akeidas Yitzchak*, Yitzchak's soul departed from him. When the heavenly voice called out, "Do not send out your hand against the lad,"[104] his soul was returned to him. As a result of that experience, Yitzchak understood the principle of *Techias Hameisim* — that all the dead will be revived in the future — and immediately recited the blessing, *Mechayei Hameisim* — that Hashem revives the dead.[105]

Based on the principle that states, "The actions of our forefathers are portents for their descendants," we may suggest that Yitzchak's revival from death was the forerunner for his descendants sharing a similar experience — i.e., when at Mount Sinai their souls momentarily left them and angels came to revive them.

Weak Start

The Gemara relates that the *maror* that grew in a certain location had six hundred thousand folds in its small interior leaves.[106] On a deeper level, the Maharshah expounds that this hints to the Jewish

---

101 *Bereishis* 33:17.

102 Rabbi Tzadok HaKohen, *Tzidkos HaTzadik* 199.

103 *Shemos* 20:1.

104 *Bereishis* 22:12.

105 *Pirkei D'Rebbi Eliezer* 31. This is why the second blessing of *Shemoneh Esrei*, which corresponds to Yitzchak, deals with the revival of the dead.

106 *Bechoros* 57b.

nation that is comprised of six hundred thousand principle souls. *Maror* is soft when it starts growing but later hardens as it matures. Similarly, when the Jewish nation was born in Egypt, they were "soft," meaning weak and susceptible to spiritual weakness.[107]

The literal translation for the word "small [interior] leaves" is *beis hameses*, which is also the word used to describe the stomach of a domesticated animal, which contains many folds. Just as the stomach is a putrid place, so were the Jewish People in Egypt enveloped in six hundred thousand folds of spiritual impurity. However, after they left Egypt and accepted the purifying and strength-giving Torah, they become spiritually firm and strong.[108]

Shavuos and Charity

"And you shall make the festival of Shavuos to Hashem, your G-d, according to the generosity of your hand."[109] What is meant by the term, "you shall *make*," and what is the connection between "making" Shavuos and generosity?

The *Ohr Gedalyahu* answers that an integral part of "making" Shavuos into a true Yom Tov is by providing for the needy.[110] The question, however, still remains. Why does the Torah stress giving *tzedakah* specifically regarding the festival of Shavous?

The Rabbeinu Bachya comments that actually the obligation to give generously to the poor applies equally to all three festivals. However, since one may erroneously assume that since Shavuos is only one day and therefore the needs of the poor are not so pressing, the Torah expresses the obligation particularly at this time.[111]

According to Rabbi Yaakov Kamenetsky, there is a direct connection between Shavuos and *tzedakah*. The Torah discusses Shavuos

---

107 Maharshah, *Bechoros* ibid.
108 Maharshah ibid.
109 *Devarim* 16:10.
110 Rabbi Gedaliah Schorr, *Ohr Gedalyahu*, end of *parashas Re'eh*.
111 Rabbeinu Bachya, *Devarim* 16:10.

next to the commandment of giving *matnas ani'im* — gifts to the poor.[112] This is because the ability of a Jew to freely give away small amounts of his money for the poor was a result of *Matan Torah*, which transpired on Shavuos. Since this is such an integral aspect of being a Jew, a Gentile who comes to convert is specifically informed about the mitzvos of *matanos ani'im*. This may also be a reason the book of Rus is read on Shavuos. The story of Rus highlights the importance of *tzedakah*, as the dynasty of Dovid HaMelech came about as a result of Boaz giving tithes to the impoverished Rus.[113]

MOUNT SINAI

Humble Conduit

Mount Sinai was chosen for the giving of the Torah because it was the humblest of mountains. This imparts an integral lesson not just regarding the quality of humility in general but also of the significance of humility as a prerequisite for receiving the Torah.

Pirkei Avos begins: "Moshe received [the] Torah from Sinai." Why does it say he received Torah *from* Sinai? It would have been more accurate to have stated, "Moshe received the Torah *on* Sinai"! Rabbi Chaim Volozhiner explains that the unusual wording conveys that the mountain itself imparts an important Torah lesson: Just as Hashem gave the Torah on Sinai because it was the humblest mountain, so too Moshe was able to receive the Torah from Sinai because he was the humblest of men.[114]

Sin or Sinai?

In the book of *Bamidbar*, the Torah calls the locality of Mount Sinai, *Midbar Sin*.[115] Several verses later, the Torah calls it *Midbar*

---

112   *Vayikra* 23:22.
113   *Emes L'Yaakov, Orach Chaim* 490:9.
114   Rabbi Chaim Volozhin, *Ruach Chaim* 1:1, s.v. "*Misinai.*"
115   *Bamidbar* 33:11–12.

Sinai.[116] The *Rokeach* comments that before the Torah was given, the area was called *Sin* (סין) to evoke the incident of the miraculous burning bush (*s'neh*) that occurred there. Later, when the Torah was given on Mount Sinai, the name of the area was changed to *Sinai* (סיני) to recall the giving of the Torah. The extra letter *yud* was added to the name since the numerical value of *yud* is ten, hinting to the Ten Commandments that were given on Sinai.[117]

Numerical Hints

The numerical value of סיני — Sinai — hints to the events leading up to the giving of the Torah there:

The numerical value of סין is 120, and י is ten. Moshe spent 120 days on Mount Sinai receiving the Ten Commandments. (Moshe spent forty days there to receive the first *luchos*, then another forty days to pray that Hashem forgive the Jewish People for the Sin of the Golden Calf, and a final forty days for the second *luchos*.)

The numerical values of the letters סיני also stand for:

- 60 — ס: ten thousands (in other words, six hundred thousand Jewish souls)
- 10 — י: received the Ten Commandments
- 50 — נ: days after leaving Egypt
- 10 — י: and another Ten Commandments, through the second *luchos*.[118]

Dry Mountain

One of the name's of Mount Sinai is *Chareivah*, which means dry or barren.[119] The *Rabbeinu Ephraim* explains that the foot of the mountain was swampy and encircled with thorn bushes. Hashem put

---

116 Ibid. 15–16.
117 *Rokeach, Bamidbar* 33:11.
118 Ibid., v. 15.
119 *Shemos* 3:1.

this barrier in place to prevent people from climbing Mount Sinai, as it was destined to be a place of extraordinary holiness. Although the bottom of the mountain was swampy, the top of the mountain was *chareivah* — dry — so it could serve as a suitable place for the presence of the *Shechinah* when He would later give the Torah atop this mountain.[120]

Encampment of Dofka

Among the encampments of *Bnei Yisrael* prior to receiving the Torah was Dofka (דפקה).[121] The *Rabbeinu Yoel* says that the name is an allusion to the verse, קול דודי דופק — "The sound of my beloved knocks!"[122] Although there was still some journey before they would reach Mount Sinai, their hearts were beating with excitement and anticipation, yearning for the great moment of *Matan Torah*.[123]

Recalling Sinai

In *parashas Masai*, the Torah records the numerous encampments of the Jewish People in the desert after the Sin of the Spies.[124] The *Rabbeinu Yoel* writes that all these places were named after the events of *Matan Torah*:[125]

- הר שפר — This alludes to Har Sinai, on which they heard the sound of the shofar (שופר). In addition, the letters שפר can be rearranged to spell שרף — burning — alluding to how Mount Sinai was aflame.[126] Finally, שפר means beautiful, since on Mount Sinai they were given אמרי שפר — beautiful words [of the Torah].

---

120 *Rabbeinu Ephraim, Shemos* 3:1, s.v. *"Kesiva Ashkenazis."* Perhaps the humility of Mount Sinai was also due to it being surrounded by thistles, as well as being barren at its peak.
121 *Bamidbar* 33:12.
122 *Shir HaShirim* 5:2.
123 *Rimzei Rabbeinu Yoel, Bamidbar* ibid.
124 *Bamidbar* 33.
125 *Rabbeinu Yoel, Bamidbar* 33:23–29.
126 *Devarim* 4:11.

- חרדה — This is a reference to the verse, ויחרד כל ההר — "And the entire mountain trembled."[127]
- במקהלות — This refers to the great assemblage of *Matan Torah*, of which the verse states, במקהלות ברכו אלקים — "In congregations [shall you] bless Hashem."[128]
- תחת — Alludes to ויתיצבו בתחתית ההר — "They stood at the bottom of the mountain."[129]
- תרח — hints to ריח מצות ותורה — "The fragrance of mitzvos and Torah." Also, beautiful fragrances accompanied each commandment when it was given on Sinai.[130]
- מתקה — This refers to the words of the Torah, which are מתוקים מדבש — "Sweeter than honey."[131]
- חשמנה — can be read as חש מנה, as if to say the Jewish People were ill (as in חש בראשו) and were given a good portion (מנה).

Although when *Bnei Yisrael* reached these places the giving of the Torah on Mount Sinai was long past, both in time as well as geographically, *Bnei Yisrael* nostalgically recalled those events wherever they traveled while also fulfilling the constant mitzvah of recalling the events of Sinai.

A Moving Experience

Hashem lifted Mount Sinai above the Jewish nation and told them that if they refuse to accept the Torah, they would be buried beneath it. Why did Hashem threaten them specifically with a mountain?

Rabbi Aharon Kotler answers that at the time of the giving of the Torah, all the mountains in the vicinity skipped like rams and young lambs in an effort to be chosen to have the Torah given on them.[132] (Rav Aharon adds that this is not a mere metaphor, but that it actually transpired.)

---

127 *Shemos* 19:18.
128 *Tehillim* 68:27.
129 *Shemos* 19:17.
130 *Shabbos* 88b.
131 *Tehillim* 19:11.
132 *Tehillim* 114:4.

Just as an extraordinary, life-altering event arouses dormant emotions, the spiritual essence of the mountains realized that their *raison d'être* was Torah and they were very moved (literally) by it.

If the Jewish People would show less appreciation for the Torah than the normally inanimate mountains, it would be fitting that they should punished by being hit by a moving mountain.[133]

MATAN TORAH —
THE GIVING OF THE TORAH ON SINAI

A Divine Marriage

At *Matan Torah,* the Jewish People became wedded to Hashem.[134] Therefore, many of the features of *Ma'amad Har Sinai* parallel those of a wedding ceremony:

- The Clouds of Glory above Mount Sinai were the *chuppah.*
- Moshe and Aharon were the *unterfirers* who led the Jewish People to the *chuppah.*
- The *luchos* were the *kesuvah.*
- Heaven and earth were the witnesses to the marriage.
- In addition, just as a *chassan* bedecks his bride with beautiful jewellery, so did Hashem adorn the Jewish nation with precious crowns.[135]

Conversely, all the customs of a Jewish wedding derive from *Matan Torah.* For example, the custom of juggling fire at a *chasunah* stems from the thunder and lightning that accompanied *Matan Torah.*[136]

---

133 *Mishnas Rebbi Aharon,* vol. 3, p. 231.
134 *Ta'anis* 26b.
135 *Rabbeinu Ephraim, Shemos* 19:1.
136 *Tashbetz Katan* 467.

When the Jewish People accepted the Torah, it was not so much a relationship of a servant to his master; rather, it was more akin to a marriage. While a slave may love his master and think he is the greatest master in the world, he still loves freedom more. On the other hand, although there are services a wife provides for her husband, she does not feel stymied because of them. She views her marriage as an ideal situation and does not desire to be relieved from her responsibilities.[137]

False Piety

Amalek waged war against *Bnei Yisrael* at Refidim. *Chazal* say that the name Refidim denotes *Sherafu yedeihem min haTorah* — their hands were lethargic from upholding the Torah.

The forty-nine days prior to *Matan Torah* were days of intense spiritual growth, and since Refidim was the last stop prior to Har Sinai,[138] by that time they were certainly on an extremely high spiritual level. So how can we understand their lapse to laxity at such an auspicious time?

Rabbi Yaakov Yitzchak Ruderman answers that sometimes the *yetzer hara* dons a cloak of "piety" and tells an upright person that he is not worthy. The *yetzer hara* came to them at Refidim and convinced them that they were not worthy of accepting the Torah. This false humility led to their despair and discouragement.[139]

Two for One

When *Bnei Yisrael* accepted the Torah, they first said נעשה — "We shall do" — and then afterward, נשמע — "We shall hear."

Hashem exclaimed, "Who revealed to My children this secret [expression] that the angels use?" And in that merit, the Jewish People received two crowns.[140]

---

137 *Peninim M'Shulchan Gavoah, Shemos* 24:7, quoting Rabbi Chaim Volozhin.
138 *Shemos* 19:2.
139 Rabbi Yaakov Yitzchak Ruderman, *Sichos Levi*, p. 76.
140 *Shabbos* 88a.

The question arises: if their act of greatness was saying נעשה before
נשמע, they should be deserving of only one crown. So why were they
rewarded with two?

Rabbi Shlomo Zalman Auerbach explains that the unique quality
of an angel is that its whole being is singularly dedicated to serving
Hashem. When the Jewish People said "we shall do" even before
hearing what they had to do, they demonstrated that fulfilling the
Torah was their entire essence and sole focus in life and thereby attained the level of angels. *Chazal* say that when a person accepts the
Torah in such a manner, he is immediately rewarded for fulfilling the
Torah even before the opportunity arises.[141] This is why *Bnei Yisrael*
deserved two rewards: one for the acceptance of the Torah and one
for its actual fulfilment.[142]

Nation of Prophets

Why was it necessary for Hashem to address the entire Jewish nation at *Matan Torah*? He could have transmitted the Torah to Moshe
individually who, in turn, would teach it to the rest of the nation, as
was done throughout the forty years in the wilderness.

Rabbi Yaakov Kamenetsky answers that the commonly accepted
belief was that any mortal to whom Hashem spoke would immediately expire. Had Moshe been the only person to receive the Divine
revelation at Sinai, he may have been suspected of being an imposter.
Therefore, Hashem spoke to everyone at *Matan Torah* to dispel any
such erroneous notion.[143]

The *Shem MiShmuel* explains the rationale of the view that *Matan
Torah* transpired on Shabbos (to the exclusion of the view of Rabbi

---

141 *Avos D'Rebbi Nasan* 22:1; *Sha'arei Teshuvah* 2:3,10.
142 *Halichos Shlomo*, Shavuos 12:1,1.
143 *B'mechitzas Rabbeinu* p. 211.

Elazar ben Azaryah that it occurred on Friday).[144] The holiness of the Torah is so intense that it should be impossible for a mortal of flesh and blood to accept it and survive. For example, the parents of Shimshon thought they would surely die for beholding an angel; even more so, the Torah itself that is on an even higher spiritual level, as it says, "The Torah and the Holy One, Blessed Be He, is one." Since Shabbos is called *yomah d'nishmasah* — a day on which the soul is prominent and the body secondary, the spiritual holiness of Shabbos elevated the Jewish People and thus enabled them to safely receive the Torah.[145]

The Malbim, citing the Rambam,[146] states that one of the greatest miracles of *Matan Torah* was that the entire nation — despite their lack of qualifications — was able to receive prophecy. This is akin to the miracle of creation, which was also a creation of something from nothing.[147] Why was such a miracle deemed necessary?

1. To counteract the prevalent attitude of that time that denied the existence of prophecy.[148]
2. To prevent a false prophet from attempting to revise the Torah, r"l. To counter such a claim, we can say that just as the original Torah was given in the presence of six hundred thousand, so too would such a massive assembly be required to alter it in any way.[149]

Virtual Shofar

"The entire people saw...the sound of the shofar" (שפר).[150] Everywhere in the Torah, the word *shofar* is spelled with the letter

---

144   See *Halichos Shlomo* 12:10.
145   *Shem Mishmuel, Bamidbar*, p. 93, s.v. *"d'kula alma."*
146   Rambam, *Mishnah Torah*, Yesodei HaTorah 7.
147   Malbim, *Devarim* 4:10, 5:21.
148   See Ramban, end of *parashas Bo*.
149   *Malbim* ibid.
150   *Shemos* 20:15.

vav (שופר), with the exception of this verse, where it is spelled lacking a letter *vav*. The *Zohar* comments that the word שפר means "beauty."[151] The verse is thereby alluding to the intrinsic beauty of Torah that the Jewish People perceived at that time.[152]

Rabbi Chaim Kanievsky suggests that the reason for the missing letter *vav* is because the shofar blast on Har Sinai was not produced by an actual physical shofar but by a virtual spiritual shofar that mimicked those sounds.[153]

One Thing to Fear

"Who leads you through the great and awesome wilderness of snake, fiery serpent, and scorpion" (נחש שרף ועקרב).[154] The Midrash relates that while the Jewish People traveled in the desert, two bolts of fire shot forth from between the two poles of the *Aron* and incinerated the dangerous snakes and scorpions in their vicinity.[155] The *Rabbeinu Ephraim* comments that the first letters of נחש שרף עקרב spell עשן — smoke. In the merit of the Jewish People accepting the Torah on Mount Sinai, which was smoking,[156] they were saved from those dangerous animals.[157]

Perhaps this can be understood as follows: Although the Jews were frightened by the smoke on Mount Sinai, they overcame their fear out of their love for Hashem. Measure for measure, Hashem spared them from all other sources of fear.

Reliving Matan Torah

The Rama cites a custom prohibiting bloodletting on Erev Yom Tov because of a demon named Tovo'ach who threatened to kill the

---

151 *Bereishis* 49:21.
152 *Zohar, parashas Yisro.*
153 *Derech Sichah, Shemos* 20:15.
154 *Devarim* 8:15.
155 *Midrash Tehillim* 22:11.
156 *Shemos* 19:18.
157 *Rabbeinu Ephraim, Shemos* ibid.

Jewish nation prior to Shavuos if they refused to accept the Torah.[158] The question arises: Since the Jewish People already accepted the Torah on Sinai, why should the demon still pose a threat today?

Rabbi Shlomo Zalman Auerbach brings a proof from this halachah that whenever we approach a holiday, we actually relive the original experience.[159] As such, it is important to rededicate ourselves to Torah each Shavuos as we originally did at Har Sinai.

Return to Sinai

The Gemara says that anyone who teaches his grandson Torah, the Torah deems it as if he had received the Torah from Mount Sinai, as it is written, "You shall make them known to your sons and grandsons" and the following verse states, "the day you stood before Hashem your God at *Chorev*."[160]

Why is specifically the grandfather who teaches his grandson singled out with this special praise?

Moshe was the consummate receiver of the Torah since he realized that the purpose of his receiving the Torah was for the sake of transmitting it to others. (This may explain why Moshe's eternal title is Moshe *Rabbeinu* — "Moshe our teacher.") Likewise, anyone who properly fulfills his obligation in transmitting Torah is also comparable to Moshe. The reason why the Torah specifically praises the grandfather in this regard is because a father teaches his son Torah because of his obligation. A grandfather, however, teaches his grandson Torah because he wants the Torah to be transmitted for eternity.[161]

We also see from this that an integral part of the mitzvah to learn Torah is to also teach it to others. Even more, the Midrash states that

---

158   Rama, *Orach Chaim* 468:10.
159   *Halichos Shlomo* 12:1.
160   *Kiddushin* 30a.
161   *Hararei Kedem*, vol. 2, chap. 122.

a rav does not receive reward for his Torah study until he teaches it to others.[162]

The Rambam rules that if a person has limited means and can only provide for either his own personal Torah study or that of his son, his own Torah study takes precedence (unless his son is more gifted than he is).[163]

In the city of Brisk, such a case came before Rabbi Chaim Brisker. He ruled that the father must support his son's Torah education rather than his own. People were surprised with his ruling, since in this particular case the son was no more intelligent than the father and the decision therefore seemed to go against the Rambam.

Rav Chaim explained that while both the father and son were equally intelligent, he discerned that the son had a greater ability in teaching others. Since the mitzvah of *talmud Torah* includes teaching it to others, the son was in the position of fulfilling the mitzvah in a more complete manner.[164]

United Effort

When the Jewish People accepted the Torah on Sinai, they said, "All the words Hashem spoke *we* will do."[165] Why did they use the plural tense in their acceptance?

The Seforno answers that the plural tense of their acceptance signifies that only through the combined efforts of the diverse services of Jews from all walks of life and situations — of both the scholar and the tradesman — is Hashem's name elevated and exalted as He intended by creation.[166]

This concept is symbolized by the branches of the Menorah. The branches on the right side of the Menorah symbolize those

---

162   *Shir HaShirim Rabbah* 8:14
163   Rambam, *Mishnah Torah, Talmud Torah* 1:4.
164   *Hararei Kedem* ibid.
165   *Shemos* 24:3.
166   Seforno, *Bamidbar* 8:2.

Jews who are involved exclusively in spiritual matters. The left ones represent those who are involved in the material world in order to obtain a livelihood. The light of the Menorah only radiates properly when the lamps of both the right and left branches face towards the center stem, demonstrating that the ideal Divine service is achieved only through the combined input of all Jews.[167]

Menorah and Shavuos

The Menorah represents the light of Torah, and it is therefore not surprising that it is also connected to the festival of Shavuos. The Arizal enumerates several ways in which the Menorah corresponds to the Torah:

- The seven branches of the Menorah correspond to the first verse in *Bereishis*, which contains seven words.
- The Menorah's eleven balls correspond to the first verse of the book of *Shemos*, which contains eleven words.
- The nine flowers correspond to the first verse of *Vayikra*, which contains nine words.
- The height of the Menorah is eighteen hand-breadths. This corresponds to the first verse of *Bamidbar*. (Although the first verse in *Bamidbar* has only seventeen words, the legs of the Menorah were actually less than a hand-breadth, so they do not have a corresponding word.)
- The total sum (in addition to the four components of the Menorah — the branches, balls, cups, and flowers) equals forty-nine. This corresponds to the forty-nine days leading up to Shavuos.[168]

---

167 Ibid.
168 See *Yismach Lev*, p. 75.

Matan Torah and the Nations

Moshe learned from the behavior of Hashem — who offered the Torah to all the nations of the world — that he should also reach out to Sichon in peace prior to waging war against his people.[169] What is the connection between Hashem offering the Torah to the nations to Moshe going into battle against Sichon?

The Maharal explains that Mount Sinai is called *Chorev*, (derived from the word חרב — destruction) because through our acceptance of the Torah, the nations were spiritually destroyed, since from that moment onwards Hashem no longer granted prophecy to the nations. Just as Hashem attempted to thwart their downfall by offering them the Torah, so did Moshe emulate His behavior by first extending a hand of peace to Sichon, instead of directly declaring war against his nation.[170]

Rabbi Yehoshua once entered into a debate with the sages of Athens. The Athenians asked him, "If a man seeks a woman in marriage and is rebuffed by her, would he then go seek another woman of higher status than the first?" Rabbi Yehoshua responded by sticking a peg in the lower part of the wall where it could not enter. Then he raised his arm and stuck the peg into a crack at a higher section of the wall, where it penetrated the wall. Rabbi Yehoshua then said, "This man, too, may chance to find his destined match."[171]

Obviously they were discussing something deeper than brides and pegs. What was the interchange really about?

According to the Vilna Gaon, the Athenians were hinting to the time when Hashem initially offered the Torah to the nations and

---

169   Rashi, *Devarim* 2:26.
170   Maharal, *Devarim* ibid., footnote 54.
171   *Bechoros* 8b.

they refused. Since Hashem only subsequently offered it to the Jewish People, it is a sign that we were Hashem's "second choice" and inferior to the other nations.

Rabbi Yehoshua replied that Hashem gives wisdom to those who value it. Although He initially offered it to the broadest group possible, it was only accepted by those of a higher caliber who were able to appreciate it.

Why did Rabbi Yehoshua choose to demonstrate his point with a peg? The Maharshah explains that a peg is useful to hang things on only when it is hung high. Therefore, Hashem only gave His Torah to a people who were not "base and rooted in downwardness," but rather a lofty nation with heavenly aspirations.[172] Alternatively, the Gra likens the spike to an animal's goad, which is used to prod the animal to produce a bountiful harvest. So too, Hashem's prod can only stimulate someone who appreciates the concept of toiling in a productive manner.

Not only did the Jewish People become elevated through *Matan Torah*, the ancient idolatrous nations (*Akum*) descended as well. The Tosfos HaRosh writes that prior to *Matan Torah*, both Jews and *Akum* were receptive to certain forms of spiritual defilement, which is an indication of spiritual sensitivity. After they rejected the Torah, they descended from that high level of spiritual refinement.[173]

When Adam and Chava ate from the forbidden Tree of Knowledge, the evil inclination sullied them with an impure *zuhamah* — "sweat" — that penetrated their bodies and limited their

---

172   Maharshah, *Bechoros* ibid.
173   *Nidah* 70b, s.v. *"ve'ayn nitziv."*

capacity to choose good. When *Bnei Yisrael* received the Torah at Sinai, the world was, as it were, recreated. As the Sages teach, the creation of the world was dependent on our future acceptance of the Torah.[174] As such, the world returned to its pristine, original state at *Matan Torah*. However, this purifying recreation only affected the Jewish nation who accepted the Torah; the nations, who did not experience *Matan Torah*, were not purged from their *zuhamah*.[175]

ASERES HADIBROS — THE TEN COMMANDMENTS

Incomplete without Man

In the Torah, the words *dibbur* and *ma'amar* are both expressions for speech. Why are the Ten Commandments called the *Aseres HaDibros* and not the *Asarah Ma'amaros*?

Rabbi Shimshon Raphael Hirsch explains the difference between a *dibbur* and a *ma'amar*:[176]

- A *dibbur* is a concise expression of a thought, an abstraction rather than a fully developed point.
- A *ma'amar* is fully comprehensible and actualized idea.

The Mishnah teaches: *B'asara ma'amaros nivrah ha'olom* — "With ten utterances the world was created."[177] The word of creation is called *ma'amar* since it immediately realizes itself in the object to which it is addressed. The word of Torah is originally a *dibbur* — it is just said — and then it awaits being accepted and carried out by man.[178]

---

174 *Avodah Zarah* 3a.
175 *Sichas Levi*, p. 5.
176 Rabbi Shimshon Raphael Hirsch, *Vayikra* 21:1.
177 *Avos* 5:1.
178 Rabbi Hirsch ibid.

Fear Factor

Why are the Ten Commandments called *Aseres HaDibros*, and not *Aseres HaDevarim*?

The *Tashbetz* explains that the numerical value of *dibros* is 612. When we add to this the commandment to fear Hashem — a mitzvah that is equal to all the mitzvos — it totals 613 (*taryag*), the sum total of all the mitzvos.[179]

What Was Given at Sinai?

What is meant by the principle that all the mitzvos, including its details, were given at Sinai?[180] This is difficult to understand, since only the *Aseres HaDibros* were said on Sinai. Even in light of the view that all 613 mitzvos are included in the *Aseres HaDibros*,[181] nevertheless, it is hard to imagine that everyone understood the entire Torah that was hinted to in those few words.

The *Ayeles HaShachar* therefore concludes that only Moshe received the entire Torah and this transpired over the forty-day period from when he ascended to heaven to receive the Torah. We use the term that "the entire Torah was given at Mount Sinai," since Moshe ascended to heaven after standing on Mount Sinai.[182]

A Familiar Tongue

אנכי ה׳ אלקיך — "I am Hashem, your God."[183] The Hebrew word for "I" is אני; אנכי is actually the Egyptian word for "I." Why did Hashem begin the *Aseres HaDibros* with an Egyptian word?

The Midrash says that it is comparable to a king whose son was captured by bandits. In the course of time, the son grew accustomed to the language of his captives and when the king finally rescued his

---

179　Rabbi Shimon ben Tzadok, 467.
180　Rashi, *Vayikra* 25:1.
181　See Rashi, *Shemos* 24:12.
182　*Ayeles HaShachar*, *Vayikra* 25:1.
183　*Shemos* 20:2.

son, he saw that his son did not comprehend what he was saying. The king therefore began to converse with his son in the language of his captors.[184] Similarly, Hashem initially addressed *Bnei Yisrael* in the language they were accustomed to as a sign of love.[185]

A Different "I"

In *Lashon HaKodesh*, the words *ani* and *anochi* both translate as "I." Nevertheless, there is a marked difference between the two words. While *ani* is similar to the word "I" and is parallel to "you," *anochi* describes one's very essence,[186] and therefore it has no parallel in the second person. The *Aseres HaDibros* begins with the word *Anochi* — "I am your Hashem," to emphasize that Hashem Himself is our G-d and that He deals with the Jewish nation directly without any emissaries. This is unlike the nations of the world to whom Hashem appoints a different angel to preside over each nation.[187]

THE GIFT OF TORAH

Time of Healing

The Chasam Sofer writes that there are 288 primary souls, all of which were present at the giving of the Torah on Sinai.[188] The numerical value of 288 equals the first letters in the words רופא חולי עמו ישראל — "The Healer of the sick of His nation, Israel." At *Matan Torah*, the entire nation was in need of healing of one sort or another and at that time all the sick were healed.

Rabbi Yosef Shalom Elyashiv once visited a sick person prior to Shavuos and told him that just as all the sick were healed on Shavuos, so too, each year on Shavuos one can access special blessings of

---

184 *Midrash Tanchumah Yashan, Yisro* 16.
185 See also *Otzer HaMidrashim* ibid.
186 See *Shabbos* 105a.
187 Maharal, *Netzech Yisrael* chap. 48.
188 *Chasam Sofer, Shabbos* 88a.

healing more than at any other time during the year. The person asked at which particular moment on Shavuos is most conducive for receiving this blessing. Rav Elyashiv responded that when the *Aseres HaDibros* are being read in shul, it is the opportune time to mentally beseech Hashem for a complete healing in all areas one needs.[189]

Power of Torah

Just as Hashem performed the miracle of splitting the *Yam Suf* when the Jewish nation left Egypt, Hashem performed a similar miracle for the Jewish nation when they first entered the Land of Israel. As they came to cross the Jordan River, Hashem made the flowing waters stand still and rise in a tall column, remaining so until the entire nation crossed on the dry riverbed.[190]

Rabbi Yechezkel Abramsky notes that there was a great difference between the two miracles:[191]

- The *Yam Suf* only parted after Nachshon ben Aminadav jumped into the water and nearly died when the water reached up to his nose.
- On the other hand, the Jordan split as soon as the feet of the *Kohanim* who were carrying the *Aron* stepped on the riverbank.

Why were these two miracles so vastly different?

Rabbi Abramsky explains that the difference between these two events is that the splitting of the *Yam Suf* occurred before the Jewish People accepted the Torah. Since they lacked the merit of Torah at that time, they therefore required the merit of great faith and self-sacrifice to be deserving of the miracle of the waters splitting. After they received the Torah, however, the power of having accepted the Torah is so great — as was symbolized by the *Kohanim* who

---

189   As told in Rabbi Yitzchak Zilbershtein, *Aleinu Leshabeiach*, 5:201.
190   *Yehoshua* 3:15–17.
191   *Chazon Yechezkel*, Sotah 8:2.

walked before the nation carrying the *Aron* — that as soon as they stepped foot in the river, the waters immediately parted.

Just Raw Materials

> "When Hashem gave the Torah to Bnei Yisrael, He gave it to them only in the form of wheat so they can make from it fine flour, and flax so they can weave out of it a garment."[192] This teaches an astounding principle — Hashem wanted us to be His partner in the creation of Torah, and only after we toil in Torah is the Torah considered fully made.[193]

Why does the Midrash compare the Torah to both wheat and flax?

Perhaps we can answer that wheat represents spiritual sustenance, just as earthly bread is the prime physical sustenance of a person. We find that wheat represents Torah, as the Gemara says that wheat bread helps a person retain Torah.[194] The Maharal comments that since wheat makes one wise,[195] and since Torah is wisdom, we therefore bring the *Shtei HaLechem*, which was comprised from wheat, on Shavuos.[196]

Flax, the material used in making fine linen clothing, represents the honor the Torah projects upon those who study it, as the Gemara relates, Rabbi Yochanan used to refer to his clothes as *mechabdosai* — "those things that honor me."[197]

Torah and the Yetzer Hara

The evil inclination (*yetzer hara*) and the Torah are inextricably intertwined, as the Torah was created as the antidote for the *yetzer hara*.[198]

---

192 *Tanna D'vei Eliyahu Zuta* 2.
193 *Mikdash Mordechai*, p. 128; *Avodah Zarah* 19a.
194 *Huryos* 13b, according to the text of the *Ein Yaakov*.
195 See *Berachos* 40a; *Sukkah* 42b.
196 *Rosh Hashanah* 16a; Maharal, *Tiferes Yisrael* 25:69.
197 *Shabbos* 113a.
198 *Kiddushin* 30b.

Rabbeinu Ephraim brilliantly demonstrates how the Torah, as well as the evil inclination, are both hinted to at the same point of the Torah:[199]

- The letter at the midpoint of the Torah is a *vav* in a word that deals with snakes,[200] which is a symbol for the *yetzer hara*.
- The letter *vav* hints to the snake as well, as the primeval snake was punished by having his limbs removed and thus resembling the straight letter *vav*.
- The *vav*, which has the numerical value of six, also corresponds to the six blessings that the snake caused Adam to lose as a result of his sin.[201] These six blessings were briefly returned at the giving of the Torah on Sinai and will ultimately be restored at the End of Days.

Torah and the Letter Vav

As mentioned above, the center of the Torah consists of the letter *vav*. This letter contains numerous references to the Torah:[202]

- The significance of the letter *vav*, which has the numerical value of six, is that it hints to the Torah that was given on the sixth day of Sivan.
- The letter *vav* is elongated to hint that the Torah is "longer than the earth and wider than the sea."[203]
- A further significance in the number six is that everything in the physical world has six sides, there are six days in creation, and the history of mankind is for six thousand years.[204]
- The letter *vav* is in the shape of a hook and in *Lashon HaKodesh* the translation of the word *vav* is a hook, as in *vavei ha'amudim* — "the

---

199   *Rabbeinu Ephraim, Vayikra* 11:42.
200   *Vayikra* 11:42.
201   *Bereishis Rabbah* 12:7.
202   *Rabbeinu Ephraim* ibid.
203   *Iyov* 11:9.
204   *Avodah Zarah* 9a.

hooks of the pillars"[205] — which upheld the curtains in the court-yard of the Mishkan. The Torah is the "hook" through which the physical world is upheld. Since the Torah is the "hook," or interface, between the physical world and the Divine "pillar of the world," there is a custom to begin each *amud* — column (lit. pillar) — of a Torah scroll with the letter *vav*.[206]

The letter *vav* is also connected to the festival of Shavuos. The Mishnah enumerates four days of judgment; Pesach, Shavuos, Rosh Hashanah, and Sukkos.[207] The *Zohar* writes that each of the four days of judgment correspond to one of the letters of the *Shem Havayah*, the ineffable name of Hashem.[208] Shavuos corresponds to the letter *vav*. Another interesting point is that the Alshich notes that every *pasuk* in the book of *Rus*, with the exception of eight, all begin with the letter *vav*.[209]

Power of Three

The number three plays a significant role in the Torah, such as the three *Avos* corresponding to the three primary spiritual qualities of Torah, *Avodah*, and *Gemilas Chasadim*, which in turn encompass the three major groupings of the Jewish nation. It is therefore not surprising that the Torah itself has numerous connections with the number three:[210]

- The Gemara states: "Blessed is the Merciful One who gave our Torah of three parts, to a threefold nation (*Kohanim, Levi'im, Yisraelim*), through a third-born person (Moshe), in the third month of the year (Sivan)."[211]

---

205 *Shemos* 38:11.
206 *Rabbeinu Ephraim, Vayikra* 11:42.
207 *Rosh Hashanah* 16a.
208 *Zohar, Vayechi*, p. 226b.
209 Alshich, introduction to *Rus*.
210 Chidah, *Devarim Achadim, Derush L'Shabbos Kallah*.
211 *Shabbos* 88a.

- Commentators explain that the three parts of Torah are Torah, *Nevi'im*, and *Kesuvim*, which were all hinted to at Sinai.[212] Alternatively, they are the stories, laws, and the mystical teachings of the Torah. According to others, it is a reference to the Oral and Written Law, as well as the hidden Kabbalistic teachings of the Torah, such as the deeper meanings of the mitzvos.[213]
- The Torah describes the *luchos* as being written with the "finger" of Hashem.[214] The *Rokeach* notes that just as a finger is comprised of three parts, so is the Torah comprised of three parts.[215]
- The Torah was given in three places:

  1. *Mitzrayim* — where *Bnei Yisrael* were taught the laws of Pesach, *tefillin*, and *bechor*,
  2. *Har Sinai* — where they were taught the *Aseres HaDibros*, *dinim*, and the construction of the Mishkan,
  3. *Ohel Moed* — where they were taught *korbanos* and the remainder of the mitzvos.[216]

- The Torah is compared to three liquids: water,[217] milk,[218] and wine.[219]

CUSTOMS

Eating Dairy

Some say that the source for the custom of eating dairy on Shavuos is because it was prohibited to consume dairy products

---

212 Rashi, *Shabbos* ibid.
213 Ritva, *Shabbos* ibid.
214 *Shemos* 31:18.
215 *Rokeach, Shemos* 8:15, s.v. "leket."
216 *Toras Kohanim*, beg. *parashas Vayikra.*
217 *Yeshayah* 55:1.
218 Ibid.
219 *Mishlei* 9:5; *Devarim Rabbah* 7:3; see also *Yalkut Shimoni, Shemos* 271.

prior to *Matan Torah*. This is because milk was originally considered *eiver min hachai* — a limb removed from a live animal — which is prohibited according to the Seven Noahide laws incumbent upon all mankind. When milk became permissible upon the giving of the Torah on Sinai, *Bnei Yisrael* were excited to try this newly permissible food and immediately consumed it on Shavuos. For this reason, we too follow suit and eat dairy on Shavuos.

The *Shemen Rokeach* disagrees with this rationale, for if milk was originally prohibited to *Bnei Noach*, Avraham would have certainly been unable to serve his guests milk and butter,[220] since it was a prohibited food item during that time.[221]

The *Mishnah Berurah* presents that the reason we eat dairy on Shavuos is to recall how the Jews only ate dairy at *Matan Torah*. This was because they were unable to properly prepare kosher meat due to its many intricate laws, such as the removal of blood and forbidden fat, proper sharpening of the *shechitah* knife, etc.[222]

If the Jewish People only heard the Ten Commandments on Sinai, how did they immediately know all these laws regarding the proper preparation of meat? The *Ayeles HaShachar* suggests that perhaps Moshe immediately taught those laws since they were pertinent immediately. He finds this approach problematic, however, since the Jewish People's diet in the desert consisted solely of manna and thus they had no need for either milk or meat.[223]

Rabbi Yaakov Kamenetsky gives a beautiful explanation for the custom of eating dairy foods on Shavuos. When the *Yidden* were

220   *Bereishis* 18:8.
221   *Shemen Rokeach, Eizehu Mekomon, Bechoros* 6b.
222   *Mishnah Berurah* 494:12.
223   *Ayeles HaShachar, Vayikra* 25:1.

commanded *shechitah* at Mount Sinai, they were unable to eat the meat already in their possession since it had the status of *neveilah* — improperly slaughtered meat. (Although they slaughtered the Pesach lamb in Egypt, they were only informed of *shechitah* that consisted of cutting the throat of the animal with a knife. However, the numerous details of *shechitah* were only given later on Sinai.) They were also unable to slaughter on Shavuos itself since they were inexperienced in the art of *shechitah* and would very likely do an improper *shechitah*. This would be prohibited to do on Yom Tov, as one is only permitted to slaughter an animal when we can reasonably assume that it will be permissible for human consumption.[224] (This is similar to the law that one who is performing a *bris milah* for the first time may not do so on Shabbos, since there is a high probability that he will not perform the act properly.)[225]

Others point out that *Bnei Yisrael* were unable to eat meat immediately after *Matan Torah* since the original Shavuos fell out on Shabbos when *shechitah* and cooking is prohibited. (The explanations cited above would follow the opinion that *Matan Torah* took place on Friday).[226]

Psalm 29

Although the general custom is to recite Chapter 24 of *Tehillim* (*L'Dovid Mizmor*), while returning the *sefer Torah* to the Torah ark when Shavuos falls out on a weekday, some have a custom to recite Chapter 29 (*Havu LaHashem*), since this chapter deals with *Matan Torah*, which transpired on Shavuos.[227]

The *Tur* explains that the reason we recite *Havu LaHashem* while returning the *sefer Torah* to the *Aron HaKodesh* on Shabbos is because this chapter discusses the giving of the Torah on Sinai, which was accompanied with the sounds of the shofar as described in that

---

224   *Emes L'Yaakov, Orach Chaim* 494:3.

225   *Orach Chaim* 331:10.

226   *Pirkei D'Rebbi Eliezer* 46.

227   *Nitei Gavriel* 28:5.

chapter. *Matan Torah* is connected to Shabbos since the Torah was given on Shabbos.[228]

Similarly, the *Mateh Efraim* writes that although when Yom Tov falls out on a weekday we ordinarily recite *L'Dovid Mizmor* while returning the *sefer Torah* to the *Aron*, an exception is made on Rosh Hashanah when we recite *Havu LaHashem*.[229] The *Elef Lamateh* explains this is because we wish to incorporate the merit of receiving the Torah on Har Sinai on this auspicious day.[230]

In Chapter 29 of *Tehillim*, the psalmist discusses numerous miracles that transpired at *Matan Torah*. In *pasuk* 6, it states: "He makes [the cedars] prance about like a calf." Why does the verse mention the prancing of a calf? It would seem more appropriate to use an analogy of a more graceful animal such as a ram?[231]

The *Ba'al HaTurim* says that the reference to the calf hints to the Sin of the Golden Calf. The verse teaches that the Golden Calf was endowed with supernatural powers that enabled it to dance like a young calf.[232]

The question arises: why should an admonition of the Golden Calf be inserted in a chapter that deals with the miraculous events of *Matan Torah*?

The answer is that the miraculous events surrounding *Matan Torah* were given to the Jewish People to provide them with the wherewithal to withstand future tests such as the Golden Calf. Had they taken due note of the unparalleled miracles that transpired at Mount Sinai — such as where the roots of the cedar trees lifted the tree upwards and began dancing as human legs — they would have been unimpressed with the paltry machinations of the prancing golden calf.

---

228 *Tur, Orach Chaim* 384, quoting *Sefer HaManhig.*
229 *Mateh Ephraim* 590:37.
230 *Elef Lamateh*, ibid. 27.
231 As employed in *Tehillim* 114:4.
232 *Ba'al HaTurim, Vayikra* 9:3.

Reading Megillas Rus

> *There are three crowns: royalty, kehunah, and Torah. The crown of priesthood was taken by Aharon and the crown of royalty was taken by Dovid HaMelech. But the third crown awaits anyone who wishes to come and claim it. Lest you say that the crown of Torah is inferior to the other crowns, the Torah therefore states, "Through me (meaning, the Torah), kings will reign."[233]*

We see from this that Dovid was worthy of royalty because of his total immersion in Torah. It is for this reason we read the book of *Rus* on Shavuos. *Rus* delineates the royal lineage of Dovid HaMelech, who merited royalty by imbuing himself with the Torah's wisdom, which was given on Shavuos.[234]

Why is *Megillas Rus* read in shul before the reading of the Torah? The Torah is read on a weekly basis and *Megillas Rus* only annually, so we should apply the principle of *tadir kodem* — that precedence is given to the more frequently performed mitzvah?

Rabbi Yosef Shalom Elyashiv answers that since *maftir* is recited on Yom Tov, one may mistakenly think that *Megillas Rus* is a second *haftorah* and erringly come to recite over it the seven blessings that one says upon reading the *haftorah*. On Purim, however, it is not a problem to read the *Megillah* after the Torah reading since there is no *maftir* recited on Purim, and thus one will not mistakenly confuse *Megillas Esther* for a *haftorah*.[235]

---

233 *Mishlei* 8:15; *Yomah* 72b.
234 *Kedushas Levi, Shavuos* s.v. *"v'od ta'am."*
235 *Chashukei Chemed, Megillah* 23a.

According to *Mesechtas Sofrim*,[236] *Rus* is read on Shavuos in two sections; the first part on the night following the first day of Shavuos, and the remainder the following night. Why should *Rus* be read on the night *after* Yom Tov?

The Midrash says that the reason *Rus* is read on Shavuos is to demonstrate that Torah is acquired only through suffering and poverty (which was how *Rus* joined the Jewish People).[237]

On Shavuos day, the Written Law was given to Israel. However, it is specifically with the Oral Law — which is acquired through toil and difficulty — that Hashem made a covenant with the Jewish People. Since the struggle to understand the Oral Law is comparable to the dark night,[238] *Rus* is also read on the night after the illuminating festival of Shavuos draws to a close.[239]

---

236   *Maseches Sofrim* 14.
237   *Yalkut Shimoni, Rus* 596.
238   *Sanhedrin* 24a.
239   *Ein Eliyahu*, p. 49.

Insights on the Book of Rus

"And it happened in the days when the judges judged." *(Rus 1:1)*

"You shall not curse a judge or curse the ruler of your people. Your *terumah* and *bikurim* you shall not delay."[240] The *Ha'amek Davar* explains the juxtaposition of these two verses as follows:

If you show proper respect to your judges and Torah leaders, then you will be blessed with an abundant harvest and be able to fulfill the commandment of bringing tithes and the first fruits. If, however, one belittles Torah scholars, then in turn one's own crops will also be cursed by pestilence. This is why the book of *Rus* begins, "It was in the days of the judges," which the Sages interpret to mean that it was in the days when the populace "judged the judges" and belittled Torah scholars. It was for this reason, the verse continues, that a hunger occurred at that time.

"There was a famine in the land, and a man went from Bethlehem in Judah, to sojourn in the fields of Moab." *(Rus 1:1)*

This information serves as a fitting introduction to the book of *Rus*, as it somewhat mitigates Elimelech's decision to leave the Land of Israel. Elimelech considered himself a private individual with no power of influence over others, as the verse states: "and *a man* [i.e., an anonymous individual] went from…Judah…to Moav."

Indeed, had Elimelech truly believed that he was merely a nameless individual with no sphere of influence, he would not have been punished.

---

240 *Shemos* 22:27–28.

However, the Sages expound the verse, "The man's name was Elimelech (אלימלך),"[241] by saying that he was wont to say אלי תבא מלכות — "Upon me will come the mantle of royalty." Since, in actuality, he viewed himself as a person of influence, he was found culpable in Heaven for shirking his responsibilities to the community.[242] So although he made himself out as if he was just *a man*, really in his heart he wished to be royalty, and so Hashem took his innermost thoughts into account and treated him accordingly.

"And his two sons were named Machlon and Chilyon." (Rus 1:2)

Our Sages say that a person's name hints to the nature of his character, as well as to his destiny. The Gemara expounds the names of Elimelech's children:[243]

- Machlon — because he made his body profane (*chulin*) by leaving the holy Land of Israel
- Chilyon — because he became worthy of destruction (*kilayon*).

In *Divrei HaYamim*, they are called by the names Yoash and Saraph:

- Yoash — because he abandoned hope (*yi'ush*) from redemption
- Saraph — because he became deserving of death by burning (*sereiphah*).

According to the *Zohar*, Machlon's name also contains a positive connotation, because Hashem eventually forgave him (*mechilah*) since he protested against the misdeeds of his father. In that merit, *yibum* was performed on his wife, and this perpetuated his name.[244]

---

241 *Rus* 1:2.
242 *Ta'ama D'kra, Rus* 1:1.
243 *Bava Basra* 91b.
244 *Zohar Chadash, Rus*.

"They married Moabite women, one named
Orpah, and the other Rus." (Rus 1:4)

Whether or not Rus and Orpah were their original birth names is a matter of dispute. When a person converts to Judaism, he is given a Jewish name. According to the *Zohar*, Rus's name before she converted was Gilis (or according to a variant text Palonisa), and Orpah's birth name was Horofoh.[245] When Machlon and Chilyon married them, they converted them to Judaism and changed their names to Rus and Orpah.

According to the variant text, we can explain that Rus's name, Palonisa, was similar to Peloni Almoni, since she was initially destined to marry him and not Boaz. Rabbi Menachem Channan suggests that the root *pelon* is an expression of sovereignty.[246] This was therefore a fitting name for Rus, who was a princess at birth and later became the great-grandmother of Dovid HaMelech, the first Jewish king from the royal tribe of Yehudah.

In the view of the Malbim, Orpah and Rus retained their former names after marrying Machlon and Chilyon, which demonstrates that they did not undergo a proper conversion.[247] According to this view, the question arises: why did Rus keep her non-Jewish name even after she properly converted upon following Naomi back to the Land of Israel?

The Gemara explains that it is because she elevated herself to such an extent that her old name was sublimated to a positive connotation.[248]

"And Orpah kissed her mother-in-law
but Rus cleaved to her." (Rus 1:14)

On this verse, the Gemara comments: "The Holy One, Blessed is He, said: 'Let the sons of the woman who was kissed (Orpah) be

---

245 *Zohar Chadash* 79a.

246 See Rashi, *Megillah* 6a, s.v. *"metropolin."*

247 Malbim, *Ruth* 1:4.

248 *Berachos* 7b: "What is the significance of the name Ruth? For she merited that Dovid descended from her, who 'satiated' the Holy One, Blessed is He, with songs and praises." (The name רות [Rus] is related to רוה [satiate].).

felled by the hand of the sons of the woman who cleaved (Rus).'"[249]
What does this mean?

In the beginning of the story of Rus, it is difficult to differentiate between the behavior of Rus and Orpah:

- Both Rus and Orpah forgave their rights for compensation from their *kesuvah* out of their love for Naomi.
- Both Rus and Orpah helped make the shrouds for their deceased husbands and both followed Naomi back towards Eretz Yisrael.
- We see it was difficult for Orpah to leave Naomi; even when she finally did, she first kissed her and took leave of her in a very dramatic parting.

The difference between Rus and Orpah was that while Orpah had strong feelings, Rus had an immutable commitment to her principles. This distinction became readily apparent in their descendants: Orpah gave birth to Golias, who blasphemed Hashem; while from Rus descended Dovid, the progenitor of Mashiach. The message of *Megillas Rus* and its connection to *Matan Torah* is to contrast the difference between a resolute dedication to Torah as opposed to a wavering one.

> *"And Rus said, 'Do not urge me to leave*
> *you...your people are my people and your*
> *God is my God.'" (Rus 1:16)*

Our Sages derive from Rus's behavior numerous laws pertaining to the acceptance of converts. We may ask, though, why it wasn't sufficient for Rus to accept Hashem's sovereignty and the fulfillment of His will ("your God is my God") in order to be accepted as a convert. Why was it necessary for her to also accept becoming socially integrated amid the Jewish People ("your people are my people")?

---

249 *Sotah* 42b.

The Rambam rules that someone who separates himself from the community of Israel and does not bear the lot of their suffering or join in their communal fasts does not receive a portion in the World to Come.[250] Accordingly, if one wishes to convert to Judaism, it is not sufficient to merely accept the yoke of Torah and mitzvos; one must also accept to become a full participating member of the Jewish community. This means that one must specifically undertake to not only join in the joy and happiness of the Jewish people, but to also share their lot during periods of suffering and tribulations.[251]

"When she saw she was determined to go (lit. to exert herself to walk) with her, she stopped arguing with her." (Rus 1:18)

Why was Naomi convinced of Rus's sincerity specifically at this point?

The Vilna Gaon compares it to the story in the life of Reish Lakish. The Gemara relates that Reish Lakish was originally a powerful highwayman who could leap great distances in a single bound. However, when he decided to repent and accept the yoke of Torah, his extraordinary strength immediately departed.[252] This was a result of the dictum that the Torah weakens the physical strength of a person.[253]

A similar reaction occurred with Rus. Naomi noticed that until this point Rus had no difficulty walking together with her. It was only now that her physical stamina suddenly diminished, and Naomi understood that this was only a result of her sincere acceptance of Torah, so she therefore refrained from dissuading her any further.[254]

---

250 Rambam, *Mishnah Torah, Teshuvah* 3:1.
251 *Hararei Kedem*, vol. 2, p. 334.
252 *Bava Metzia* 84a.
253 *Sanhedrin* 26b.
254 Vilna Gaon, *Davar B'ito*, p. 94.

> *"May Hashem reward your actions,*
> *and may your payment be full from*
> *Hashem, the G-d of Israel." (Rus 2:12)*

A righteous convert has a distinct advantage over one born into the Jewish faith. When Hashem redeemed the Jewish People from slavery in Egypt, we became indebted to Him in servitude. Since a slave is the property of his master and fully indentured to him, it is inappropriate for a slave to seek compensation for his work.

A convert, however, who was not enslaved in Egypt but rather chose to serve Hashem on his own accord, has every right to request full payment for his service. This is why Boaz told Rus, "May Hashem reward your actions, and may your payment be full from Hashem, the G-d of Israel." Boaz was confident that she would be greatly rewarded for her good deeds from "under whose wings you have come to seek refuge."[255] Since Rus was a righteous convert, her relationship to Hashem was not one of a maidservant to her Master, and she therefore could expect to be rewarded handsomely for her good deeds.[256]

> *"And [Rus] said, 'The name of the man for*
> *whom I have done today is Boaz.'" (Rus 2:19)*

Shouldn't the verse have stated the reverse, "The name of the man *who has done for me* today is Boaz," since it was Boaz who charitably gave wheat to Rus and not vice versa?

The Midrash derives from here that more than the wealthy man does for the poor person, the poor man does for the wealthy person. Rabbi Aharon Kotler points out that the Midrash is not only referring to heavenly reward, but also to the numerous tangible pleasures the benefactor experiences in this world as a result of

---

255 *Rus* 2:12.
256 Vilna Gaon, *Peninim M'Shulchan HaGra*, p. 408.

his largesse.[257] The prophets compare *Gehinom* to a leech,[258] and to an insatiable wide-gaping mouth.[259] If a person lives a greedy, self-centered life, his entire existence becomes a living purgatory due to his unmet desires. It is generosity that generates immense pleasure.

"The name of the man...is Boaz." (Rus 2:19)

When the angels came to save Lot and his family from Sodom, they said, "Whom else do you have here (פה)?"[260] The numerical value of פה is eighty-five and hints to Boaz (בועז), whose name has the same numerical value. This signifies that it was in the merit of Boaz — through his eventual marriage with Lot's descendant, Rus — that Lot and her daughters were saved. The significance of this number is further indicated in that there are eighty-five verses in the book of *Rus*.[261]

"And he said, 'blessed are you unto Hashem, my daughter, [for] your second kindness is greater than your first.'" (Rus 3:10)

What was Rus's first act of kindness to which Boaz alluded?

The Bach explains that her first act of kindness was her conversion to Judaism.[262] A sincere convert adds another holy soul to the ranks of the Jewish People, which strengthens the Jewish nation and spreads more light upon the world. For this reason, a convert is referred to as a "benefactor."[263]

---

257 *Mishnas Rebbi Aharon al HaTorah*, p. 313.
258 *Mishlei* 30:15.
259 *Yeshayah* 5:14.
260 *Bereishis* 19:12.
261 *Rabbeinu Ephraim, Breishis* 19:12.
262 In his commentary *Meishiv Nefesh*, quoted in *Hararei Kedem*, vol. 2, 127:1.
263 *Sukkah* 49b and Rashi there.

Megillas Rus speaks about the numerous acts of kindness that Rus performed. However, when one analyzes them, he finds that all those acts benefited her as much as they did others. For example,

- Naomi said to Rus, "Hashem should do *chesed* with you as you have done with the deceased."[264] Would one consider a loving relationship with one's spouse an act of kindness?
- Next, Naomi told Rus that her marriage with Boaz will be beneficial to her, yet Boaz tells Rus that what she was performing was an act of kindness.[265] Would one call the efforts to obtain a *shidduch* with a person one keenly desires as an act of kindness?

Since the prophet nevertheless considers all these acts as *chasadim*, we may derive from this that regardless whether one has self-serving interests or ulterior motives, an act done for the benefit of others is still deemed an act of kindness.[266]

"I have also acquired Rus, the Moabite, the wife of Machlon, as my wife." (Rus 4:10)

Throughout *Megillas Rus*, Rus's name, "Rus the Moabite," is spelled fully, with a letter *vav* (רות המואביה). An exception is the last time her name is mentioned, which is in this verse (וגם את רות המאביה אשת מחלון). The reason for this is that once Boaz ruled that Moabite women converts are exempted from the prohibition of marrying a Jewish man, her Moabite status was diminished and hence is lacking the letter *vav*.[267]

We may suggest that this missing *vav* was transferred into verse 4:18, ואלה תולדות פרץ — "These are the descendants of Peretz." The Midrash explains that the Torah always writes the word *toldos*

264 *Rus* 1:8.
265 Ibid. 3:10.
266 Rabbi Yeruchem Levovitz, *Da'as Chochmah U'Mussar*, vol. 3, p. 173.
267 *Ta'ama D'kra*, p. 161.

without a letter *vav* (תולדת) with the exception of two places: "These are the *toldos* (descendants) of Peretz," and "These are the *toldos* (chronicles) of heaven and earth."[268] The reason the word *toldos* is written "full" (inclusive of the letter *vav*) regarding the creation of heaven and earth is because the Angel of Death had no power at that point. After the sin of Adam, mankind was subject to death, henceforth all future descendants (*toldos*) are deficient (lacking the letter *vav*).

The reason why "the descendants of Peretz" is written full (with a *vav*) is because Mashiach will be descended from Peretz, and in his time death will again cease from mankind.[269] Since Mashiach's birth was dependent upon Rus's marriage to Boaz, it is appropriate that the *vav* from her name be used in the verse that hints to the birth of Mashiach.

"They named him Oved." *(Rus 4:17)*

Regarding the mitzvah of *yibum*, the *pasuk* states: "The firstborn that she bears shall arise in the name of the dead brother."[270] The Ramban explains that this does not mean that the child of the union of *yibum* must necessarily be named after the deceased husband. As proof, he cites the story of Rus, whose son was named Oved and not Machlon.[271] The Abarbanel suggests that Rus indeed named her son Machlon,[272] but that her neighbors called him Oved (the one who serves),[273] since he devotedly took care of Naomi in her old age.

---

268   *Bereishis* 2:4.
269   *Bereishis Rabbah* ibid.
270   *Devarim* 25:6.
271   Ramban, *Devarim* ibid.
272   Abarbanel, *Devarim, parashas Ki Seitzei.*
273   *Rus* 4:17.

The Three Weeks and Tishah B'Av

The Month of Av

The *Churban* — destruction — of the Holy Temple, as well as many other tragedies in Jewish history, occurred during the month of Av. There are numerous reasons offered as to why the month was given this specific name:

- Av means "father." The month of Av is considered the "father" of all Jewish suffering, due to the many tragedies that occurred during this month.[1]
- When Hashem punishes us, it is with love, just as a father who wants only what is best for his child and therefore disciplines him with fatherly love.
- Hashem is deemed a King only while the Temple stands. As a result of the *Churban*, He is no longer perceived as a King, but merely as a Father.[2]

---

1   See *Midrash HaChefetz*, cited in *Torah Sheleimah, Parashas Bo, Miluim*, p. 177.
2   Maharshah, *Berachos* 3a.

HINTS IN THE TORAH

The Mabul

The period between the seventeenth of Tamuz and the ninth of Av was predisposed for tragedy from the dawn of history. Tosfos says that Noach opened the window of the ark after the deluge on the seventeenth of Tamuz.[3] On this day, Noach sent out the dove but it did not find a place to rest.[4] On this same day, a similar scenario would repeat itself to the Jewish People, who are compared to a dove. The seventeenth of Tamuz commenced a period of exile in which the children of Israel would be "unable to find a place to rest their feet."[5]

In the view of the Malbim, Noach opened the window of the ark after the *Mabul* on the tenth of Av.[6] According to his view, this hints that immediately following a period of great destruction begins a new era of rebuilding and renewal.

Gid HaNasheh

The *Zohar* writes that the 365 negative commandments in the Torah correspond to the 365 days in the solar year. The commandment that corresponds to the day of Tishah b'Av is the prohibition of eating the *gid hanasheh* — the sinew of the hind quarter of an animal. This prohibition came as a result of the angel of Eisav successfully dislocating Yaakov's thigh while engaging him in mortal combat. This served as a prelude for the day of Tishah b'Av becoming an ominous time for the children of Israel falling into the hands of Eisav.[7]

Ya'aros Devash adds that since an animal has a *gid hanasheh* on the thigh of both hind legs, the *gid hanasheh* on the other hind leg corresponds to the Fast of Gedaliah, as the death of *tzadikim* is

---

3   *Da'as Zekeinim M'Ba'alei Tosfos, Bereishis* 8:3.
4   Ibid., v. 9.
5   Da'as Zekeinim ibid.
6   *Bereishis*, v. 6.
7   *Zohar, Vayishlach*, pp. 170a–b.

equivalent to the destruction of the Temple.[8] Branching out of each *gid hanasheh* is another sinew that is rabbinically prohibited. These two sinews correspond to the secondary fast days of the tenth of Teves and the seventeenth of Tamuz.[9]

"על כן לא יאכלו בני ישראל את גיד הנשה" — Therefore the Jewish People are not to eat the displaced nerve."[10] The *Zohar* explains that the reason for this prohibition is that the nerve touched by the angel of Eisav is seen as the place where evil has a strong influence.[11] According to the *Sefer HaChinuch*, this mitzvah teaches that a Jew must never despair, despite the devastating onslaughts of our enemies in exile.[12] Just as the angel of Eisav only succeeded in inflicting pain upon Yaakov, but was unable to defeat him, and ultimately the sun shone upon him to heal him, so too will the sun of the Mashiach shine for us, and he will heal us of all our suffering in exile.

The *Rimzei Rabbeinu Yoel* writes that the above verse also hints to other fast days over the course of the year:[13]

- ג (3) — corresponds to the third day in Tishrei, which is Tzom Gedaliah
- י (10) — corresponds to the tenth of Teves
- גיד — is the numerical value of seventeen, hinting to the seventeenth of Tamuz
- את גיד הנשה — the numerical value of the first letters of these words is nine, alluding to the ninth of Av. Also, the words את גיד הנשה, have the same numerical value as תשעה באב.

---

8   *Ya'aros Devash*, 7, p. 111.
9   Ibid.
10   *Bereishis* 32:33.
11   *Zohar, parashas Vayishlach*, pp. 170a–170b.
12   *Sefer HaChinuch* 3.
13   *Rimzei Rabbeinu Yonah, Bereishis* ibid.

Further Hints

There are additional hints in the Torah to the destruction of the Beis HaMikdash:

The *pasuk* says: "And the anger of Hashem was kindled on that day [the ninth of Av]."[14] The words "that day" signify that henceforth the ninth of Av would be a day suited for calamity.[15]

In the episode of the Sin of the Spies, *Bnei Yisrael* cried during the night on the ninth of Av. Similarly, both the First and Second Temples were also destroyed on the ninth of Av at night (albeit by the Second Temple, it was the night following the ninth of Av).

The Torah mentions that the spies traveled to Eretz Yisrael by traversing the boundary of Edom. The Torah mentions this detail of their travels to hint that the destruction of the Temple, which was a result of the Sin of the Spies, would be brought through the hands of Edom [Rome].

The only person whom the Torah mentions the month in which he died is Aharon HaKohen. The Torah relates that Aharon passed away in the month of Av as an allusion that the Temple service, which will be performed by the descendants of Aharon, would also come to an end in this month.[16]

---

14   *Bamidbar* 32:10.
15   See *Sanhedrin* 104b.
16   *Nifla'os M'Toras Hashem Yisbarach, Ma'amar Chofer Matmunei Ha'Avos*, chap. 18.

From Destruction to Redemption

SIN OF THE SPIES

Disconnected from Israel

The Midrash says that when the Jewish People accepted the spies' evil report about the Land of Israel, Hashem decreed at that moment that the Beis HaMikdash would be destroyed and that the Jewish People would go into exile.[17] The following difficulty arises: the Gemara enumerates various sins for which the Temple was destroyed,[18] but no mention is made of the sin of the *meraglim*!

The Maharal answers that had the Sin of the Spies not transpired, the Jewish People would have been ineradicably bound to Hashem and the Land of Israel. Even if they were to later commit grievous sins, Hashem would mete out to them various forms of punishment, but they would have still stayed in Eretz Yisrael and the Beis HaMikdash would have remained intact. But when they disparaged the Land of Israel, they severed their intrinsic connection with it. As a result, the punishment for their future sins would be in the form of exile and the destruction of the Beis HaMikdash.[19]

Blinded to the Facts

In the book of *Eichah*, the verses follow each other in alphabetical order. An exception is made in chapter two, where the verse

---

17   *Bamidbar Rabbah* 16:12.
18   *Shabbos* 31a, *Yomah* 9b.
19   *Peninim M'Shulchan Gavoah, Bamidbar* 14:1.

beginning with the letter *peh*, פצו עליך פיהם — "They jeered at you with their mouths"[20] — precedes that beginning with the letter *ayin*. The Gemara explains that this is because of the Sin of the Spies, who spoke with their mouths (the Hebrew word for "mouth" is *peh*) against the Land of Israel, about what they had not seen with their eyes (the word for "eye" in Hebrew is *ayin*).[21]

Rabbi Betzalel Ashkenazi observes that the punishment is measure for measure. It is difficult to wrongfully embarrass a person while directly looking at him, so it is common to close one's eyes when degrading another. In a similar way, the enemies of Israel open their mouths against the Jews while blindly "closing their eyes" to the plain facts that clearly demonstrate how their accusations are based on lies.[22]

Unaccepted Repentance

After Hashem pronounced the punishment upon the generation of the wilderness that they be prevented from entering the Land of Israel as a result of the Sin of the Spies, the Jewish People repented and prayed to Hashem to recant His decree.[23] Why didn't Hashem accept their prayer and repentance?

The Seforno explains that it was because their sin entailed *chilul Hashem*, for which repentance alone does not achieve atonement but rather death is required to achieve full atonement.[24] Alternatively, *Bnei Yisrael* repented only after Hashem's punishment was decreed and were thus motivated out of fear of retribution. This lower level of repentance (*teshuvah meyirah*) is not sufficient to annul a decree, as we find by Kayin, the sons of Eli HaKohen, and Shaul HaMelech.[25]

---

20   *Eichah* 2:16.
21   *Sanhedrin* 104b.
22   Rabbi Betzalel Ashkenazi, *Derashos U'ma'amarim*, pp. 324–325.
23   *Devarim* 1:45.
24   Seforno, *Bamidbar* 13:2.
25   Seforno, *Devarim* 1:45–46.

THE FIRST TEMPLE

Golden Calf

The sins that destroyed the First Temple were rooted in the Sin of the Golden Calf. As the Gemara interprets the verse, "On the day I make My account, I shall bring their sin [of the Golden Calf] against them,"[26] as referring to the destruction of the First Temple.[27] How do we reconcile this concept with the statement of the Sages that says the first Temple was destroyed because the Jews transgressed the three cardinal sins?

Rabbi Gedaliah Schorr answers that while the Sin of the Golden Calf was primarily one of idolatry, it also included strains of murder and immorality as well.[28] Although Moshe's intervention rectified the sins of the Golden Calf to a certain degree, nevertheless the root of the sins were never totally eradicated and later resurfaced during the First Temple period.[29]

Unsatisfying Service

The worth of our actions can be accurately measured by how much *ratzon* — satisfaction — they bring Hashem. "Life results from His satisfaction,"[30] and conversely, Hashem's displeasure with man's actions results in destruction.[31] The degree of satisfaction our Torah and mitzvos give to Hashem is commensurate with one's relationship with Hashem and the manner and objective of one's Divine service.[32]

During the time of the First Temple, the Torah was studied diligently and the Sages and the prophets were therefore at a loss

---

26   *Shemos* 32:34.
27   *Sanhedrin* 102a; see Rashi there.
28   Rashi, *Shemos* 32:6.
29   *Ohr Gedalyahu, Devarim*, p. 175.
30   *Tehillim* 30:6.
31   See *Bereishis* 6:6–7.
32   See *Tehillim* 50:16.

to understand why *Bnei Yisrael* deserved to be exiled. Hashem answered them by saying that it was because they lacked an appreciation for the Torah.[33] Without proper appreciation for the Torah, Hashem's *ratzon* was also minimized, and this caused the Divine Presence to depart and ultimately led to the loss of the land.[34]

Animal Lessons

The prophet Yeshayah rebuked Israel prior to the *Churban*, saying: "An ox knows his owner and a donkey his master's trough, but Israel does not know."[35] Why does Yeshayah give these two specific animals as examples when there are numerous other animals that also demonstrate this same behavior?

The *Mekor Chochmah* answers that idolatry and laxity in separating tithes were among the prominent sins that led to the *Churban*.[36] When Eliyahu brought a *korban* on Mount Carmel, he also gave the prophets of the *Ba'al* an identical twin cow for them to sacrifice for their idol. The Sages relate that the cow assigned for the prophets of *Ba'al* refused to budge, since it did not want to have any part in their idolatrous practices.[37] The Gemara also relates how the donkey of Rabbi Pinchas ben Yair refused to eat produce that was not tithed. It is now understandable why Yeshayah singled out these two specific animals; it was specifically these two animals that demonstrated more regard than Israel in refraining from the sins that would lead to exile.

Mirror Punishment

Hashem miraculously drove the Canaanites out of Eretz Yisrael by sending upon them an insect that afflicted them with blindness

---

33   Ran, *Nedarim* 81a.

34   *Mishnas Rebbi Aharon al HaTorah, Bereishis* 6:6–7.

35   *Yeshayah* 1:3.

36   Rabbi Chaim Ozer Kohen, cited in *Peninei Kedem, Devarim* 11:17.

37   *Midrash Tanchumah, parashas Masai.*

as well as sterility. Hashem warned *Bnei Yisrael* that if they would not completely drive the Canaanites out of Eretz Yisrael, "They shall be pins in your eyes and thorns in your sides…and it shall be that what I had meant to do to them, I shall do to you."[38] The *Rokeach* explains this to mean that when Hashem will drive *Bnei Yisrael* into exile for their sins, He will utilize the very same punishment He had earlier exacted upon the Canaanites.[39] This was fulfilled by the blinding of King Tzidkiyahu,[40] and Daniel, Chananyah, Mishael, and Azaryah being made sterile upon serving as courtiers to the King of Bavel.[41]

Choose Your Fast

"Thus said Hashem, Master of Legions: The fast of the fourth [month], the fast of the fifth, the fast of the seventh, and the fast of the tenth…"[42] The Midrash says that the fast of the fourth month is the seventeenth of Tamuz, the fifth month is the ninth of Av, the seventh Tzom Gedaliah, and the tenth is the tenth of Teves. Why didn't the prophet explicitly state the exact date of the fast day on each of these months?

The *Minchas Chinuch* deduces from this that the prophets merely obligated a person to fast one day in each of these months to commemorate the tragedy that occurred during that month, but each individual was able to choose which day during that month on which to fast. Only after the destruction of the Second Temple did the rabbis regulate a uniform practice that everyone fast on a specific day in each of those months.[43]

---

38 *Bamidbar* 33:55–56.
39 *Rokeach, Bamidbar* ibid.
40 *Melachim II* 25:7.
41 See Rashi, *Tehillim* 64:2.
42 *Zechariah* 8:19.
43 *Minchas Chinuch* 301:7; *Tashbetz* 2:271.

THE SECOND TEMPLE

Tishah B'Av in the Second Temple

How was Tishah b'Av observed during the era of the Second Temple?

It is unclear whether Tishah b'Av was observed as an official fast day, since the destroyed Temple was rebuilt.[44] In any event, it appears that there was still an element of mourning on this day, as the Second Temple lacked numerous features that were present in the First Temple. This is consistent with the view of Rabbi Yaakov Kamenetsky, who posits that the Second Temple was never viewed as a replacement for the first Beis HaMikdash, but rather as an aid to ease the Jewish People in their transition into exile.[45] For this reason, the Second Temple was not constructed according to the specifications of Yechezkel's prophecy of the final Messianic Temple.

Disharmony through Discontent

The Ramban comments that the admonitions found in the book of *Vayikra* deal with the sins that led to the destruction of the First Temple, while the ones in *Devarim* refer to those of the Second Temple era.[46] Rashi writes that the curses in the book of *Vayikra* come as a result of not toiling in Torah.[47] This, in fact, is what led to the Temple's destruction — a lack of proper appreciation for Torah study.[48]

The destruction of the Second Temple was a result of the sin of baseless hatred. Where is a hint to this sin found in the curses in the book of *Devarim*? There, it is written that the curses will come "because you did not serve Hashem amid gladness and goodness of heart."[49] A happy person is generally content and sees the good in

---

44 See Rambam, Commentary to Mishnah, *Rosh Hashanah* 1:3; cf. *Tashbetz* 2:271.
45 *Emes L'Yaakov, Avos* 1:1.
46 Ramban, *Vayikra* 26:16.
47 Rashi, *Vayikra* 26:3,14.
48 *Yirmiyah* 9:12; *Bava Metzia* 85b.
49 *Devarim* 28:47.

himself as well as in others. A malcontent not only hates himself but his hatred extends to others as well.[50]

Misplaced Piety

There is a debate between Beis Shammai and Beis Hillel regarding the *muktzah* status of bones and shells. The *Tosefta* writes that Rabbi Zechariah ben Avkilos was undecided as to whom the halachah should follow and therefore acted stringently, taking into account both views. The *Tosefta* cryptically concludes: "Rabbi Yosi said, 'the humility of Rabbi Zechariah ben Avkilos destroyed the Sanctuary.'"[51]

Commentators explain that just as Rav Zechariah was in doubt regarding the *muktzah* status of bones and shells, he was also in doubt regarding the permissibility of bringing a sacrifice with a minor blemish, which tragically resulted in the destruction of the Second Temple.[52]

What is the connection between these two disparate cases?

The message is that it is not always an act of piety to act stringently; rather, it is incumbent upon a person to gain clarity in order to be able to act in a decisive manner. Sometimes, one who consistently rules stringently "to be on the safe side" is not guided by piety but rather by misplaced humility.[53]

Deadly Naiveté

The Seforno comments that the Egyptian exile was a result of Yosef's lack of foresight in not considering the ramifications of relaying negative reports about his brothers to his father. A trace of youthful naiveté (on Yosef's high level) ultimately led him and his entire family going down to and eventually becoming slaves in Egypt.[54]

---

50 See Rabbi Nosson Wachsfogel, *Kovetz Sichos*, vol. 4, p. 179.
51 *Tosefta, Shabbos* 17:4.
52 See *Gittin* 56a.
53 *Derech Sichah*, p. 431; *Chazon Yechezkel, Shabbos* 17:4.
54 Seforno, *Bereishis* 37:2.

Similarly, the death knell of the remnant of the Jewish presence in Israel after the destruction of the First Temple resulted from the superficial attitude held by the righteous Gedaliah ben Achikam, who was appointed the governor of Israel by King Nevuchadnetzar. When Gedaliah was warned that a traitor by the name of Yishmael ben Netanya planned to kill him, he "piously" refused to consider their "*lashon hara*" [derogatory report] and failed to take the necessary precautions to prevent his own assassination. After Gedaliah was killed, the Jews remaining in Israel fled the land out of fear of reprisal from King Nevuchadnetzar.[55]

The Second Temple was also destroyed because of a lack of foresight on the part of Rabbi Zechariah ben Avkilos who did not consider the full repercussions of not accepting the blemished sacrifice offered by the Caesar. When the Roman Emperor heard that the Jews refused to accept his Temple offering, he took it as an act of rebellion and immediately dispatched his army to attack Yerushalayim.[56]

Lashon Hara and the Cardinal Sins

> *Why was the First Temple destroyed? Because of the sins of murder, idolatry, and immorality that were among them. But the Second Temple, where the people occupied themselves with Torah, mitzvos, and acts of kindness, why was it destroyed? Because of the baseless hatred that was among them. This teaches that baseless hatred is tantamount to the three cardinal sins.*[57]

Although *Chazal* specifically mention the sin of baseless hatred, the Chofetz Chaim says it actually includes the sin of speaking *lashon hara*.[58] How, then, is *lashon hara* tantamount to the three cardinal sins?

---

55   See *Nidah* 61a; Rabbi Nosson Wachtfogel, *No'am HaMussar*, pp. 229–230.
56   See *Gittin* 55b.
57   *Yomah* 9b.
58   *Sefer Chofetz Chaim*, introduction.

- Among the sins one transgresses when speaking disparagingly of others is the prohibition against haughtiness, which is akin to idol worship.[59]
- The Chofetz Chaim also recounts how *lashon hara* led to the murder of countless people.[60] When Doeg HaAdomi told Shaul HaMelech that the *Kohen Gadol* who lived in Nov was loyal to his enemy, Dovid, Shaul ordered that all the *Kohanim* of Nov be executed.[61]
- We may suggest that *lashon hara* is akin to immorality, based on the verse in *Shmuel* that states that the sons of Eli HaKohen sinned with married women.[62] But, as the Gemara explains, they did not actually sin but merely delayed the bringing of the women's bird offerings, which extended the time of separation between husband and wife.[63] When one person belittles another, it may lead the victim's spouse to look down upon him as well. So we see from the Gemara, therefore, that creating a rift between a husband and wife, whether it be through actions or negative speech, is tantamount to committing adultery.

Fox on the Mount

The Talmud relates that several sages were once walking near the Temple Mount when they saw a fox emerge from the site of the Holy of Holies.[64]

Why did Divine Providence orchestrate for a fox, rather than any another animal, to appear before these great men?

---

59 *Chofetz Chaim, Lavin* 5.

60 Ibid., preface.

61 In addition, the Chofetz Chaim there quotes the *Zohar* that states that when a person speaks *lashon hara*, it arouses negative spiritual forces that unleash death and bloodshed upon the earth.

62 *Shmuel I* 2:22.

63 *Yomah* 9a.

64 *Makkos* 24b.

The *Aruch Laner* answers that this incident parallels a strikingly similar episode that occurred at the destruction of the First Temple.[65] The Sages of that era prayed for the evil inclination of idol worship to be removed from the hearts of Israel, since it was because of the sin of idolatry that the Temple was destroyed. The Sages realized that their prayers were accepted when they saw a lion emerge from the Holy of Holies. The significance of a lion is that just as the lion is a powerful and formidable adversary, so was the temptation of idolatry an overpowering urge at that time.

The sin that led to the destruction of the Second Temple was baseless hatred. This sin is appropriately comparable to the sly and cunning fox, since the evil inclination tricks even a righteous person into thinking that his friend is a sinner worthy of being despised.

Why Was Kamtza Guilty?

"Because of Kamtza and Bar Kamtza Jerusalem was destroyed."[66]

The Gemara relates that there was a certain man who had a friend named Kamtza and an enemy named Bar Kamtza. The man made a banquet and told his attendant to summon Kamtza, but the attendant mistakenly invited Bar Kamtza. When the host saw his enemy sitting at his party, he publicly shamed Bar Kamtza and threw him out of the banquet hall. Bar Kamtza was incensed that the rabbis who were present at the feast did not protest the injustice done against him, so he decided to take revenge by slandering the Jews before the Roman emperor.

It is readily understandable why Bar Kamtza was guilty of causing the destruction of Yerushalayim, since he went to the emperor and told him that the Jews were rebelling against him. It's also plain to us that the host was also to blame for cruelly shaming Bar Kamtza and throwing him out of his house.

---

65   Rabbi Yaakov Etlinger, *Aruch Laner*, *Makkos* ibid.
66   *Gittin* 55b.

But why is Kamtza blamed if he wasn't even involved in the story? Commentators present several different possibilities:

1. The Gemara is simply stating the concrete events that led to the destruction of Yerushalayim. The Gemara states similarly: "As a result of [the incident involving] a rooster and a hen, Har HaMelech was destroyed; as a result of the side of a carriage, Beitar was destroyed." Kamtza was no more culpable than the rooster, the hen, or the side of the carriage.

2. Kamtza derives from the word "separate" (as in *kemitzah*, which is the flour separated from the rest of the *korban minchah* to be offered up on the *Mizbei'ach*). He initiated the concept of creating private clubs that excluded other people. The host followed Kamtza's example by making an exclusive party for his in-group. These cliques caused outsiders to feel isolated and rejected, and it was for this sin of *sinas chinam* that the Beis HaMikdash was destroyed.[67]

3. When a person is involved in a quarrel, he usually turns to his friends for support. The responsibility of a good spiritual friend is to try to quell the dispute by restoring peace and by soothing his friend's hurt feelings. Kamtza is faulted for not attempting to persuade the host to appease and beg forgiveness from Bar Kamtza.

4. The *Yalkut Meam Loez* says that Kamtza was the father of Bar Kamtza (*bar* means son of). Kamtza derives from the word *kamtzan* — a miser. Kamtza was a miser and did not want to spend money to teach his son Torah, which would have helped him learn to manage his explosive temper. Therefore, the father is also held accountable for his son's behavior.

5. In response to this question, Rabbi Chaim Soloveitchik would say: "*A gutte freint kumpt ohn an einladunge* — A good

---

67   Cf. Maharal, *Chidushei Aggados*, Gittin 55b.

friend comes [to a *simchah*] without an invitation." The reason the host of the party was in such a poor frame of mind was because he received a double blow: his enemy came and his friend did not. Had Kamtza not stood on ceremony but instead come to the *simchah*, the host's anger would not have flared as much, since he would have consoled himself that at least his friend Kamtza also attended his *simchah*.

Destruction of Tenth of Av

The Romans set fire to the Beis HaMikdash on the ninth of Av towards evening, and it continued to burn the entire day of the tenth of Av. For this reason, Rabbi Yochanan commented that had he been present in the generation that fixed the date for commemorating the Temple's destruction, he would have designated the fast to be on the tenth of Av instead of on the ninth.[68]

The Chasam Sofer explains the rationale of the rabbis who fixed the date based on when the fires began. There is a principle that כיון שפרצום נעשו חול — once the vessels of the Temple are misappropriated, they become mundane.[69] Therefore, once the Romans set the Temple aflame, the building immediately lost all its sanctity and it would be pointless to mourn its loss on the tenth, since it was just an ordinary building at that point. According to the view of Rabbi Yochanan, however, this principle only applies to sanctified *vessels*; the Temple *building* retains its holiness as long as it is not completely destroyed.[70]

Churban in the Talmud

The Aggadic portions found in each tractate of the Talmud are intentionally placed in their specific locations, as they directly connect to the theme of the specific tractate. For example, the Aggadata that

68   *Ta'anis* 29a.
69   *Nedarim* 62a.
70   *Chasam Sofer, Orach Chaim* 33; *Devarim*, pp. 15–16.

discusses the giving of the Torah on Sinai is found in Tractate *Shabbos*, since *Matan Torah* occurred on Shabbos. The feast for the righteous that will transpire at the future redemption is in Tractate *Pesachim*, whose laws deal with the redemption from Egypt. Also, a discussion about the *yetzer hara* is found in Tractate *Sukkah* because of its connection to the *simchah* of being free of sin during the holiday of Sukkos.

The story of the *Churban* is fittingly placed in tractate *Gittin*, since the *Churban* created a rift in our relationship with Hashem, akin to a divorce between a husband and wife.[71] However, just as a divorce is reversible, so can our relationship with Hashem be restored. This can perhaps explain why the cures for various ailments are discussed at great length in this particular tractate.[72]

Surviving Exile

The Seforno comments that the way to survive *Galus Edom* — the Roman exile (of which we are currently suffering) is through subservience to our enemies. This is based on the historical precedent of our forefather Yaakov, who prostrated himself on the ground when encountering his estranged brother Eisav who harbored murderous intentions against him. This act immediately aroused Eisav's compassion and changed his attitude towards Yaakov to one of compassion and kindness.[73]

The prophet Achiyah HaShiloni cursed the Jewish People before their advent into exile that they be similar to a reed that sways in the wind. This was actually a blessing in disguise, for this trait would guarantee their survival in exile. Had the zealots heeded the council of Rabbi Yochanan ben Zakai and humbly submitted themselves to the authority of the Romans, the siege against Jerusalem would have been averted and the Second Temple would not have been destroyed.[74]

---

71   Rabbi Dovid Kronglass.
72   See *Gittin* 67b–70b.
73   Seforno, *Bereishis* 33:4.
74   Seforno ibid.

DESTROYERS OF THE TEMPLE

Fitting Punishment

Hashem punished both Nevuchadnetzar and Titus for destroying the Temple, each in a manner befitting his crime:

- Nevuchadnetzar destroyed the Temple that was constructed in seven years, so he was therefore forced to roam among the animals for seven years.[75]
- Titus exiled the Jewish nation who is compared to a dove, and therefore the gnat that gnawed at his brain grew to the size of a dove.[76] In addition, the Temple is compared to the head and the brain.[77] Since he ravaged the head and brain of the Jewish nation, so were his head and brain destroyed as well.[78]

Taking the Wrong Message

"Your enemies have roared amid Your meeting place, they took their signs for signs."[79] When Titus entered the Temple, he stabbed the curtain of the Holy of Holies with his sword, and miraculously blood began to flow from it. Titus took this as a sign that he had slain Hashem himself.[80] The blood was actually a Divine sign for Israel — that Hashem was joining in their suffering over their tragic plight. Thus "they" [the Romans] "took their signs" [the ones intended to encourage Israel] for favorable "signs" [for themselves] (i.e., that Hashem had been rendered impotent to help Israel).[81]

---

75   *Daniel* 4:29.
76   *Sefer Chasidim* 1:151.
77   *Zohar Chadash, Shir HaShirim* 75a; *Zohar* 2:108b.
78   Rabbi Shaul Yedidyah Taub, *Yisah Berachah*, vol. 3, p. 144.
79   *Tehillim* 74:4.
80   *Gittin* 56b.
81   Seforno, *Tehillim* ibid.

Nothing Left to Do

"From on high He sent a fire into my bones."[82] The Midrash explains that Hashem Himself sent a fire to burn the Temple so that the heathens could not boast that they themselves had destroyed it.

The Arizal comments that this is the meaning of the verse: "[The enemies said] 'Indeed, this is the day we longed for; we have found, we have seen.'"[83] The enemy had hoped for the day when they could burn the Temple themselves. They were disappointed because "*we found, we saw*," meaning they found that Hashem had already sent down the fire that burned the Temple.[84] This is a cause for comfort as well; just as Hashem burned the Temple Himself, so will He Himself rebuild the Temple with fire.[85]

MOURNING THE DESTRUCTION

It's Alive!

"Whoever mourns over the destruction of Jerusalem merits seeing its joy."[86] Why does the Gemara use the present tense "seeing" instead of the future tense "to see"?

The Chasam Sofer explains that Hashem implanted into the nature of human beings the tendency to forget a deceased relative after a year of mourning.[87] If so, how do we still mourn the Temple's destruction, which occurred thousands of years ago? The answer is that although the Temple is physically destroyed, it is still spiritually alive. Since it presently exists in the heavenly, spiritual dimension,[88] we are therefore unable to forget it and if we are worthy we can even

---

82   *Eichah* 1:13.

83   Ibid. 2:16.

84   *Kinos* (Artscroll Publications), p. 31.

85   *Nachem*, addition to *Shemoneh Esrei* of *Minchah* on Tishah b'Av.

86   *Ta'anis* 30b.

87   *Chasam Sofer*, *Ta'anis* ibid.

88   See Rashi, end of *Sukkah* 41a.

perceive an inkling of its majestic glory. Perhaps it is for this reason Tishah b'Av is called a *Moed* — a festival,[89] since through our mourning we can also sense the joy of its future rebuilding.

Feeling the Churban

The *Tumim* writes that if a person truly comprehended the magnitude of the *Churban*, he would go out of his mind from pain. Some bring a proof to this idea from the *din* that one must remove knives from the table while reciting *Birchas Hamazon*. This law is based on an event that once occurred when an individual was so disturbed over the *Churban* while *bentching* that he stabbed himself with a knife that was lying on the table.[90] Would the Sages make a law based on a solitary event that occurred to one disturbed individual? Apparently, the Sages considered his reaction totally rational; it is our apathy that is abnormal.

The pain of the *Churban* was so real to the early generations that the Midrash relates that Rabbi Yochanan expounded sixty interpretations on the verse, "Hashem swallowed and showed no mercy," while his predecessor, Rebbi, only interpreted twenty-four explanations on that verse.[91] The Midrash concludes that it was not because Rabbi Yochanan was more prolific than Rebbi, but rather that since Rebbi lived closer to the time of the *Churban*, he would stop and cry more frequently and was unable to continue his discourse.[92]

True Mourners

Rabbi Yeruchem Levovitz observes that while we cry when reciting the lamentation describing the death of Rabbi Akiva and his colleagues, the lamentation of *Alei Tzion*, which describes the desecration of the Holy Temple, is chanted like a pleasant song.[93] This

---

89   See *Shulchan Aruch, Orach Chaim* 559:4.
90   *Mishnah Berurah* 180:11.
91   *Eichah Rabbah* 2:4.
92   *Derech Sichah*, p. 610.
93   Rabbi Yeruchem Levovitz, *Da'as Chochmah U'Mussar* 2:67.

demonstrates that we are indifferent to how the spiritual loss of the *Churban* directly impacts our lives. The rabbis instituted the laws of mourning on Tishah b'Av so that we should feel that we are truly mourners in a very real and literal sense. The importance of properly mourning the *Churban* can be appreciated in light of the remarkable statement by Rabbi Yaakov Emden, who said that all the tragedies the Jewish People suffer in exile are a direct result of not properly mourning the *Churban* of the Beis HaMikdash.[94]

The Mother We Never Met

One of the reasons why it is difficult for us to properly mourn the Beis HaMikdash can be illustrated by the following parable: There was once a mother who developed serious complications during childbirth and was forced to choose whether she would live and the child would die, or the reverse. She decided to forfeit her life for the sake of her child, but made a condition that her child be informed of her supreme sacrifice. When the child grew up, relatives told him what his mother had done and took him to his mother's burial plot. Since the child never met his mother, he looked on apathetically and did not even shed a tear. We are like that child. Hashem smote wood and stones of the Temple edifice to spare the Jewish People, but since we have never met this "mother" — i.e., the Temple that was sacrificed for our sake — we lack any feelings for her.[95]

Sacrifice of the Beloved

> *Let a beloved, the descendant of a beloved, come and build a beloved, for a beloved, in the portion of a beloved, and those who are beloved will receive atonement in it.*[96]

---

94   *Siddur Beis Yaakov, Dinei Tishah b'Av, Chalon* 6:16.
95   Rabbi Bentzion Yadler.
96   *Menachos* 53a.

The Gemara explains the meaning of this cryptic statement as follows: "Let King Solomon, a descendant of Avraham, come and build a Temple for the Holy One, Blessed is He, in the portion of Binyamin, and the children of Israel will receive atonement in it."[97] The Gemara goes on to cite verses showing how King Solomon, Avraham, the Temple, etc. are all called "beloved."

Rabbi Eliezer Ginzberg explains that the definition of "beloved" is someone who is selfless and sacrifices something dear to him for the benefit of his beloved.[98] The reason the Temple is called "beloved" is because it allowed itself to get destroyed (so to speak) in order to spare the Jewish People from destruction.[99]

Painful Aftershocks

Most of *Eichah* deals with the suffering of the Jewish People that resulted from the Temple's destruction, but very little is devoted to the destruction of the Temple itself. Rabbi Chaim Kanievsky comments that this is because the Temple's destruction was actually a benefit for Israel, for Hashem let out His anger, so to speak, on wood and stones and thereby saved the remnant of Israel.[100] The Midrash comments: "The day the Temple was destroyed was one of joy, since the great debt of sin that hung over the Jewish People was finally repaid."[101] Since it was only the aftershocks of the Temple's destruction that were truly bad, it is the human suffering that resulted from the Temple's destruction that is the primary focus of the prophet's lamentations.[102]

---

97   Ibid.

98   Rabbi Eliezer Ginsburg, *Mesilas Maharshah, Bereishis* 43:30.

99   See *Eichah Rabbah* 4:14.

100 *Eichah Rabbah* 4:14.

101 *Bereishis Rabbah* 42:3.

102 *Derech Sichah*, pp. 607–608.

Same Event, Different Perspective

Rabbi Avigdor Miller gives a beautiful analogy how three people can wail over the *Churban* in an identical manner, but essentially their cries are entirely different:

> *There was once a Yid who lived in the forest whose po-*
> *ritz — landlord — offered him the rights to cut all the*
> *lumber in the forest for the mere sum of three hundred*
> *rubles. The Yid quickly calculated that this deal would*
> *make him an instant fortune, so he ran to his home to*
> *bring the poritz the three-hundred-ruble notes he had*
> *saved under his mattress. Unbeknownst to him, his child*
> *had just discovered the valuable notes and began playing*
> *with them by putting them in the fire. After the last note*
> *was burned, the child became distressed and began to*
> *cry because he had none left to burn. When the mother*
> *came into the room to assist the child, she immediately*
> *understood what transpired and also began crying. Just*
> *then her husband arrived home, and after seeing what*
> *had happened, he too started to cry. The three cryings*
> *are incomparable: one is crying because he lost his toy,*
> *the second is crying over the loss of a significant amount*
> *of money, and the third because of the loss of the oppor-*
> *tunity of a lifetime.*

Excessive Mourning

The laws of mourning the *Churban* are stricter than the laws pertaining to a mourner who loses a relative of flesh and blood. While the Rambam discourages mourners from expressing excessive grief for the deceased,[103] he considers it an act of piety to mourn the *Churban*

---

103   Rambam, *Mishnah Torah*, Avel 13:11.

in an excessive manner.[104] In addition, on Tishah b'Av we recite lamentations to evoke emotions of pain and tears, which has no parallel in relation to mourning the loss of human life. (*Hespedim* — eulogies — are said to recall the greatness of the deceased and to feel the void of his loss, which is different to the *Kinos* recited on Tishah b'Av, whose sole function is to arouse crying for its own sake.)

The reason why excessive crying is an integral part of mourning the *Churban* is to rectify the Sin of the Spies when *Bnei Yisrael* cried needlessly.[105]

A Long Exile

"When the Temple was destroyed for the second time, many Jews became ascetics and resolved not to eat meat or drink wine."[106] Why didn't those who lived in the generation after the destruction of the First Temple also do the same?

Ben Yehoyada explains that everyone knew that the exile after the destruction of the First Temple would last for only seventy years. Since the exile would be short-lived, they did not feel it necessary to enact measures of self-denial to mourn the Temple. However, it was not revealed how long the exile following the destruction of the Second Temple would last. As a result, many feared that it would perhaps last for a thousand, even thousands of years. As such, the people in that era were in greater distress over the loss of the Temple, and the ascetics among them felt it fitting at that time to take drastic measures to remember the Temple's destruction.[107]

Diminishing Kingship

The Gemara relates that whenever the Jewish People in exile say *Amen Yehei Shemei Rabbah* during *Kaddish*, Hashem

---

104 Ibid., Ta'anis 5:9.
105 *Hararei Kedem*, vol. 2, 148:2.
106 *Bava Basra* 60b.
107 Ibid.; *Har Tzvi, Yomah* 9b.

[metaphorically] nods His head and says, "Fortunate is the King who is praised this way in His house. What is there for the Father who has exiled His sons, and woe to the sons who have been exiled from their Father's table."[108] The Maharshah notes that Hashem refers to himself as a King only while the Temple is standing, but after the destruction of the Temple, His status is diminished to that of a Father.[109]

While Hashem's Kingship is eternal, the specific aspect of His Kingship that became diminished due to the *Churban*, is *kavod Malchusoh* — the honor of Hashem's Kingship. The Gra writes that this alluded to in the Gemara, which says that while the Beis HaMikdash existed angels possessed six wings but that after the *Churban* two of their wings vanished.[110]

How is this so?

The *Gra* explains that the six wings correspond to the six words ברוך שם כבוד מלכותו לעולם ועד — "Blessed is the name of His Glorious kingdom for all eternity." In exile, כבוד מלכותו — "the glory of His Kingdom" is lacking, and though the emissaries of Hashem continue to do His bidding as before, they do so in a manner in which Hashem's glory is concealed.[111] Since it is particularly this aspect of Hashem's kingship that is diminished in exile, we therefore pray: "Reveal the *glory of Your Kingship* upon us."[112]

Rabbi Yaakov Kamenetsky elaborates how while the Beis HaMikdash stood, the glory of Hashem's kingship was readily apparent. When one crossed the threshold of the Sanctuary, one entered a dimension that transcended the laws of nature, as the Mishnah records the constant miracles that transpired there.[113] A

---

108 *Berachos* 3a.
109 Maharshah, *Berachos* ibid.
110 *Chagigah* 13b.
111 *Siddur HaGra, Avnei Eliyahu, Musaf* of Yom Tov.
112 *Musaf* of Yom Tov.
113 *Avos* 5:7.

person came to the Beis HaMikdash "to see and be seen." Hashem's presence was so keenly felt in the Beis HaMikdash that people would desist from transgressing *aveiros* throughout the year so as not to feel embarrassed when appearing before Hashem's presence during the pilgrimage festivals.

The service of the *Kohanim* and the singing of the *Levi'im* that was performed with devotion, alacrity, and precision also made a tremendous impression on everyone present. For example, Josephus records that even the Romans were overwhelmed by the decorum of the Temple service; each Kohen knew his responsibility so perfectly that the entire Temple service was conducted in total silence.[114]

The Hardest Blow

The climax of the Tishah b'Av morning *Kinos* is the lament *Alei Tzion*, which ends, "*Alei Shimchah asher chulal* — Alas for Your Name that is desecrated." This final stanza sums up the essence of our mourning on Tishah b'Av. Of all the excruciating pain and anguish that the Jewish People experienced in exile — such as the destruction of the Beis HaMikdash, the massacre of our people throughout the generations, and our past and present exile — the aspect that causes a Jew to scream out in the greatest pain is the desecration of Hashem's name in exile.[115]

For this reason, the Chofetz Chaim says that when we pray and long for the redemption, our primary focus should be for the sake of Hashem's honor. Moreover, Hashem in His mercy allows this desecration of His name to stimulate us to repentance. If we do not utilize the exile to stimulate us to *teshuvah*, then we are partly to blame for causing Hashem's name to be desecrated in vain.[116]

---

114   *Emes L'Yaakov, Devarim* 6:4.
115   *Hararei Kedem*, vol. 2, p. 312.
116   Rabbi Eliyahu Dessler.

Revival of Dead Mourners

The Gemara says that all who mourn for Yerushalayim will merit to witness her joy, but those who eat meat and wine at the meal prior to the advent of Tishah b'Av will have "their sins on their bones"[117] — alluding to the fact that their bones will not rise at the time of the resurrection of the dead.[118]

The Ritva explains that *Techias Hameisim* — the resurrection of the dead, will come about in two stages. The first stage will take place at the beginning of the Messianic redemption and will be reserved for those who have awaited the coming of Mashiach in exile. Since they yearned for the rebuilding of the Beis HaMikdash during their lifetimes, they will merit seeing its construction, which will take place upon the arrival of Mashiach.[119]

Those who did not mourn for the Temple will not arise at this time, but only at the "Great Day of Judgment," which will take place at the end of the Messianic period.[120]

BRINGING THE REDEMPTION

Power of Tears

The *Zohar* states that the redemption of the Jewish People in exile is solely dependent on our tears. The reason why all the tears shed during our exile have not yet achieved the redemption is because Hashem must first finish repaying the reward owed to Eisav for the tears he shed.[121]

What does this refer to?

The Midrash relates that when Eisav discovered that his brother Yaakov surreptitiously seized the blessings of his father, he cried

---

117 *Yechezkel* 32:27.
118 *Ta'anis* 30b. See Rashi there.
119 *Ta'anis* ibid.
120 Ritva to *Ta'anis* ibid. See also Appendix to Artscroll *Sanhedrin*, vol. 3.
121 *Zohar, Shemos* 12b.

three tears. One dropped out of his right eye, one from his left, and the third he kept back. Those three tears aroused Hashem's mercy, and as a result, Eisav merited sovereignty over the entire world, tranquility in this world, and also caused that the Jewish People taste the bitter tears of exile in threefold measure.[122]

The Jewish People plead before Hashem: "Master of the World, if You were immediately filled with compassion when the wicked Eisav cried two tears, all the more so we who constantly cry in exile are deserving of Your mercy." Hashem responds that after the wicked Eisav is completely repaid, the time for the Jewish nation to become eternally elevated will then come.[123]

Power of Prayer

The Midrash says that on the day the dynasty of Dovid HaMelech was split during the era of the First Temple, the Jewish People denied three things: HaKadosh Baruch Hu, the Beis HaMikdash, and the monarchy of the House of Dovid. The redemption will only arrive when the Jewish People will beseech Hashem that these three matters be restored.[124] The *Shibolei HaLeket* writes that it is for this reason that the Sages instituted, both in the *Shemoneh Esrei* prayer as well as in *Birchas Hamazon*, a prayer for the restoration of Hashem's kingship, for the rebuilding of the Beis HaMikdash, and for the uplifting of the royal house of Dovid HaMelech.[125]

Seeking the Temple

It was customary for idol worshipers to place their idols and temples on high mountains so that they could be seen and accessed with ease. In contrast, the Beis HaMikdash was not

---

122   *Midrash Tehillim* 80; *Midrash Tanchumah, Toldos* 24.
123   *Tanchumah* ibid.
124   *Midrash Shmuel* 13:4.
125   *Shibolei HaLeket, Birchas Hamazon* 157.

located on the highest peak in Yerushalayim,[126] as the Torah requires: לשכנו תדרשו ובאת שמה — "to *seek out* the place of His presence and come there."[127] Rabbi Yeruchem Levovitz explains that "searching" is a prerequisite for "coming," since in the spiritual realm, the only way to find the place of the *Shechinah* is by first searching for it.

The requirement of *derishah* — seeking — applies even after the destruction of the Beis HaMikdash. The Gemara states: "'She is Tzion, there is none who seek her'[128] — from this, it is implied that she requires seeking."[129] Just as while the Beis HaMikdash stood, the act of seeking enabled us to find the *Shechinah*'s place, so too seeking the Mikdash after its destruction helps us achieve a connection to that place.

Building for Life

All of the workers who were involved with the building of the Beis HaMikdash were blessed with miraculous success. Throughout the entire period of the construction, not one worker became ill or died, neither did any of their tools ever become the slightest bit damaged. Even the shoelaces of the workmen's shoes never tore![130]

The Torah discusses the reward of longevity adjacent to a commandment dealing with building a new house to hint that those who are involved with building the future Beis HaMikdash will merit a rewarding long life.[131]

---

126 *Zevachim* 54b.
127 *Devarim* 12:2–5, Rabbi Itzile M'Volozhin, cited in *Peninim M'Shulchan Gavoah, Devarim* ibid.
128 *Yirmiyah* 30:17.
129 *Rosh Hashanah* 30a.
130 *Pesikta Rabasi* 6.
131 *Devarim* 22:7–8. See *Ba'al HaTurim; Rabbeinu Ephraim* there.

Era of Mashiach

והיה עקב תשמעון — "This shall be the reward when you hearken [to these ordinances]."[132] The numerical value of והיה עקב equals the words בא הקץ — "the time of the redemption has arrived." This hints that after the number of years of עקב (172), starting from the time of the destruction of the Temple (3828), begins the era suitable for Mashiach to arrive (3828 + 172 = 4,000). As our Sages say, after four thousand years from Creation begins the era of Mashiach.[133] That Mashiach has still not arrived is only the result of our numerous sins.[134]

Kindness

There is a form of *gematriah* called *osios ne'elamos* — hidden letters — which are the pronounced but unwritten letters of each letter. (For example, the hidden letters in the letter א are ל and ף.) The *Rabbeinu Ephraim* says that the hidden letters that comprise the word חסד, kindness, are ת, מך, and לת. The sum of these letters equal 890, which is the total numbers of years from when the Jews left Egypt until the First Temple was destroyed.[135] This hints that the Jewish People went into exile because the trait of lovingkindness was "hidden" from them. Just as laxity in *chesed* caused the destruction of the Temple, so will acts of kindness bring the final redemption.[136]

Charity and Justice

"Judges and officers shall you appoint (תתן לך) in all your cities."[137] The numerical value of תתן is 850, which is the number of years the Jewish nation lived in the Land of Israel during the First Temple period. The *Rabbeinu Ephraim* explains that in the merit of maintaining

---

132 *Devarim* 7:12.
133 *Avodah Zarah* 9a.
134 *Rabbeinu Ephraim, Devarim* 7:12.
135 Rabbeinu Ephraim, *Devarim* 7:12.
136 See *Avos D'Rebbi Nasan* 4.
137 *Devarim* 16:18.

justice, the Jewish People lived peacefully throughout all the cities of Israel, but when they stopped pursuing justice they were immediately exiled.[138] *Bnei Yisrael* will be redeemed and return once again to their land in the merit of justice, as it states, "Tzion will be redeemed through justice."[139]

However, justice alone is insufficient to bring about the future redemption; it requires acts of charity as well. This is demonstrated by the conclusion of that same verse: ושביה בצדקה — "And those who return to her through *tzedakah*."[140] This means that in addition to repentance for one's sins (שביה has the same root as *teshuvah*), one must also give *tzedakah* to merit the ultimate redemption. *Rabbeinu Ephraim* notes that this is also alluded to in the *pasuk*: צדק צדק תרדף — "*Tzedek tzedek* shall you pursue."[141] The numerical value of צדק צדק is למשיח, since through *tzedakah* we will merit the arrival of Mashiach.[142]

Love and Peace

"Pray for the peace of Yerushalayim."[143] The Psalmist urges us to seek true, lasting peace of Yerushalayim. What is the secret as to how this elusive dream can become a reality? The answer is contained in the conclusion of the same verse: "Those who love you should be serene."

Who are these beloved ones who are the true lovers of Tzion? They are the pious, G-d fearing Jews who toil in the study of Torah and mourn the desecration of the Temple's destruction. It is specifically the lack of concord within this group that led to the destruction of the Temple and is delaying its rebuilding. Since Satan knows that this is the key to redemption, he exerts much effort to induce discord among the G-d fearing — especially prior to the advent of Mashiach,

---

138 *Rabbeinu Ephraim, Devarim* ibid.; *Midrash Tanchumah* ibid.
139 *Yeshayah* 1:27.
140 *Yeshaya* ibid.
141 *Devarim* ibid.
142 *Rabbeinu Ephraim, Devarim* 16:20.
143 *Tehillim* 122:6.

as our Sages say, in the generation when Mashiach is due to arrive there will be baseless ill-feeling between Torah scholars.[144]

A TIME FOR COMFORT

My Portion, My Hope

"'Hashem is my portion,' says my soul, 'therefore I have hope in Him.'"[145] What is the connection between the first and second half of the verse?

We will present two approaches:

- The Midrash compares this to a king who visited one of his provinces together with his royal entourage. One villager decided to befriend the king's prime minister so that the minister would always come to his aid in his time of need. Another villager chose to befriend the king's chief military commander to be assured of protection if the need would ever arise. There was one wise person among the villagers who reflected, "All the king's officers and advisors can be discharged at the king's will. I will only choose the king to be my protector and benefactor, since his rule is everlasting." Similarly, the nations of the world choose Hashem's servants as their savior — some serve His angels, others serve the constellations, or His creations of wood and stone. Israel chooses Hashem as their sole patron and so they expectantly await His salvation with confidence.[146]

- It is the natural order of the world that when a part is separated from a whole, the smaller part seeks to be reunited with its source (for example, all rivers flow into the sea). A case in exception is Hashem and the Jewish People. Our souls are

---

144 *Kesuvos* 112b. Rabbi Tzvi Pesach Frank, *Har Tzvi, Yomah* 9b.
145 *Eichah* 3:24
146 *Eichah Rabbah* 3:8.

but a miniscule portion of the One most High. Yet, in His great love for us, He constantly yearns to be united with *us* more than we yearn for Him. This is what the prophet means when he says, "'Hashem is *my* portion,' says my soul." That Hashem constantly seeks to be connected with me makes it apparent — from the vantage point of the soul — that Hashem is the small portion of the soul. "Therefore I hope to him," if Hashem loves me in such an unnatural and excessive manner, I am certain that He will come to my salvation and will never forsake me.[147]

Tishah B'Av Festival

In *Eichah*, the prophet Yirmiyah calls Tishah b'Av a *moed* — a festival.[148] How can this most tragic time be considered a festival?

Rabbi Yaakov Naiman says that it is comparable to a son who is walking in a forest with his father. The son notices a delicious-looking berry bush in the distance and without his father's permission, he wanders off to collect the berries. After he finishes, he tries to return to his father but gets lost and cannot find his way back. The son cries bitterly and the father, hearing the cries, begins to search for his son. When he eventually finds his son, he gives him a hard slap and berates him for running off on his own. The son is so happy to be reunited with his father that he focuses on the closeness to his father and ignores the slap and his father's scolding.[149]

While *moed* is generally translated as a "festival," a more literal translation would be "a time for meeting." The primary reason why the Temple festivals were such joyous occasions was because the Jews would go up to Yerushalayim to have a personal encounter with Hashem. In our present exile, too, although our suffering and

---

147 *Chazon Yechezkel, Tanach*, p. 342.
148 *Eichah* 1:15.
149 Rabbi Yaakov Naiman, *Darkei Mussar* p. 184.

persecution is extremely painful, the awareness that our loving Father is together with us and is the One who is smiting us provides us a certain degree of solace. For this reason, we may rightfully call the bittersweet period of this encounter a *moed*.

Love amid Pain

The sages of Athens once presented Rabbi Yehoshua with two eggs and asked, "Which is the egg of a black hen and which is the egg of a white hen?"

Rabbi Yehoshua brought them two types of cheese and asked in return, "Which is of the milk of a black goat and which is of a white goat?"[150]

The Maharshah explains that an egg represents a twenty-one day period, since the gestation period of a chicken embryo is twenty-one days. The intent of the Athenians' seemingly absurd question is: of what benefit is there in the product of the white hen — i.e., the twenty-one-day period between Rosh Hashanah and Hoshanah Rabbah, when the sins of the Jews are absolved — if there is a corresponding black hen — i.e., the three week period of mourning and destruction between the seventeenth of Tamuz and ninth of Av.

In reply, Rabbi Yehoshua presented cheeses produced from the milk of two different goats. The two goats represent the two goats brought in the Temple on Yom Kippur. The "white" goat represents the one sacrificed to Hashem as a sin offering, while the "black" goat is the one sent to Azazel, where it is thrown off a barren cliff to its death. Just as both goats produce the same "white cheese," in that together they help cleanse Israel of sin, so too do both the black and white hen lay identical white eggs. The purity and cleansing achieved as a result of suffering and exile during the three-week period of mourning equals the level of atonement and closeness to Hashem one attains between Rosh Hashanah and Hoshanah Rabbah.

---

150 *Bechoros* 8b.

Rabbi Yisrael Simchah Schorr notes that Tishah b'Av falls out on the twenty-second day from the seventeenth of Tamuz, which is akin to the actual laying of the egg — the sum product of the twenty-one-day gestation period. This corresponds to the day of Shemini Atzeres, which is the twenty-second day from Rosh Hashanah and the climax of the twenty-one day Tishrei period. On Shemini Atzeres, *Bnei Yisrael* experience an unparalleled loving closeness with Hashem. Tishah b'Av parallels Shemini Atzeres because as a result of the suffering on Tishah b'Av, we attain the same level of loving closeness. This is why when the nations destroyed the Temple and entered the Holy of Holies, they found the *Cherubim* embracing each other,[151] which demonstrated the loving relationship between Hashem and Israel.

The Greatest Holidays

As the *luchos* were broken on the seventeenth of Tamuz, the fast on this day primarily focuses on the loss of Torah as a result of the *Churban*. The ninth of Av focuses on the loss of the Beis HaMikdash, through which we lost an integral aspect of Divine service (*avodah*) as well as the unifying source of the Jewish nation.

Corresponding to these days of tragedy, Hashem gave us two special holidays — Yom Kippur and the fifteenth of Av. On Yom Kippur, we received the second *luchos*, through which the Torah, which was formerly lost, was now returned. The various reasons given in the Talmud for the cause of festivities on the fifteenth of Av all relate to reinstating the Temple service, which had been previously lost, and to the unifying of the nation after a period of painful separation.[152]

---

151   See *Yomah* 54a–b.

152   *Keren Orah, Ta'anis* 30b.

See *Ta'anis* 30b, which enumerates the reasons for the festival of the fifteenth of Av:

A.   On this day, the Sages ruled that the tribes were permitted to marry members of another tribe.

B.   On this day, the tribe of Binyamin was permitted to marry into the congregation of Israel (following a ban that was issued after the incident of the *Pilegesh b'Givah*).

The Gemara says that there were no holidays in Israel like the holidays of Yom Kippur and the fifteenth of Av.[153] These holidays are so spiritually lofty that it manifested itself in the custom of women dancing in the vineyards to find their *shidduch*, which is the earthly equivalent of the great Kabbalistic unifications that are concurrently transpiring in the heavenly realms at this time.[154]

Symbol of Peace

"There were no Yomim Tovim in Israel like the fifteenth of Av and Yom Kippur."[155] It is interesting that both festivals shared a common feature in that on both days linen garments were worn. (On Yom Kippur, the *Kohen Gadol* performed the Yom Kippur service while wearing linen clothing, and on the fifteenth of Av maidens wore linen garments when going out into the vineyards in search of their *shidduch*.)

One who wears pure linen clothing demonstrates a desire to distance himself from wearing *shatnez*. The prohibition against *shatnez* stems from the tragic episode of Kayin and Hevel. Hevel brought a sheep as an offering to Hashem and Kayin brought an offering of flax, from which linen is made. The volatile combination between wool and linen led to Kayin murdering his brother.[156] The *Zohar* says that one who is careful in separating between wool and linen brings peace upon himself and upon the entire world.[157] Since the prohibited combination of *shatnez* leads to jealousy and strife, which is the

---

C.   On this day, those who were destined to die in the wilderness stopped dying.

D.   On this day, Hoshea ben Elah removed the sentries that Yaravam ben Nevat had stationed on the roads to prevent Jews from ascending to the Temple on the pilgrimage festivals.

E.   On this day, the slain Jews of Beitar were afforded burial.

F.   On this day, they completed the mitzvah of felling the wood for the fire on the altar.

153   *Ta'anis* ibid.
154   See *Keren Orah* ibid.
155   *Ta'anis* 26b.
156   See *Pirkei D'Rebbi Eliezer* 21.
157   *Zohar* 3, 86b–87a.

antithesis of these two festivals, whose sole purpose was to bring peace between Hashem and one's fellow man, the garments worn on these days were made exclusively from linen.[158]

Double-Measure Comfort

Because they sinned in a double measure, they were punished in a double measure; and since they were punished in a double measure, they will be comforted in a double measure, as it is written, "Nachamu, nachamu ami — Be comforted, be comforted, My people."[159]

The *Binyan Shlomo* explains that their sinning in a "double measure" refers to the two sins that led to the destructions of the two Temples.[160] The primary sin of the First Temple period was a lack of appreciation for Torah study, as the prophet *Yirmiyah* revealed: "For what reason did the land perish and become parched as a desert without a passerby? And Hashem said, 'Because of their forsaking my Torah.'"[161] No mention is made of their transgressing the three cardinal sins since Hashem would have overlooked those major transgressions and allowed *Bnei Yisrael* to remain in Israel had they appreciated and studied the Torah properly.[162]

The "second" measure of sin refers to the prime sin of the Second Temple era, which was baseless hatred. Since they sinned in a double measure, they were also punished in a double measure, namely through the destruction of the First and Second Temples.

To merit the rebuilding of the Third Temple, one must rectify the lapses that brought about the destruction of the first two. The prophet Zechariah says: "Thus said Hashem...the fast of the fourth

---

158 *Mikdash Mordechai, Bereishis* 4:4.
159 *Yeshayah* 40:1. *Midrash Eichah Zuta* 1.
160 *Binyan Shlomo*, vol. 2, pp. 567–569.
161 *Yirmiyah* 9:11–12. See *Nedarim* 81a, Ran there.
162 *Binyan Shlomo* ibid., citing *Pesichah, Eichah Rabasi*.

[month, i.e., the seventeenth of Tamuz] and the fast of the fifth [month, i.e., the ninth of Av]...will be...for joy and for gladness and for happy festivals. [Only] *love truth and peace.*"[163] "Truth" refers to Torah,[164] and peace is the opposite of baseless hatred. This is to say, that in the merit of love of Torah study and love of one's fellow man, the fast days commemorating the destruction will be turned to gladness with the coming of Mashiach.

The double measure of comfort is that the Third Beis HaMikdash will be restored for eternity, and the Jewish People are assured that they will never revert to the sins that destroyed the first two Temples, as the prophet says regarding the era of the future redemption: "All your children will be students of Hashem (and will have the proper appreciation for Torah), and your children's peace will be abundant (meaning, that they will love and pursue peace)."[165]

Destruction and Rebirth

The Midrash relates a story about a Jew who lived far away from Yerushalayim who was tilling his field with his ox on the day the Beis HaMikdash was destroyed. His ox let out a cry, and just then an Arab who understood the language of oxen passed by. "What nation are you from?" inquired the Arab of the ox's owner. "I am a Jew," he replied. "In that case, you should untie your ox and stop working, since the Temple of the Jews was destroyed today." When the Jew began untying his ox, the ox cried out again. The Arab then told him, "You can retie your ox and your plow since your redeemer has just been born."[166]

In the famous dispute between the Ramban and a representative of the Catholic Church before the King of Aragon, this Midrash was cited by Pablo Christiani, a convert from Judaism to Christianity,

---

163 *Zechariah* 8:19.
164 *Berachos* 5b.
165 *Yeshayah* 54:13; *Binyan Shlomo* ibid.
166 *Eichah Rabbah* 1:51.

as a "proof" that their "Messiah" had already been born during the period of the Mishnah. Among the Ramban's responses was that he does not believe in the literal reading of this Midrashic text, but that rather it is to be taken allegorically. Some understand the intent of the Midrash as conveying that Divine Providence orchestrates that at the moment of the greatest destruction, the seeds of the future salvation are planted.

LAWS OF THE THREE WEEKS

Shehechiyanu Blessing

The *Shulchan Aruch* rules that one should preferably refrain from reciting a *Shehechiyanu* blessing over a new garment or fruit during the Three Weeks.[167] The Vilna Gaon comments that this is an excessive stringency, since the mourning period of the Three Weeks cannot be stricter than that of a mourner mourning the loss of his father, who does recite *Shehechiyanu* if he becomes the beneficiary of an inheritance.[168]

According to the Netziv, a distinction can be made between the *Shehechiyanu* recited over a new fruit and that recited over a new garment. This is because the *Shehechiyanu* blessing over a new fruit celebrates the produce of the new harvest and praises Hashem for having allowed one to live to that point to experience it. Since the Three Weeks is a sad period of time, it would be inappropriate to recite *Shehechiyanu* for this period. On the other hand, the *Shehechiyanu* blessing for a new garment is not related to any time period but rather expresses one's personal joy over acquiring a new item. Since this form of the *Shehechiyanu* blessing is not related to the mourning period of the Three Weeks, a *Shehechiyanu* for a new garment can be recited even at this time.[169]

---

167 *Shulchan Aruch, Orach Chaim* 551:17.
168 *Biur HaGra, Orach Chaim* ibid.
169 *Ha'amek Sheilah* 171:10.

Fasting or Mourning?

During the Nine Days, we refrain from bathing for pleasure and from consuming meat and wine. The Maharshal makes a distinction between the two prohibitions. Abstaining from meat and wine constitutes a minor form of fasting, while the prohibition of bathing is in order to act in the manner of mourners as a result of the Temple's destruction.[170]

A practical difference between the two categories is whether a person who made a vow to refrain from meat and wine for the entire three weeks prior to Tishah b'Av would be permitted to bathe during that time. Since abstaining from wine and meat is considered a miniature fast, it is an appropriate expression of pain over what the Jewish People endured during the three weeks between the seventeenth of Tamuz and the ninth of Av. Bathing, however, is an expression of mourning and is therefore only appropriate for the time immediately preceding the day commemorating the Temple's destruction. For this same reason, bathing is permissible on the seventeenth of Tamuz as well as on the other minor fast days.

LAWS OF THE NINE DAYS AND TISHAH B'AV

Mourning Variations

Why is it that during the Nine Days it is permissible to study Torah, but eating meat and drinking wine is forbidden, whereas the laws concerning an ordinary mourner are the opposite — Torah study is prohibited but consuming meat and wine are permissible?

Rabbi Shlomo Zalman Auerbach explains that with a personal loss, mourning is a natural reaction, and wine and meat will not distract him from his mourning.[171] A mourner may not study Torah, though,

---

170   Maharshal 92.

171   This does not contradict the verses in *Mishlei* (31:6–7) that encourage giving wine to a mourner to mitigate his pain. Since when a mourner drinks wine it does not give him joy — it merely dulls his excessive pain — he is still able to demonstrate proper respect

since Torah gladdens a person's heart and will totally remove him from his mournful state.

On the other hand, since the destruction of the Temple occurred millennia ago, one does not naturally feel pained about it. Therefore, it requires external stimuli such as refraining from eating meat and drinking wine to help arouse our feelings of mourning. The rabbis did not see fit to prohibit Torah study for the duration of the Nine Days, though, for on the contrary, the Torah gives us the strength to persevere in our difficult exile and through it merit complete redemption. They therefore limited the prohibition of Torah study only to the day of Tishah b'Av itself.[172]

Meals Prior to Tishah B'Av

There is a custom to eat a large *seudah* prior to the *seudah hamefsekes* (which consists only of a boiled egg with bread) in order to give one strength to fast for a twenty-four-hour period. This parallels the *seudah* eaten prior to Yom Kippur where one also partakes of a large meal for the same reason.[173] Other *Acharonim* frown upon this custom, since an elaborate meal diminishes the spirit of mourning which is appropriate at this time.[174]

One can bring support to the custom to have the meal from the *Yerushalmi* that says that after Rav finished eating "all that he needed," he would then dip his bread in ash and say, "This is the *seudah* for Tishah b'Av."[175] This implies that it is indeed proper to eat one's fill prior to the *seudah hamefsekes*.

The *Magen Avraham* gives an additional reason for the first large meal. During the period of the Second Temple, Tishah b'Av was turned into a Yom Tov and was celebrated with a festive meal. We

---

for the dead.
172   *Halichos Shlomo* 14:28.
173   Rama, *Orach Chaim* 552:9.
174   *Mishnah Berurah* 552:22.
175   *Ta'anis* 4:6.

commemorate this with a larger meal to reaffirm our belief that the day of Tishah b'Av will once again be turned into a day of rejoicing with the rebuilding of the Beis HaMikdash.[176] Accordingly, the first meal corresponds to the prior and future redemption, while the paltry *seudah hamefsekes* relates to our present reality of Tishah b'Av as a day of mourning.

It is questionable whether women are obligated to eat the first large meal prior to Tishah b'Av.

Rabbi Akiva Eiger raises a similar question whether women are required to eat the meal prior to Yom Kippur.[177] The *Mekor Chaim* cites the Maharil who says that if a woman made a vow not to eat meat and drink wine other than on Shabbos and Yom Tov, she is permitted to eat meat and drink wine on Erev Yom Kippur.[178] Although women are absolved from time-dependent mitzvos, since they are obligated to fast on Yom Kippur, they are also obligated to fulfill the requirements in preparation for the fast, namely eating. According to the opinion cited above, which equates the meal prior to Tishah b'Av with the meal prior to Yom Kippur, we may conclude that women are indeed obligated to eat on Erev Tishah b'Av as well.

There is also a question whether women are obligated to eat the *seudah hamefsekes*. At first glance, it would appear to fall into the category of a time-dependent mitzvah from which women are absolved. On the other hand, one may argue that the *seudah hamefsekes* is part of the obligation of mourning on Tishah b'Av in which women are obligated. The *Mekor Chaim* argues that one is not *obligated* to eat a *seudah hamafsekes*; the Sages just made a stipulation for those

---

176 *Magen Avraham, Orach Chaim* 552:11.
177 Rabbi Akiva Eiger, responsa 16.
178 *Mekor Chaim* 604:1.

who wish to eat how to properly do so.[179] Accordingly, since the *seudah hamafsekes* isn't even obligatory for men, certainly women are exempt. However, from the *Yerushalmi* cited above, it appears that the *seudah hamafsekes* is not a voluntary act but rather an actual obligation.[180]

No Birchas Kohanim

On Tishah b'Av morning, *Kohanim* do not recite *Birchas Kohanim* (even in communities where they customarily recite it daily), nor does the chazzan recite the *Kohanim's* blessing during his repetition of *Shemoneh Esrei*.

There are numerous reasons offered for this:[181]

- On Tishah b'Av, *Kohanim* mourn the destruction of the Beis HaMikdash, and a mourner does not recite *Birchas Kohanim*.
- The verse says, regarding the destruction, "When the *Kohanim* will lift their hands [in blessing] I will remove My eyes from them,"[182] meaning that *Birchas Kohanim* will not be accepted.
- On Tishah b'Av, it is not permitted to greet a person with "Shalom," so it is prohibited to recite *Birchas Kohanim* that contains the blessing of Shalom.
- A drunken person is prohibited to recite *Birchas Kohanim*. On Tishah b'Av (as well as other times when one experiences pain and distress), one obtains the status of one who is intoxicated since they are "inebriated with pain."[183]
- The prophet Yirmiyah says, regarding Tishah b'Av, "The day will not be blessed,"[184] so it is inappropriate to say the blessing of the *Kohanim* on this day.

179 *Mekor Chaim* 552:1.
180 *Hararei Kedem*, vol. 2, 140, s.v. *"v'yeish l'hosif."*
181 *Nechamas Yisrael*, p. 190, footnote 274.
182 *Yeshayah* 1:15.
183 See *Midrash Eichah* 3:15.
184 *Yirmiyah* 20:14; see Malbim.

No Torah Study

On Tishah b'Av, one may only learn the portions of Torah that deal with the topics of *Churban* and mourning. Rabbi Yaakov Kamenetsky is unresolved as to whether one is *required* to learn those areas of Torah in order not to transgress the prohibition of *bitul Torah*, or whether the general obligation of Torah study is altogether lifted on Tishah b'Av.

Rabbi Shlomo Zalman Auerbach states that since there is absolutely no obligation of Torah study during *aveilus*, this would logically extend equally to Tishah b'Av.[185] (Rav Shlomo Zalman would disapprove of mourners who would spend significant amounts of time studying permissible portions of Torah, as this detracts from the mourners' primary responsibility of mourning the deceased.) This could explain the custom of several *Gedolim* who would compose poetry and other forms of literature on Tishah b'Av that were meaningful to the day.

Tallis and Tefillin

There are opinions that one should not wear a *tallis* on Tishah b'Av,[186] based on the Midrash that interprets the verse, בצע אמרתו — "He completed his decree,"[187] to read: בזע פרפוריה דיליה — "He tore the hem of his distinguished garment."[188] (The word בצע is related to בזע, which means "to tear," and אמרת can also be translated as "a garment.")[189]

The *Maharam M'Rotenberg* rules that one should not wear *tefillin* on Tishah b'Av, based on the Midrash that applies the verse, "He cast down from heaven to earth the glory of Israel,"[190] to be referring to *tefillin*.[191] According to the Rambam, the custom not to wear the

---

185 *Shalmei Mo'ed*, p. 496.

186 *Sefer HaMinhagim*, Av 79.

187 *Eichah* 2:17.

188 *Eichah Rabbah* 1:1.

189 *Be'er Mayim Chaim, Bamidbar* 15:38.

190 *Eichah* 2:1

191 Cited by *Tur, Orach Chaim* 555:1.

tefillin on Tishah b'Av applies only to the *tefillin shel rosh*.[192] This is because the component of *tefillin* that is termed "glory" is specifically the head *tefillin*, since it is a distinguished head ornament.[193]

Although a mourner is required to wear *tefillin*, save for the first day of the death of his relative, Tishah b'Av is equivalent to the to the first day of mourning where the mourner's dead lies before him,[194] as there is no day as bitter as the day of the destruction of the Temple.

Rabbi Shashne Gaon writes that since nowadays so many years have passed from the time of the destruction and we have become accustomed to the loss, Tishah b'Av is no stricter than a mourner during the remaining week of his mourning when one is obligated in *tallis* and *tefillin*.[195]

In practice, we adopt a combination of both opinions by wearing *tallis* and *tefillin* at *Minchah*.

As mentioned above, the reason why *tallis* and *tefillin* are not worn on Tishah b'Av is because on the day of the destruction of the Temple we are equivalent in status to an *onein* — a mourner on the first day of mourning. The *Toras Chaim* asks: an *onein* is also absolved from all mitzvah obligations, such as prayer and reading the *Shema*. If we are like an *onein* on Tishah b'Av, why aren't we absolved from all other mitzvos as well?

The *Toras Chaim* therefore understands the rationale for not wearing *tallis* and *tefillin* in an entirely different light. Our Sages say that just as we wear *tallis* and *tefillin*, so does Hashem. Our *tefillin* bespeak of our love of Hashem, and in turn Hashem's *tefillin* speak

---

192   *Ta'anis* 5:11.
193   See *Targum Yonansan, Yechezkel* 24:17.
194   *Taanis* 30b.
195   *Otzer HaGaonim, Eruvin* 96a. Rabbi Shashne Gaon lived approximately 1,350 years ago.

about His love of the Jewish nation.[196] Therefore, when a Jew sins, it so-to-speak severs Hashem's connection to His *tefillin*. This is why when a person is in pain, as a punishment for his sins, Hashem says, "My head is heavy, My arm is heavy."[197] The head and arm are singled out since those are the places the *tefillin* are worn.

At the time of the destruction, *bitza emrasoh* — Hashem tore the *tzitzis* off the hem of His garment and cast His *tefillin* — which contains verses that describe the glory of Israel — to the ground. Since Hashem removed His *tallis* and *tefillin* on Tishah b'Av, we follow suit and do not wear them on those days as well.[198]

Sneakers

Some suggest that the reason one is forbidden to wear leather shoes on Tishah b'Av is because they are comfortable, and we wish to minimize our comfort on this sad day. If that is the case, asks Rabbi Shlomo Zalman Auerbach, why is it permissible to wear sneakers and slippers, as many find them even more comfortable than leather shoes?

He therefore understands the prohibition of wearing leather shoes is because they demonstrate the dominion of man over the natural world.[199] One may not wear shoes on the Temple Mount, since all signs of rulership have no place in Hashem's presence. Likewise, in times of mourning, as well as on Yom Kippur when our lives are hanging in the balance, it is also not appropriate to flaunt our power, as it states: "There is no dominion on the day of death."[200] This reason would equally apply to Tishah b'Av, since it is the time we mourn the destruction of the Temple.[201]

---

196 *Berachos* 6a; *Rosh Hashanah* 17b.

197 *Chagigah* 15b.

198 Rabbi Avraham Chaim Shur, *Toras Chaim, Bava Kama* 59b.

199 See *Tehillim* 8:7, "You give him dominion over Your handiwork, You placed everything *under his feet.*"

200 *Koheles* 8:8.

201 *Shalmei Mo'ed*, chap. 94.

Chinuch in Fasting

There is no mitzvah of *chinuch* to train a child to fast on a fast day.[202]
There are several reasons given:

- Anything that is not inherently prohibited, but only becomes forbidden at certain times, is exempted from the obligation of *chinuch*.[203]
- We do not obligate a child in mitzvos that involve pain.[204]
- We are not stringent in training children in Rabbinic commandments. Therefore, when it comes to Rabbinic fast days, due to the danger inherent in fasting, a healthy child need only fast for a short period, and a weak child need not fast at all.[205]

Sanctity of the Kosel

There is a prohibition to break off a piece of the stone from the Altar, walls, or other Temple structures.[206] There is a debate among the *poskim* whether this prohibition would presently apply to the stones of the *Kosel* — the Western Wall.

According to the Chasam Sofer, breaking off a part of the *Kosel* would be permitted,[207] based on the principle that "lawless people came into it, and defiled it," which means that when Gentiles overran

---

202 *Mishnah Berurah* 550:5.

203 *Chayei Adam* 1:66:10. Although we do train children not to eat *chametz* on Pesach, a distinction can be made between prohibitions such as *chametz* on Pesach, where the object is prohibited (איסור חפצא), for which *chinuch* does apply, as opposed to those prohibitions that impose a behavior upon on an individual (איסור גברא), such as fasting, for which children are exempt from *chinuch*.

204 *Chachmas Adam* 152:17; cf. *Chachmos Adam* ibid., who notes that an exception is made for the fast of Yom Kippur, which, due to the severity of this fast, one is *mechanech* children to fast for a few hours.

205 *Rama M'Panu* 111; *Sherashei HaYom* 1:171b.

206 *Sifri, Devarim* 61:3.

207 *Chasam Sofer, Yoreh Deah* 264.

the Temple its sanctity was removed.[208] When King Yechaniah and his entourage were exiled from Jerusalem, they took along with them some Temple stones and later incorporated them into a synagogue which they built in Bavel. How were they able to decrease the sanctity of the Temple stones by using them to build a shul? The answer is that when the Babylonians desecrated the Temple, its sanctity departed.

Rabbi Moshe Feinstein disagrees: The Midrash relates that Hashem swore that the Western Wall will never be destroyed and will always remain the resting place for the Divine Presence. Since the *Kosel* was never destroyed by the Romans, the wall never lost its original sanctity and the prohibition to destroy its stones remains intact.[209] In his view, there is no proof from the story of King Yechaniah. King Yechaniah did not use Temple stones to construct a shul in exile; he took unsanctified stones from Jerusalem. They carried ordinary stones from the Land of Israel with them into exile in order to fulfill the dictum,[210] "For Your servants have cherished her stones and favored her dust."[211]

Rabbi Yosef Shalom Elyashiv was asked whether it is proper to clean the stones of the *Kosel* with sandblasting, as well as the stones of the *Kosel* plaza. He makes a distinction between the surroundings of the *Kosel* and the actual wall itself. Regarding the plaza, since it is a place where people come to pray, it has the status of a place of prayer, of which it is proper that its floor be washed and swept.[212]

On the other hand, even if sandblasting would not remove any particles from the wall, it is still preferable to leave it in its natural

---

208   *Avodah Zarah* 52b.
209   *Igeres Moshe, Yoreh Deah* 4:63.
210   *Tehillim* 102:15.
211   Cited in *Mesivtah, Peninei Halachah, Bechoros* 15b.
212   *Shulchan Aruch, Orach Chaim* 151:9.

state as it has appeared since the time of the Temple's destruction. Viewing the grime and vegetation on the site of the House of Hashem will cause one's heart anguish and arouse him to fervently pray to Hashem that the Temple be speedily rebuilt.[213]

---

213   Rabbi Yosef Shalom Elyashiv, *Ashrei HaIsh, Orach Chaim* 3, p. 500.

IN LOVING MEMORY OF MY DEAR PARENTS

Yehuda ben Yitzchok

and Yentel bas Naphtali, a"h

WHO GAVE US THE LEGACY
OF THE TORAH'S CENTRALITY IN OUR LIVES

Jan Fishman and Family

IN APPRECIATION AND RECOGNITION OF

HaRav Wurzburger, shlita

FOR HIS TREMENDOUS DEVOTION AND EFFORTS
OVER MORE THAN THREE DECADES
ON BEHALF OF THE KOLLEL,
THE MELBOURNE JEWISH COMMUNITY
AND BEYOND, כן ירבו.

לעילוי נשמת
הורינו
ר׳ אריה בן ר׳ דוד ז״ל
ומרת מניה בת ר׳ אברהם ז״ל
ליפקס

וזקננו
ר׳ דוד בן ר׳ חיים אליעזר ז״ל
ר׳ אברהם בן משה חיים ז״ל
ומרת לאה בת ר׳ ישעיה לייב ז״ל
ומרת חנה טויבע בת משה ז״ל
ליפקס-ווינשטיין

ת.נ.צ.ב.ה.

לע״נ
ר׳ ברוך
ב״ר יהודה אריה ע״ה
בייקער

ור׳ חיים אהרן יעקב
ב״ר ישראל אליהו ע״ה
שידלא

WE WOULD LIKE
TO EXPRESS OUR
DEEP RESPECT AND
APPRECIATION FOR
THE ROSH KOLLEL
FOR HIS DEDICATED
TORAH GUIDANCE AND
LEADERSHIP OF THE
MELBOURNE JEWISH
COMMUNITY.
MAY HASHEM GRANT HIM
CONTINUED STRENGTH TO
BE MARBITZ TORAH AND
PRODUCE MANY MORE
BEAUTIFUL TORAH WORKS.

Mr. and Mrs.
Yechiel Baker

WITH IMMENSE GRATITUDE TO THE

Rosh HaKollel and the Rebbitzen, shlita

Moishe and Miri Landau and family

לעילוי נשמת הורינו היקרים ז״ל

ר׳ אפרים דב בן ר׳ יוסף חיים הלוי LANDAU
ר׳ יוסף אלחנן בן ר׳ שמעון ומרת רחל לאה בת ר׳ יהודה VALENT

ר׳ מרדכי דוד בן ר׳ יקותיאל ומרת יהודית הדסה בת ר׳ יוסף FRIEDMAN
ר׳ יהודה בן ר׳ יהודה ומרת שפרינצע בת ר׳ משה SCHLESINGER

ר׳ יוסף חיים בן ר׳ אברהם מאיר הלוי ומרת חיה טובה בת ר׳ ישראל יעקב LANDAU

Dedicated by Moishe and Miri Landau

WITH DEEP GRATITUDE
TO

Rav Wurzburger

FOR HIS TIRELESS EFFORTS
ON BEHALF OF THE KOLLEL
AND THE BROADER
MELBOURNE COMMUNITY

Anonymous

WITH OUR
ENDURING THANKS
AND APPRECIATION TO OUR
MOIREH DERECH,

Rabbi Wurzburger, shlita

FOR HIS 20-20 VISION
OVER MANY YEARS.
WE LOOK FORWARD
TO THE SEQUEL OF THIS SEFER.

Harry and Celia Grossman

About the Author

Rabbi Binyamin Wurzburger studied at Talmudical Yeshiva of Philadelphia and Beth Medrash Gevoha of Lakewood, New Jersey. In 1981, he moved his young family to Melbourne, Australia, to cofound the first overseas Lakewood community *kollel*. Rabbi Wurzburger has served in the position of *Rosh Kollel* of Kollel Beth HaTalmud/Yehudah Fishman Institute of Melbourne for over thirty-five years.

About Mosaica Press

Mosaica Press is an independent publisher of Jewish books. Our authors include some of the most profound, interesting, and entertaining thinkers and writers in the Jewish community today. Our books are available around the world. Please visit us at www.mosaicapress.com or contact us at info@mosaicapress.com. We will be glad to hear from you.